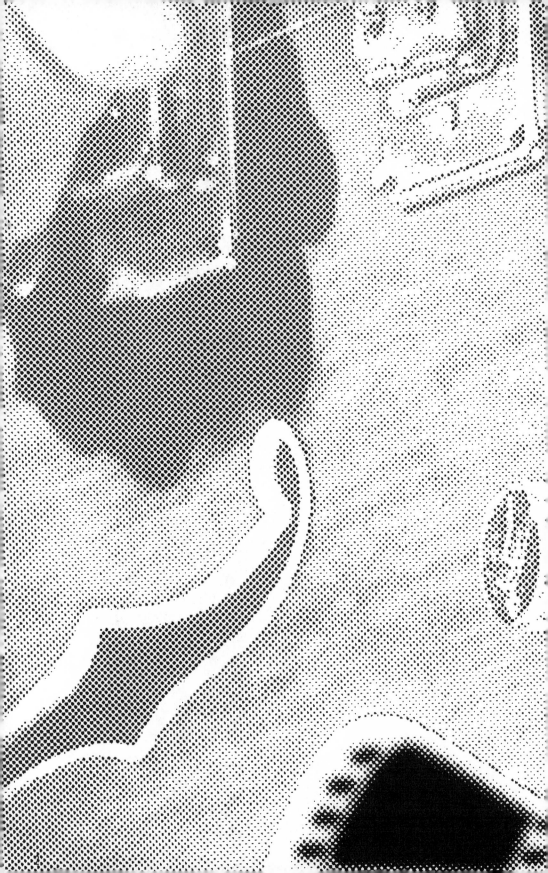

HOLLYWOOD ROCK

MARSHALL CRENSHAW

EDITED BY TED MICO

HarperPerennial
A Division of HarperCollinsPublishers

AN AGINCOURT PRESS BOOK

President: David Rubel
Art Director/Design: Tilman Reitzle
Editor: Sarah B. Weir

The posters, lobby cards, and stills reproduced in this book
appear courtesy of the Alan Betrock Collection.

HarperCollins books may be purchased for educational, business, or sales promotional use. For information, please write: Special Markets Department,
HarperCollins Publishers, Inc., 10 East 53rd Street, New York, NY 10022.

FIRST EDITION

ISBN 0-06-273242-0 (pbk)

94 95 96 97 98 **RRD** 10 9 8 7 6 5 4 3 2 1

GREW UP IN THE DETROIT AREA, where the local music had a certain unnameable yet distinctive quality—at least while I lived there. You could sometimes feel a sense of lunacy and meanness in the air and hear it in the music of the Stooges, say, or the MC5, whom I saw open for Jimi Hendrix when I was 14.

The television around Detroit was also unique. It was the *best* bad TV. You could always tune in lots of offbeat things—Lemmy Caution movies, for instance, which starred actor Eddie Constantine as a sort-of Euro James Bond. It seemed that when I was growing up, people in Detroit had a tireless need to watch gangster movies and rock'n'roll movies on TV.

I remember this station in Windsor, Ontario, that showed lots of British movies, the station being Canadian. It showed many of the movies in this book, like *Rock around the World* and *Gonks Go Beat.* Looking back now, it seems odd that *Rock around the World*, Tommy Steele's life story, was even

made—and odder that I saw it so often in Detroit. But it has stuck in my memory, as random things from childhood often do, and I haven't forgotten the taste of the TV dinners that I used to eat as I watched it. So I want to dedicate this book to the memory of all the hours I spent as a kid having my senses assaulted and my worldview informed by the sights and sounds of Detroit TV. I don't live there anymore, but Detroit is always in my thoughts.

Don't take the title of this book literally. The films included here are diverse, beginning chronologically with Louis Jordan's *Beware* in 1946. There are Mexican films, Australian films, German films, and others that are off the beaten track. After days, weeks, months of researching and consulting with fans all over the globe, we now bring you this volume of information and opinion about rock films—the good, the bad, and the heinous.

We've divided *Hollywood Rock* into a number of sections. In the main review section, you will find complete reviews of more than three hundred films. Each of these is rated (on a scale of 1 to 5) in each of three categories: Music, Attitude, and whether the movie is Fun to Watch. The music category is self-explanatory. The Attitude rating is meant to reflect how well the movie succeeds on its own terms. In other words, did the reviewer think the film was cool. The Fun to Watch rating is meant to gauge whether the film works as an entertainment overall. Each review is then followed by one or more features: Scenes, Lines, Cameos, and Songs. The Scenes feature (usually followed by a time signature to locate its position within the film) calls your attention to particular highlights in a film. The Lines feature captures classic bits of dialogue. The Cameos feature lists famous or otherwise noteworthy people who appeared in the film, yet whose roles were to small to merit a listing in the cast. The Songs feature lists all the songs actually performed in each film. (Songs merely appearing on the soundtrack are not listed here.)

The appendix that follows the main review section has itself been divided into three subsections covering More Rock Films, Concert Films & Rockumentaries, and a Rock Actors Filmography. (For more information on the preparation of the appendix, see the introduction on page 261. Following the appendix, you will find the Cameo Glossary, which offers a brief description of each person listed in the Cameos feature. There is a also a list of sources *(Where to Find It)* for some of the hard-to-find films reviewed in this book. And finally, a Performer Index that lists all the bands that appear in the movies reviewed here, both in the main review section and the appendix.

We picked which movies to include in this book using only two objective criteria: the films had to be released theatrically, and rock'n'roll had to be an essential, indispensable element. Other than that, we went by our gut. We consulted every available book on the subject, and everyone who worked on *Hollywood Rock* was polled for suggestions. If the scale tilted at a certain point, the film was in.

We had already agreed that, for a film to be included in the main review section, the reviewer had to watch it firsthand. So the next task was to find all these films, in itself a Herculean task. For instance, I first heard about *Mondo Daytona* from Jay Schwartz and immediately became obsessed with tracking it down. I'm a big fan of Billy Joe Royal and the Swinging Medallions, both of whom appear in this movie, so I just had to see it.

ATT: MARSHALL CRENSHAW

FROM: FIFA RICCOBONO

DATE: 16TH SEPTEMBER 1993

RE: THE EASYBEATS

Dear Marshall

I have tried to find out about "Between Heaven and Woolworths" for you and the information is not great.

Yes, there was such a film made by Peter Clifton. It was originally called "SOMEWHERE BETWEEN HEAVEN AND WOOLWORTHS" and later changed to "Easy Come, Easy Go". It was a twenty minute documentary of the Easybeats in England, as is supposed to be excellent.

The last time it was sighted was at a rock concert held in 1970 in Wallacia (Australia) - NOBODY HAS SEEN IT SINCE! Peter Clifton has scoured Australia as has Glenn A. Baker but no-one knows of it's whereabouts. No doubt it's been buried in some company's film vault and no-one probably even knows it's there!

I'm sorry I can't be of more help, but I too would love to get my hands on it.

All the very best with your book. Best regards

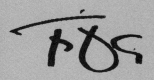

The first thing I did was tap into the collectors' network by calling a few specialists whom I know. They have ways of getting their hands on especially hard-to-find stuff. Some of their methods are aboveboard, while others are sneaky and devious and involve all sorts of undercover activities. Whenever I want to see a movie that's unavailable through normal rental channels, I call these people. If one of them doesn't have the film, he or she usually puts me on to someone who might. Eventually, I found out that in 1970 *Mondo Daytona* had been intercut with clips of Grand Funk Railroad and remade into another film called *Weekend Rebellion.* After a few more calls, I located a collector of early '70s video who's also a big Grand Funk fan. Somehow he had gotten a fourth- or fifth-generation copy of *Weekend Rebellion.* That's the copy that was reviewed for this book.

It took another considerable effort for Domenic Priore to locate, and then get permission to watch, *One Man's Challenge.* He viewed perhaps the only existing copy of that film in the offices of Dick Clark Productions in Los Angeles. Meanwhile, I watched *Groupies* at the New York office of the film's producer, Joseph Cates, in a storage room where tape decks and little monitors had been set up. (I finally hooked up with Cates after half a dozen telephone calls to people who had distributed *Groupies* at one time or another.)

At other times, we weren't so fortunate. Jay Schwartz, who first told me about *Mondo Daytona*, also hinted at the existence of a movie starring the Easybeats, that great Australian rock band from the '60s who sang "Friday on My Mind." Just as with *Mondo Daytona*, I started the ball rolling by calling a few collectors. I also called Domenic Priore, our beach movie specialist, who talked to some of his friends, and Dennis Diken, the Smithereens drummer, who told me about an Australian expert on beach and biker movies named Stephen J. McParland. (Whenever there's a great reissue album or a new rock history book, you'll usually find Dennis's name somewhere in the acknowledgments.) An exchange of faxes directed me to Albert Productions, the Australian company that represents two former members of the Easybeats, Harry Vanda and George Young, who are still active as songwriters and producers. I faxed the company, and they faxed me back with the bad news that the film hadn't been seen since 1970.

Many of the writers who contributed to this book were drawn from this same network of rock film enthusiasts. Most of them are friends of mine who, like me, are ardent rock'n'roll fans and happen to have a variety of writing credits and accomplishments. In general, we looked for people who specialized in a particular area of interest and matched them up with it. For example, I found out about Bruce Eder, our British movie expert, from an article he wrote about British rock films in *Goldmine* magazine. When I read that article, I knew we had to have him. And while I don't want to pigeonhole any of these people, Domenic Priore is really passionate about beach movies and early '60s California youth culture, while Art Fein thinks they haven't really got it right since 1957. Tony Paris, who appeared in *D.O.A.: A Right of Passage* as well as reviewing it here, might make the same argument about 1977.

In other words, we thought partisanship on the part of the reviewers was not a bad thing, as long as it was coupled with an expertise. We wanted there to be an enthusiastic tone to this book, and I was particularly concerned that we didn't necessarily bash and bury stuff that I personally despised. To the extent

that we could, we found people to review films who were positive about and had an affinity for the material they were watching.

I want to emphasize that no attempt was made to enforce a uniformity of opinion here. For example, Domenic Priore thinks Frankie Avalon has a fine comedic talent, while Ben Vaughn makes it clear in his review of *Grease* that he would beg to differ.

Because we were determined that all the reviews in the main section be based on firsthand viewing, we used the appendix at the back of this book to take up the slack. Among other things, it covers films we heard about but couldn't find, no matter how hard we tried. And we really tried. Compiled by the one-man film festival that is Jay Schwartz, the appendix evaluates those films to the extent that we can.

So, why did we do this? Out of love, of course. The love of fast cash, laughs, film, art, Americana, and rock'n'roll. Thanks for your interest.

Marshall Crenshaw
November 1993

A ny project of this scope necessarily involves the efforts of many people. Among those who have kindly given of their time and advice are Michael Ackerman, Julia Banks, Tom Benton of Video Cave (Hudson, NY), Alan Betrock, Shawn Brighton and Jan Muenzler of the Joe Meek Appreciation Society (U.S.), Dave Brown, Mark Cantor, Joseph Cates, Tom Cherwin, Traci Collins, Jack Conklin, Dennis Diken, Distortions Records, Sheri Fitzsimons of ABBA World (Scottsdale, AZ), Joanne Frank, Gary Giddins, Phil Grodski, Mike Hoffman, Tom Hudgins, Barbara Jacobs, Caroline Kaplan and Jonathan Sehring of Bravo, Ira Kaplan, Michael Krumper, Rich Leighton, Herschell Gordon Lewis, Mark Lewis, Richard Lieberson, Michael Lucas, Jim Luckett, David Markey, Jimmy Maslin, Joe McLaughlin, Billy Miller, Movies Unlimited, Ray Murray, Laura Nugent, Jay Mike Perkins, Todd Phillips, Jim Pike, Tricia Provost, Laura-Ann Robb, Will Roberts, Tony Sanchez, Ken Sharp, Irv Slifkin, Beth Smith, David Snyder, Robert Walker, Cathy Watson, Michael Weldon, Steve White, Edwin Wong, and Peter Zaremba.

Kent Benjamin is the programming director for three Austin Community Television public access stations as well as a television, rock, and video commentator. His collection of music on television totals about 2,800 hours of material.

Mark Blackwell is a former senior editor of *SPIN* and now a freelance journalist for many of the finest publications in the land. He can be heard semi-frequently on radio and television professing to know very much about things he secretly confesses he knows very little about.

Jason Cohen writes about film, books, and music for such publications as *Details*, *Rolling Stone*, *SPIN*, and *Option*. He is the co-author (with Michael Krugman) of *Generation Ecch!* (Fireside).

Marshall Crenshaw is a former snowmobile factory worker, now a professional rock musician. His songs and performances are included in several of the films mentioned in this book.

Erin Culley currently works for *US Magazine* and serves as the music editor for *Detour*. She lives in L.A. with her bulldogs, Claudius and Julius—the only things in the world she loves more than music.

Bruce Eder has written for the *Village Voice, Newsday, Goldmine,* and *Current Biography.* He is a contributing editor at *Video Magazine* and has produced laserdisc editions of *A Hard Day's Night, Help!,* and *Monterey Pop.*

Art Fein is best known for his book, *The L.A. Musical History Tour* (Faber & Faber), and his TV show, "Art Fein's Poker Party."

Michael Goldberg is a contributing editor at *Rolling Stone*. These days, when he's not rocking out to Captain Beefheart, the American Music Club, or Souls of Mischief, he can be found watching *Touch of Evil* (a true rock classic!).

Robert Gordon is a producer, a video maker, a regular contributor to music magazines around the globe, and an Aquarius. He is currently writing *It Came from Memphis*, a book on Memphis music to be published by Faber & Faber.

Howard Hampton writes music and movie criticism for *L.A. Weekly, Film Comment,* and other publications. He is currently writing *Badlands*, a study of the Reagan era for Harvard University Press.

Andy Langer is a regular contributor of music features and reviews to the Austin *Chronicle*. After his upcoming graduation from the University of Texas, he expects to have more time available to spend watching rock'n'roll movies.

Johnny Legend is a writer, wrestling manager, actor *(Children of the Corn III)*, filmmaker, and songwriter (whose cult hits include "Pencil Neck Geek"). He continues to wage a one-man war against a no-win world with new recordings, including his vocal version of "Pipeline" and the long-awaited "Run, Geek, Run."

Amy Linden is a frequent contributor to the *New York Times, People, Vibe,* and *Mirabella*. She writes mainly about R&B.

Tara McAdams is a freelance writer who has contributed to *Pulse* and *L.A. Weekly*. She really feels sorry for Elvis.

Stephen J. McParland has been documenting the surfer, beach, and hot rod genres for well over twenty years. In addition to writing for and editing such magazines as *California Music, Gonna Hustle You,* and *Beach Boys Australia,* he has authored a number of books including *It's Party Time* and *Beach Street and Strip.*

Ted Mico is the former features editor of *Melody Maker* and currently the president of Shattered, a mixed-media works.

Tony Paris is an Atlanta-based writer who has been covering music since before he knew any better. To relax and get his mind off the music business, he travels to the Middle East to enjoy a less stressful environment. He believes music should be "heard and not seen."

Domenic Priore is the author of *"Look! Listen! Vibrate! SMILE!",* the story of Brian Wilson's unreleased 1966 masterpiece *Smile.* He is also the producer of "It's Happening"—today's answer to "Shindig," "Ready Steady Go," and "Hollywood a Gogo"—featuring live bands and kids from the rockabilly, garage, and mod undergrounds.

Tilman Reitzle is a graphic artist and rock musician. He is the electronic maniac and producer for the Hoboken-based band Liarface.

David Rubel is the president of Agincourt Press. Among his writing credits is a children's biography of Elvis Presley, and he has visited Graceland. Twice.

Tony Sanchez has been a collector of '60s garage music for more than a decade. He currently resides in San Diego, where he manages a bookstore and writes for *Ugly Things,* an independent magazine about music with a wild teenage sound.

Andy Schwartz is the former editor and publisher of *New York Rocker,* a national monthly magazine of alternative music. A resident of New York City, he is associate director of media services for Epic Records.

Jay Schwartz is a Philadelphia-based writer who has contributed to *New York Rocker, Trouser Press,* and other long-defunct publications. He also programs the Secret Cinema, a popular film series showcasing forgotten cult oddities.

Mike Stax moved from England to San Diego in 1980 to join a '60s garage band. Since 1983, he has published *Ugly Things,* covering the ugliest and wildest unsung heroes of punk's rock'n'roll past.

Ben Vaughn is a songwriter, recording artist, and record producer whose production credits include Arthur Alexander and Charlie Feathers for Elektra/Nonesuch and *Johnny Otis: The Capital Years,* which he compiled and annotated. He has released five albums of his own music on Restless Records and a collection of home recordings on Bar None.

Sarah B. Weir is a writer and editor whose film criticism appears in *The Motion Picture Guide.* She has recently accepted that it's too late for her to become a rock star.

Karen Woods is a Vancouver-based writer who gave up the daily grind and the foreign desk to devote her life to alternative music. She now hopes that someday she will no longer be in need of a day job.

ABBA: THE MOVIE (1977)

CAST: Anni-Frid Lyngstad, Benny Anderson, Björn Ulvaeus, Agnetha Faltskog, Robert Hughes, Stig Anderson; DIR: Lasse Hallström; PROD: Stig Anderson; SCREENPLAY: Bob Caswell, Lasse Hallström; STUDIO: Warner; 95 min., color (Warner)

MUSIC ★★★★★
ATTITUDE ★★★★
FUN ★★★★

The blues had a baby.
ABBA were magicians in the recording studio (usually Polar Music Studios, Stockholm) and masters of escapist entertainment at its most potent. With Anni-Frid and Agnetha's multitracked harmonies to the fore, ABBA created a sound that most of the world's record buyers fell in love with between 1974 and 1982. Today, songwriters and record producers everywhere worship the names of Björn, Benny, Agnetha, and Anni-Frid. They invented Europop. Most phenomenally successful pop/rock acts eventually make the Cash-In Movie, and ABBA made theirs in 1977. Here's the plot: Sydney DJ Ashley (Robert Hughes) chases ABBA all over Australia during a sold-out concert tour trying to get an in-depth interview with the group. His station's prestige and his job are at stake, but since he's forgotten his press card, he's constantly thwarted until the last minute when dumb luck intervenes, and he gets the interview with ABBA. It's just that interesting. Ashley also interviews many ABBA fans, all of whom seem to be over 50 or under 10. One gentleman claims to like ABBA for their "clean-cut beat." Many of the fans comment on the group's tidy appearance. (MC)

SCENES
After a hard day of being abused by ABBA's security guards, Ashley takes a nap in his hotel room. He dreams that he's alone with Anni-Frid and Agnetha as they sing "The Name of the Game" just for him.

SONGS
The Tiger, S.O.S., Money Money Money, He Is Your Brother, Waterloo, Mamma Mia, Rock Me, I've Been Waiting for You, The Name of the Game, Why Did It Have to Be Me, When I Kissed the Teacher, Get on the Carrousel, I'm a Marionette, Fernando, Dancing Queen, So Long, Eagle, Thank You for the Music (ABBA)

ABSOLUTE BEGINNERS (1986)

CAST: Eddie O'Connell, Patsy Kensit, David Bowie, James Fox, Ray Davies, Lionel Blair, Steven Berkoff, Mandy Rice-Davies; DIR: Julien Temple; PROD: Stephen Wooley, Chris Brown; SCREENPLAY: Christopher Wicking, Richard Burridge, Don MacPherson; STUDIO: Virgin; 107 min., color (HBO)

MUSIC ★★★★
ATTITUDE ★★★
FUN ★★★

A 19-year-old photographer in pre-Beatles London.
For 20 years, numerous celebrated directors attempted (and failed) to bring Colin MacInnes's seminal story of teen angst in '50s London to the silver screen. Julien Temple's brave, stylized musical interpretation highlights why everyone else gave up. The director's complex three-and-a-half-minute continuous shot, which opens the film (and is cited in Robert Altman's *The Player*), serves as warning that every scene was designed for maximum visual impact—the constant struggle of style over substance.

Temple assembled a cast of pop stars, very British icons, and arcane Brit quiz show hosts with the sole purpose of providing the audience with intrigue—you never know who is going to pop up next. The elaborate dance numbers walk a fine line between mockery and reverence for '50s musicals. The elaborate "That's Motivation" dance number is symbolic of the film's ambiguity: The presence of the great *Bowie* tells you they're kidding, but are they? He looks *very* comfortable as the singin' businessman (p'raps he'll retire—soon!—to stage musicals), and the film-makers make the scene so attractive you're not sure whether it's a sendup or an homage. The half-baked romantic plot turns ugly and congested at the end when racism becomes the film's focus, and squalor and violence threaten to sully the film's seamy, but upbeat tone. In the end, all the in-jokes and self-parodies combine to make the movie a little too foreign, and ambitious, for American audiences. (AF)

ALICE'S RESTAURANT   (1969)

CAST: Arlo Guthrie, Pat Quinn, James Broderick; **DIR:** Arthur Penn; **PROD:** Hillard Elkins, Joe Manduke; **SCREENPLAY:** Venable Herndon, Arthur Penn; **STUDIO:** MGM/United Artists; 111 min., color (CBS/Fox)

MUSIC ★★
ATTITUDE ★★
FUN ★★

The prequel to the song.
As a song, Arlo Guthrie's semi-autobiographical ballad was 18-and-a-half minutes long. As a movie, it had to be longer, so Arthur Penn added a new story line about the hippie community that gathers at the Berkshire County home (a converted church) of Ray and Alice Brock. Inevitably, the new material takes over from the song. It's a full hour, for instance, before Arlo gets to eat "the Thanksgiving dinner that couldn't be beat," which leads to his arrest for littering and later his deliverance from military service.

Penn's real subject is Ray and Alice's dream of hippie community. Although the movie, like the dream, fails, it's not for lack of trying. For a picture shot in 1969, *Alice's Restaurant* is remarkably prescient. But like most '60s artifacts, it's difficult to watch for too long. There are genuine hippies everywhere, which makes the film something of an historical curiosity. But their self-righteousness solipsism (endemic by this point) get to you after a while. Good song, though. (DR)

SCENES Pete Seeger and Arlo performing "Pastures of Plenty" and "Car-Car Song" in Woody Guthrie's hospital room (0:47)

LINES Arlo to Alice: "Just what I always wanted." Alice: "A restaurant?" Arlo: "No, a friend with a restaurant."

CAMEOS Pete Seeger, Stockbridge police chief William Obanhein (Officer Obie) as himself, M. Emmet Walsh, Alice Brock (the eponymous Alice)

AMERICAN GRAFFITI   (1973)

CAST: Richard Dreyfuss, Ron Howard, Paul Le Mat, Charlie Martin Smith, Candy Clark, Mackenzie Phillips, Cindy Williams; **DIR:** George Lucas; **PROD:** Francis Ford Coppola; **SCREENPLAY:** George Lucas, Gloria Katz, Willard Huyck; **STUDIO:** Universal; 112 min., color (MCA)

MUSIC ★★★★★
ATTITUDE ★★★★★
FUN ★★★★★

Play it again for the Wolfman.
It's no accident that George Lucas set *American Graffiti* on the last night of the summer of 1963. Looking back, it was quite a poignant time: Kennedy was still

president (but not for long), Vietnam was still a geography lesson away, and the waitresses at the drive-ins still wore roller skates. This particular night is also special because it's the last that high school buddies Curt Henderson (Richard Dreyfuss) and Steve Bolander (Ron Howard) will spend in the San Joaquin Valley. They leave their hometown for an eastern college in the morning.

A lot happens from dusk to dawn in this coming-of-age story, which set the standard for films like *Stand By Me* that also trade on a musical moment in time. While chasing after a beautiful blonde in a white T-bird, Dreyfuss gets kidnapped by the local JDs. Howard breaks up, then gets back together with his girlfriend (Cindy Williams), while their twenty-something friend John Milner (Paul Le Mat) cruises the town in his lemon yellow hot rod, wondering why life seems to have passed him by. Suffice it to say that the memories are so real, you'd swear they were your own. This movie is so good that it's genuine experience. Watching it is living it. (DR)

Dreyfuss visiting the Wolfman, whose singular presence seems to jump out of every car radio (1:37) **SCENES**

Wolfman Jack, Harrison Ford, Suzanne Somers **CAMEOS**

AMERICAN HOT WAX (1976)

CAST: Tim McIntire, Fran Drescher, Jay Leno, Laraine Newman; **DIR:** Floyd Mutrux; **PROD:** Art Linson; **SCREENPLAY:** John Kaye; **STUDIO:** Paramount; 91 min., color (Paramount)

MUSIC	★★★
ATTITUDE	★★★★
FUN	★★★

A stylized version of the last days of pioneering disc jockey Alan Freed.
Tim McIntire is magnificent as Freed, who first made a name for himself on the radio in Cleveland playing black music for white kids. While other DJs played white cover versions of R&B songs, the uncompromising Freed played only the black originals. Some, especially Freed, even credit him with naming the music "rock'n'roll."

In September of 1954, Freed's skyrocketing career brought him to New York's WINS-AM, where he began promoting a now-legendary series of rock'n'roll shows at the Brooklyn *Fox* and *Paramount* theaters. The plot of *American Hot Wax* revolves about the last of these shows, which ended when Freed became the fall guy for the 1960 payola scandal. A subplot features Laraine Newman as the young Carole King. Don't try to sort out this film's cockeyed chronology, though, because you'll miss all the fun. There's an awful lot of whitewashing, but the movie still manages to capture Freed's charm and that of his time, the eve of Camelot, when doo-woppers really did sing on street corners and Buddy Holly's death meant a lot to some people. Anyway, you know it's a fairy tale when—after the cops confiscate the ticket money—that notorious penny-pincher Chuck Berry (who plays himself) agrees to perform for nothing. That's right—free. Only in the movies. (DR)

The D.A.: "One more demonstration and I'll close you down." Freed: "Look, you can close the show. You can stop me. But you can never stop rock'n'roll. Don't you know that?" **LINES**

Chuck Berry, Jerry Lee Lewis, Frankie Ford, Screamin' Jay Hawkins, Cameron Crowe, Brenda Russell **CAMEOS**

Come Go with Me, Rock'n'Roll Is Here to Stay (Planotones); *Mr. Lee, Maybe* (Delights); *Why Do Fools Fall in Love?* (Chesterfields); *Mister Blue* (Timmy and the Tangerines); *Reelin' and Rockin', Roll Over Beethoven* (Chuck Berry); *Great Balls of Fire* (Jerry Lee Lewis) **SONGS**

American Graffiti

AMOR A RITMO DE GO-GO   (1967)

MUSIC ★★★
ATTITUDE ★★★★★
FUN ★★★★

ENGLISH TITLE: *Love to the Beat of the Go-Go*
CAST: Javier Solis, Rosama Vazquez, Leonorilda Ochoa, Eleazar Garcia Chelelo, Raul Astor; **DIR:** Miguel M. Delgado; **PROD:** Jesus de Eduardo Galindo; **SCREENPLAY:** Adolfo Torres Portillo; **STUDIO:** Peliculas Mundiales Y.T.A; 90 min., color (no video release)

Rock's Creeping Terror.
Little is known about this wonderfully obscure Mexican rock film. Ads billed the movie as "The Mexican *T.N.T. Show*," but in truth it's more like *Rock, Rock, Rock* or *Go Johnny Go*—an extremely low-budget flick thrown together to capitalize on the newfound popularity of teen films. Its flimsy plot serves primarily as a springboard for would-be rock tunes in a choreographed dance-club format. But in the grand tradition of such awful horror films as *The Creeping Terror*, *Amor a Ritmo de Go-Go* is truly enjoyable, at least for its music sequences.

The plot features a voluptuous teenage girl named Lupe and an old man to whom she introduces rock'n'roll and go-go dancing. Along the way, there's a subplot involving several driving instructors. They do pointless things in cars with two steering wheels and figure in a big fight scene at the club, the Cafe A Go-Go, which features nice imitation-American pop art backdrops and go-go dancers doing identifiable trendy American steps. The delightful musical numbers are choreographed and played in the style of mid-'60s garage bands from north of the border. Actually, the "original" tunes are blatant ripoffs of American hit records. Sam the Sham and the Pharoahs' "Wooly Bully" gets the treatment it has always deserved as a great Mexican garage band, Los Rockin' Devils, translates the song into Spanish and performs it as go-go dancers strut their stuff in cages. If you live in a town with a Spanish-language TV station, watch for this highly entertaining film in the late-night listings. (KHB)

SCENES A Mexican garage band plays a modified version of the McCoys' "Hang On Sloopy" called "Hey Lupe." Later, when the curvaceous young Lupe takes the old man to her apartment, she puts an orchestral version of the song on her record player and tries to teach him the latest steps.

THE AMOROUS SEX   (1957)

MUSIC ★★
ATTITUDE ★
FUN ★★

CAST: Sheldon Lawrence, Julie Amber, Irv Bauer, Al Burnett, David Browning; **DIR:** Ronnie Albert; **PROD:** William Mishkin; **SCREENPLAY:** Ron Ahran; **STUDIO:** Constitution; 63 min., b/w (Something Weird)

British beauty lured to New York by promise of big job.
This cheap quickie is included because of the lip-synched performances by Billy Myles, the Mello-Kings, and Fred Parris and the Satins (a.k.a. the Five Satins—Fred was lead singer but couldn't take the name when he left). Also included are several pop songs by the film's female protagonists. This was a very soft skinflick designed for peep-show audiences. There are two exotic strippers, one tit shot in a dressing room, and some almost-tit in a couple of brief (probably edited for U.S. release) clinch scenes. And then, apparently, someone at Herald-Ember Records decided to give their acts exposure in a movie that already had some. It didn't work, and this film languished unknown for more than 30 years. (AF)

SONGS *In the Still of the Nite* (Fred Parris and the Satins); *The Joker* (Billy Myles); *Tonite Tonite* (Mello-Kings)

ANOTHER STATE OF MIND (1983)

CAST: Youth Brigade, Social Distortion, Minor Threat; DIR: Adam Small, Peter Stuart; PROD: Adam Small, Peter Stuart; SCREENPLAY: Adam Small, Peter Stuart; STUDIO: Coastline; 83 min., color (Magnum)

MUSIC ★★★
ATTITUDE ★★★★
FUN ★★★★

All the young punks.

This well-paced, shot-on-video feature follows two hardcore bands, Social Distortion and Youth Brigade, on their first cross-country tour. It provides a valuable and entertaining chronicle of an all-ages, D.I.Y. music environment that is now all but extinct. It begins with the crew happily converting an old school bus for the trip and making other vital preparations, like shaving their heads and dyeing their hair. One musician decides to color his hair a different hue for each week of the tour—maintaining an outrageous appearance was serious business in those heady days. As Social Distortion leader Mike Ness notes with a superior air, "Most guys don't know how to wear makeup."

In between concert segments (which include subtitled lyrics for the often indecipherable thrash tunes), the documentary charts the great expectations and disappointments of the young travelers. They find kindred spirits at a Calgary punk house (complete with backyard skateboard ramp), where they are offered lodging and ominous-looking pots of chili. The gung-ho feeling weakens as the bus breaks down, they get stiffed by promoters, and some crew members catch the next Greyhound home. Finally, the ailing bus (and tour) grinds to a halt amid flaring tempers. Youth Brigade's Scott Stern declares the trip a financial disaster but a moral victory. Although most of the entourage has deserted him, he may be right. (JS)

Washington, D.C., scene deity Ian Mackaye at his day job scooping Häagen Dazs ice cream, long before his later band Fugazi entered the Billboard Hot 100

SCENES

Ness, after his road-weary band bails out and flies home: "I might have to get new members.... I *will* keep the name Social Distortion, and I *will* keep the songs." The mascara-ed singer made good on his threat.

LINES

Keith Morris

CAMEOS

Fight to Unite, You Don't Understand the Sickness, Violence (Youth Brigade); *Telling Them, Mommy's Little Monster, Mass Hysteria, Another State of Mind* (Social Distortion); *In My Eyes, Minor Threat* (Minor Threat)

SONGS

THE APPLE (1980)

CAST: Catherine Mary Stewart, George Gilmour, Vladek Sheybal, Grace Kennedy, Allan Love; DIR: Menahem Golan; PROD: Menahem Golan, Yoram Globus; SCREENPLAY: Menahem Golan; STUDIO: Cannon; 90 min., color (Paragon)

MUSIC ★
ATTITUDE ★
FUN ★★★★

1984 *meets* Xanadu.

During their early-'80s reign at Cannon Films, Israeli-born cousins Menahem Golan and Yoram Globus cranked out schlocky films by the score. They specialized in quickie action flicks, vulgar sex comedies, and tacky musicals like *The Apple*, which is perhaps the pinnacle of their art form. This film opens at the 1994 Worldvision song contest, where the crowd is literally mesmerized by Bim, a futuristic troupe of rock musicians and swishy dancers who resemble a cross between Labelle and the cast of *Rocky Horror*. Controlling the performance from behind the scenes is super rock svengali Mr. Boogaloo, whose servants electronically monitor the dazed crowd for brain activity and heart rate (just like when disco DJs fretted over "BPM" counts!).

When Bim are nearly upstaged by the super-clean duo Alphie and Bibi, mind-altering subsonic tapes are used to turn the audience violently against Alphie and Bibi's saccharine-sweet singer-songwriter crap. Afterwards, Mr. Boogaloo attempts to coopt the pair by signing them to his world-dominating entertainment conglomerate. Bibi is thrilled ("He made Pandi and Dandi...he made everybody!"), but Alphie smells a rat and refuses to sign. Undaunted, Boogaloo makes Bibi a solo star, while Alphie, now alone, continues to write his own terrible songs. He attends a promotional party/orgy in an attempt to win Bibi back but gets slipped hallucinogens and must pass through a gauntlet of drag queens in order to escape. Eventually, Bibi rejects her new, hollow life, and the pair find refuge at a secret hippie commune in the forest. A year later, Boogaloo and his goon squad discover and surround the commune. Then, just in time, God (called "Mr. Topps" here) appears in a white luxury car to lead the good people to heaven. (JS)

SCENES   Alphie's lovable, stereotypical landlady: "Vy doncha write the kind of shit they like so you can sell it and pay me the rent?"

SONGS   *Hey Hey Hey Bim's on the Way, The Speed* (Bim); *Love the Universal Melody* (Alphie, Bibi); *You're Made for Me, The Magic Apple* (Dandi); *Life Is Nothing but Showbiz, I Know How to Be a Master* (Mr. Boogaloo); *Where Has Love Gone?* (Alphie); *Alphie Where Are You Now?* (Bibi); *I'm Coming, Something's Happened to Me* (Pandi); *Light My Way Child of Love* (Hippies)

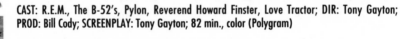

ATHENS, GA.: INSIDE OUT   (1986)

MUSIC ★★★
ATTITUDE ★★★★
FUN ★★

CAST: R.E.M., The B-52's, Pylon, Reverend Howard Finster, Love Tractor; DIR: Tony Gayton; PROD: Bill Cody; SCREENPLAY: Tony Gayton; 82 min., color (Polygram)

Cutting-edge capital or hippie refuge?

This sprawling look at the famous college town/rock scene covers many bases and is a good travelogue of Athens in the mid-'80s. Scene definers The B-52's and R.E.M. are paid proper homage—there's early Super-8 footage of the former, while R.E.M. bits include a lip-synched "Swan Swan H" done in an abandoned building, Michael Stipe tap dancing, and Peter Buck giving a tour of his house. Equal time is given to the artists and poets of this slacker capital, including Stipe's old art teacher Jim Herbert and "naive" artists like Reverend Howard Finster.

Most of the other musical acts featured do little to validate the making of this film. The members of the B-B-Que Killers, Time Toy, the Kilkenny Cats, and the Squalls seem amiable enough in their interviews, but their songs demonstrate why these groups are all but forgotten a few short years later. The best music here is by the B-52's and the fondly remembered Pylon, whose relatively thrilling live clip is punctuated by non-nostalgic interviews with members of the then-defunct band (they briefly re-formed after this film). All in all, this documentary will either make you feel you belong to a continuing tradition, or it will confirm why you hate "college rock." For a complete history of the Athens scene, read Rodger Lyle Brown's excellent book, *Party Out Of Bounds* (NAL-Dutton). (JS)

SCENES   A seemingly catatonic Vanessa Briscoe (ex-Pylon vocalist), barely remembering (or even believing) her previous life as a punk rock star

"We met at a party. None of us knew how to play our instruments when we formed," says every band in this film. *LINES*

I'm a Juvenile Delinquent (Dexter Romweber); *Swan Swan H.* (R.E.M.); *Work That Skirt, 52 Girls* (B-52's); *Oh Shit, Hunchback in the Morning* (B-B-Que Killers); *Windowsill, Hi* (Time Toy); *Crazy Hazy Kisses, Jet Tone Boogie* (Flat Duo Jets); *Steps* (Dreams So Real); *Fun to Be Happy, Got to Give It Up* (Love Tractor); *Room 101, Nightfall* (Kilkenny Cats); *Na Na Na Na, Elephant Radio* (Squalls); *Stop It, Italian Movie Theme* (Pylon) *SONGS*

BABY SNAKES   (1979)

CAST: Frank Zappa, Terry Bozzio, Adrian Belew, Tommy Mars, Ed Mann, Peter Wolf, Patrick O'Hearn; DIR: Frank Zappa; PROD: Frank Zappa; SCREENPLAY: Frank Zappa; STUDIO: Intercontinental Absurdities; 165 min., color (Honker)

MUSIC	★★★★★
ATTITUDE	★★★★★
FUN	★★★★

Frank Zappa's live, streamlined tour de force.
Relying on the principle that reality is often stranger than fiction, Frank Zappa decided to get real. In *Baby Snakes*, everyone becomes an actor and every situation a performance. Keeping track of it all is Zappa himself, who emcees the proceedings, making copious use of his razor-sharp wit. The action was filmed in 1977 during Halloween concerts at New York's Palladium. At these shows, Zappa delivers something largely missing from his earlier movies: his uniquely stunning and underrated guitar work. The humor and musical prowess of his band shine as well, especially drummer Terry Bozzio, who is the secret star of this film. Released in 1979, *Baby Snakes* was shown nonstop around the clock in a New York City theater before disappearing, like much of Zappa's best work, into commercial oblivion. A full hour was later cut from the film in a futile effort to please a potential distributor, but the original work is now available on video. At nearly three hours, it's the *Ben-Hur* of rock. (TR)

Interludes featuring the hallucinatory, obsessive clay animation of Bruce Bicksford, who also delivers some hilarious commentary, donating the phrase "disco out-freakage" to the English language *SCENES*

Warren Cucurullo, Janet the Planet *CAMEOS*

Baby Snakes, Broken Hearts Are for Assholes, I'm So Cute, Disco Boy, Bobby Brown Goes Down, I Have Been in You, City of Tiny Lites, Flakes, King Kong, Punky's Whips, Jones Crusher, Titties'n'Beer, Dinah-Moe Humm, Camarillo Brillo, Muffin Man, San Ber'dino, Black Napkins (Frank Zappa) *SONGS*

BACK TO THE BEACH   (1987)

CAST: Frankie Avalon, Annette Funicello, Laurie Laughlin, Tommy Hinkley, Demian Slade, Joe Holland, John Calvin, David Bowe, Connie Stevens; DIR: Lyndall Hobbs; PROD: Frank Mancuso Jr.; SCREENPLAY: Peter Krikes, Steve Meerson, Christopher Thompson; STUDIO: Paramount; 92 min., color (Paramount)

MUSIC	★
ATTITUDE	★★
FUN	★★

Frankie and Annette shut down the Mondos.
This reunion of Frankie Avalon and Annette Funicello is a lot better than anyone could have expected. It's funny, if only for the exaggerated self-parody. If you thought '60s beach movies made surfers look foolish, how about *Back to the Beach*, with its full complement of fake punk rockers and garish neon clowns? Annette shows her class by refusing to sing the rancid disco version of "Pajama Party" pre-

sented here. Instead, she performs "Jamaica Ska" with Fishbone, which is the only cool musical scene in the film. This hilarious, forgotten album track from 1964 became popular when DJ Rodney Bingenheimer (who cameos here) started playing it during the '80s mod/ska revival. It should be no surprise, however, that Annette remained hip—her independent-label 45 of "The Night Before Christmas" with the Ventures in 1980 proved her talent had been dormant for too long.

Frankie Avalon's comedic brilliance shines during the climax: While riding a tidal wave, he fusses with his hair, swings a golf club, and signs an autograph. Avalon also sings a cheesy version of the Rivieras' "California Sun" on-screen with none other than Dick Dale providing hot surf guitar. Then Stevie Ray Vaughan joins Dick on "Pipeline." They won a Grammy for this swill, but it really should have gone to the Chantays in '63. Pee Wee Herman hacks up the Trashmen's "Surfin' Bird" as multicolored afro wigs sway in the background. Cameos fill out the rest of the movie: Connie Stevens, Barbra Billingsley, Tony Dow, Jerry Mathers, Don Adams, Bob Denver, Alan Hale Jr., Edd "Kookie" Byrnes, O.J. Simpson, and Drew Steele (of the Surf Punks). But where were Candy Johnson, Jody McRea, Donna Loren, John Ashley, and Mary Hughes? They probably just weren't drawn by the sound of rock'n'roll, kids. Harvey Lembeck, rest in peace! (DP)

SCENES Avalon to a short-boarding mondo thrash surfer: "Boy, back in my day, a surfboard was about nine feet long, weighed 50 pounds, not like this sissy job. You had to be a real man to handle one of those babes. Ya know, I think this board has become a little bit effeminate, don't you think, huh?"

SONGS *California Sun* (Frankie Avalon, Dick Dale); *Pajama Party* (Cast); *Jamaica Ska* (Annette Funicello); *Pipeline* (Stevie Ray Vaughan, Dick Dale); *Surfin' Bird* (Pee Wee Herman); *Some Things Don't Ever Change* (Connie Stevens, Annette Funicello, Frankie Avalon)

BE MY GUEST   (1964)

MUSIC ★★★
ATTITUDE ★★★
FUN ★★★★

CAST: David Hemmings, Steve Marriott, Avril Angers, Ivor Salter, Jerry Lee Lewis, The Nashville Teens, The Zephyrs, Kenny and the Wranglers, The Nightshades; DIR: Lance Comfort; PROD: Lance Comfort; SCREENPLAY: Lyn Fairhurst; STUDIO: Rank; 82 min., b/w (no video release)

Seaside rock'n'rollers.

A follow-up to *Live It Up*, *Be My Guest* (same director/producer, screenwriter, studio, and male leads) has an equally contrived plot—all about a family that takes over a seaside resort and tries to put it on the map with help from some local and international rock'n'roll talent. It's reasonably well handled, helped by the fact that Hemmings and Marriott are probably the best acting leads ever to grace this sort of picture, and Jerry Lee Lewis (in an appearance that was shot the same afternoon he arrived in London) is in top form performing "My Baby Loves Nobody But Me." He's backed by the Nashville Teens, with whom he cut an amazing live album (*Jerry Lee Lewis: Live at the Star Club Hamburg*) that same year. (BE)

SCENES Hemmings and his band playing the title song, with Marriott on drums mimicking Keith Moon

LINES One shifty music biz type to another: "I'm telling you, the Mersey Sound can move over. From here on, it's the Brighton Beat."

SONGS *Be My Guest* (Nightshades); *My Baby Loves Nobody but Me* (Jerry Lee Lewis, Nashville Teens); *She Laughed* (Zephyrs); *Gotta Get Away Now* (Joyce Blair); *Somebody Help Me* (Kenny and the Wranglers); *Whatcha Gonna Do* (Nashville Teens)

BEACH BALL (1965)

CAST: Edd Byrnes, Chris Noel, Robert Logan, Aron Kincaid, Mikki Jamison, Don Edmonds, Brenda Benet, Gayle Gilmore, Anna Lavelle, Dick Miller, Lee Krieger, James Wellman, Jack Bernardi, Bill Samson, John Hyden, Rita D'Amico, Ron Russell, Brian Cutler, Sid Haig; DIR: Lennie Weinrieb; PROD: Bart Patton; SCREENPLAY: David Malcom; STUDIO: Paramount; 83 min., color (no video release)

MUSIC ★★★★
ATTITUDE ★★★★
FUN ★★★★★

Hot rod rally meets Gloop City.
Beach Ball is the most obvious bad ripoff of A.I.P.'s successful "beach party" format. Unlike the A.I.P. films, *Beach Ball* (and director Lennie Weinrieb's follow-ups *Out of Sight* and *Wild Wild Winter*) lack the continuity in humor and kinetic rock'n'roll staging that enlivens the A.I.P. films. Still, Weinrieb's choice in bands more than excused the lack of rock 'em, sock 'em dialogue. The Supremes are an absolute crack-up here. Not only do they sing the real cool "Surfer Boy" and "Beach Ball," but Diana Ross's wonderful hairdo looks like the left half of Salvador Dali's mustache.

The Hondells are a real gas here as they arbitrarily warm up with Brian Wilson's "My Buddy Seat," and the Four Seasons perform one of their finest tunes, "Dawn." The Walker Brothers groove on stage at a real hot rod show in Long Beach (as do the Righteous Brothers, the Supremes, and a fake band called the Wigglers). Someone who keeps popping up in these films is stock Beach Bunny deluxe Chris Noel. Her introduction to the Hondells is a classic in offhand, take-it-for-granted stupidity that makes junk pictures like this work so well. In the final analysis, *Beach Ball* is no knockout, but you wouldn't want to miss it. It's like entering a good junk store: Some of the stuff may be cheap, but it will stick out on your shelf for years to come. Viewing this 1965 hot-rod show on the big screen is like reading Tom Wolfe's *Kandy-Kolored Tangerine Flake Streamlined Baby*. (DP)

Edd "Kookie" Byrnes has one of the best lines ever during a teen nightclub dance sequence. When asked by a girl to leave the dance floor so they can talk, Edd replies, "Don't bug me, baby, I'm in orbit."

S C E N E S

I Feel Good, Surfin' Shindig, Wigglin' Like You Tickled, We Got Money (Wigglers); *Come to the Beach Ball with Me, Surfer Boy* (Supremes); *Dawn* (Four Seasons); *My Buddy Seat* (Hondells); *Baby What You Want Me to Do* (Righteous Brothers); *Doin' the Jerk* (Walker Brothers)

S O N G S

BEACH BLANKET BINGO (1965)

CAST: Frankie Avalon, Annette Funicello, Deborah Walley, Harvey Lembeck, John Ashley, Jody McRea, Donna Loren, Marta Kristen, Linda Evans, Timothy Carey, Don Rickles, Paul Lynde, Earl Wilson, Bobbi Shaw, Buster Keaton; DIR: William Asher; PROD: James H. Nicholson, Samuel Z. Arkoff; SCREENPLAY: William Asher, Leo Townsend; STUDIO: American International; 98 min., color (HBO)

MUSIC ★★★
ATTITUDE ★★★
FUN ★★★★

A mermaid needs Deadhead, while everyone needs Donna Loren.
Jody McRea (as Deadhead) finally gets a starring role in this, the fourth of A.I.P.'s *Beach Party* pictures. By this time, the beach gang themselves were becoming stars, so *Beach Blanket Bingo* cleans up their act a little after the raunch of *Bikini Beach*. The Hondells (whose "Little Honda" was a hit at the time) are the featured rock'n'roll act here, and they play in a posh setting as the cast goes high class. Donna Loren shows great beauty and tremendous talent belting out "It Only Hurts When I Cry." Linda Evans special guest stars as Sugar Cane and sings some of the better tunes, including "Fly Boy" and "New Love" with the Hondells. Her

singing voice is ghosted by Robin Ward, who had a hit with "Wonderful Summer" in '63. Annette's material is better than usual this time around as she bashes out the Wall of Sound-alike "I'll Never Change Him." Frankie Avalon blesses us with "These Are the Good Times," and Don Rickles gives a great performance as Big Drop (the plot centers on sky-diving). Deborah Walley makes her A.I.P. debut here (she was Gidget in *Gidget Goes Hawaiian*). After this, she became a beach gang regular. Not to be overlooked is the sinister role of South Dakota Slim, played intuitively by Timothy Carey.

A well-remembered hit from the era, *Beach Blanket Bingo* made tons of money. But the vitality of the *Beach Party* pictures was beginning to fade. All these nice kids, all cleaned-up and talking about their futures—producer Samuel Z. Arkoff must've known it was getting stale. The rest of the *Beach Party* flicks he put out all had some crazy twists of format, including *Ski Party, Pajama Party* (sci-fi), and *How to Stuff a Wild Bikini* (voodoo with Buster Keaton!). Frankie and Annette wouldn't star together again until *Fireball 500*, and in that film she ends up with Fabian! (DP)

Beach Blanket Bingo, I Think You Think (Frankie Avalon, Annette Funicello); *It Only Hurts When I Cry* (Donna Loren); *I Am My Ideal* (Harvey Lembeck); *New Love, Fly Boy* (Linda Evans); *These Are the Good Times* (Annette Funicello); *The Cycle Set* (Hondells)   **SONGS**

THE BEACH BOYS: AN AMERICAN BAND   (1985)

DIR: Malcolm Leo; PROD: Leo Peterson, Bonnie Peterson; SCREENPLAY: Malcolm Leo; 103 min., color (Vestron)

MUSIC	★★★★★
ATTITUDE	★★★
FUN	★★★

Castles made of sand fall into the sea, eventually.
You wouldn't expect an authorized Beach Boys documentary to dwell too heavily on the dark side of their Southern California myth. Thus, *The Beach Boys: An American Band* always looks for the silver lining while tracing the group's oft-cloudy history from 1961 until the mid-'80s. By this time, Brian Wilson is a 300-pound-plus Beached Boy. From bed, he responds to an interviewer's questions in a sincere but stilted monotone. The other band members—Carl Wilson, Dennis Wilson, Mike Love, Al Jardine, and Bruce Johnston—mostly recite from writer/director Malcolm Leo's script. A long sequence in which Carl visits a car dealer to the accompaniment of "409" nearly stops the movie in its tracks.

As Leonard Cohen once sang, "We are ugly, but we have the music." And the best of the Beach Boys still ranks with the finest American pop music of the past four decades. The performances in *The Beach Boys: An American Band* are culled from network television, early promotional films, and home movies. They range from a variety show lip-synch of "California Girls" to revelatory scenes of the *Pet Sounds* recording sessions. Other scenes include the band on tour in Czechoslovakia shortly after the Soviet invasion of 1968. The Beach Boys dedicate "Breakaway" to the deposed Czech president Alexander Dubcek. For a PBS special hosted by Leonard Bernstein, Brian Wilson performs an aching'y pure and tender "Surf's Up" alone at the piano. In 1971, the Beach Boys recast the Robins' "Riot in Cell Block #9" as "Student Demonstration Time" for a massive anti-Vietnam War rally in Washington, D.C. A decade or so later, they're back in the nation's capital playing an equally massive July 4th concert at the personal invitation of President and Mrs. Ronald Reagan. (AS)

Surfin' U.S.A., Little Surfer, Fun Fun Fun, I Get Around, Little Honda, Girls on the Beach,   **SONGS**
California Girls, Help Me Rhonda, In My Room, Dance Dance Dance, Wouldn't It Be Nice, Sloop John B., God Only Knows, Good Vibrations, Do It Again, Rock'n'Roll Woman, Breakaway, Student Demonstration Time, Okie from Muskogee, Heroes and Villains, Surfer Girl, Rock'n'Roll Music, You Are So Beautiful (Beach Boys); *Surf's Up* (Brian Wilson)

BEACH GIRLS AND THE MONSTER   (1965)

MUSIC ★★★★★
ATTITUDE ★★★
FUN ★★★★

ALTERNATE TITLE: *Monster from the Surf*
CAST: John Hall, Sue Casey, Walker Edmiston, Arnold Lessing; DIR: Jon Hall, PROD: Edward Janis; SCREENPLAY: Joan Gardiner; STUDIO: U.S. Films; 70 min., b/w (Sinister Cinema)

Rubber monster attacks sand-twisting teens!
More than 40 beach exploitation movies have been made over the years, but the soundtrack of *Beach Girls and the Monster* has got to rank up there among the best. Sure, "Malibu Run" by Gary Lewis and the Playboys in *Out Of Sight,* "Bikini Drag" by the Pyramids in *Bikini Beach,* and "The Gasser" by the Hondells in *Ski Party* were memorable moments. But in this film, no fewer than 13 different sections of full bore, deep-reverb tank surf instrumentals throb the soundtrack. But there's a mystery here: the band, always offscreen, is also nameless, as are all the songs! The main theme is reprised three times, but the best one has to be the second one, which is probably the longest surf instrumental ever performed by any band. Wild drum breaks and a wide variety of attack-guitar stanzas blend in with a montage of excellent surfing footage shot by a real surf filmmaker. Another great scene is the nighttime beach dance (to a song perhaps called "Beach Bongo Bo"), which is a stock bikini dance to a drenched Bo Diddley beat.

The star of this movie, filmed in glorious black and white, is John Hall, whom you may remember from *Girls on the Beach*. This is his masterpiece. He delivers each line of dialogue so stiffly that he's beyond criticsm. He's an idiot savant, perhaps, but an idiot nonetheless. The rubber-suited "monster," who kills four peole, turns out to be John Hall's father, further proving that it's always the parents' fault. (DP)

S O N G S   *More Than Wanting You, Monster in the Surf* (Frank Sinatra, Jr.)

BEACH PARTY   (1963)

MUSIC ★★★★★
ATTITUDE ★★★★★
FUN ★★★★★

CAST: Annette Funicello, Frankie Avalon, Dorothy Malone, Robert Cummings, Morey Amsterdam, Eva Six, Harvey Lembeck, John Ashley, Jody McRea, Dick Dale and his Del-Tones, Candy Johnson; DIR: William Asher; PROD: James H. Nicholson, Lou Rusoff; SCREENPLAY: Lou Rusoff; STUDIO: American International; 101 min., color (Warner)

Archeologist discovers lost surfer artifacts.
This is the blueprint for a film genre that in the course of three years spawned more than 40 clones and then vanished. Itself an exploitation of the dollars made from both *Gidget* (1959) and *Where the Boys Are* (1960), *Beach Party* banked on the same ingredients that made these cherry bombs explode: rock'n'roll combined with teenage junk culture, for which A.I.P. had an incredible feel. The formula worked, fooling everyone (including surfers) in the process. Along the way, Frankie Avalon unintentionally proved that he was a better comic actor than singer. Meanwhile, Annette Funicello found that there was indeed a world outside easy-goin' Disney vehicles. Helping them out in the *Beach Party* movies were comedians of the highest rank: Morey Amsterdam, Don Rickles, Buddy Hackett, Buster Keaton, and many more. In this one, Bob Cummings makes his mark as an anthropologist studying the tribal habits of surf dwellers.

So-called sophisticates who dismiss these films must realize what they're missing is the beat. *Beach Party* features Dick Dale and his Del-Tones. So does *Beach Party*'s follow-up, *Muscle Beach Party*. Do not advance on the later pics until you've seen both these beachers, because the continuity of the storyline is important. In *Beach Party*, we get the basic lesson: surf dwellers are a true subculture, and this is what they do. Real California surfers attending the premiere of *Beach Party* turned away in disgust. Such a criminal misrepresentation was considered a desecration of everything they held sacred. Things got so bad in the theater that Malibu legend (and surfing stuntman) Mickey Dora released a jar of moths, which promptly covered the screen. But 30 years later, *Beach Party* is one of the few places you can still see "hot curl" art, Tiki culture teen clubs, and Dick Dale playing lead guitar on Gary Usher-penned songs like the brilliant "Secret Surfin' Spot." Candy Johnson dances up a storm, Jody McRea rules as Deadhead, and Harvey Lembeck is preposterous as motor-sickle gang leader deluxe Eric Von Zipper. Kick open the doors! (DP)

Vincent Price   C A M E O S

Beach Party (Annette Funicello, Frankie Avalon); *Secret Surfin' Spot, Surfin' and a-Swingin'*   S O N G S
(Dick Dale and his Del-Tones); *Promise Me Anything, Treat Him Nicely* (Annette Funicello); *Don't Stop Now* (Frankie Avalon)

BEAT GIRL   (1960)

CAST: Noelle Adam, David Farrar, Adam Faith, Gillian Hills, Shirley Ann Field, Christopher Lee; DIR: Edmond T. Greville; PROD: George Willoughby; STUDIO: Times Films, 92 min., b/w (no video release)

MUSIC   ★★★★
ATTITUDE ★★★
FUN   ★★★★★

Mundane delinquent flick saved by Faith.
In most respects, *Beat Girl* is a conventional juvenile delinquency drama. Teenager Noelle Adam rebels when her father (David Farrar) remarries, and she ends up hanging out with the wrong crowd. The film's real value derives from the presence of Adam Faith, one of a handful of pre-Beatles British rockers who really had potentially world class talent. He isn't quite the Elvis Presley figure the producers would have wanted, but he does sing convincingly (his songs rock), and he is a better-than-average actor. (Faith later starred in the cult British comedy series "Budgie.") *Beat Girl* also offers a rare look at the beatnik scene in London's Chelsea district (glimpsed in pictures like *The Day the Earth Caught Fire* and the seldom-seen *The Party's Over*), which was a revelation to millions of American and British teenagers alike. The picture's grimy, realistic look doesn't hurt, either. (BE)

Beat Girl, I Did What You Told Me, It's Legal (Adam Faith); *Made You, The Stripper* (John   S O N G S
Barry Seven)

Beat Girl

BECAUSE THEY'RE YOUNG (1960)

MUSIC ★★
ATTITUDE ★★
FUN ★★★

CAST: Dick Clark, Doug McClure, Michael Callan, Tuesday Weld, Victoria Shaw, Warren Berlinger; DIR: Paul Wendkos; PROD: Jerry Bresler; SCREENPLAY: James Gunn; STUDIO: Columbia; 102 min., b/w (no video release)

Dick Clark as a quarterback who's too clever by half.
If you can't believe "American Bandstand" host Dick Clark as a high school quarterback, then how 'bout as a sensitive schoolteacher? In this film, Clark actually plays a star QB whose career is tragically ended by a car wreck that killed his brother and sister-in-law. Determined to make amends and stabilize his life, Clark becomes a history teacher and attempts to win custody of his orphaned nephew. Naturally enough, Dick runs afoul of the despotic principal, the crusty old football coach, *and* the student heavy. Meanwhile, he falls for the principal's frosty secretary, saves a student from a terrible home situation, and foils an armed robbery. Tuesday Weld shines as an archetypal good girl/bad girl, while Warren Berlinger (of "Kilroy" fame) and a very young Doug McClure fill out the excellent cast. Although its script never really surprises, *Because They're Young* is clever enough to rise above its genre. (KHB)

SCENES   Duane Eddy's performance at the school dance, one of his rare film appearances; Clark taking on a JD with a blade

LINES   Clark to the principal's secretary: "That wasn't chivalry. That was lust."

SONGS   *Swingin' School* (Bobby Rydell); *Shazam* (Duane Eddy and the Rebel Rousers); *Because They're Young* (James Darren)

BELOVED INVADERS (1965)

MUSIC ★★★★★
ATTITUDE ★★★
FUN ★★★★

DIR: George M. Reid; PROD: George M. Reid; SCREENPLAY: Junko Terayama; STUDIO: Interfilm; 80 min., b/w (Toshiba-EMI)

Instrumental action with the Ventures.
If you consider the number of great rock instrumental combos from the '50s and '60s—bands like Johnny and the Hurricanes, the Fireballs, Eddie and the Showmen, the Lively Ones, and the Revels—and how few of them are preserved on film, you'll realize how important *Beloved Invaders* is. This movie captures the Ventures on tour in Japan at their peak during the recording of *The Ventures on Stage* (their last significant album). By this time, the group had wielded its influence twice: the first time in 1960 when it defined the Fender guitar band sound that was quickly adopted by the surf scene, and later with *The Ventures in Space* LP, which irreversibly affected the destinies of hordes of aspiring guitarists (Jeff Beck included).

    Beloved Invaders is the best rundown of the group's material you could ask for. It's also a definitive summary of the rock instrumental genre. (The Ventures' cover of the Surfaris' "Wipe Out" is especially tenacious.) Ventures Don Wilson and Bob Bogle are regular American joes, and it's great to see Japanese kids celebrating the band for just the right reason: its music. Nokie Edwards is probably the most unconscious rock god ever. Almost stealing the show is the montage introduction: a Japanese boy thrills over the sound of "Outer Limits" on the jukebox while records are pressed, sleeved, and boxed; sheet music is bought; guitars are sampled; and more than seven Japanese garage bands bash out raving instrumentals. It's the meaning of life captured on film. (DP)

Out of Limits, Beloved Invaders Theme, So Good Now That You've Come Back Home, The Cruel Sea, **SONGS**
Walk Don't Run '64, Apache, Wipe Out, House of the Rising Sun, Telstar, Slaughter on 10th Avenue,
Penetration, Bumble Bee, Pipeline, Diamond Head, Caravan (Ventures)

BEWARE (1946)

CAST: Louis Jordan, Frank Wilson, Dimples Daniels, Valerie Black, Milton Woods; DIR: Bud
Pollard; PROD: Berle Adams, R.M. Savini; SCREENPLAY: John E. Gordon; STUDIO: Astor; 60 min.,
b/w (no video release)

MUSIC ★★★★★
ATTITUDE ★★★★★
FUN ★★★★

Louis Jordan is such a god of American culture that his face should be on the $50 bill.
Between 1941 and 1950, Louis Jordan was a huge star and sold millions of records
to black and white fans alike. The first generation of rock'n'roll artists of the 1950s
absorbed and loved Jordan's music. His influence on early rock was all-pervasive.
It only takes one listen to such Jordan's hits as "Saturday Night Fish Fry,"
"Barnyard Boogie," and "Reet, Petite, and Gone" to realize that he practically
started it all, and that nobody since has done it better.

Jordan also had a feature-film career, making cameo appearances in major studio films (such as *Follow the Boys* and *Swing Parade of 1946*) and starring in three
full-length, low-budget films (and one fifteen-minute featurette) for Astor
Pictures. *Beware* was the first, with a plot that involves Jordan and his band on
their way to New York to headline at the Paramount. Their train gets delayed for
a few hours in Ware, Ohio, which just happens to be where Louis's alma mater,
Ware College, is located. Louis visits the school and learns that it's in financial
trouble. He resolves to help bail them out, but meanwhile there's some business
to take care of with an old flame and a former rival. In every scene in this film,
Louis performs at least one of his steady-rocking hits. For those interested in
reading more about Jordan, try *A Separate Cinema: Fifty Years of Black Cast
Posters* (Farrar, Straus & Giroux) by John Kisch and Edward Mapp. It includes
an essay by Donald Bogle that traces the evolution and history of black cinema.
A must for film fans. (MC)

Louis's appearance in the film is preceded by a long montage put together by Fred **SCENES**
Barber. We see trains rushing in every direction, close-ups of Jordan's hit Decca
78s, theater marquees with his name in giant letters, newspaper headlines, and
magazine covers, all attesting to Jordan's awesome fame. This montage is so great
that the producers used it again in Louis's third feature, *Look Out Sister.*

How Long Must I Wait for You, Good Morning Heartache, Land of the Buffalo Nickel, Hold On, **SONGS**
*You've Gotta Have a Beat, Don't Worry 'bout That Mule, Long Legged Lizzie, Salt Pork West
Virginia, Beware, I've Got That Old-Fashioned Passion* (Louis Jordan)

BEYOND THE DOORS (1983)

ALTERNATE TITLE: *Down on Me*
CAST: Gregory Allen Chatman, Riba Meryl, Bryan Wolf, Sandy Kenyon; DIR: Larry Buchanan;
PROD: Murray M. Kaplan; SCREENPLAY: Larry Buchanan; STUDIO: Omni-Leisure International;
117 min., color (Unicorn)

MUSIC ★
ATTITUDE ★
FUN ★★★★

It's beyond us as well.
This mind-numbingly inane movie purports to reveal a secret CIA plot to stifle
'60s youth dissent by assassinating "the three pied pipers" of rock'n'roll: Jimi
Hendrix, Janis Joplin, and Jim Morrison! The scandalous story is told in docudrama flashbacks, although apparently no money was spent to re-create the magic of

the period. A small club stage and an audience of two dozen stands in for the Fillmore, nothing and nobody looks like the '60s, and the original songs (written, no doubt, to sidestep royalty payments) are consistently awful pastiches of Woodstock-era rock. This moronic, pretentious film captures a vibe all right: that of watching an evening of dreadful tribute acts at a local cover-band nightclub (which is no doubt where this movie's "stars" were discovered).

Gregory Allen Chatman's Hendrix is weak, but he's great compared to the other members of the Experience played by two '70s dudes with floppy hats. Actually, Chatman acts like Olivier compared to Riba Meryl, whose portrayal of Joplin is limited to spouting vulgar cracks and crying in her gin about how lonely she is. Best of all is Bryan Wolf, who even resembles Morrison a little and talks like a retarded stoned surfer. Wolf creates some on-the-spot poetry about "boners against denim" and delivers his stage lines ("Is everybody in?") like Pauly Shore. The '70s drive-in style of *Beyond the Doors* makes room for lots of gratuitous profanity, nudity, sex, and even Jimi's vomit. (JS)

SCENES   Jimi's appearance at Woodstock, which in this movie takes place indoors! After his revolutionary performance of "The Star-Spangled Banner" (no expensive copyright here), the fake Hendrix collapses backstage. Two musicians ponder the moment. A white guy: "Man, what was he trying to tell us out there?" A black guy (holding in his toke): "What he was trying to tell us was that the fire next time is gonna be one...hot...mother!"

LINES   A Bill Graham type yelling at a lackey: "This isn't summer stock or a state fair! It's rock'n'motherfuckin'roll!"

CAMEOS   Stuart Lancaster

BEYOND THE VALLEY OF THE DOLLS (1970)

MUSIC ★★★★★
ATTITUDE ★★★★★
FUN ★★★★★

CAST: Dolly Read, Cynthia Myers, John La Zar, Michael Blodgett, David Gurian, Marcia McBroom, Edy Williams, The Strawberry Alarm Clock; DIR: Russ Meyer; PROD: Russ Meyer; SCREENPLAY: Roger Ebert; STUDIO: 20th Century-Fox; 109 min., color (CBS/Fox)

Forget whatever you thought you knew about Roger Ebert.
Not merely a corpulent TV star and Pulitzer Prize-winning film critic, Roger Ebert is also the screenwriter of *Beyond the Valley of the Dolls*, perhaps the greatest movie ever made. This film is loaded with surprises, and I'd hate to give any of them away, so I'll just say that *Beyond the Valley of the Dolls* is a hilarious black comedy about an all-girl rock group, the Carrie Nations, and their rise to the top. Ebert describes it as a "camp sexploitation horror musical." Trivia fans might also like to know that Lynn Carey, who sings most of the songs here (and is the daughter of actor MacDonald Carey), once recorded with a band called Mama Lion.

After this film, Ebert and director Russ Meyer remained friends and developed several other projects together, including *UP!* (1976) and *Beneath the Valley of the Supervixens* (1979). Two projects that never panned out are also worth mentioning here: One was to be a story about Elvis Presley losing his sex drive (the remedy was found eventually in the pituitary glands of the female beaver). The other was *Who Killed Bambi?*, a film starring the Sex Pistols and Marianne Faithfull that aborted after just a few days of shooting. The rumors surrounding the termination of this project include stories of financial problems, creative differences, and gunplay on the set.

Another Russ Meyer film that I highly, fervently recommend to rock film fans is *Faster Pussycat! Kill! Kill!*, which features much desert scenery in glorious black-

and-white. An action-packed, riveting saga of three bisexual go-go girls on a mur-
derous spree, *Faster Pussycat!* has been described by filmmaker (and film fan) John
Waters as "beyond a doubt, the best movie ever made...possibly better than any
film that will be made in the future." Maybe you've heard the Cramps' cover of
that film's theme song (originally sung by the Bostweeds). (MC)

SONGS *In the Long Run, Look Up at the Bottom, Beyond the Days of Now and Then, Come with the Gentle
People, Sweet Talkin' Candy Man, Find It, Once I Had You* (Carrie Nations); *A Girl from the City,
I'm Comin' Home, Incense and Peppermints* (Strawberry Alarm Clock)

THE BIG BEAT   (1957)

MUSIC ★★★
ATTITUDE ★★★
FUN ★★★

CAST: William Reynolds, Andra Martin, Gogi Grant, Jeffrey Stone, Rose Marie, The Diamonds,
The Del Vikings, Fats Domino, Charlie Barnet, The Four Aces, Harry James, The Mills Brothers,
George Shearing, Cal Tjader, Russ Morgan; DIR: Will Cowan; PROD: Will Cowan; SCREENPLAY:
David P. Harmon; STUDIO: Universal; 82 min., b/w (no video release)

Fake Beatnik Saves Day!
The Big Beat is one more of those late-'50s films whose plots centered on square
music-biz types struggling to cash in on the youth market. Here, Joe Randall—
head of Randall Records, a successful big band LP label—allows his son Johnny
(William Reynolds) to talk him into releasing rock'n'roll 45s. To find some good
acts, Johnny begins palling around with his secretary/love interest and her bohemian friends in Greenwich Village. One cat in particular, an older dude named
Vladimir, stands out as a bonafide hungry artist/nut case.

In the best '50s rock movie tradition, *The Big Beat* pauses for performances by
both rockers (Fats Domino, the Del Vikings, the Diamonds) and squares (Russ
Morgan, the Four Aces, Harry James). Turns out that Johnny's rock'n'roll business is losing lots of money, which does not make Dad and the Randall stockhold-
ers very happy. It all looks like a bust until Johnny discovers that Vladimir is really
supermarket magnate V.J. Carson, who likes to disappear underground for
months at a time. Sympathetic to Junior's problem, V.J. agrees to distribute
Johnny's records to every store in his national chain. Everybody loves Johnny
again, and all is cool. (BV)

SCENES Fats Domino performing the title tune and *dancing*

SONGS *All My Life* (Russ Morgan); *You're Being Followed* (Mills Brothers); *Can't Wait* (Del Vikings);
You've Never Been in Love, Call Me (Gogi Grant); *The Big Beat, I'm Walkin'* (Fats Domino); *It's
Great When You're Doing a Show* (Rose Marie, Cast); *Where Mary Goes, Little Darlin'*
(Diamonds); *Lazy Love* (Gogi Grant, Harry James); *Nobody Else But Me* (Four Aces)

BIG TIME   (1988)

MUSIC ★★★★★
ATTITUDE ★★★★★
FUN ★★★★

CAST: Tom Waits, Michael Blair, Ralph Carney, Greg Cohen, Marc Ribot, Willie Schwarz; DIR: Chris
Blum; PROD: Luc Roeg; STUDIO: Island Visual Arts; 87 min., color (Fries)

Tom Waits for no man...so watch him closely.
Big Time is based on concert footage from Waits's widely acclaimed 1987 tour.
The film itself is a dream sequence of events featuring songs from Waits's early
'80s trilogy of albums—*Swordfishtrombones, Rain Dogs,* and *Frank's Wild Years.*
The performances are intertwined with a subplot centered on Frank O'Brien, a
character out of Waitsian mythology, who has always dreamed of "a life in the
entertainment business." As Frank's career progresses from usher at a two-bit

movie house to ticket-taker at a once-majestic old theater, Waits appears onstage, a masked Lone Ranger of the downtrodden and misbegotten, spouting bullets of wisdom, which are just as often shots in the dark. As time ticks away, the viewer is absorbed into Frank's dreamworld, then jolted back into reality by the melodious cacophony of the onstage performances.

Big Time is about dreams, real and deferred, and the tick, tick, tick of time as it passes us by. The film is in constant flux between what is real and what isn't, what is attainable and what is lost. Waits is superb in a dual role, knocking the breath out of you with his quick onstage jabs as Frank rides his dream (however small) to the end of the line. (TP)

LINES Waits onstage: "The Lord is a very busy man, but I'll do what I can. Jesus is always looking at the Big Picture, but He helps us out of the little jams, too." "I feel like I know you, individually and as a whole room." "I saw a place that sells used erotica. What? Do they clean it? Who cleans it? Are they licensed?"

SONGS *Frank's Wild Years, Shore Leave, Way Down in the Hole, Hang On St. Christopher, Telephone Call from Istanbul, Cold Cold Ground, Straight to the Top, Strange Weather, Gun Street Girl, Ninth and Hennepin, Clap Hands, Time, Rain Dogs, Train Song, 16 Shells from a Thirty-Ought-Six, I'll Take New York, More Than Rain, Johnsburg Illinois, Innocent When You Dream, Big Black Mariah* (Tom Waits)

THE BIG T.N.T. SHOW (1966)

DIR: Larry Peerce; PROD: Phil Spector; STUDIO: American International; 93 min., b/w (no video release)

MUSIC ★★★★★
ATTITUDE ★★★★★
FUN ★★★★

Phil Spector meets A.I.P. on the Sunset Strip.
Originally billed as *The T.A.M.I. Show II* in preview hype, this repeat performance delivers on every level. The Lovin' Spoonful, Bo Diddley, Ray Charles, and the Ronettes all contribute riveting, electric performances in front of raging, screaming kids. Everyone has a ball with Roger Miller's underrated country numbers, and most of all, the church of Ike and Tina Turner can be built on this rock. *The T.A.M.I. Show* ended with a dramatic show-stopping contest between James Brown and the Rolling Stones, but *The Big T.N.T. Show* has no such competition, except for maybe Bo. Ike and Tina's blazing set, especially their performance of "Goodbye So Long," should wipe away 30 years of Ike's disrepute and then some. The Byrds' segment is legendary, and Petula Clark's rendition of "Downtown" is also astonishing. But the quality of the music should be no surprise, because Phil Spector produced the live orchestra. Joan Baez even turns up in a couple of numbers. For cameo appeal, Sky Saxon of the Seeds appears twice, perhaps only days after "Pushin' Too Hard" was cut.

There's only one thing missing here, and that's a future. Things would change very soon, and it's in *The Big T.N.T. Show* that we first begin to see the dividing line between '50s and '60s rock'n'roll and post-Monterey "rock." For an entire night, everyone jumps around, dances, and goes ape. Then Donovan takes the stage and suddenly the same audience sits down patiently and *listens*. That's the difference between a hot, boppin' sock hop and an arena seat, and this new seriousness can be seen as heralding rock'n'roll's decline. The closing of the film admonishes the viewer to "be sure to tune in for next year's show," but next year never came. *Big T.N.T.* captures that final, tantalizing moment. (DP)

SCENES The opening sequence with all the groups, kids, and dancers gallivanting on the Sunset Strip (during its peak) to Spector's M.F.Q. production "This Could Be The Night"

Roger Miller being interupted by a heckler: "Most of my songs are written about things that happened to me maybe when I was a kid, 'cause I was a kid for 11 years back in...that's right, HIPPIE!"

SONGS *This Could Be the Night* (Modern Folk Quartet); *Satisfaction* (David McCallum); *What'd I Say, Georgia on My Mind, Let the Good Times Roll* (Ray Charles); *Downtown, You're the One, My Love* (Petula Clark); *Do You Believe in Magic?, You Didn't Have to Be So Nice* (Lovin' Spoonful); *Hey Bo Diddley, Bo Diddley* (Bo Diddley); *500 Miles, There but for Fortune* (Joan Baez); *You've Lost That Lovin' Feelin'* (Joan Baez, Phil Spector); *Be My Baby, Shout* (Ronettes); *Dang Me, Engine Number Nine, King of the Road, England Swings* (Roger Miller); *Turn! Turn! Turn!, The Bells of Rhymney, Mr. Tambourine Man* (Byrds); *The Universal Soldier, The Reflections of a Summer Day, Bert's Blues, Sweet Joy* (Donovan); *Shake!, It's Gonna Work Out Fine, Please Please Please, Goodbye So Long* (Ike and Tina Turner); *One Two Three* (Ray Charles Orchestra)

BIKINI BEACH (1964)

MUSIC ★★★★★
ATTITUDE ★★★★★
FUN ★★★★★

CAST: Frankie Avalon, Annette Funicello, Martha Hyer, Don Rickles, Harvey Lembeck, John Ashley, Candy Johnson, Meredith McRae, Keenan Wynn, Danielle Aubrey, Little Stevie Wonder, Dolores Wells, Donna Loren, Paul Smith, James Westerfield; DIR: William Asher; PROD: James H. Nicholson, Samuel Z. Arkoff; SCREENPLAY: William Asher, Leo Townsend, Robert Dillon; STUDIO: American International; 99 min., color (Embassy)

Siesta by the Sea suffers the Pyramid Stomp.
What we get here is a cheaper version of the successful A.I.P./ *Beach Party* formula that's less expensive because it uses fewer big names and even leaves out s few regular cast members. Its absolute highlight is an appearance by the Pyramids, an authentic garage-surf band. This colorful group first hit in 1963 with the reverb-pumped "Penetration." Sometimes they'd arrive at their gigs in a helicopter, and one time they pulled up in front of the ballroom on an elephant! In *Bikini Beach* as well, they do not disappoint. Reacting to the Mop Top craze of 1964, the Pyramids appear onstage in Beatles wigs. A fishing line from above jerks the mops straight off to reveal shaven baldy beans as the band crashes into "Record Run." Taking another step in the right direction, A.I.P. allowed the band to play an instrumental, "Bikini Drag," and a great one it is. This Gary Usher tune, the "Miserlou" of the '90s, has been covered by such current surf acts as the Phantom Surfers, the Finks, and the Boardwalkers, almost 30 years after its debut in this film.

Often overlooked is a scene that best captures the spirit of the A.I.P. beachers. It features Donna Loren wigging out in the middle of a circle of kids, dancing to her girl-group shouter "Love's a Secret Weapon." The Exiters (later Candy Johnson's onstage go-go band) really stomp here, too, with "Gotcha Where I Want Ya." And Little Stevie Wonder must have had so much fun doing *Muscle Beach Party* that he returned to sing "Happy Feelin'" in this one. As a rule of thumb, you can forget about the plot in these movies, but be sure you see enough to tell people about Don Rickles's take as Big Drag. Annette Funicello rules as usual, singing the title song, another Usher classic. The only flub here is committed by Frankie Avalon, who is great in his usual role but makes an ass out of himself when he puts down the British Invasion. (DP)

CAMEOS Boris Karloff

SONGS *Bikini Beach* (Cast); *Love's a Secret Weapon* (Donna Loren); *Gimme Your Love, How about That* (Frankie Avalon); *Because You're You* (Frankie Avalon, Annette Funicello); *This Time It's Love* (Annette Funicello); *Record Run, Bikini Drag* (Pyramids); *Gotcha Where I Want You* (Exiters); *Happy Feelin'* (Little Stevie Wonder)

AMERICAN INTERNATIONAL'S
The BIG T.N.T SHOW
JAMES H. NICHOLSON, SAMUEL Z. ARKOFF & HENRY SAPERSTEIN · PHIL SPECTOR · LARRY PEERCE
BAEZ
CLARK
SPOONFUL
RONETTES
Tina TURNER
DIDDLEY
MODERN
QUARTET
McCALLUM
© 1966 AMERICAN INTERNATIONAL PICTURES

Blackboard Jungle

THE BLACKBOARD JUNGLE   (1955)

CAST: Glenn Ford, Anne Francis, Sidney Poitier, Vic Morrow; DIR: Richard Brooks; PROD: Pandro S. Berman; SCREENPLAY: Richard Brooks; STUDIO: MGM; 101 min., b/w (MGM/UA)

MUSIC ★
ATTITUDE ★★★★
FUN ★★★

The first rock film.
When Bill Haley and his Comets released "Rock Around the Clock" during the summer of 1954—the summer that Elvis first stumbled into Sun Records in Memphis—the song went nowhere. A year later, rereleased, it topped *Billboard*'s pop chart for eight straight weeks. What made the difference? Clearly, *The Blackboard Jungle*, one of the first teenage exploitation flicks. Haley's R&B ripoff, the one bit of music in the entire picture, plays only during the opening and closing credits. But that was enough to make it the first rock'n'roll mega-hit by a white band. Of course, it didn't hurt the song's popularity that riots in movie theaters all over the country made *Blackboard Jungle* national news.

The story is classic: Glenn Ford plays a returning, idealistic World War II vet beginning his first teaching job at the '50s version of a dangerous, inner-city high school. The school, North Manual Trades, is populated entirely with switchblade-wielding JDs of every ethnicity. There are blacks (most notably Sidney Poitier), Irish (Vic Morrow), Italians (a very young Paul Mazursky), and Hispanics, too. Most of them have it in for Glenn, who only wants "to reach them." Watching *Blackboard Jungle*, you get the feeling that when the schlockmeisters in Hollywood saw this film for the first time, they shot right up out of their seats and shouted, "Yes! That's it!" (DR)

BLAST-OFF GIRLS   (1967)

CAST: Dan Conway, Ray Sager, The Faded Blue, Charlie, Sharon Camille; DIR: Herschell Gordon Lewis; PROD: Herschell Gordon Lewis; SCREENPLAY: Herschell Gordon Lewis; STUDIO: Creative Film Enterprises; 85 min., color (Something Weird)

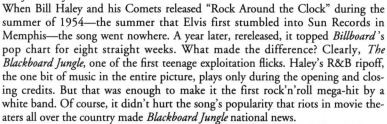

MUSIC ★★★★★
ATTITUDE ★★★
FUN ★★★★

The garage rock Citizen Kane.
Few films include appearances by genuine garage bands—local groups that flourished in every American city throughout the 1960s, all trying to emulate the Beatles and the Stones. Most of these groups never played a show larger than a Battle of the Bands at the local shopping center. Even fewer left behind a single or two on a regional label. *Blast-off Girls*, however, is a full-length feature actually *starring* two such Chicago bands. And it's directed by none other than the celebrated Wizard of Gore, Herschell Gordon Lewis. This film is almost too good to be true.

The sleazy world of rock seems a perfect subject for exploitation king Lewis, but in fact *Blast-Off Girls* has no violence or viewable sex. What we get instead are generous helpings of the bands, both of whom pass through the greedy hands of crooked manager Boojie Baker (nicely played by Dan Conway). Charlie, a raw garage combo, perform a cool song called "Bad Day" (the 45 was released on the Vision label) and a rock version of "Goodnight Ladies," which they turn into "Goodnight Boojie" after the manager tries to rip them off. Undaunted, Boojie finds another young band he can exploit, the Faded Blue, which he discovers in the Mother Blues club (complete with posters advertising Howlin' Wolf and Otis Rush).

A note for trivia fans: Chris Wolsky, the Faded Blue's Cordovox player, was a founding member of the New Colony Six, but his dad made him quit the band after a bad report card (he was still in high school). His poor grades thus forced him to miss out on what would become one of the Windy City's hottest musical exports. At least he got to star in this movie. Charlie's lead singer, Steve White, who wrote "Bad Day" because "at the time I was heavily into dope," also got to appear in Herschell Gordon Lewis's *She Devils on Wheels* and *Just for the Hell of It*, in which he plays a nihilistic delinquent (as did Faded Blue drummer Ralph Mullin). The Faded Blue are on display throughout this movie: live, in the studio, rehearsing, and even doing some real acting. They're wonderful, and *Blast-Off Girls* is a lasting monument to their glory. There's even a promotional clip of sorts at the end, with the band clowning around Chicago's Lincoln Park Zoo in *A Hard Day's Night* fashion. Charlie are great, too. (JS)

CAMEOS Colonel Harlan Sanders

SONGS *Bad Day, Goodnight Ladies* (Charlie); *The Next Time, You Got Me Where You Want Me, Stop Hear What I Say, Noise, Blast-Off, Go _____ Yourself, If Only I Could Find a Way* (Faded Blue)

BLONDE ON A BUM TRIP (1968)

CAST: Alexis Wassel, Don Nevins, Barbara Spiegelber, Carole Trent; DIR: Ralph Mauro; PROD: Jack Bravman, Ed Adlum; STUDIO: Nile Street; 64 min., b/w (no video release)

MUSIC ★★★★
ATTITUDE ★★★★
FUN ★★★★

100% hippie-free LSD movie.
Although it bears all the hallmarks of a student film project—shaky, handheld camerawork; badly dubbed dialogue; poor sound effects; hopelessly stilted acting—the deliciously titled *Blonde on a Bum Trip* still has a lot to offer fans of B-movie trash and rock'n'roll subculture. Such as: college girls in black lace underwear, a solid garage band soundtrack, plenty of gratuitous sex (or at least dry humping), and authentic dance club scenes filmed at the Rolling Stone Discotheque in New York City. It's an acid movie unlike any you've ever seen. In fact, unless its low budget and amateurish style offend you, it's anything but a bum trip.

Although released in 1968, the movie has a look and feel more in keeping with 1966. The short-haired, clean-shaven college boys wear sweaters and slacks and date back-combed, bouffanted girls with heavy eyeliner and pointy bras. No acid rock here, either; the music is straight garage-punk. The nightclub action features a band that looks every inch like a junior-league Young Rascals. Although they don't appear in the film, San Jose's E-Types play on the soundtrack, and their "Put the Clock Back on the Wall" is reprised what seems like a hundred times in the film. You can also hear Long Island's own Vagrants, featuring future Mountainous fat boy Leslie West. (MS)

SCENES A roomful of dancing, bongo-beating teens chanting "LSD's got a hold on me."

SONGS *Put the Clock Back on the Wall* (E-Types); *I Love You Yes I Do* (Vagrants); *Out of Sight Out of Mind, Is It On Is It Off?* (Bit a Sweet)

BLOW-UP (1966)

CAST: David Hemmings, Vanessa Redgrave, Sarah Miles, Verushka, Jane Birkin; DIR: Michelangelo Antonioni; PROD: Carlo Ponti; SCREENPLAY: Michelangelo Antonioni, Tonio Guerra (English dialogue by Edward Bond); STUDIO: MGM; 102 min., color (MGM/UA)

MUSIC ★★★★★
ATTITUDE ★★
FUN ★★★

Chic alienation and groovy decay in swinging London.
Director Michelangelo Antonioni, celebrated for his arty mood movies about the moral emptiness of the rich and famous, wanted to go where the decline-of-the-West action was. So he set this story of an arrogant, bored young fashion photog-

rapher (David Hemmings), who may (or may not) have captured a murder on film, in the mid-'60s capital of pop-star glamour and hedonism.

The supposedly shocking images of miniskirted mod waifs, affectless sex, and joints being passed about are quaint and rather charming: snapshots of a manic pop scene just before it was swept into the discard bin of history. Except for Vanessa Redgrave's long limbs and piercing, aristocratic stare, the movie's square "head trips" and phony objectivity are a pain. But just when the eyes start to glaze over at the ham-fisted ennui of it all, the Yardbirds materialize out of thin air. Tearing into a feedback-drenched "Stroll On" (actually "Train Kept A-Rollin'" refitted with new lyrics for copyright reasons), in three frantically exciting minutes they trashed the club right along with most of the movie's pretentions. (HH)

Redgrave does a herky-jerky dance and then is introduced to pot (0:46); A smirking Jeff Beck and a babyfaced Page play "Stroll On" to an audience of motionless zombies. Then Beck smashes his guitar (ripping off the Who at Antonioni's insistence), the crowd abruptly comes to life, and a riot breaks out (1:27). **SCENES**

Stroll On (Yardbirds) **SONGS**

BLUE HAWAII (1961)

CAST: Elvis Presley, Joan Blackman, Angela Lansbury, Nancy Walters, Roland Winters, John Archer; DIR: Norman Taurog; PROD: Hal B. Wallis; SCREENPLAY: Hal Kanter; STUDIO: Paramount; 101 min., color (Key)

MUSIC ★★★★
ATTITUDE ★★
FUN ★★

Elvis does Hawaii I—by land.
Elvis's eighth film did reasonably well at the box office, often shown on a double bill with Ricardo Montalban's Spanish-Italian movie *Desert Warrior*. It was the first of the King's Hawaiian trilogy (along with *Paradise Hawaiian Style* and *Girls, Girls, Girls*), all of which boast uncannily similar story lines. Of the three, this one's probably the most difficult to watch, often losing the viewer as it ventures deep into that familiar surreal world of the generic Elvis musical.

Chad Gates (Elvis) has just returned to Hawaii from serving in the Italian army and becomes embroiled in the classic young man's struggle to find himself. Most of the time, he winds up finding a lot of girls and sticky situations involving girls. Angela Lansbury plays one of Chad's hapless parents (she's not gonna solve any murders in this one), whom Elvis avoids like the plague to keep from having to work at his pop's fruit company. No matter how sexist Elvis gets (he's actually not too bad in this one), he makes it up as usual by hitting another jerk to defend a girl's honor. Chad eventually realizes that the one thing he can do is find his way around, so he opens a tourism service called Gates Of Hawaii: conclusive proof that travel doesn't necessarily broaden the mind. (MB)

Elvis lovingly singing "Can't Help Falling in Love" to the tune of an Austrian music box (0:32); Elvis spanking a girl over his knee (1:32) **SCENES**

Mrs. Prentice: "Do you think you can satisfy a school teacher and four teenage girls?" Elvis: "Well, uh, I'll sure try, ma'am. I'll do all I can." **LINES**

Flora Hayes, Howard McNear **CAMEOS**

Blue Hawaii, Almost Always True, Aloha Oe, No More, Can't Help Falling in Love, Rock-a-Hula Baby, Moonlight Swim, Ku-u-i-Po, Ito Eats, Slicin' Sand, Hawaiian Sunset, Beach Boy Blues, Island of Love (Kauai), Hawaiian Wedding Song (Elvis Presley) **SONGS**

CORN
BREAD

SHORT RIBS

Blues Brothers

THE BLUES BROTHERS (1980)

CAST: John Belushi, Dan Aykroyd, John Candy, Henry Gibson, Carrie Fisher, Charles Napier; DIR: John Landis; PROD: Robert K. Weiss; SCREENPLAY: Dan Aykroyd, John Landis; STUDIO:Universal; 133 min., color (MCA)

MUSIC ★★★★
ATTITUDE ★★★
FUN ★★★

Cars crash as solid characters fall victim to bulk.

Ahead of its time with large budgets, action sequences, and a big-name director, *The Blues Brothers* was an ambitious and groundbreaking step for modern musicals. Belushi and Aykroyd's deadpan humor and zany live performances should have been enough for this weakly plotted but entertaining movie. But director John Landis is perhaps too ambitious. He feels it necessary to justify this big-screen adaptation of the "Saturday Night Live" skit by doing things live television can't—specifically, car chases followed by the inevitable car crashes. Brilliant cameo performances by James Brown, John Lee Hooker, Aretha Franklin, Cab Calloway and Ray Charles make *The Blues Brothers* a classic, but these great scenes are spread too thin by unnecessary action. At over two hours, there's more quantity than quality. And wouldn't one more Ray Charles song have been worth a ten-police-car pileup? Perhaps Landis was confusing Bo Diddley and Bo ("Dukes of Hazzard") Duke. (ALa)

The requested "Theme from Rawhide" at Bob's Country Bunker (1:08)　　*SCENES*

Blues Brothers: "We're on a mission from God."　　*LINES*

James Brown, Cab Calloway, Aretha Franklin, Ray Charles, John Lee Hooker　　*CAMEOS*

The Old Landmark (James Brown); *Cuando* (Murph and the Magic Tones); *Boom Boom* (John Lee Hooker); *Think* (Aretha Franklin); *Shake a Tail Feather* (Ray Charles); *Minnie the Moocher* (Cab Calloway); *Somebody to Love, Sweet Home Chicago, Jailhouse Rock, Gimme Some Lovin', Theme from Rawhide, Stand by Your Man* (Blues Brothers)　　*SONGS*

BOP GIRL GOES CALYPSO (1957)

CAST: Judy Tyler, Bobby Troup, Margo Woode, Mary Kaye Trio, The Goofers, Lord Flea, Nino Tempo, The Titans; DIR: Howard W. Koch; PROD: Aubrey Schenk; SCREENPLAY: Arnold Belgard; STUDIO: Bel-Air/United Artists; 79 min., b/w (no video release)

MUSIC ★
ATTITUDE ★
FUN ★

Caucasians in disgrace.

In early 1957, there was a flurry of speculation that calypso music might displace rock'n'roll and become the next teen music fad. This was partly due to the success of records of Americanized calypso music by Harry Belafonte, the Tarriers, and others, and partly because the show business establishment wanted to see rock'n'roll eliminated. Three films were made to cash in on the emerging calypso "trend": *Calypso Joe, Calypso Heat Wave* (courtesy of Sam Katzman), and the odious *Bop Girl Goes Calypso*.

This film opens with Nino Tempo tearing his clothes off and playing "Horn Rock," the same song he played in *The Girl Can't Help It.* Seated near the stage is Bobby Troup (the man who penned "Route 66"), a psychologist who's researching his thesis that rock'n'roll is dying, that calypso is gaining popularity, etc. Troup is searching for that sensational new star who can spearhead calypso's rise to preeminence. It takes a lot of doing, but in the end he convinces his new love, Jo, a singer, to forsake rock'n'roll, put on a straw hat, tie her shirt up at the waist, and sing with a fake Jamaican accent. It works. She becomes an instant star. Never watch this movie. (MC)

SONGS *Horn Rock* (Nino Tempo); *Rhythm in Blues, So Hard to Laugh So Easy to Cry* (Titans); *Fools Rush In, Calypso Rock* (Mary Kaye Trio); *Calypso Jamboree* (Lord Flea); *Hard Rock Candy Baby* (unidentified girl); *Wow, I'm Gonna Rock and Roll 'Til I Die* (Goofers); *Oo Ba Lo, Way Back in San Francisco, Rain, Calypso Boogie, Rovin' Gal* (Judy Tyler)

BORDER RADIO   (1987)

MUSIC ★★★★
ATTITUDE ★★★
FUN ★★

CAST: Chris D., John Doe, Luana Anders, Chris Shearer, Dave Alvin, Texacala Jones; DIR: Allison Anders, Dean Lent, Kurt Voss; PROD: Marcus De Leon; SCREENPLAY: Allison Anders, Dean Lent, Kurt Voss; STUDIO: Coyote; 84 min., b/w (Pacific Arts)

Even cowpunks get to live out their B-movie fantasies.
Daytime film noir? West Coast kitchen sink? You can bet that the three UCLA students who made this 16mm black-and-white project were well-versed in stylish genres of film, and style seems to be the main currency here. After a few reels of watching John Doe (of the band X) shuffle through abandoned drive-ins and piloting old trucks through the desert, you may think this is really a continuous loop of Levi's commercials. What plot does exist is eventually abandoned in favor of pretentious "interview" clips during which the characters talk to the camera in documentary style. But *Border Radio* does score high in hipness quotient, with a musician-filled cast that also includes Chris D. (Flesheaters, Divine Horsemen), Dave Alvin (Blasters), and other L.A. scene fixtures from the golden age of Slash Records. (The film was made three years before its 1987 release.)

Three rockers go into hiding after breaking into the safe of a nightclub that stiffed them. Dean (Doe), a guitar player, gets caught by some punk rock thugs who beat him, but Jeff (Chris D.), the band's enigmatic leader, escapes to Mexico, where he sits alone and sings to statues of Elvis. Meanwhile, Jeff's wife (Luana Anders) tries to piece together what happened. But that doesn't stop her from fooling around with the band's goofy roadie (Chris Shearer). People wear cowboy hats, set fire to old acoustic guitars on the beach, and swig beers in carefully staged shots framed by high voltage power lines. Eventually, everyone goes to Mexico in search of Jeff, and then the movie just sort of stops. Doe gives the best performance, but let's face it, shrugs and mumbling ain't exactly Shakespeare. Green on Red are seen here playing at the Hong Kong Cafe, while something called Billy Wisdom and the Hee Shees camp it up in a rehearsal studio. The soundtrack includes music by the Flesheaters, Tony Kinman, Los Lobos, Lazy Cowgirls, Divine Horsemen and Doe. (JS)

SCENES Jeff's roadie, offering a theory for Jeff's odd behavior: "You gotta understand. It's tough being a seminal L.A. rock artist."

BORN TO BOOGIE   (1972)

MUSIC ★★★★
ATTITUDE ★★★★★
FUN ★★★★★

CAST: Marc Bolan & T. Rex, Elton John, Ringo Starr, Geoffrey Bayldon, George Claydon, Miss Chelita; DIR: Ringo Starr; PROD: Ringo Starr; STUDIO: Apple; 75 min., color (MPI)

The glitter king glows and a Starr sparkles.
One of the better rock films of the '70s, this little known documentary about the late glitter-rocker Marc Bolan was produced and directed by Ringo Starr in Britain during the height of T. Rextacy—a teen craze every bit as potent as Beatlemania was in the '60s. The movie's structure is engagingly disjointed: Film of a Wembley concert cuts away to surreal *Magical Mystery Tour*-style clips, which actually work better than the original. Bolan plays opposite a monkey-costumed actor and a

dwarf—and later sings "Jeepster," "Get It On," and "The Slider" in a field accompanied by a string quartet. There's also a live studio session in which the band, backed by Elton John on piano and Ringo on drums, rips through surprisingly effective renditions of Little Richard's "Tutti Frutti" and Bolan's own "Children of the Revolution," surrounded by mirrors. The overall effect is a stunning testimony to Bolan's talent at its most appealing and dynamic. Ringo and Bolan—who died in a car crash in 1977—obviously had a great time making this movie, and it shows in every frame, down to the staggeringly funny end credits. Even for non-fans, this is a keeper. (BE)

SONGS

Jeepster, Baby Strange, Tutti Frutti, Children of the Revolution, Look to the Left, Space Ball Ricochet, Telegram Sam, Cosmic Dancer, Hot Love, Bang a Gong (Get It On), Let's Have a Party, The Slider, Chariot Choogle (Marc Bolan)

BREAKING GLASS   (1980)

CAST: Phil Daniels, Hazel O'Connor, Gary Tibbs, Peter-Hugo Daly, Mark Wingett, Jonathan Pryce, Jon Finch; DIR: Brian Gibson; PROD: Davina Belling, Clive Parson; SCREENPLAY: Brian Gibson; STUDIO: Paramount; 94 min., color (Paramount)

MUSIC ★
ATTITUDE ★★★
FUN ★

British post-punk piffle.
Breaking Glass is the fatuous tale of a Bette Midler lookalike in bad makeup (and with half the talent) who discovers the high emotional cost of fame. It's not that the film's acting performances are bad; it's just that the story is *stupid!* The film is incredibly dated (it bellows early '80s London), and unfortunately it's hilariously obvious. Danny (Phil Daniels), a young promoter/chart fixer, discovers Kate (Hazel O'Connor) hanging up gig posters in the street and decides to make her into a star. What follows is a silly, morose chronicle of her rise to fame in which Jonathan Pryce puts in a welcome turn as her heroin-addicted saxophonist. O'Connor wrote and composed all the songs that she performs here, which may explain why the music is so unbearable. (EC)

SCENES

An exec at Kate's record company (appropriately named Overlord Records) tells her she can't use the lyric "kick him in the ass" in a song. "How about 'bum'?" he suggests in all seriousness. "Or how about 'When I get my chance, I'm going to punch him in the nose, nose, nose'?" Sell-out Kate is indeed singing it his way by the end of the film.

SONGS

Have You Seen the Writing on the Wall?, You Are a Program, I Am the Black Man, When I Get My Chance/Kick It in the Ass, Top of the Wheel, Whoever Writes the Song Calls the Tune, You Drink Your Coffee I'll Sing My Tune, Behold What I Have Done (Hazel O'Connor)

THE BUDDY HOLLY STORY   (1978)

CAST: Gary Busey, Charles Martin Smith, Don Stroud, Maria Richwine, Amy Johnston, Conrad Janis, Dick O'Neill; DIR: Steve Rash; PROD: Freddy Bauer; SCREENPLAY: Robert Gittler; STUDIO: Columbia; 113 min., color (RCA/Columbia)

MUSIC ★★★★
ATTITUDE ★★★★
FUN ★★★★★

The Lubbock legend lives again.
Although it occasionally veers from the historical record, *The Buddy Holly Story* delivers a compelling search for the emotional truth behind the rise and fall of this unlikely rock'n'roll star. As Buddy, Gary Busey contributes the performance of his career, skillfully conveying the singer's restless creativity and relentless ambition. Busey's singing and guitar playing also make the songs here something more than

mere reminders of Holly's hits. On the road to success, Holly had to overcome parental doubts, religious fundamentalism, and Nashville studio dogma. Once he made it, however, things didn't work out nearly as well. The movie recounts the breakup of the Crickets, Buddy's marriage to Maria Elena, and the February 1959 plane crash outside Clear Lake, Iowa, that killed him. The Epic soundtrack album (now out of print) featured Busey's lead vocals on an assortment of Holly hits and medleys. Angered by the filmmakers' sometimes-casual attitude toward certain facts, ex-Cricket Sonny Curtis later released a single called "The Real Buddy Holly Story" on Asylum. (AS)

SCENES Buddy working out "Peggy Sue" in the back of a car (0:18); a garage recording session of "Everyday" (0:30); the very white Crickets playing the very black Apollo Theater (0:45); Buddy romancing Maria at a 3-D movie (1:05)

CAMEOS Paul Mooney

SONGS *Mockingbird Hill, Rock Around with Ollie Vee, That'll Be the Day, Everyday, Oh Boy, It's So Easy, Rave On, Words of Love, Maybe Baby, Well All Right, True Love Ways, Not Fade Away* (Gary Busey); *Whole Lotta Shakin' Goin' On* (Gary Busey, Jerry Zaremba)

BUMMER   (1973)

MUSIC ★
ATTITUDE ★★★★★
FUN ★★★★

CAST: Carol Speed, Kipp Whitman, Dennis Burkley, Connie Strickland, David Ankrum, David Buchanan, Diane Lee Hart; DIR: William Allen Castleman; PROD: David F. Friedman, William Allen Castleman; SCREENPLAY: Alvin L. Fast; STUDIO: Entertainment Ventures; 90 min., color (Magnum)

Exactly like real life.
This is how the band's manager describes Butts, the 250-pound bass player: "He's a PIG! The groupies don't dig him. Even his own mother don't dig him!" The other guys in the band have to fight off the groupies, yet Butts never gets any attention. Instead, he has to settle for voyeurism and visits to his mother's massage parlor. Finally, Butts's self-loathing consumes him. He snaps and ends up raping and killing until he's shot in the stomach at point-blank range by one of the groupies. Dying, he begs for an answer to the repeated question, "Why? Why? Why?" *Bummer* supplies the answer plus a great deal of hard-boiled action, nudity, and a few cheap laughs. (MC)

SONGS *Yes I Know, So It Goes, Like I Can, Search the Sky, This Time* ("The Group")

BYE BYE BIRDIE   (1963)

MUSIC ★★★★★
ATTITUDE ★★★★★
FUN ★★★★★

CAST: Ann-Margret, Bobby Rydell, Paul Lynde, Jesse Pearson, Dick Van Dyke, Janet Leigh, Maureen Stapleton, Ed Sullivan; DIR: George Sidney; PROD: Fred Kohlmar; SCREENPLAY: Irving Brecher; STUDIO: Columbia; 112 min., color (Columbia)

Rock'n'Roll Hall of Fame membership for Conrad Birdie now!
There are various theories as to how and why Elvis Presley was drafted in 1958, but we know this much: If Elvis hadn't been railroaded into the army, then this fine musical satire wouldn't exist. Based on the Broadway smash, *Bye Bye Birdie* is a film about what happens when a teen idol of godlike proportions gets his draft notice. If a 1962 issue of *Mad* magazine had been made into a movie, this would have been it. The Cold War, middle-American sensibilities, families, love, TV, and rock'n'roll are all held up as targets for goofy satire. Also, Bobby Rydell's hair makes its first, and last, big-screen appearance here.

Early in the film, Conrad Birdie (played by the great Jesse Pearson) makes one of the all-time classic movie entrances: hauling ass on a motorcycle flanked by his two lieutenants, each with a candy-apple-red Fender Jazz Bass strapped to his back. The three of them screech to a halt as the two sidemen dismount and raise their Jazz Basses over their heads to form an Arc de Triomphe through which Conrad slowly walks. Wow! (MC)

SCENES

When Conrad sings his first song, "Honestly Sincere," he starts it off with a chord on his Fender Jaguar that just drips with echo and tremolo. As Jeff Bridges once said, "Phew!... Rock'n'roll!"

SONGS

Bye Bye Birdie, Lovely to Be a Woman (Ann-Margret); *Goin' Steady, We Love You Conrad, Kids, Everything Is Rosie* (Cast); *Honestly Sincere, One Last Kiss* (Jesse Pearson); *One Boy* (Bobby Rydell, Ann-Margret, Janet Leigh); *Put On a Happy Face* (Dick Van Dyke, Janet Leigh); *Gotta Lotta Livin' to Do* (Jesse Pearson, Bobby Rydell, Ann-Margret)

CANDY MOUNTAIN (1988)

CAST: Kevin J. O'Connor, Harris Yulin, David Johansen, Roberts Blossom; DIR: Robert Frank, Rudy Wurlitzer; PROD: Ruth Waldburger; SCREENPLAY: Rudy Wurlitzer; STUDIO: Xanadu, Les Films du Plain, Chant Vision; 91 min., color (Republic)

MUSIC ★★
ATTITUDE ★
FUN ★★

The road goes on forever.
This seemingly interminable road movie trades on its numerous cameos of music scenesters in much the same way that Alex Cox's *Straight to Hell* did. (Co-director Rudy Wurlitzer, who wrote the cult classic *Two-Lane Blacktop*, also penned Cox's *Walker*.) But unlike *Straight to Hell*, which was a self-indulgent in-joke, *Candy Mountain* aspires to much more The result is a long-winded, humorless film filled with embarrassingly awkward cliches that add up to very little.

Kevin J. O'Connor plays Julius, a loser rock musician in New York who's better at growing and grooming cool sideburns than at honing his craft or earning a living. (Marshall Crenshaw also read for this role.) O'Connor's distant, wooden performance is the only convincing aspect of the film. At a rehearsal studio, Julius overhears a conversation between a rock star (David Johansen) and his middle-aged handlers about legendary guitarmaker Elmore Silk, who has vanished. Julius bluffs that he knows Silk and is given some money to help locate Silk and his wondrous, valuable guitars. Julius begins a long journey northward, tracking down various relatives and acquaintances of the missing luthier, all of whom are cantankerous oddballs played by the likes of Tom Waits, Leon Redbone, and Dr. John. Curiously, musical director Hal Wilner's preference for "authentic" roots music makes this a rock movie with virtually no rock'n'roll. If you stay awake until the end of this ponderous, phony nonsense, you'll probably wish you hadn't bothered. (JS)

CAMEOS Tom Waits, Leon Redbone, Dr. John, Joe Strummer, Arto Lindsay, Tony Machine, Rockets Redglare

CAN'T STOP THE MUSIC (1980)

CAST: The Village People, Steve Guttenberg, Valerie Perrine, Bruce Jenner, Paul Sand, Tammy Grimes, June Havoc, Barbara Rush, Marilyn Sokol, The Ritchie Family; DIR: Nancy Walker; PROD: Alan Carr, Jacques Morali, Henri Belolo; SCREENPLAY: Bronte Woodard, Alan Carr; STUDIO: EMI; 118 min., color (HBO)

MUSIC ★★★★
ATTITUDE ★
FUN ★

Alan Carr's wretched tour de force.
The liner notes to *The Village People: Greatest Hits* (Rhino) say that that the creator of the group, record producer Jacques Morali, got the idea for the band while watching a group of men in macho costumes dance together at 12 West, a gay disco in Greenwich Village. The Village People's visual image (one guy dressed as a cop, another as a construction worker, etc.) was conceived as a simultaneous personification and parody of male stereotypes. It surprised and puzzled Morali when the group became popular among mainstream consumers. Nevertheless, for about three years, the Village People were more or less the most popular singing group in the world on the strength of records like "Macho Man," "Y.M.C.A.," and "In the Navy." In the hearts and minds of many, these records are classics. Then, just as their popularity began to wind down (and their original lead singer, Victor Willis, bailed out), they made this movie.

I was sure that any picture with as horrible a reputation as this one had would be fun to watch. But it just didn't work for me. I blame: 1) the principal actors, who give shrill and idiotic performances; 2) director Nancy Walker, who made them do it; and 3) producer/screenwriter Alan Carr. But not the Village People. They rock. (MC)

I Love You to Death, Magic Night, O Danny Boy, Y.M.C.A., Liberation, Milkshake, Can't Stop the Music, Sound of the City, Samantha (Village People); *Give Me a Break* (Ritchie Family)   **SONGS**

CARNIVAL ROCK   (1957)

CAST: Susan Cabot, Brian Hutton, David J. Stewart, Dick Miller, The Platters, Bob Luman, David Houston; DIR: Roger Corman; PROD: Roger Corman; SCREENPLAY: Leo Leiberman; STUDIO: Howco International; 75 min., b/w (Rhino)

MUSIC ★★★★★
ATTITUDE ★★★★★
FUN ★★★★★

Slap echo and the Eternal Triangle.
Christy Christakos is a former vaudeville clown who owns a sleazy carnival night-club. Natalie Cook (Susan Cabot) is his featured singer, and Christy is totally obsessed with her. But she's in love with Stanley, a small-time gambler. When Stanley learns that Christy's creditors are about to move in for the kill, he lures him into a card game and wins control of the nightclub. This, of course, sends Christy drifting out of control toward spiritual ruin and madness.

Carnival Rock is a typical Roger Corman '50s film. It was shot on a five-figure budget, in a few days, in one location. It's not a typical '50s rock-exploitation picture, however, because *Carnival Rock* actually has some interesting characters and a real story. And the music is mostly outstanding: Rockabilly gods Bob Luman and David Houston are in fine form, and their lead guitarist is the legendary James Burton. Here, he looks to be about 15 years old and, as the saying goes, he plays his ass off. (MC)

The cat-fight scene between Natalie and Celia, a Vivian Vance-type who is   **SCENES**
Christy's former vaudeville partner

This Is the Night, All Night Long (Bob Luman); *Teenage Frankie & Johnny, One and Only* (David   **SONGS**
Houston); *Remember When* (Platters); *Ou-Shoo-Bla-O, There's No Place Without You* (Susan Cabot); *Carnival Rock* (Blockbusters)

CATALINA CAPER (1967)

MUSIC ★★★★
ATTITUDE ★★★
FUN ★★★★

CAST: Tommy Kirk, Del Moore, Peter Duryea, Robert Donner, Ulla Stromstedt, Jim Begg, Sue Casey, Peter Mamakos, Lyle Waggoner, Venita Wolf, Mike Blodgett, Brian Cutler, Donnie Comann, James Almanza; DIR: Lee Sholem; PROD: Bond Blackman, Jack Bartlett; SCREENPLAY: Clyde Ware; STUDIO: Crown International; 84 min., color (no video release)

Little Richard presides over hot bikinis.

Catalina Caper is tantalizing. It's like squeezing the last bit of something good out of a tube. There's hardly anything left, but it still gives you that last fix. An unlikely joy is the chance to see one of San Diego's few hitmaking bands, the Cascades, onstage in five different sequences. It had been five years since "Rhythm of the Rain," and here some of their swell, underappreciated later work can be enjoyed. Ray Davies gave the Cascades a couple of previously unrecorded Kinks tunes (ca. 1967), and one of them, "There's a New World," is only available in this film. Another great songwriter, Carol Connors, steps onstage with the Cascades to perform her collaboration with Roger Christian, "The Book Of Love." Connors was an important shadow figure in the L.A. surf vocal scene, although she was better known as the lead vocalist of the Teddy Bears (with Phil Spector) on "To Know Him Is to Love Him." Her performance is an unexpected gift for surf music fans.

Catalina Caper also benefits from the superb fashions for which the mid-'60s have become best known. The 1966-67 era featured some of the coolest swimsuits ever, and plenty are featured here. (For more swimsuit action, check out the frantic *The Day the Fish Came Out.*) None of the rock'n'rollers in this film would be caught dead without their swimwear—except for his highness, Little Richard, who is too hot, hot, HOT in his performance of "Scuba Party." Richard cut some fantastic, neglected recordings during the mid-'60s (such as "Bama Lama Lu"), but film appearances were rare. The hidden star here is choreographer Michael Blodgett, host of a live beach L.A. dance program called "Groovy." Most likely, he pulled the girls featured here right from that show's daily bikini contest. It's hard to tell by watching *Catalina Caper* that 1968 is just two seconds away. (DP)

SONGS *Scuba Party* (Little Richard); *There's a New World* (Cascades); *Book Of Love* (Carol Connors); *Never Steal Anything Wet* (Mary Wells)

CHANGE OF HABIT (1969)

MUSIC ★★★
ATTITUDE ★★★
FUN ★★★

CAST: Elvis Presley, Mary Tyler Moore, Barbara McNair, Jane Eliot, Leora Dana, Doro Merande, Regis Toomey; DIR: William Graham; PROD: Joe Connelly; SCREENPLAY: James Lee, S.S. Schweitzer, Eric Bercovici; STUDIO: Universal; 93 min., color (MCA)

Fewer Elvis songs make better Elvis films!

The contemporary 1969 content of this good-conquers-all ghetto drama hasn't aged well. Elvis puts in a surprisingly believable performance as Dr. Carpenter, assisted by three plain-clothed nuns led by Sister Michelle (Mary Tyler Moore), but the Black Power banter between Sister Irene (Barbara McNair) and some neighborhod brothers contains the N-word and will make contemporary audiences squirm, as will the vomit-inducing cutesy Elvis song "Have a Happy."

It's ironic that for his last film—or next-to-last (its follow-up, *The Trouble with Girls*, hardly included him)—Elvis finally breaks out of character, while Moore remains "Mary." Elvis is rail-thin, and his hair is weird: For the first time, it's parted and combed forward,. But its indecisiveness—no Beatle-cut for Elvis!—often makes it bizarre, especially in his final confrontation with Moore, where it looks as though he has a pinwheel pompadour. (AF)

The final scene during which Moore teeters between Elvis and God has quick film cut-ins of Jesus that anticipate Madonna's "Like a Prayer" video.

SCENES

Ed Asner, Timothy Carey, Darlene Love (singing and clapping with the Blossoms)

CAMEOS

Change Of Habit, Rubberneckin', Have a Happy, Let Us Pray (Elvis Presley)

SONGS

CHARLIE IS MY DARLING (1966)

CAST: The Rolling Stones; DIR: Peter Whitehead; PROD: Peter Whitehead; STUDIO: Lorrimer; 60 min., b/w (no video release)

Debut Stones documentary needs fresh Eire.
Watching Peter Whitehead's documentary on the Rolling Stones, shot during the band's 1966 Irish tour, is a frustrating experience, mostly because almost no music is heard in a well-recorded or even audible form. The one exception is a sequence that uses a portion of "Goin' Home" (from the *Aftermath* album) as background while they're (you guessed it!) going home. The group is shown coping with over-ardent fans, hangers' on—and generally dealing with their offstage world in a Dylanesque manner. The problem is that Jagger & Co. aren't nearly as articulate as Dylan, so the results are less interesting. The images are dark and grainy like the band, but the film is an honest portrayal of the group, warts and all. Even without any good live performance footage, it's worth a look. (BE)

CHARRO! (1969)

CAST: Elvis Presley, Ina Balin, Victor French, Barbara Werle, Solomon Sturges, Lynn Kellogg; DIR: Charles Marquis Warren; PROD: Charles Marquis Warren; SCREENPLAY: Charles Marquis Warren; STUDIO: National General; 98 min., color (Warner)

Elvis's last dramatic film.
Elvis wasn't one of those sissy actors. Nearly every Elvis film has at least one good, serious fistfight. In this one, besides the fistfights, he ropes and rides a wild horse. It's really him doing it. Elvis also has a beard in this picture, and it looks great. Some people have suggested that this movie was a flop in its time because Elvis's fans didn't care to see him in a nonsinging, dramatic role. That may be true. But it's also true that *Charro!* is nearly impossible to sit through. It's badly written and basically just horrible. Don't waste your time when you could be watching *Flaming Star* instead. (MC)

Charro! (Elvis Presley)

SONGS

CHUCK BERRY: HAIL! HAIL! ROCK'N'ROLL (1987)

CAST: Chuck Berry, Johnny Johnson, Keith Richards, Little Richard, Bo Diddley, The Everly Brothers, Jerry Lee Lewis, Bruce Springsteen, Roy Orbison; DIR: Taylor Hackford; PROD: Stephanie Bennett, Chuck Berry; STUDIO: Universal; 120 min., color (MCA)

The real king of rock'n'roll.
It's pretty safe to say that Chuck Berry is the single most influential figure in the history of rock'n'roll. He simply did marvelous work. Even Jerry Lee Lewis's

Chuck Berry: Hail! Hail! Rock'n'Roll

mother said so. In 1985, director Taylor Hackford made this film about Chuck Berry's life and music on the occasion of his 60th birthday. It's more than just a rock film.

Any self-respecting electric guitarist gets angry as hell if someone else messes with his or her amplifier settings without permission—and Chuck Berry has self-respect. Shown here rehearsing for his birthday tribute concert, Chuck gets into a shouting match over his settings with the concert's musical director, Keith Richards. It's obvious that Chuck doesn't think he needs anyone to help him figure out how to express himself—and he's right. On the other hand, could this film have gotten financing without the *Last Waltz*-style presence of Richards, Eric Clapton, and other contemporary rock stars? One reason why there's never a dull moment im this film is that all of its conflicts are laid out right there on the screen in front of you. In one of the film's great concert sequences, Clapton tears up the house playing an early Chuck blues ballad called "Wee Wee Hours." Then Etta James practically steals the picture with her version of "Rock and Roll Music."

Some of the film's interview subjects give long-winded, ill-conceived "explanations" of the origins of Chuck's music, but not Little Richard. True, you can't win an Oscar for Best Interview in a Musical Documentary. Still, for my money, Richard deserves one for his contributions here. What star power! John Lennon also puts in a memorable appearance in a clip from the old "Mike Douglas Show." As one of Mike's co-hosts, Lennon introduced Chuck Berry in 1974 as "the greatest rock'n'roll poet." As an interview subject, Chuck himself is no slouch, delivering the film's most thoughtful and insightful comments despite his flat-out refusal to discuss personal matters (such as jail). (MC)

LINES
Jery Lee Lewis on Chuck: "He's the Hank Williams of rock'n'roll." Chuck on his music: "Rock'n'roll. . . it's freedom."

SCENES
The ending, with Chuck all alone (except for the camera crew, I guess) playing the lonesome blues on an out-of-tune pedal steel guitar

SONGS
Come On (Robert Cray, Ingrid, Chuck Berry); *It Don't Take but a Few Minutes* (Eric Clapton, Chuck Berry); *Back in the U.S.A.* (Linda Ronstadt); *Johnny B. Goode* (Julian Lennon); *Brown Eyed Handsome Man* (Robert Cray); *Wee Wee Hours* (Eric Clapton); *Rock and Roll Music* (Etta James); *I'm Through with Love, Roll Over Beethoven, Almost Grown, Maybellene, Cosmo Blues, School Day, Carol, A Cottage for Sale, Deep Feeling, Memphis Tennessee, Little Queenie, Too Much Monkey Business, No Particular Place to Go, Sweet Little Sixteen, No Money Down, Nadine* (Chuck Berry)

CLAMBAKE   (1967)

CAST: Elvis Presley, Shelley Fabares, Will Hutchins, Bill Bixby, Gary Merrill, James Gregory; DIR: Arthur Nadel; PROD: Jules Levy, Arthur Gardner, Arnold Laven; SCREENPLAY: Arthur Browne Jr.; STUDIO: United Artists; 97 min., color (MGM)

MUSIC	★★
ATTITUDE	★★
FUN	★★

Keep your finger on the fast-forward.
A colorful music-ridden Elvis romp in which a millionaire's son, played by Presley, switches places with a young but eerily addled ski instructor (Will Hutchins, who in the late 1980s was a bicycle messenger at a Hollywood studio). Elvis wants to find out whether anyone likes him for himself. Hilarious complications ensue, during which Elvis wins the big boat race and the girl.

Set in garish Miami (though Elvis's scenes were all done in L.A.), this "Love Boat" predecessor rings in many has-beens: Gary Merrill, Shelley Fabares, an ex-Gildersleeve, and Bill Bixby, whose age and shellacked hair make him look weird in his role as a predatory playboy. Elvis's hair is its usual swept-back anachronism. And though not fat, he looks a little puffy. (AF)

COCKSUCKER BLUES

SCENES   Worst moment by far is the interminable *Seven Brides for Seven Brothers*-like musical production of "Confidence," in which Elvis dances around a playground.

CAMEOS   Jack Good, Sam Riddle, Red West

LINES   Gary Merrill: "I've always missed not having a son."

SONGS   *Clambake, The Girl I Never Loved, Confidence, A House That Has Everything, Hey Hey Hey, Who Needs Money, You Don't Know Me* (Elvis Presley)

COCKSUCKER BLUES (1972)

MUSIC ★★★★★
ATTITUDE ★★★★★
FUN ★★★★

Stones '72 tour exposed.

CAST: The Rolling Stones; DIR: Robert Frank; PROD: Marshall Chess; STUDIO: (unreleased); 95 min., color (no video release)

With the release of their definitive album *Exile on Main Street*, the Stones sought to document their own burgeoning celebrity and self-mythology by hiring renowned photographer-filmmaker Robert Frank (known for his documentary study of madness *Me and My Brother* as well as the brilliant cover photography for *Exile* itself). The resulting movie was at once so dreamy and harsh—crowded with scenes of the Stones nodding out, roadies balling groupies, and assorted tour hangers-on shooting up—that the band refused to permit its release. Eventually Frank secured the right to screen it once a year, but it has only appeared on video in bootleg form.

From the snatch of the corrosive, never-issued title song which Mick Jagger sings plaintively under the opening credits, it's clear this isn't quite your standard rock star propaganda. Sure, the music's good (ruthless calculation undermined by bursts of naked abandon), but the movie mostly takes place on the periphery, in the soft white underbelly of glamour and fame. It's as bleak and unforgiving as the Stones' best music—like the version of "Brown Sugar" here, which Jagger twists into an ode to a teen drag queen. (HH)

SCENES   Naked girl being groped in the Stones' jet as they impassively look on, squealing "I'm all slippery!"; Mick the epicure contemplating the South from his limo: "It's one of the few parts of America where you can really eat."

CAMEOS   Tina Turner, Dick Cavett, Andy Warhol, Terry Southern

SONGS   *Uptight, Satisfaction* (Stevie Wonder, Mick Jagger); *Brown Sugar, Midnight Rambler, All Down the Line, Happy, Street Fighting Man* (Rolling Stones)

COLLEGE CONFIDENTIAL (1960)

MUSIC ★
ATTITUDE
FUN ★

A professor's sex survey lands him in hot water.

CAST: Steve Allen, Jayne Meadows, Mamie Van Doren, Walter Winchell, Herbert Marshall, Cathy Crosby, Conway Twitty; DIR: Albert Zugsmith; PROD: Albert Zugsmith; SCREENPLAY: Irvin Shulman; STUDIO: Universal; 91 min., b/w (no video release)

At least this picture is balanced: absolutely *nobody* in it is believable. Steve Allen plays the professor, his real-life wife Jayne Meadows plays an investigative reporter, and Mamie Van Doren and Conway Twitty are (yes) college students! The plot's tenuous logic quickly collapses when students discover a stag movie that's been planted at the prof's house. One outraged student snaps, "I'm going to tell my parents." Yeah, right. (AF)

Elisha Cook Jr. (as Van Doren's father), Herbert Marshall, Rocky Marciano *CAMEOS*

College Confidential Ball (Conway Twitty); *College Confidential, Playmate* (Randy Sparks) *SONGS*

COMEBACK (1982)

CAST: Eric Burdon, Julie Carmen, Michael Cavanaugh, Jory Pfennigwerth, John Aprea, Louisiana Red; DIR: Christel Buschmann; PROD: Joachim von Vietinghoff; SCREENPLAY: Christel Buschmann; STUDIO: Von Vietinghoff; 96 min., color (MGM/UA)

MUSIC ★★
ATTITUDE ★★
FUN ★★

Rock loser burns transcontinental bridges.

Rocco is a washed-up L.A. rock star (played a little too convincingly by Eric Burdon) who's trying to stage a successful comeback with the help of a new manager (Michael Cavanaugh). Only problem is, Rocco is about as self-destructive as they come and the manager's favorite slogan (repeated about a zillion times in this film) is "When you're dead, you're great." As a matter of fact, said manager's last three clients are all residing in rock'n'roll heaven.

The plot (if you want to call it that) involves Rocco being stalked by the German boyfriend of an obsessive groupie, the groupie killing herself, and Rocco beating up his manager. Rocco then escapes to Berlin in the company of the stalking boyfriend, who is now his pal (that's right). Throw in an on-again, off-again relationship with a stupid L.A. model type who's got a death wish (played with no emotion by Julie Carmen), and you pretty much get the whole shebang right there. Besides watching Rocco pal around with expatriate bluesman Louisiana Red in Berlin, the scenes of Burdon on stage in leather pants and a Sex Wax T-shirt bellowing "Who Gives a Fuck" (a recurring theme song) are worth the price of admission alone. Let's just hope he's acting. (BV)

Do You Feel, Who Gives a Fuck, The Road (Eric Burdon) *SONGS*

THE COMMITMENTS (1991)

CAST: Robert Arkins, Michael Aherne, Angeline Ball, Maria Doyle, Dave Finnegan, Branch Gallagher, Felim Gormley, Glen Hansard, Dick Massey, Johnny Murphy, Kenneth McCluskey, Andrew Strong, Colm Meaney; DIR: Alan Parker; PROD: Roger Randall-Cutler, Lynda Myles; SCREENPLAY: Dick Clement, Ian LaFrenais, Roddy Doyle; STUDIO: 20th Century-Fox; 116 min., color (CBS/Fox)

MUSIC ★★
ATTITUDE ★★★
FUN ★★★★

Irish kids come of age with a little bit of soul.

Roddy Doyle's novel *The Commitments* was a rarity in fiction: It captured the spiritual essence and physical energy of rock'n'roll using nothing but prose. Alan Parker's film brings Doyle's world to life with a uniformly terrific ensemble cast, but it leaves a lot less to the imagination. What sounded so cool through Doyle's hyperactive bursts of capital letters, hyphens, and Irish slang turns out to be a plain old covers group, separated from the Michael Boltons of the world by just a few notches, albeit very significant notches. Andrew Strong and Maria Doyle can really sing, and because the music lacks Hollywood's usual sheen of technological modernism, the band's heart-and-soul seems genuine.

In portraying the embryonic stages of a low-level band, *The Commitments* is about dreams, about the void music can fill in otherwise ordinary and sometimes desperate lives. Parker drives this point home with cloying shots of dole queues, charwomen, cheery neighbors, and factory drudgery. Band manager Jimmy Rabbitte (Robert Arkins) is happiest while conducting mock interviews with himself about his impending fame. But what it's *really* all about is sex, as old, ugly saxman Joey "The Lips" Fagin (Johnny Murphy) proves: He's the only member of the band with true soul, and thus the one who sleeps with all three female band members. (JC)

SCENES   The audition montage where a slew of ornery goofs offer up bad influences (Spandau Ballet, Wings, U2) and bad cover versions (The Smiths) (0:11); the public transport performance of "Destination Anywhere" (0:29)

LINES   Jimmy on the reason they can play R&B: "The Irish are the blacks of Europe," an observation that's more P.C., but also far less meaningful, than Doyle's original "The Irish are the niggers of Europe."

CAMEOS   Sean Hughes, Alan Parker

SONGS   *Needles and Pins, 24 Hours from Tulsa, Mustang Sally, Do Right Woman, Too Many Fish in the Sea, Mr. Pitiful, Show Me, Bye Bye Baby, Take Me to the River, Dark End of Me Street, Hard to Handle, Chain of Fools, I Never Loved a Man, Try a Little Tenderness, In the Midnight Hour* (Commitments)

THE CONCERT FOR BANGLA DESH   (1972)

DIR: Saul Swimmer; PROD: George Harrison, Allen Klein; STUDIO: Apple; 95 min., color (HBO)

MUSIC ★★★★★
ATTITUDE ★★
FUN ★

The first of the major rock'n'roll superstar benefit concerts.
In 1971, Ravi Shankar asked George Harrison to help the famine-stricken people of Bangla Desh. The ex-Beatle responded to his sitar instructor's plea by coaxing some friends onto the stage at Madison Square Garden for a benefit concert. Having just recently stepped out of the shadows of Lennon and McCartney with the release of *All Things Must Pass*, Harrison called on those musicians who'd helped him with the album. Counting Eric Clapton and Bob Dylan among his guests, George created a blueprint for Live Aid and all the rest. At the time, these two mainstays of today's benefits were virtual hermits, the former junked out in hiding at his English manor and the latter in Woodstock.

As an historical document, *The Concert for Bangla Desh* captures a great moment in rock'n'roll. Yet today it's a labor to sit through the film from beginning to end. What's most worthy of attention now is what was criticized then—Ravi Shankar's set. The soundtrack album is better. (TP)

SCENES   The guitar interplay between Clapton and Harrison (0:52); the urgent, inspired performance of "Bangla Desh" (1:30)

LINES   Ravi Shankar, upon hearing the applause from the rock'n'roll audience as he the other Eastern musicians start to play: "Thank you. If you applaud the tuning so much, I hope you will enjoy the playing more." A journalist to Harrison: "Of all the problems in the world, why did you decide on this one?" Harrison to the journalist: "I was asked."

CAMEOS   Phil Spector

Bangla Dhun (Ravi Shankar); *Wah Wah, My Sweet Lord, Awaiting on You All, While My Guitar Gently Weeps, Here Comes the Sun, Something, Bangla Desh* (George Harrison); *That's the Way God Planned It* (Billy Preston); *It Don't Come Easy* (Ringo Starr); *Beware of Darkness* (George Harrison, Leon Russell); *Jumpin' Jack Flash, Youngblood* (Leon Russell); *A Hard Rain's A-Gonna Fall, It Takes a Lot to Laugh It Takes a Train to Cry, Blowin' in the Wind, Just Like a Woman* (Bob Dylan)

SONGS

THE COOL ONES   (1967)

CAST: Debbie Watson, Gil Peterson, Roddy McDowall, Phil Harris, Robert Coote, Nita Talbot, George Furth, Mrs. Miller, Jim Begg, James Milhollin, Phil Arnold, Melanie Alexander; DIR: Gene Nelson; PROD: William Conrad; SCREENPLAY: Joyce Geller; STUDIO: Warner; 96 min., color (no video release)

MUSIC ★★★★
ATTITUDE ★★★★★
FUN ★★★★

Do the Tantrum.

Debbie Watson plays a pent-up go-go dancer itching for her big break. She's up for a spot on the network rock'n'roll show "Whizbam," a detailed send-up of both *Shindig* and *Hullabaloo*, but the studio bosses keep giving her the shaft. So Deb wigs out, escapes from her go-go cage, and steals the mike from Glen Campbell, who's singing onstage at the time. While Glen does all he can to stop this crazy nonsense on live TV, Deb shakes and shimmies her way out of impending hand-cuffs. The audience goes wild, imitating her moves, and when a misdirected camera sends the message out to the nation, a new dance craze is born—the Tantrum! Enter Roddy McDowall as a parody of Phil Spector, a teen tycoon to manage her booming career. Deb gets fired from "Whizbam," but her go-go dancing pals take her to Palm Springs, where they see the Leaves perform "In the House of Dr. Stone." (The Leaves had hit with the garage punk version of "Hey Joe" earlier that year.) She soon meets out-of-step teen idol Cliff Donner (Gil Peterson), with whom she forms a duo. There are in-jokes aplenty in this wonderfully rockin' bombshell-in-wimpster-clothing. (DP)

The Bantams (and tons of other aspiring acts) sneaking onto Tony's floor of the Sunset Tower, trying to "get signed"

SCENES

McDowall ending an argument: "It's getting *warm* standing here."

LINES

The Cool Ones, Up Where the Air Is Thin, Have a Tantrum, It's Your World, When You Touched My Hand, Baby Love Is All I Need (Debbie Watson, Gil Peterson); *In the House of Dr. Stone* (Leaves); *Birth of the Blues, Secret Love, What Is This Thing Called Love?, This Town, Bad Woman Love* (Gil Peterson); *Just One of Those Things* (Glen Campbell); *This Town* (Debbie Watson); *Hey Hey Ronnie* (T.J. and the Fourmations); *I'm So Happy* (Bantams); *Where Did I Go Wrong?* (Roddy McDowell, Cast); *It's Magic* (Mrs. Miller)

SONGS

CROSSROADS   (1986)

CAST: Ralph Macchio, Joe Seneca, Jamie Gertz; DIR: Walter Hill; PROD: Mark Carliner; SCREENPLAY: John Fusco; STUDIO: Columbia; 100 min., color (RCA/Columbia)

MUSIC ★★
ATTITUDE ★★
FUN ★★

Devil's food that's hard to stomach.

In a music business full of larger-than-life characters, blues great Robert Johnson stands apart. His "crossroads" deal with Satan, exchanging his soul for talent, may be the biz's most repeated legend. It's difficult to imagine anybody in 1986 screwing up the story. But *Crossroads* does exactly that. A limp contemporary adventure, it sends 17-year-old guitar prodigy Ralph Macchio (*The Karate Kid*) to rescue

Johnson's elderly friend Willie Brown (Joe Seneca) from his own crossroads deal. Excellent opportunities to feature real blues legends and bars are wasted. Instead, bluesmen are made to look like petty criminals as the generation-gapped duo hitchhikes from New York to Mississippi. Despite the picturesque journey, *Crossroads* is essentially a one-scene movie—a sizzling guitar duel for Brown's soul between ex-Frank Zappa and David Lee Roth guitarist Steve Vai and a Ry Cooder-enhanced Macchio (1:24). Even this one exciting scene is probably best suited for serious players or fans of instrumental guitar music. Little else in the movie offers anything remotely revealing about the blues. So if you haven't heard Johnson's story yet, get it somewhere else. (ALa)

SCENES   Brown to Macchio's cocky guitar-playing Eugene Martone: "You ain't even the beginning of a pimple on that late great Robert Johnson's ass."

SONGS   *Cotton Needs Pickin', Maintenance Man* (Wonders); *Willie Brown's Blues* (Joe Seneca, Wonders, Ry Cooder); *Feelin' Bad Blues* (Ry Cooder); *Butler's Bag, Head Cuttin' Duel* (Steve Vai, Ry Cooder); *Eugene's Trick Bag* (Steve Vai); *Walkin' Blues* (Sonny Terry, Ry Cooder)

CRY BABY   (1990)

MUSIC ★★★★★
ATTITUDE ★★★★★
FUN ★★

CAST: Johnny Depp, Amy Locane, Ricki Lake, Iggy Pop, Traci Lords, Darren E. Burrows, Kim Maguire, Polly Bergen, Susan Tyrell, Stephen Maker; DIR: John Waters; PROD: Rachel Talalay; SCREENPLAY: John Waters; STUDIO: Universal; 86 min., color (MCA/Universal)

Many a tear has to fall.
Trash film guru John Waters uses the standard '50s teen film format to document faithfully the perversity of American culture. "Drape" king Wade "Cry Baby"

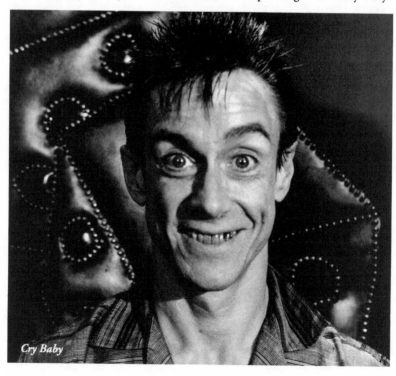

Cry Baby

Walker (Johnny Depp) and "Square" queen Alison Vernon Williams (Amy Locane) fall for each other while getting booster shots. She's captivated by the solitary tear drifting down his cheek. Mayhem ensues as one protagonist changes so that the course of true love can run smoothly. Will it be Cry Baby? Think again. We're talking Johnny Depp here. So Alison makes the transition from Square to Drape (Scrape?)—despite opposition from the entire Square population—with the help of the Cry Baby Girls: sister Pepper Walker (Ricki Lake), town tease Wanda (ex-porn star Traci Lords) and the appropriately named Hatchet Face (Kim Maguire). And yes, there is a drag race or two. (KW)

Alison, about to ride off into the sunset on the back of Cry Baby's motorcycle: **SCENES**
"Just one night of happiness is all I ask," to which her grandmother (Polly Bergen) replies, "But what if you get your dress dirty?"

Willem Dafoe   **CAMEOS**

Cry Baby (Beth Anderson, Susie Benson); *Sh-Boom* (Gary Beckley, Timothy B. Schmit, Andrew   **SONGS**
Gold); *King Cry Baby, High School Hellcats, Teardrops Are Falling, Doin' Time for Bein' Young*
(James Intveld); *Mister Sandman* (Rachel Sweet, Gary Beckley, Timothy B. Schmit); *Bunny Hop*
(Ray Anthony Band); *Please Mister Jailer, A Teenage Prayer* (Rachel Sweet)

DADDY-O (1959)

CAST: Dick Contino, Sandra Giles, Bruno Vesoto, Gloria Victor, Ron McNeil, Jack McClure; DIR:
Elmer C. Rhoden Jr.; PROD: Lou Place; SCREENPLAY: David Moessinger; STUDIO: Imperial; 74
min., b/w (RCA/Columbia)

MUSIC ★★★★
ATTITUDE ★★★
FUN ★

Anything goes, Daddy-O.
The reason you've never heard of any of the cast members is that they were all run out of Hollywood the day this film was released. Boy (Dick Contino) meets girl (Sandra Giles) when she tries to run his truck off the road. Boy (he's called Phil) meets girl (she's called Janet) again at a nightclub. They have a drag race. She wins; he loses his driver's license. Meanwhile, his best friend is run off the road by the bad guys and dies in the crash. Our heroes then put on their detective hats and go undercover at a rival nightclub (run, of course, by the bad guys). Phil poses as the singer Daddy-O, while Janet pretends she's just a cigarette girl. They manage to solve the crime, but the real mystery is how. Special awards may be sent to people who can prove they made it all the way through this film. (KW)

Rock Candy Baby, Angel Act, Wait Till I Get You Home (Daddy-O)   **SONGS**

DARKTOWN STRUTTERS (1974)

CAST: Trina Parks, Roger E. Mosley, Edna Richard, Bettye Sweet, Frankie Crocker; DIR: William
Whitney; PROD: Gene Corman; SCREENPLAY: George Armitage; 85 min., color (Charter)

MUSIC ★★★
ATTITUDE ★
FUN ★

Foxy mama uncovers a cloning ring.
Sirena (Trina Parks) is bad and beautiful. Cruisin' around town on a three-wheeler, dressed like Labelle, she's looking for her kidnapped mother. Beyond that, it's unclear what's going on, thanks to a style of editing and dubbing obviously copped from Russ Meyer's *Vixens* period. Among the nonsensical scenes are Klansmen wearing bikini underwear, a Colonel Sanders lookalike cloning prominent black leaders in his basement, and the Dramatics performing "What You See Is What You Get" from inside a jail cell.

Chock-full of stupid Keystone Kops-type chase scenes and ridiculous acting, this is a black exploitation film that even "Kung Fu" dialogue couldn't save. The only real highlight is the scene in which an a capella group strolls through the park singing a beautiful version of the Mad Lads' "I Don't Have to Shop Around," one of the greatest soul songs ever written. (BV)

SONGS   *I Don't Have to Shop Around* (John Gary Williams and the Newcomers); *What You See Is What You Get* (Dramatics)

Dean Reed–American Rebel

DEAN REED–AMERICAN REBEL   (1985)

MUSIC ★★★★
ATTITUDE ★★★★★
FUN ★★★★★

DIR: Will Roberts; PROD: Will Roberts; STUDIO: United Documentary/Ohio River; 93 min., color (no video release)

Move over, Joe Strummer!
What can you say about a pop singer who leaves American capitalism behind and defects to East Germany? It's a weird story to say the least, and it makes this documentary a must-see for comrades and imperialist running dogs alike. Dean Reed's story begins in the late '50s when he leaves Colorado for Hollywood in search of fame and fortune as a rock'n'roll star. Capitol Records signs him up and releases a bunch of singles that fail to chart—in the States, that is. In South America, Dean (now a personal friend of Phil Everly's) has a succession of Number One hits. He leaves for a tour south of the border and digs it so much that he moves there and becomes a man of the people. Before you know it, Dean is singing socialist protest songs, getting thrown in jail, and eventually has to leave. He makes a bunch of

spaghetti westerns in Italy before meeting a famous East German actress, with whom he falls in love. Settling down with her in the G.D.R., Dean lives the life of a socialist megastar as he continues to make hit records and films. Every so often, he travels to Russia, Nicaragua, and Chile to "spread the word" with his socialist rock performances.

This may sound like outrageous opportunism, but after watching Dean Reed in action, you might think differently. Filmmaker Will Roberts spent six years putting together this deeply intriguing human-interest story. Reed was planning a 1987 tour of U.S. college campuses to promote the film, but in June of 1986, he disappeared mysteriously and, a few days later, was found dead, sitting fully clothed in his car at the botom of a lake. His death was officially ruled a suicide, but it remains an inexplicable mystery to his friends and family. (BV)

An old clip of Dean from his 1962 appearance on "Bachelor Father"; Phil Everly's revelation that he voted for Reagan **SCENES**

A DEGREE OF MURDER (1966)

CAST: Anita Pallenberg, Hans P. Hallwachs, Manfred Fishbeck; DIR: Volker Schlondorff; PROD: Rob Houner; SCREENPLAY: Volker Schlondorff, Gregor Von Rezzori; STUDIO: Universal; 87 min., color (no video release)

MUSIC ★★★★
ATTITUDE ★★★★★
FUN ★★★★

Brian Jones' and his psycho-delic soundtrack.
Brian Jones of the Rolling Stones never got closer to finishing a solo project than he did scoring this dark, offbeat drama about a woman (Anita Pallenberg) who accidentally kills her former lover and then recruits a group of men to help her dispose of the body. The music (played by Jones, Steve Marriott, Ian McLagen, and other members of the Rolling Stones/Andrew Loog Oldham orbit) surges in strange psychedelic oscillations throughout the movie. In one bar scene a bluesy, Dylanesque song is heard, sung (evidently by Jones) faintly in the background. Director Volker Schlondorff was one of Germany's leading New Wave filmmakers at the time. His stylish approach makes this an extremely watchable and fascinating film, over and above its music content. (BE)

DESPERATE TEENAGE LOVEDOLLS (1984)

CAST: Jennifer Schwartz, Hilary Rubens, Steve McDonald, Tracy Lea, Kim Pilkington; DIR: David Markey; SCREENPLAY: David Markey, Jennifer Schwartz, Jordan Schwartz; STUDIO: We Got Power; 60 min., color (We Got Power)

MUSIC ★★★★
ATTITUDE ★★★★★
FUN ★★★★★

Let's make a movie.
Shot in grainy Super-8, this completely homemade effort has some scenes that are overexposed or out of focus, and you can occasionally hear the camera's motor whir. The actors are all amateurs, so they sometimes smile when they shouldn't. Much of the incidental music was freely appropriated from records and TV shows. To top it off, the whole mess was sloppily transferred to video with ugly, computer-generated titles. It's got to be the lowest-budget project in this book (it cost $250 to make). It also may be the cleverest, funniest film and should inspire you to make your own movie. It proves that none of the technical stuff matters if you've got some good ideas. *Desperate Teenage Lovedolls* was filmed with members of various mid-'80s L.A. underground bands (Redd Kross, Bangles, Black Flag) and their friends in suburban backyards and on the graffiti-scarred streets of Hollywood. This

movie and its sequel (*Lovedolls Superstar*) will seem too in-jokey to some folks, but they should strike resounding chords with Generation Xers everywhere who spent their formative years in front of a TV, fortified by Pop Tarts.

The dialogue and music are a hilarious regurgitation of the choicest bits of '70s TV shows (especially "The Brady Bunch"), news stories, bubblegum and heavy metal, antidrug commercials, punk rock lifestyles, and sundry other trash culture. (JS)

LINES   Kitty's mother (throwing a tantrum): "I'm trying to be both a mother and father to you!" to which Kitty replies, "Well, go fuck yourself then!"

CAMEOS   Annette Zilinskas, Vicki Peterson, Dez Cadena

SONGS   *Legend, Ballad of a Lovedoll* (Lovedolls)

DESPERATELY SEEKING SUSAN (1985)

MUSIC ★★
ATTITUDE ★★★★
FUN ★★★★

CAST: Rosanna Arquette, Madonna, Aidan Quinn, Mark Blum, Robert Joy, Laurie Metcalf; DIR: Susan Seidelman; PROD: Sarah Pillsbury, Midge Sanford; SCREENPLAY: Leora Barish; STUDIO: Orion; 107 min., color (HBO)

Downtown bad girl liberates suburban housewife.
Post-"Like a Virgin" and pre-"Material Girl," *Desperately Seeking Susan* is a must for Madonna watchers. As the title's Susan, Madonna hasn't gone bionic yet. She's curvy, dark, and raw. Although in 1985 one might not have been able to predict Madonna's vertiginous success, her fresh sex appeal is what fuels this film. Susan's alter ego is the unfulfilled housewife Roberta (Rosanna Arquette). When Roberta becomes obsessed with Susan through reading messages she and her boyfriend Jim (Robert Joy) exchange in the personal ads, her comfy, non-orgasmic suburban existence explodes—but sweetly. In Susan's wake, Roberta encounters infidelity, mafia hitmen, 42nd Street dives, and prison, yet the movie remains innocently zany. The airiness sometimes turns to ether, but it's still fun to see Roberta break out of her domestic bondage and even better to peep at the early Madonna. (SBW)

SCENES   Madonna drying her armpits with a hot-air blower in the Port Authority Bus Terminal toilets (0:09); the Spanish-language version of Roberta's nerdy husband's hot tub commercial (1:10)

CAMEOS   Arto Lindsay, John Turturro, Steven Wright

D.O.A.: A RIGHT OF PASSAGE (1981)

MUSIC ★★★★★
ATTITUDE ★★★★★
FUN ★★★★★

DIR: Lech Kowalski; PROD: Lech Kowalski; STUDIO: High Times; 89 min., color (no video release)

Punk—it's the real thing.
Forget whatever the revisionists have to say about punk. In its day, it was a threat. A sociological and cultural phenomenon as much as a musical upheaval, punk was about overthrowing (destroying) everything (including rock'n'roll). The idea was to destroy the world, sweep the rubble into the dustbin, and start over again. In America, where life was just too comfortable, punk never enjoyed the impact that it had in England. Still, even in this country, punk was more than a fashion statement. *D.O.A.* is a documentary about punk's assault on America set against the

bleak backdrop of British daily life that spawned the movement. Its focus is the first and only American tour of the Sex Pistols.

Were punks in it for the money? Of course, but Johnny Rotten's sneer seemed destined for greater things. That this slipshod footage is all that remains is a testament to the fact that punk scared the music business as well as the American public. Had it been safer, this would have been a six-camera shoot with a pay-per-view broadcast. The message would have been diluted and compromised but so much more saleable. And then it would have been forgotten like yesterday's news. The Sex Pistols? They were great, both in person and in this film, and their chaos, their frenzy, their energy—it's all here. (TP)

The American debut of "Anarchy in the U.S.A." performed in Atlanta (0:06); the Pistols arriving in Memphis on Elvis's birthday (0:33); the first of many interview bits with Sid Vicious and Nancy Spungen, Sid on the nod (0:54)   **SCENES**

An interviewee: "They suck—like shit." Bob Regehr, the Warner exec who signed the Pistols in America: "There hasn't been a rock'n'roll band to hate in a very long time."   **LINES**

Tony Paris   **CAMEOS**

Nightclubbing (Iggy Pop); *Anarchy in the U.S.A., God Save the Queen, Lies, I Wanna Be Me, Pretty Vacant, No Fun, New York New York, Holidays in the Sun, EMI, Bodies* (Sex Pistols); *Oh Bondage Up Yours!* (X-Ray Spex); *Pretty Vacant* (Rich Kids); *Police and Thieves* (Clash); *Kiss Me Deadly* (Generation X); *Untitled* (Terry and the Idiots); *Rip Off, Borstal Breakout* (Sham 69); *I Wanna Be a Boy/Hey Little Girl* (Dead Boys)   **SONGS**

DON'T KNOCK THE ROCK (1957)

CAST: Bill Haley and his Comets, Alan Dale, Alan Freed, The Treniers, Little Richard, Dave Appell and the Applejacks, Jana Lund; DIR: Fred F. Sears; PROD: Sam Katzman; SCREENPLAY: Robert E. Kent, James B. Gordon; STUDIO: Columbia; 84 min., b/w (no video release)

MUSIC ★★★
ATTITUDE ★★
FUN ★★

The not very good old days.
Don't Knock the Rock was producer Sam Katzman's follow-up to *Rock Around the Clock* (the first rock-exploitation picture), and it's a souvenir from a time when it was generally taken for granted that Old Mean White Guys should be in charge of everything and have all the power. This film deals with the generation-gap conflict inspired by rock'n'roll that had the nation in such a tizzy back in the mid-'50s. Alan Dale appears here as Arnie Haines, America's top rock'n'roll idol. There were no reports of his being burned in effigy, and no theaters were ripped to shreds during screenings of *Don't Knock the Rock*. This suggests that rock film fans of the time were a patient, sedate lot and that they were willing to sit through an excruciating hour of bogus sermonizing and lame ersatz rock'n'roll in order to see just a few minutes' worth of Bill Haley and his Comets (who look more like a bunch of bus drivers than a rock'n'roll band). Comets lead guitarist Frank Beecher was one of the best players of his era, so it's a good thing that the band plays lots of instrumentals here. Haley's hillbilly music is hokey, but the jumped-up way it's delivered here makes it exciting. *Don't Knock the Rock* also features a group that Haley particularly admired and borrowed from, the Treniers, who break up the house with their wild, lounge-band antics. And finally, Little Richard and the Upsetters don't just steal this picture, they transcend it.

A final note: In the early '60s, after their popularity in most of the world had faded, Haley and the Comets continued to be hugely successful in Mexico. During

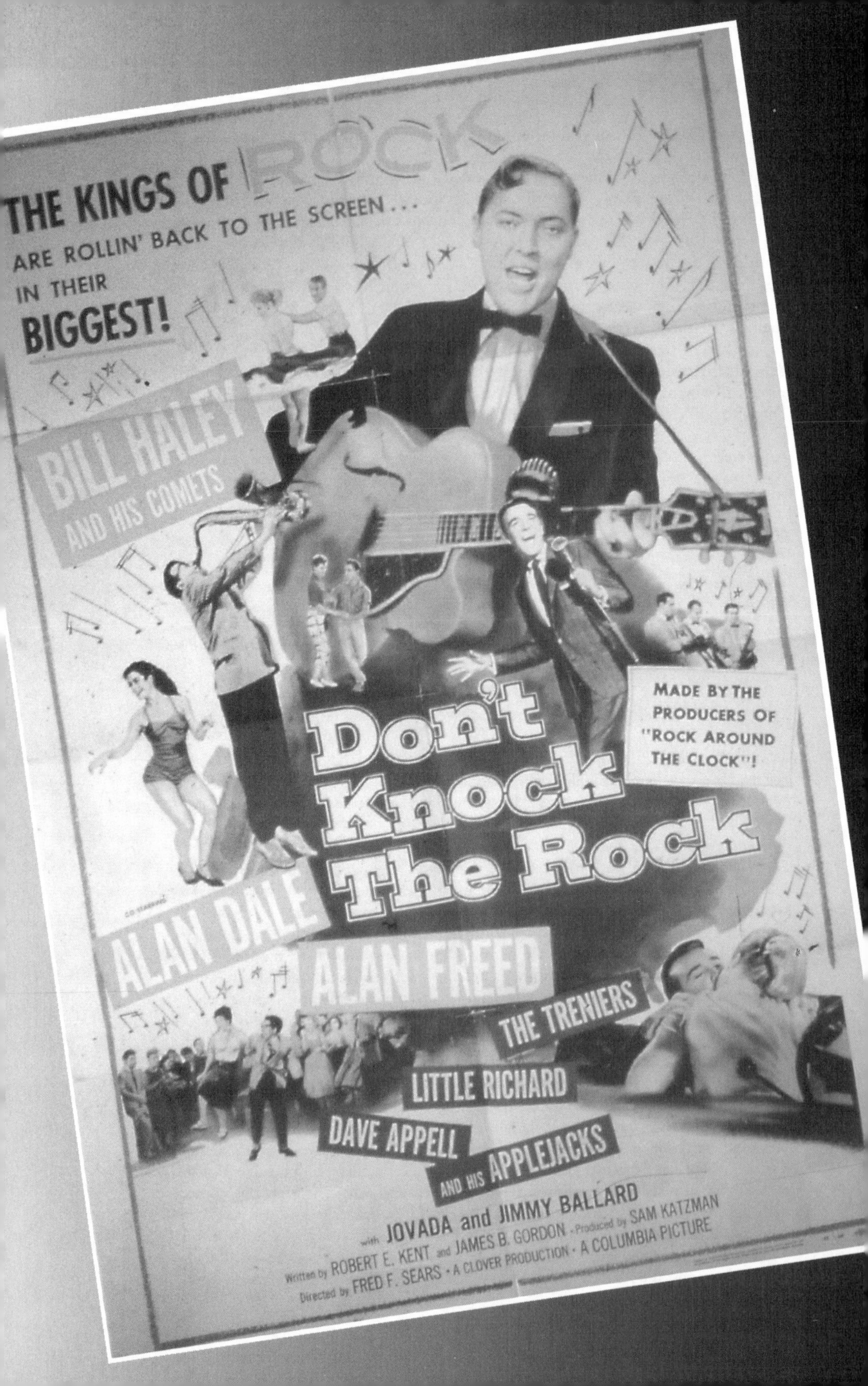
THE KINGS OF ROCK
ARE ROLLIN' BACK TO THE SCREEN...
IN THEIR
BIGGEST!
BILL HALEY
AND HIS COMETS
MADE BY THE
PRODUCERS OF
"ROCK AROUND
THE CLOCK"!
Don't Knock The Rock
ALAN DALE
ALAN FREED
THE TRENIERS
LITTLE RICHARD
DAVE APPELL
AND HIS APPLEJACKS
with JOVADA and JIMMY BALLARD
Written by ROBERT E. KENT and JAMES B. GORDON · Produced by SAM KATZMAN
Directed by FRED F. SEARS · A CLOVER PRODUCTION · A COLUMBIA PICTURE

these years, they appeared in a handful of Mexican films, including one called *Jovenes y Rebelde*. Even rock film fans who don't understand Spanish might find this film more fulfilling than *Don't Knock the Rock*. (MC)

Calling All Comets, Hot Dog Buddy Buddy, Rip It Up, Hook Line and Sinker (Bill Haley and his Comets); *Tutti Frutti, Long Tall Sally* (Little Richard); *I Cry More, One of These Days* (Alan Dale); *One of These Days, The House Will Rock* (Treniers) **SONGS**

DON'T KNOCK THE TWIST   (1962)

CAST: Chubby Checker, Mari Blanchard, Lang Jeffries, Georgine Darcy, Barbara Morrison, James Chandler, Stephen Preston, Mydia Westman, Hortense Petra, Frank Albertson, Elizabeth Harrower; DIR: Oscar Rudolph; PROD: Sam Katzman; SCREENPLAY: James B. Gordon; STUDIO: Columbia; 86 min., b/w (no video release)

MUSIC ★★★★
ATTITUDE ★★★
FUN ★★★★★

Do you wanna dance?
It probably took about two seconds flat to put together this follow-up to *Twist Around the Clock*. By this time (ca. 1962), it was already obvious that the Great Dance Craze had replaced JD rock'n'roll, so producer Sam Katzman probably figured he could afford to spend a little more on this quickie. The bigger budget paid for more acts and better sets. Tikis pop up in just about every room. There are some brilliant choices for guest stars as well. Gene Chandler as the Duke of Earl would be a shocker anytime...monocle, top hat, cap, bustier, and all. A great surprise are the Carroll Brothers stomping out a surfy version of "Bo Diddley." Linda Scott, whose universally loved version of "I Told Every Little Star" hit big that year, sings the follow-up "Yesiree." And the Dovells perform both "The Bristol Stomp" and a bonus track, "Doin' the New Continental." This song reemerged later in John Waters's *Hairspray*, but you can dig the real thing here. Gratefully, Chubby Checker's gyrations keep popping up in place of actual dialogue. (DP)

Don't Knock the Twist, We're Goin' Twistin', Let's Twist to the Pretty Melody of Love, I Love to Twist with You, The Fly (Chubby Checker); *The Bristol Stomp, Doin' the New Continental* (Dovells); *Little Altar Boy* (Vic Dana); *Mashed Potato Time* (Dee Dee Sharp); *Duke of Earl* (Gene Chandler); *Bo Diddley* (Carroll Brothers); *Yes-sir-ee* (Linda Scott); *Slow Twistin'* (Chubby Checker, Dee Dee Sharp) **SONGS**

DON'T LOOK BACK   (1967)

DIR: D.A. Pennebaker; PROD: Don Court, Albert Grossman; STUDIO: Leacock-Pennebaker; 96 min., b/w (Paramount)

MUSIC ★★★★
ATTITUDE ★★★★★
FUN ★★★★★

D.A. Pennebaker does Dylan's 1965 English tour.
Until 1965, Bob Dylan was best known as a folksinger. He'd written several hits for Peter, Peter, and Mary, most notably "Blowin' in the Wind," and most folkies thought he was the Second Coming. That spring, however, the 24-year-old Dylan released *Bringing It All Back Home*, the first folk-rock album. And while the "Subterranean Homesick Blues" single rewrote the rules of popular music in America, Dylan scooted to Britain for what would be his last major tour as a "folk" singer. In *Don't Look Back*, Dylan performs solo in the Pete Seeger style, using just an acoustic guitar and harmonica. But the performance footage really isn't the point here. Instead, what Pennebaker skillfully offers is a rare and mesmerizing glimpse behind Dylan's facade. Half the movie takes place in hotel rooms, where reporters keep asking Bob insipid questions like "What's your real message?"

There are countless good bits, but two scenes stand out. The first (0:39) is an extended sequence during which Dylan's manager, Albert Grossman, conspires with British booking agent Tito Burns to rook the BBC into coughing up more money for a Dylan TV appearance. The other (1:09) revolves around Donovan, who, as the "new" Dylan, is the film's running joke. When Donovan finally appears in Bob's hotel room and sings a bland ballad, Dylan is unimpressed. "Hey, that's a good song, man," he says with a smirk. Then he takes the guitar from Donovan and plays "It's All Over Now, Baby Blue." In the NBA, they call that a facial. (DR)

SCENES Allen Ginsberg loitering in the background during the classic "Subterranean Homesick Blues" opening; a snippet of pirate Radio Caroline over the limo radio (0:24); Bob berating a *Time* magazine reporter (1:17)

SONGS *Only a Pawn in their Game, The Times They Are a-Changin', The Lonesome Death of Hattie Carroll, Lost Highway, Don't Think Twice It's All Right, It's All Over Now Baby Blue, Talking World War III Blues, It's Alright Ma, Love Minus Zero/No Limit* (Bob Dylan); *Percy's Song, Love Is Just a Four-Letter Word* (Joan Baez); *To Sing for You* (Donovan)

THE DOORS   (1991)

CAST: Val Kilmer, Meg Ryan, Kyle MacLachlan, Kevin Dillon, Frank Whaley, Kathleen Quinlan, Michael Madsen, Michael Wincott, Mark Moses, Billy Idol; DIR: Oliver Stone; PROD: Bill Graham, Sasha Harar, A. Kitman Ho; SCREENPLAY: J. Randall Johnson, Oliver Stone; STUDIO: Carolco; 138 min., color (Carolco)

MUSIC ★★★★
ATTITUDE ★★★
FUN ★★

Jim Morrison's lust for death.
The legend of Morrison (Val Kilmer) gets the full over-the-top Oliver Stone treatment. We meet Jim as a plucky film student, courting eventual wife Pamela (Meg Ryan) and bonding with kindred soul Ray Manzarek (Kyle MacLachlan) to form the Doors. As the group takes off, the ensuing fame, sex, and drugs devour the death-fixated singer. Consumed by the fire the Doors lit, Morrison ends up a serene corpse in a Paris bathtub at 27.

This could have been a great movie—the Doors' music spanned the most exciting and most numbing aspects of the '60s counterculture. The film is obviously a labor of love for director/cowriter Stone, but he still can't resist spoiling it with rancid symbolism and Hollywood corn. Stone's operative premise seems to be that the Doors (as prophets of rock hype) were too subtle to begin with, so the movie underlines every Deep Thought with hyperventilating pulp. Despite this, the unlikely Val Kilmer manages a quite convincing version of Morrison's self-destructive narcissism (for an earlier incarnation of the project, John Travolta was set to play the Lizard King), and some of the concert scenes are very dramatic. Stone shot them like war scenes, which in a way they were. But as an epitaph for a band that acted out the lost promises of a heady decade, the most indelible image *The Doors* offers is of pathetic, rag-doll Pamela screaming to Jim, "You killed my duck!" (HH)

Witch-lover Patricia Keneally (Kathleen Quinlan) to Jim: "Ever try drinking blood?" Morrison's final line in the movie: "C'mon, let's get some tacos."   *LINES*

Patricia Keneally, John Densmore, Bill Graham, Mimi Rogers, Paul Williams, Crispin Glover (as Andy Warhol, no less)   *CAMEOS*

Break On Through, The End, Light My Fire, Back Door Man, Not to Touch the Earth, The Soft Parade, Five to One (Doors, with additional vocals by Val Kilmer)   *SONGS*

THE DOORS ARE OPEN   (1968)

CAST: Jim Morrison, Ray Manzarek, Robby Krieger, John Densmore; DIR: John Sheppard; PROD: Jo Dunden-Smith; STUDIO: Granada Television; 56 min., b/w (Warner)

MUSIC ★★★
ATTITUDE ★★★★
FUN ★★★

The Doors live in 1968.
Performance footage of the Doors playing London's Roundhouse is intercut with bits of mumbled interviews and lots of pseudo-relevant film clips showing LBJ, police battling demonstrators, and the general chaos of an era the group supposedly personified.

This made-for-British-TV documentary is a mess, but then so were the Doors. The music is all crossed wires: lofty ambition scrambled with low cunning, zit-creme Top 40 meets Artaud's Theatre of Cruelty. Jim Morrison presides over the show like a hanging judge doffing his robes in the go-go cage of a leather bar. But as ludicrous as his overripe baritone and drama school posturing could get, he certainly knew how to hold an audience. His synthesis of violent invocations, druggy pillow talk, and poetic mystification remains seductive to this day, even if death alone spared Morrison's "soft parade" from winding up in Vegas opening for Roseanne Arnold. (HH)

LINES   Morrison to an interviewer: "I think, uh, these days, especially in the States, you have to be a politician or assassin . . . to really be a superstar."

SONGS   *When the Music's Over, Five to One, Spanish Caravan, Hello I Love You, Back Door Man, Light My Fire, The Unknown Soldier* (Doors)

DOUBLE TROUBLE   (1967)

MUSIC ★★★
ATTITUDE ★★
FUN ★★

CAST: Elvis Presley, Annette Day, John Williams, Yvonne Romain; **DIR:** Norman Taurog; **PROD:** Judd Bernard, Irwin Winkler; **SCREENPLAY:** Jo Heims; **STUDIO:** MGM; 92 min., color (MGM/UA)

Elvis does the underage thing.

Elvis stars as Guy Lambert, a nightclub singer and ladies' man out on the town in this mystery/musical. Guy is living in Germany when he meets the enigmatic Jill (Annette Day), who won't reveal her last name. Soon he finds out why: Jill is only seventeen. Her guardian Gerald Waverly (John Williams) is not pleased about their relationship. Chivalrous Guy leaves Jill alone, but she pursues him relentlessly. To fill out the plot, Jill is followed herself by threatening thugs who try to harm her whenever she is alone. It's up to snazzy Guy to protect Jill. In the process, he falls in love with her.

One can't help wondering whether *Double Trouble* is a rewrite of the Elvis-and-Priscilla story: 1967, after all, was the year of their marriage. The downfall of Jerry Lee Lewis's career was marriage to his 13-year-old cousin Myra, and Priscilla was just fourteen when she met Elvis, then a soldier in Germany. Perhaps there was the need to prove once and for all that Elvis was indeed the perfect American boy—the good soldier, the noble protector of young womanhood, the sexless knight. It sure didn't do his music any good, as this vapid soundtrack proves. Maybe if he had stayed hounddogging in Memphis with Jerry Lee, we would have had more Elvis and less Guy Lambert. (TM)

SCENES   Guy fights with a murderer and, ever natty, neatly takes his jacket off in mid-tussle (0:55)

LINES   A friend to Guy about Guy's success with women: "Must be the maternal instinct you bring out in chicks. Them mothers can't live without you!"

SONGS   *Double Trouble, If You Give Me All Your Love, Could I Fall in Love, Long-Legged Girl with a Short Dress On, City by Night, Old MacDonald, One in Every Town, There's So Much World to See* (Elvis Presley)

THE DRILLER KILLER   (1979)

MUSIC ★★
ATTITUDE ★★★★★
FUN ★★★★

CAST: Jimmy Laine, Carolyn Day, Rhodney Montreal, Tony Coca-Cola and the Roosters; **DIR:** Abel Ferrara; **PROD** Rochelle Weisberg; **SCREENPLAY:** Nicholas St. John; **STUDIO:** Navaron; 90 min., color (Magnum)

Licensed to drill.

New York City's East Village circa 1979 is the setting for this tale of Reno, a struggling, tortured artist plagued by the pressures of the artist's life and his own inner demons. What plagues him the most, though, is the rock band that rehearses in his apartment building (Tony Coca-Cola and the Roosters). They rehearse day and night and they *suck*. They rehearse some more, and they still suck. It just goes on like that: They rehearse, they suck, rehearse, suck, etc. Finally, Reno does what anyone would: He becomes a homicidal maniac and roams the East Village, randomly killing people with a power drill.

Driller Killer doesn't have an ending, but it does have lots of bad rock music, bleeding, drilling, and dying, and lots of real East Village/late '70s ambience (the characters go to Max's Kansas City a lot). I didn't think the scenes of drilling and mutilation were the most grotesque part of this film. (I'm pretty sure they were all faked.) For me, the worst part was the scene in which Reno, Carol, and Pamela—eating a pizza with everything on it—start throwing pieces of it at one another. (It's definitely real pizza.) But really, the strangest thing about this movie is that Reno doesn't murder the band. (MC)

DU-BEAT-E-O   (1984)

CAST: Ray Sharkey, Derf Scratch, Nora Gaye, Joan Jett, Len Lesser, Johanna Went, Linda Texas Jones, Zachary, El Duce; DIR: Alan Sacks; PROD: Alan Sacks; SCREENPLAY: Marc Sheffler; STUDIO: Fox Hills; 84 min., color (Fox Hills)

MUSIC ★★★
ATTITUDE ★★
FUN ★

Dead Beat-E-O. Watch the Weather Channel instead.
The late, great, criminally misused Ray Sharkey plays the filmmaker Du Beat-E-O, who has been given money by a bad guy with a funny European accent (Len Lesser) to make a movie about Joan Jett. Or sort of about Joan Jett—we see lots of pictures of her, anyway. Well, Du Beat-E-O falls behind schedule, so the guy with the accent gives him just 31 hours to complete said film. Right away, Du heads to the local flophouse, where he drags his Nyquil-addicted editor/sidekick Benny (Derf Scratch) out of a stupor. Meanwhile, we're in the annoying company of some people offscreen who keep talking about the making of a film about the making of a film. They never *shut up*. Do Du-Beat-E-O and Benny finish the film in time? Who cares? Unless you really dig Ray Sharkey or Joan Jett, save your money. (KW)

Benny's "dream sequence," which is a performance by the high priestess of weird, Johanna Went

SCENES

"I am Du-Beat-E-O. My real name is Alan Shapiro."

LINES

Chuck E. Weiss

CAMEOS

You Don't Know What You've Got, I Want You, Tell Me, You Can't Get Me, We're All Crazy Now (Joan Jett); *Hour of Darkness, Creeps, It's Not a Pretty Picture* (Social Distortion); *You're My Next Victim* (Modifiers); *Stickball* (Ray Sharkey); *Lock Me Up* (Tex and the Horseheads); *Sidekick* (Chuck E. Weiss); *A Little Lesson in the Movie Biz* (Zachary); *Theme to Benny's Nightmare* (Johanna Went); *Get Up and Die* (Mentors); *Up Your Ass* (Dr. Know); *We Suck* (Even Worse); *Sure Sure* (Rainbow Smith); *No Bikers Just Punkers* (Alan, Jodi, and Derf)

SONGS

Easy Rider

EASY COME, EASY GO (1967)

CAST: Elvis Presley, Dodie Marshall, Pat Priest, Pat Harrington, Skip Ward; DIR: John Rich; PROD: Hal B. Wallis; SCREENPLAY: Allan Weiss, Anthony Lawrence; STUDIO: Paramount; 95 min., color (Paramount)

MUSIC ★
ATTITUDE ★
FUN ★

Elvis dives for sunken treasure.
Here the Elv is an underwater demolition expert (specializing in unexploded mines, by golly) who finds an old shipwreck on the eve of his naval discharge. As a civilian, he tries to salvage the booty, but first he has to contend with a no-good rich girl ("Munsters" chick Pat Priest) and a "kooky" beatnik (Dodie Marshall). When the coins Elvis recovers turn out to be worth a few grand instead of a few million, he discovers that money isn't everything and turns over his share to help start an arts center for the local hep cats.

This flick offers major rubber-fetish action—especially frogman Elvis in his glistening wet suit—and little else. You'd think a movie in which the King comes face to face with the counterculture, modern performance art, and flaming homosexuality (he can't make heads or tails of them) would be way more fun than this waste of cheap film stock. It just goes to show you should never underestimate the forces of entropy and decay at work in a Presley picture. If they could turn him into Spam, what chance has anything else got? (HH)

No one who has seen Elsa Lanchester's dotty cameo singing "Yoga Is as Yoga Does" will ever forget it, although they'll spend the rest of their lives trying. (HH)

SCENES

Easy Come Easy Go, Love Machine, Stop, You're Wrong Again, Sing Children Sing, I'll Take Love (Elvis Presley); *Yoga Is as Yoga Does* (Elsa Lanchester)

SONGS

EASY RIDER (1969)

CAST: Peter Fonda, Dennis Hopper, Jack Nicholson, Karen Black, Toni Basil; DIR: Dennis Hopper; PROD: Peter Fonda; SCREENPLAY: Peter Fonda, Dennis Hopper, Terry Southern; STUDIO: Columbia; 94 min., color (RCA/Columbia)

MUSIC ★★★★
ATTITUDE ★★★★★
FUN ★★★

Looking for America circa 1969.
As *Easy Rider* opens, longhairs Wyatt (Peter Fonda) and Billy (Dennis Hopper) are shown wrapping up a major cocaine deal with a fashionable pusher played by reclusive record producer Phil Spector in a rare cameo. Although it's a cloudy day, they're all wearing the most incredible shades. Calmly, Wyatt and Billy collect their money, hop on their Harleys, and ride off into America with Steppenwolf's "Born to Be Wild" urging them on. Their first stop is a failing hippie commune, but their ultimate destination is Mardi Gras in New Orleans. Along the way, they meet Jack Nicholson in a small town jail. Nicholson plays a malcontent lawyer, the drunken scion of a prominent local family, who shares the boys' frustration with the straight Establishment. After springing them, Nicholson joins Wyatt and Billy on their trip.

For much of *Easy Rider*, Fonda and Hopper try to equate their lack of conformity with a lack of dialogue, but Nicholson cures that with a number of memorable speeches, especially one on the subject of freedom (1:10). It seems that Wyatt and Billy may practice freedom, but they don't understand it. Nicholson's performance notwithstanding, much of the drama in *Easy Rider* doesn't hold up too well. But if you've forgotten what the country was like during the Age of Aquarius (especially what it looked like), there are few films so evocative or authentic. (DR)

SCENES Nicholson's motorcycle helmet (0:52); the acid trip scene against which all others are now measured (1:23)

LINES Peter Fonda to a small-*c* communist spreading seed over hard, sandy ground: "Get much rain here, man?"

EAT THE DOCUMENT (1972)

DIR: Bob Dylan, Howard Alk; SCREENPLAY: Bob Dylan; STUDIO: Leacock/Pennebaker; 55 min., color (no video release)

MUSIC ★★★★★
ATTITUDE ★★★★★
FUN ★★★★★

Bob Dylan and Garth Hudson electrify the U.K.
Eat the Document captures Bob Dylan at the peak of his creative powers as he tours England during 1966 with the Hawks (later renamed the Band). It's tempting to pigeonhole this film as the color follow-up to D.A. Pennebaker's *Don't Look Back*, but *Eat the Document* has much more to it. At the 1965 Newport Folk Festival, Dylan's electric set shocked the folk purists in the audience, and the same things happens to the British folkies here. Pennebaker often turns his camera on the disgusted and disappointed British college students who call Dylan a "traitor" and suggest that he should have left his electric band in America. Pennebaker later shows one of these students bursting into tears when Dylan lashes out with a stunning electric rendition of "Like a Rolling Stone."

In *Don't Look Back*, Dylan behaved like a punk, taking on the critics with pointed jibes, and casting off musical foibles at the drop of a supreme song. In *Eat the Document*, however, Dylan makes no excuses and lets his music do the talking instead. By this time, Dylan had learned to dismiss his detractors with a laugh. In one instance, he denies an audience member an autograph with the retort, "No, you booed." Other fun times include an improvised duet at the piano with Johnny Cash on "I Still Miss Someone" and Richard Manuel's attempt to trade his jacket for a mod guy's girlfriend (with Dylan silently pressuring the poor lad).

The film was originally shot for an ABC-TV special keyed into the publication of Dylan's novel *Tarantula*. When the networks execs saw the footage, however, they flipped out and failed to air it. *Eat the Document* was later "released" on the underground theater circuit in 1971. By that time, the Band had become superstars, and Dylan a myth. *Eat the Document* remains cutting edge, ahead of its time, and out of sight. (DP)

SCENES A *Revolver*-era John Lennon sitting in the back of a cab with a *Blonde on Blonde*-era Dylan

EDDIE AND THE CRUISERS (1983)

CAST: Michael Paré, Tom Berenger, Ellen Barkin, Joe Pantoliano; DIR: Martin Davidson; PROD: Joseph Brooks, Robert K. Lifton; SCREENPLAY: Martin Davidson, Arlene Davidson; STUDIO: Embassy; 100 min., color (Embassy)

MUSIC ★★★★
ATTITUDE ★★★★
FUN ★★★★★

Come back, Jimmy Dean. All is forgiven.
Michael Paré shines as Eddie Wilson, a working-class Rimbaud from the Jersey shore, whom we meet in a series of flashbacks to the early 1960s. He's got the black leather jacket, the attitude, and even a band, but the music doesn't come together for him until he meets Frank Ridgeway (Tom Berenger), the Word Man, a real college graduate who knows how to spell Rimbaud. With Wilson's tunes

and the Word Man's lyrics, Eddie and the Cruisers climb the charts. Then, with success in their grasp, Eddie drives his car off a bridge. His body is never found.

The movie's action begins 20 years later when an entertainment reporter (Ellen Barkin) convinces her editor that Eddie may have faked his death in order to disappear. The key to the mystery, she decides, are tapes of the band's last, unreleased album, *A Season in Hell*, which disappeared the day after Eddie's accident. Is Eddie alive? Does he have the tapes? Will Tom Berenger sleep with Ellen Barkin? These are puzzles well worth your attention. *North by Northwest* it's not, but *Eddie and the Cruisers* will keep you guessing while the acting and the ambience take you back. And for those who like Bruce Springsteen soundalikes, John Cafferty's original music sure makes the film go down easy. (DR)

SONGS *On the Dark Side, Tender Years, Down on My Knees, Wild Summer Nights, Boardwalk Angel, A Season in Hell* (John Cafferty); *Betty Lou's Got a New Pair of Shoes* (Kenny Vance)

Eddie and the Cruisers

EEGAH! (1962)

CAST: Arch Hall Jr., Marilyn Manning, Richard Kiel, William Watters; DIR: Nicholas Merriwether; PROD: Nicholas Merriwether; SCREENPLAY: Bob Wehling; STUDIO: Fairway International; 92 min., color (Rhino)

MUSIC ★★★
ATTITUDE ★★★★
FUN ★★★★

Arch de triomphe.
For the details on Arch Hall, Jr., and "Archmania," check out the review of *Wild Guitar* elsewhere in this book (or get Kicks magazine's Bobby Fuller issue). *Eegah!* was made by the same creative team responsible for *Wild Guitar* with one notable exception: That film's director, Ray Dennis Steckler, doesn't do the honors here, and consequently *Eegah!* comes up short in terms of pacing and atmosphere. Arch, Jr., however, is in fine form, rocking out on the same white Fender Jazzmaster (wearing the same clothes, too, I believe) as in *Wild Guitar*.

Richard Kiel appears in the title role as Eegah, a caveman from some long-past millenium. He wanders down from the mountains into Palm Springs, California (ca. 1962), where he meets and falls in love with the tantalizing Roxy Miller. In the end, he gets shot to death by cops for stealing food from a country club. (MC)

SCENES Ray Dennis Steckler getting thrown into a swimming pool by the caveman

SONGS *Vicki, Valleri, The Brownville Road* (Arch Hall, Jr.)

ELVIS (1979)

CAST: Kurt Russell, Shelley Winters, Bing Russell, Robert Gray, Pat Hingle, Season Hubley; DIR: John Carpenter; PROD: Anthony Lawrence; SCRENPLAY: Anthony Lawrence; STUDIO: Dick Clark Pictures; 117 min., color (Vestron)

MUSIC ★★★★
ATTITUDE ★★★★★
FUN ★★★★★

Former Disney prince enters another magical Kingdom.
About a year and a half after Elvis Aron Presley is said to have bid our world adieu, he was spotted again—February 11, 1979, at 8 P.M. on ABC television. Kurt Russell turns in an excellent documentation (good accent, terrible lip-synching) of the life and times of the King in this TV movie that digs up the singer's trials and tribulations from a kid in 1945 to his Las Vegas stage comeback in 1969. The film moves at breakneck pace through all the familiar subjects (Ed Sullivan, the movies, the pink Cadillacs, Graceland, the army stint, Priscilla, the TV target practice, etc.) as the rocker grows increasingly erratic and often violent. The movie emphasizes Elvis's relationship with his mother, as well as his tendency to be rather insecure. Ending with his Vegas triumph on July 26, 1969, it never touches upon his beached whale/pharmaceutical era. Which is just fine, since it's a lot less depressing that way.

It's impossible to tell whether every little detail here is accurate, but rumor has it that Priscilla Presley received $50,000 as a consultant for the movie. Incidentally, Kurt Russell married the actress who plays Priscilla (Season Hubley) a month after the movie aired. Like the King and his bride, they were later divorced. (MB)

LINES A humble Elvis about to make his first recording: "I don't sound like nobody."

CAMEOS Ed Begley Jr., Joe Mantegna, Ellen Travolta

SONGS *Mystery Train, Good Rockin' Tonight, Old Shep, My Happiness, That's All Right, Blue Moon of Kentucky, Lawdy Miss Clawdy, Blue Moon, Tutti Frutti, Long Tall Sally, Heartbreak Hotel, Rip It Up, Unchained Melody, A Fool Such as I, Crying in the Chapel, Pledging My Love, Until It's Time for You to Go, Bosom of Abraham, Suspicious Minds, Are You Lonesome Tonight?, Sweet Caroline, Blue Suede Shoes, The Wonder of You, Burning Love, An American Trilogy* (Ronnie McDowell)

ELVIS: THAT'S THE WAY IT IS (1970)

DIR: Denis Sanders; PROD: Herbert F. Solow; STUDIO: MGM; 109 min., color (MGM/UA)

MUSIC ★★★★
ATTITUDE ★★★★★
FUN ★★★★★

The way we'll always remember him.
This 1970 documentary is a must-see for everyone, Elvis fan or not. It's almost shocking to see Elvis like this after all his deadly dull films of the '60s. He's vibrant, funny, and bright, although not slim. His backup singers are the Sweet Inspirations (featuring gospel great Cissy Houston, Whitney's mom), and there

are glimpses of the Memphis Mafia, the group of homies who always accompanied Elvis.

Director Denis Sanders uses his material to its greatest advantage. Early in the film, he intercuts scenes of a playful Elvis rehearsing with serious fan interviews (as only Elvis fans can be serious). One of these fans talks about her cat's fondness for Elvis's Vegas album: "She likes it 'cause it's got a lot of action in it." There are also interviews with dreadful Vegas PR people and earnest hotel workers. When Elvis is on stage, his performances are intercut with footage of impersonators in Luxembourg, showing both the immensity of his fandom and the phenomenal, obsessive hero worship the King has inspired. However, despite the exciting music, Elvis's career at this point was feeding only off itself. It was just a matter of time before he starved. (TM)

SCENES The credits, in which shots of Elvis are intercut with crying fans, some not more than eight years old; one of Elvis's guys walking through rehearsal rooms papered with thousands of Elvis pictures (0:04); people getting married in a Vegas chapel so that they can catch Elvis's show on their honeymoon (0:33)

LINES One fan on Elvis: "He sets my Phi Beta Kappa key to jangling." Another: "He should rank with Marconi and Bell."

SONGS *That's All Right, I've Loved You, Patch It Up, Love Me Tender, You've Lost That Lovin' Feelin', Sweet Caroline, The Girl Is Gonna Stay, King of the Jungle, Bridge Over Troubled Water, Heartbreak Hotel, One Night with You, Blue Suede Shoes, All Shook Up, Polk Salad Annie, Suspicious Minds, Can't Help Falling in Love* (Elvis Presley)

THE ENDLESS SUMMER (1965)

CAST: Robert August, Mike Henson; DIR: Bruce Brown; PROD: Bruce Brown; STUDIO: Bruce Brown Films; 90 min., color, (Pacific Arts)

MUSIC ★★★★★
ATTITUDE ★★★★★
FUN ★★★★

Who says there's no surf in Tahiti?
"With enough time and enough money, you could spend the rest of your life following the summer around the world." That's just what Bruce Brown captures in the surfing subculture's most classic film, *The Endless Summer.* Surfing itself existed in ancient Hawaii, but it wasn't rediscovered until the 1890s. At first, the focus was on the preservation of a cultural tradition, but in the late '50s, several elements jelled, including the advent of teenage rebellion and rock'n'roll. Artists like Rick Griffin and Ed "Big Daddy" Roth, bands like the Bel Airs and Dick Dale and his Del-Tones, and filmmakers like Bruce Brown and John Severson (who founded *Surfer* magazine) happened along at just about the same time that transistor radios did. As a result, rock'n'roll was able to hit the beach...dig?

Surfing films had a major influence on rock'n'roll because surf music was inadvertently born at their screenings. Surf filmmakers often narrated their footage live in front of their audiences. For background music, they used either West Coast jazz or rock instrumentals. Henceforth, the music of Duane Eddy, the Fireballs, the Revels, and the Ventures was irreversibly associated with surfing. The garage surf groups of the early '60s followed suit.

The Endless Summer is the best introduction to this sandy bohemia. In it, Brown follows surfers Mike Henson and Robert August as they surf their way around the world, visiting the virgin beaches of Africa, Australia, New Zealand, and Tahiti. The best locations in California and Hawaii are featured as well, along with surfing legends Mickey Dora, Lance Carson, Butch Van Artsdalen, and Phil Edwards. The Sandals are the groovy group on the soundtrack, and Brown's surf heptalk is the cherry on top. The elapsed-time sunset surf introduction could be one of the most beautiful scenes in movie history. Films like this were buried for over 30 years due to contempo surf thrash mondo negligence. Today, the catalogs of Bruce Brown, Greg Noll, John Severson, Dale Davis, and Bud Browne are being reissued, and there's always the hope that more will be forthcoming (including Thomas Edison's 1895 footage shot at Waikiki). Without surf films, surf music wouldn't exist. So get with it, squid! (DP)

SCENES The best moments are the "perfect wave" at Cape St. Francis, South Africa; the marathon rides at Raglund, New Zealand; John Whitmore's goatee; and a soundtrack tune that resembles a Tahitian "Telstar."

LINES "The only words they know in English are 'Hang Ten.'"

SONGS *Theme from the Endless Summer, Wild as the Sea, Good Grieves, Six-Pack* (Sandals)

EXPRESSO BONGO (1959)

MUSIC ★★★
ATTITUDE ★★★★
FUN ★★★★★

CAST: Laurence Harvey, Cliff Richard and the Shadows, Sylvia Syms, Yolande Donlan, Meier Tzelniker, Wilfred Owen; DIR: Val Guest; PROD: Val Guest; SCREENPLAY: Wolf Mankowitz; STUDIO Britannia/Conquest; 111 min., b/w (no video release)

The best British rock'n'roll movie of the '50s.
Expresso Bongo is probably the best rock'n'roll movie made in England prior to *A Hard Day's Night* despite the fact that its script shows utter contempt for the music. Adapted from a stage play that was loosely inspired by Tommy Steele's rise to fame, *Expresso Bongo* is a delightfully sleazy tale about a two-bit theatrical agent (Laurence Harvey) who tries to parlay Soho singer Cliff Richard into a national sensation until he is undone by his only marginally more upright girlfriend. The rock songs aren't among Richard's best (although "Bongo Blues" is pretty cool), and there are too many songs from the stage play, but the grittiness of the story, and its surprisingly earthy attitude toward sexuality, make this a seminal rock'n'roll movie. (BE)

Bongo Blues, Love, The Shrine on the Second Floor, A Voice in the Wilderness (Cliff Richard)

THE FAT SPY (1966)

MUSIC ★★
ATTITUDE ★
FUN ★★

CAST: Phyllis Diller, Jack E. Leonard, Brian Donlevy, Jayne Mansfield, The Wild Ones, Johnny Tillotson, Lauree Berger; DIR: Joseph Cates; PROD: Everett Rosenthal; SCREENPLAY: Matthew Andrews; STUDIO: Phillip/Magna; 75 min., color (Discount)

Stop making scents!
This farfetched farce concerns a perfume manufacturer (Brian Donlevy) who's trying to bottle the Fountain of Youth, which he's discovered on his own private island. The producers of this bizarre independent production—shot in Cape Coral, Florida—must have believed that the unusual cast would make for a hilarious movie. They were wrong.

When a group of teenagers (including the Wild Ones and Johnny Tillotson) arrives on the island for a weekend treasure hunt, Donlevy dispatches his daughter (Jayne Mansfield) and a scientist (Jack E. Leonard) to investigate. Leonard also plays the scientist's twin brother, who's in cahoots with a rival manufacturer (Phyllis Diller). The badly dated humor of nightclub comedians Leonard ("Answer the phone...or I'll cut your nose off!") and Diller consistently falls flat.

There are several times when characters look at the camera attempting to get laughs and dumb, jokey title cards throughout. Screen veteran Donlevy reads his lines awkwardly, as though he didn't bother to memorize the script.

The film includes several musical numbers, ranging from the mediocre to the awful. The now-forgotten Wild Ones (who sang the great theme song for the underrated black comedy *Lord Love a Duck*) contribute some generic fun-in-the-sun tunes, as well as an angry folk song that precedes the main title. Wild One Jordan Christopher also sings some bland duets with Lauree Berger (their characters are named Frankie and Nanette), and Johnny Tillotson adds some schmaltzy, Anka-type ballads. Even Leonard and Mansfield attempt to hold a note (Jayne fails badly). One eerie, laugh-killing moment comes when Tillotson (as Dodo), beckoned by a mermaid, walks into the sea and drowns!

A footnote for trivia fans: Jordan Christopher briefly gained some notoriety when he married Richard Burton's ex-wife (whom Burton had just dumped for Liz after *Cleopatra*). Sybil Burton Christopher then opened a swinging New York discotheque called Arthur. The Wild Ones' next album (on United Artists) was called *The Arthur Sound.* (JS)

People Sure Act Funny, Come On Down, Let's Dance Let's Dance, Do the Turtle, Wild Way of Living **SONGS**
(Wild Ones); *Nanette, I'll Always Love You* (Jordan Christopher, Lauree Berger); *Where Is the Girl for Me, If I See You Again* (Johnny Tillotson); *You Haven't Changed a Bit* (Jack E. Leonard); *I'd Like to Be a Rose in Your Garden* (Jayne Mansfield); *The Nicest Way You Can* (Lauree Berger)

FEAST OF FRIENDS   (1968)

DIR: Paul Ferrara; **PROD:** The Doors; 40 min., color (no video release)

MUSIC ★★★★
ATTITUDE ★★★★
FUN ★★★★★

Jimbo spins his tale.
Knowledgeable Doors fans can trace the band's headiness back to the days it spent immersed in neo-intellectualism at the U.C.L.A. film school. In that context, *Feast of Friends*, the group's reentry into the cinematic world, has a sort-of roots thing going on. The film opens to the Cheez Whiz organ chords of "Strange Days" and a title card that looks more like a graphic from a California Highway Patrol film than the beginning of a pretentious art statement. Our trip through the Doors'collective psyche gets well underway when a WWII veteran begins spouting some great bumpkin anti-Vietnam philosophy as the band storms into "Moonlight Drive." There follows a great encapsulation of the song's lyrics, with outer-space imagery and a spinning musical presentation of the band miming the song.

A performance of "Wild Child" at a small outdoor concert full of various hippie derelicts and Hell's Angels goes way beyond the glorified image commonly presented of the Doors in these later days. The actual pandemonium surrounding them can be grasped firsthand during their arena performances of "Five to One" and "Not to Touch the Earth," as the Doors cinematically clue in the viewer to how the madness feels from the inside. Morrison "runs" to the lyrics as the audience charges the stage and the cops bust heads,. Eventually, Morrison gets busted himself. The most impressive bit is some unannounced Morrison poetry, mumbled then screamed: "Earth, air, fire, water, mother, father, sons and daughters, it has been said that on birth we are trying to find a proper womb for the growth of our Buddah nature and that on dying we find a womb in the tomb of the Earth!" Psycho Jimbo at his most brilliant. The film closes with a performance of "The End" live from the Hollywood Bowl. Oliver Stone pilfered a lot from this movie, but he couldn't touch it. (DP)

Strange Days, Wild Child, Moonlight Drive, Five to One, Not to Touch the Earth, The End (Doors)   **SONGS**

FERRY 'CROSS THE MERSEY   (1965)

CAST: Gerry Marsden, Deryck Guyler, Jimmy Saville; DIR: Jeremy Summers; PROD: Michael Holden; SCREENPLAY: David Franden; STUDIO: United Artists; 88 min., b/w (no video release)

MUSIC ★★★★
ATTITUDE ★★
FUN ★★★

Have Mersey!
A Hard Day's Night was a guileless look at the Beatles and the phenomenon of their success. In contrast, *Ferry 'Cross The Mersey* is a styless attempt to make the same kind of movie about Gerry and the Pacemakers. Director Jeremy Summers made regular visits to the set of *Hard Day's Night*, but they did him little good. Flat action is a major problem here, but balancing that flaw is some surprisingly good music, including superior versions of several songs that were hits at the time. Cilla Black and the other Liverpudlians featured in musical numbers are forgettable. So is the gimmick of having the boys lose their instruments and nearly miss the big show. It's just too ridiculously contrived to take with a straight face. (BE)

SONGS   *Ferry 'Cross the Mersey, It's Gonna Be Alright, Why Oh Why, Fall in Love, This Thing Called Love, Baby You're So Good to Me, She's the Only Girl for Me, I'll Wait for You* (Gerry and the Pacemakers); *Is It Love* (Cilla Black); *I Love You Too* (Fourmost); *I Got a Woman* (Black Knights); *Shake a Tailfeather* (Earl Royce and the Olympics)

FESTIVAL   (1970)

DIR: Murray Lerner; PROD: Murray Lerner; STUDIO: Peppercorn-Wormser; 98 min., b/w (no video release)

MUSIC ★★★★
ATTITUDE ★★★★
FUN ★★★★★

Hand me down my walkin' cane...I think I'm gonna fly.
From the opening credits, it's immediately obvious that *Festival* is the first link in a movie chain that evolved into *Monterey Pop* before climaxing with *Woodstock*. The film compiles highlights from the '63, '64, '65, and '66 Newport Folk Festivals. Son House plays Dobro and tells the blues. Peter, Paul, and Mary deliver powerful performances of "If I Had a Hammer" and "Blowin' in the Wind." In a

very rare appearance, Howlin' Wolf busts out "Howlin' for My Darlin'." And, of course, Dylan "goes electric." These are but some of the highlights from a very full and fast-moving film.

The overal effect is so intensely powerful because the Newport festivals show-cased the best stuff from the folk boom of the early '60s. *Festival* interweaves the political content of many of the songs with a use of dialogue that was unprecedented (matched only by Bob Dylan's *Eat the Document*). In the best example, the dialogue elaborates on the depth of Dylan's electric revolution. Sequences of the maestro rehearsing his group (featuring Paul Butterfield, Mike Bloomfield and Al Kooper) are intercut with bits of charming old folkie ladies (who can barely move) singing some amazing a capella broadsides.

Onstage, Dylan and the band blast through "Maggie's Farm" despite hollered catcalls. Rumor has it Pete Seeger was so outraged that he tried to chop Dylan's amplifier leads with an ax! The excitement's so great that you almost miss a young Judy Collins. Her version of "Turn, Turn, Turn" anticipates the hit her recording partner Jim McGuinn later had with the Byrds. The final moment of note is Joan Baez singing "Farewell Angelina" at the '64 festival before introducing a virtually unknown Bob Dylan to the world (he sings "All I Really Want to Do"). (DP)

SONGS

Improvised Rag (Jim Kweskin Jug Band); *Come and Go with Me to That Land, If I Had a Hammer, Blowin' in the Wind, The Times They Are a-Changin'* (Peter, Paul, and Mary); *Green Corn, Deep Blue Sea, Down by the Riverside* (Pete Seeger); *Codine* (Buffy Sainte Marie); *Go Tell It on the Mountain* (Joan Baez, Peter Yarrow); *All I Really Want to Do* (Bob Dylan); *My Trials Will Soon Be Over, Farewell Angelina, Pack Up Your Sorrows* (Joan Baez); *And the War Drags On, Vietnam, Colours* (Donovan); *Turn Turn Turn, Anathea* (Judy Collins); *Trouble in Mind* (Odetta); *Highway Blues* (Sonny Terry and Brownie McGhee); *Candy Man* (Mississippi John Hurt); *Maggie's Farm* (Bob Dylan and the Paul Butterfield Blues Band); *Up Above My Head, I Ain't Gonna Let No One Turn Me Around, Go Tell It on the Mountain* (Staple Singers); *Freedom, We Shall Overcome* (Freedom Singers); *I Was Born in Chicago* (Paul Butterfield Blues Band); *Howlin' for my Darlin'* (Howlin' Wolf); *I Walk the Line* (Johnny Cash); *Ruby* (Tex Logan and the Lilly Brothers); *Every Day's a Holiday* (Paul Stookey)

FIREBALL 500 (1966)

CAST: Frankie Avalon, Annette Funicello, Fabian, Chill Wills, Harvey Lembeck, Julie Parrish, Sandy Reed, Doug Henderson, Baynes Barron, Vin Scully, Mary Hughes; DIR: William Asher; PROD: James H. Nicholson, Samuel Z. Arkoff; SCREENPLAY: William Asher, Leo Townsend; STUDIO: American International; 92 min., color (no video release)

MUSIC ★★★
ATTITUDE ★★★★
FUN ★★★

Hot rod derbies meet surf sensations Avalon and Fabian.

It's a pure thrill to see Fabian and Frankie Avalon brutally beat the hell out of each other in this late, late *Beach Party* entry. L.A. Dodgers broadcaster Vin Scully opens the film with a great voiceover to claymation (created by Art Clokey, the man who brought you "Gumby") and footage of stock car racing. Avalon sings a memorable title song over the credits as he wheels into Harvey Lembeck's garage. Later, Annette jumps onstage at a carnival sideshow to sing "Step Right Up." Don Randi Trio Plus One is the hillbilly band backing her, and they contribute their own instrumental, "Country Carnival." (Randi is best known as the L.A. session keyboard player featured in Phil Spector's Wall of Sound.)

A.I.P. staff songwriters Guy Hemric and Jerry Styner contributed some great tunes to the beach pictures, and they pen all the songs performed here. Avalon delivers the plot-oriented "My Way" and "Turn Around," a Wall of Sound-style duet with romantic interest Julie Parrish. The movie also has a pretty decent plot about hot rodders using their cars for illegal moonshine runs. It's funny to see A.I.P's accountants at work during the "racing" scenes, in which stock footage is used, shall we say, generously. Finally, it should be noted that *Fireball 500* marks the end of a long and successful run of A.I.P. movies starring Frankie Avalon and Annette Funicello. (DP)

SONGS   *Fireball 500, My Way* (Frankie Avalon); *Step Right Up* (Annette Funicello); *Country Carnival* (Don Randi Trio Plus One); *Turn Around* (Frankie Avalon, Julie Parrish)

THE FIVE HEARTBEATS (1991)

MUSIC ★★★
ATTITUDE ★★★★
FUN ★★★★

CAST: Robert Townsend, Michael Wright, Leon, Tico Wells, Chuck Patterson, Harold Nicholas, Hawthorne James, Harry J. Lennix, Diahann Carroll; **DIR:** Robert Townsend; **PROD:** Loretha C. Jones; **SCREENPLAY:** Robert Townsend, Keenen Ivory Wayans; **STUDIO:** 20th Century-Fox; 120 min., color (CBS/Fox)

A composite black music legend, black Hollywood style.

Energetic performances, good *faux*-Motown music, and loads of period detail make *The Five Heartbeats* an enjoyable, if superficial, drama tracing the tumultuous 20-year career of a black vocal group. Writer/director Robert Townsend spent months researching this film, much of that time travelling with the Dells, who have been together since 1953 with but one change in personnel. Townsend also threw in character and plot details from the careers of the Temptations, among others.

We first meet the Five Heartbeats at a raucous Detroit amateur show circa 1963. The principal characters are quickly, if sketchily, established: the hard-living, hard-loving Eddie (read: David Ruffin); the shy, choir-boy falsetto (read: Eddie Kendricks); Townsend himself as the group's songwriter and musical director. Next, the Five Heartbeats take on a manager and a veteran choreographer (played by Harold Nicholas of the legendary Nicholas Brothers dance team), and they land a deal with a scrappy black-owned label (read: Motown or VeeJay). Then come the hits, the tours, the money, the broads, the booze, the rivalries, the failed solo careers, the "accidental" death of the manager, the breakup, and finally the loving reunion. (Townsend even throws in a born-again rehabilitation for Eddie, although David Ruffin wasn't that lucky.) Along the way, the sound of the Five Heartbeats evolves from the circa-`64 Temptations to circa-`72 Spinners to circa-`76 Parliament under the direction of George Duke, the picture's music supervisor. (AS)

SCENES   An Apollo Theater battle of the bands (0:22); an onstage fight that becomes an established stage routine (0:57); a singer being brutally beaten when he demands overdue royalties from Big Red (1:09); Eddie, broke and beaten, pleading with the other Heartbeats to take him back (1:30)

SONGS   *I Got Nothing but Love, A Heart Is a House for Love* (Five Heartbeats); *Stop Runnin' Away* (Bird and the Midnight Falcons); *We Haven't Finished Yet* (Kid Sister); *I Feel Like Going On* (Church Choir)

FLAME (1974)

MUSIC ★★★★
ATTITUDE ★★★★
FUN ★★★

CAST: Slade, Tom Conti, Alan Lake, Johnny Shannon, Nina Thomas; **DIR:** Richard Loncraine; **PROD:** Gaverick Losey; **SCREENPLAY:** Andrew Birkin, David Humphries; **STUDIO:** Goodtimes Enterprises; 91 min., color (no video release)

It's a wig!

During the early '70s, a brief succession of British bands were presented to American consumers as "the next Beatles": T. Rex (with Marc Bolan), the Bay City Rollers, and Slade. Of the three, Slade were far and away the biggest British success story and the biggest American flop. Here, Slade received little but scorn and rejection. With hindsight, one might suggest that Slade were too strange looking and hideously dressed to make it as American teen idols and too "pop" to gain an older FM audience. But who can say why KISS and AC/DC made it big and Slade didn't. That's just the way it happened. Later, in 1983, a nondescript metal band from L.A. called Quiet Riot remade Slade's "Cum On Feel the Noize" into a monster hit, so maybe Slade were musically ahead of their time.

To cash in on their massive fame in Britain (where they are still revered), Slade made this film in 1974. Oddly enough, the film is a very somber affair about a rock group called Flame circa 1967. They form, have a hit, get conned, manipulated, and screwed at every turn, break up, and that's that. The film ends, and everybody goes home. You might expect a Slade movie to be action-packed, hilarious, balls-out fun (like their U.K. hit singles), but this film isn't. It is, nevertheless, a well-written, well-made movie for Slade fans, past and present. (MC)

SCENES Flame travel to a radio station for an interview. To get there, they take a freezing-cold boat ride out to the shabby barge from which the station broadcasts. This is based on reality. While British rock was dominating the charts all over the world (1964-67), there were no legally sanctioned commercial pop stations in England. Instead, British rock fans listened to "pirate" operations like Radio Caroline and Radio London, broadcasting from platforms anchored outside Britain's territorial waters. You've got to hand it to those crafty British renegade entrepreneurs.

SONGS *How Does It Feel, If Pigs Culd Fly, So Far So Good, Better Day, Wishing U Were Heer, Far Far Away* (Slade)

FLAMING STAR   (1960)

CAST: Elvis Presley, Steve Forrest, Barbara Eden, Delores Del Rio, John McIntire; DIR: Don Siegel; PROD: David Weisbart; SCREENPLAY: Clair Huffaker, Nunnally Johnson; STUDIO: 20th Century-Fox; 92 min., color (Key)

MUSIC	★
ATTITUDE	★★★
FUN	★★★★

Elvis's entry in the great race debate.
Upon his discharge from the army in 1960, Elvis Presley plunged into nearly a decade of cookie-cutter films. Both *GI Blues* and *Flaming Star* were made in the year of his return to civilian life. It's difficult to imagine two more different films. *GI Blues* is a light musical capitalizing on Elvis's military status, while *Flaming Star* is a dramatic film with no music and a big Message. *Flaming Star* features Elvis as Pacer, a young man born to a white father (John McIntire) and an Indian mother (Delores Del Rio). As tension between the white settlers and the local tribe mounts, Pacer and his family are persecuted and torn apart.

Like John Ford's 1956 classic *The Searchers, Flaming Star* attempts to address issues of race and racism. Unfortunately, *Flaming Star* lacks both the subtlety and the grandeur of Ford's film. Delores Del Rio's Hispanic accent is intrusive, Pacer's almost supernatural senses of sight and sound are at times laughable, and the dialogue is ponderous. But casting Elvis, the man who brought together blues and country, as a doomed half-breed is an interesting statement. If Elvis's early musical career epitomized a successful heterogeneity, this film suggests the difficulty of translating such blendings to mainstream America. (TM)

LINES Pacer and a brave trade Hollywood Indian truisms too hokey even for a "Kung Fu" episode: "I will return, then, when the sun has killed the stars in the sky."

SONGS *Flaming Star, A Cane and a High Starched Collar* (Elvis Presley)

FM

FM (1978)

MUSIC ★★★
ATTITUDE ★★
FUN ★★

CAST: Michael Brandon, Eileen Brennan, Alex Karras, Martin Mull, Cassie Yates, Norman Lloyd; **DIR:** Jon A. Alonzo; **PROD:** Rand Holston; **SCREENPLAY:** Ezra Sacks; **STUDIO:** Universal; 104 min., color (MCA/Universal)

This could have been radio's Spinal Tap.

If *FM* weren't so concerned with painting radio as a good guy in the battle against corporate America, a little extra wit might have made this movie *Spinal Tap*'s natural forerunner. Instead, *FM* will have to settle for second billing as a throwaway "WKRP in Cincinnati" episode. Too bad. *FM* wastes a slam-dunk opportunity to exploit the humor and personality of '70s radio. Not that fine musical performances by Jimmy Buffet and Linda Ronstadt don't reflect the era's inclusive nature, but a few less personal references to characters we hardly know and a few more moments like the hilariously misguided Tom Petty interview could have been the difference between an enjoyable radio reminder and a footnote in TV sitcom history. (ALa)

LINES Station manger Brandon invites Lloyd of the corporate office to a Jimmy Buffet concert. Says Lloyd, "Great, I love buffets. What are they serving?"

CAMEOS Linda Ronstadt, Jimmy Buffett, Tom Petty, REO Speedwagon

FOOTLOOSE (1984)

MUSIC ★★★
ATTITUDE ★★★★★
FUN ★★★★

CAST: Kevin Bacon, Lori Singer, John Lithgow, Dianne Wiest, Christopher Penn, Sarah Jessica Parker; **DIR:** Herbert Ross; **PROD:** Daniel Melnick; **SCREENPLAY:** Dean Pitchford; **STUDIO:** Paramount; 107 min., color (Paramount)

A city boy loosens up the Bible Belt.

The key to enjoying most Hollywood movies, especially the sentimental ones, is what Freud called the "willing suspension of disbelief." Of course elephants can't fly, but most people let themselves believe Dumbo can, at least while the lights are out. Similarly, *Footloose* can be a terrific, upbeat rental. You just have to believe that the Kenny Loggins tunes on the soundtrack are really rock'n'roll. Kevin Bacon plays a teenager from Chicago who is relocated after his parents' divorce to a small town where rock'n'roll and dancing are illegal. There he falls for Lori Singer, the rebellious daughter of the town's crusading preacher (John Lithgow), whose only son died in a rock-related accident. Bacon and Lithgow clash when Bacon tries to organize a high school dance.

Okay, the movie's just a *little* over the top, but Lithgow is remarkably thoughtful as the preacher, and Bacon turns in another seamless performance. Believe it or not, there's real energy here, especially during the dance sequences. *Footloose* is essentially a souped-up Elvis film: the rocker, misunderstood, emerges triumphant and purified. But, hey—if you've got a great formula, work it, baby. (DR)

FOR THOSE WHO THINK YOUNG   (1964)

CAST: James Darren, Pamela Tiffin, Paul Lynde, Woody Woodbury, Tina Louise, Bob Denver, Nancy Sinatra, Robert Middleton, Claudia Martin, Ellen McRae, Sammy Tong; DIR: Lesley H. Martinson; PROD: Hugh Benson; SCREENPLAY: James O'Hanlon, George O'Hanlon, Dan Beaumont; STUDIO: United Artists; 96 min., color (no video release)

A beach flick in which Bob Denver plays kelp—uh, Kelp.
On the surface, this beacher/sleeper can easily be dismissed as lightweight fare. The title itself suggests casual adult fancy, taken from early '60s Pepsi ads. No famous-name rock acts perform their tunes. Yet lurking beneath the surface are strange, unexplained things. Originally a post-*Gidget* vehicle for James Darren, *For Those Who Think Young* relishes in its accidental flavor and finally reaches Beach-O-Rama's ridiculous summit in the person of Bob Denver as Kelp.

Denver plays a freak (somewhere on the spectrum between Maynard G. Krebs and Gilligan). He's ably supported in this role by sidekick/girlfriend Nancy Sinatra. The lately realized greatness of Woody Woodbury as a teen leader and nightclub comedian also helps to keep the film going. A rare appearance by Richard Delvy and Randy Nuart of the Challengers ("K-39") alongside Paul Johnson of the Bel-Airs ("Mr. Moto") adds a true surf music segment to the spice. They back an unidentified singer sweatin' out "Gonna Walk All Over This Land"...sheesh! It's Denver, however, who injects the most howling rock'n'roll and steals the show with his recitation of the tribal surf stomp "Ho Daddy" while a dancing circle of surf-dwellers wave their arms and chant, "HO-DADDY, SURF'S UP!" It's preposterous, inane, and overdone...just the way we like it! (DP)

For Those Who Think Love (James Darren); *Ho Daddy* (Bob Denver); *I'm Gonna Walk All Over This Land* (unidentified vocalist with Bel-Airs/Challengers band)   **SONGS**

FRANKIE AND JOHNNY   (1965)

CAST: Elvis Presley, Donna Douglas, Harry Morgan, Sue Ane Langdon, Audrey Christie, Nancy Kovack; DIR: Fred De Cordova; PROD: Alex Edward Small; SCREENPLAY: Alex Gottlieb; STUDIO: United Artists; 88 min., color (MGM/UA)

The King's courtship carousel.
A musical remake of a 1938 film by the same name, this film has the flaccid charmlessness of a Branson, Missouri, nightclub act. Elvis plays Johnny, a gam-

blin', fun-lovin', night club singin' ne'er-do-well who is advised by a gypsy to team up with a red-haired woman for luck at the gaming tables. So, for no other reason, Johnny starts flirting with redheaded siren Nellie Bly. This angers his girlfriend Frankie (Donna Douglas, who played Ellie Mae on "The Beverly Hillbillies"). It also annoys Nellie's boyfriend Blackie (Robert Strauss), who happens to be Johnny's boss. Thus begins a humorless musical chairs of partner swapping that ceases only with the much-wished-for ending. This movie has been bloated to a merciless 88 minutes, and Elvis also seems to have a swollen, shiny look to him. All the songs suck, too. (TM)

SONGS *Gypsies* (Elvis Presley, Harry Morgan); *Frankie and Johnny* (Elvis Presley, Donna Douglas, Sue Ane Langdon); *Lookout Broadway* (Elvis Presley, Donna Douglas, Harry Morgan, Audrey Christie); *Beginner's Luck, When the Saints Go Marchin' In, Get Happy, Hard Luck, Please Don't Stop Lovin' Me, Let's Go Along with the Show, Make Petunia's Tulips Mine, What Every Woman Lives For* (Elvis Presley)

FUN IN ACAPULCO (1963)

CAST: Elvis Presley, Ursula Andress, Elsa Cardenas, Paul Lukas; DIR: Richard Thorpe; PROD: Hal B. Wallis; SCREENPLAY: Allan Weiss; STUDIO: Paramount; 97 min., color (Key)

MUSIC ★★
ATTITUDE ★★
FUN ★★★★

Another installment in the endless grind of Elvis pulp.
Fun in Acapulco stars Elvis as Mike Winwood, a drifter who ends up as a part-time lifeguard and singer in a fancy hotel. He wavers in his affection between the passionate Delores Gomez (Margherita Dauphin), a female bullfighter of Latin appetites (yeah, right), and a blond ex-princess (Ursula Andress), who really is the right girl for Mike. Soon it's revealed that Mike has a history. Because of an unfortunate trapeze incident in his recent past, he's terrified of heights. That's why he has taken the lifeguard job—so that he can learn to jump off the high dive and thus rid himself of the acrophobic demons that haunt him.

   Fun in Acapulco glories in its own camp, especially during the scene in which Elvis (dressed completely in black) climbs on the high board to conquer his fears. Or the scene in which Elvis and Delores try romance in her tiny car, inspiring the truly tasteless song "No Room to Rhumba in a Sports Car." (TM)

SCENES Elvis frenetically dancing and playing the organ and bongo in his number "Bossanova" (0:58)

LINES Delores Gomez, bullfighter, flirts with Mike: "You want to play papa in my house?"

SONGS *Acapulco, Viva el Amor, I Think I'm Gonna Like It Here, Life Begins When You're in Mexico, El Torro, Margherita, Pedro the Bull, No Room to Rhumba in a Sports Car, Bossanova, You Can't Say No, Guadalajara* (Elvis Presley)

GET CRAZY (1983)

CAST: Daniel Stern, Allen Goorwitz, Malcolm McDowell, Gail Edwards, Miles Chapin; DIR: Allan Arkush; PROD: Hunt Lowry, Herbert Solow; SCREENPLAY: Danny Opatoshu, Henry Rosenbaum, David Taylor; 98 min., color (Embassy)

MUSIC ★
ATTITUDE ★
FUN ★

Andy Hardy and the gang put on a rock'n'roll show.
I'd suspect this farce was meant for the prepubescent crowd if it weren't for the language and the gratuitous nipple shots. This piece of schlock is so bad that it's

beyond the crowd that likes Beavis and Butt-Head. If anything, it's for numskulls *like* Beavis and Butt-Head. Allen Goorwitz plays a promoter (not unlike Bill Graham) on the day of his big New Year's Eve show. His main attraction is a Mick Jagger clone named Reggie Wanker (Malcolm McDowell). There's excitement in the air, especially because the dastardly Colin Beverly (Ed Begley Jr.) *has planted a bomb in the theater!* Do you think it will go off? Not soon enough, I promise you. (DR)

SCENES Lou Reed plays Auden, the Dylan character. His living room (0:21) is an exact replica of the cover art from *Bringing It All Back Home*. It's hard to believe that Reed let himself be associated with this film.

CAMEOS Ed Begley Jr., Bobby Sherman, Fabian Forte, Franklyn Ajaye, Howard Kaylan, John Densmore, Lou Reed, Paul Bartel, Mary Woronov

GET YOURSELF A COLLEGE GIRL   (1964)

CAST: Mary Ann Mobley, Joan O'Brien, Nancy Sinatra, Chris Noel, Chad Everett; DIR: Sidney Miller; PROD: Sam Katzman; SCREENPLAY: Robert E. Kent; STUDIO: MGM; 87 min., color (no video release)

MUSIC ★★★★
ATTITUDE ★★
FUN ★★★

The screen magic that is Sam Katzman.
This is another tune-filled romp from drive-in mogul Sam Katzman, whose films have probably put more rock bands on celluloid than any other producer's. *Get Yourself a College Girl* is ostensibly about a songwriting coed (Mary Ann Mobley) who's nearly expelled for penning a scandalous song about the sexual sophistication of college babes! Meanwhile, she's pursued by a song publisher (Chad Everett), as well as a politician seeking the youth vote via a musical telethon. Katzman threw together a varied bill of musical acts for *Get Yourself a College Girl*, the release of which straddled two very distinct eras in pop history. In addition to some very happening British invaders (the Dave Clark Five and the Animals, who perform their debut U.S. 45), he's also included Stan Getz with Astrud Gilberto, the Jimmy Smith Trio, and the Standells (in their frat-rock phase). All this, and Freddie Bell and the Bellboys, too?! (JS)

SCENES A hypnotic rendition by Getz and Gilberto of "The Girl from Ipanema," the song that sparked the Bossa Nova craze, in which Gilberto stares straight into the camera and rocks way harder than the lame DC5 scenes

SONGS *Blue Feeling, Around and Around* (Animals); *Get Yourself a College Girl* (Mary Ann Mobley); *Bony Moronie, The Swim* (Standells); *The Girl from Ipanema* (Stan Getz, Astrud Gilberto); *Sweet Rain* (Stan Getz); *The Sermon, Comin' Home Johnny* (Jimmy Smith Trio); *Talkin' about Love* (Freddie Bell and the Bellboys, Roberta Linn); *Whenever You're Around, Thinking of You Baby* (Dave Clark Five)

THE GHOST GOES GEAR   (1966)

CAST: The Spencer Davis Group, Nicholas Parsons, Dave Berry; DIR: Hugh Gladwick; PROD: Harry Field; SCREENPLAY: Roger Dunton, Hugh Gladwish; 41 min., color (no video release)
M4, A3, F2

MUSIC ★★★★
ATTITUDE ★★
FUN ★★★

Gimme some Group therapy.
The Spencer Davis Group is the only reason to watch this aborted feature film which, in its final confused form, unintentionally anticipates *The Magical Mystery*

Tour in all of its worst attributes. The plot has something to do with raising money to keep an ancestral estate afloat, but you'd be hard put to glean that from what survives of the original 80-minute (proposed) feature. (BE)

THE GHOST IN THE INVISIBLE BIKINI (1966)

CAST: Tommy Kirk, Deborah Walley, Aron Kincaid, Susan Hart, Boris Karloff, Harvey Lembeck, Jesse White, Claudia Martin, Nancy Sinatra, Basil Rathbone, Patsy Kelly; DIR: Don Weis; PROD: James H. Nicholson, Samuel Z. Arkoff; SCREENPLAY: Louis H. Hayward, Elwood Allman; STUDIO: American International; 83 min., color (no video release)

MUSIC ★★★
ATTITUDE ★★★
FUN ★★★

Boris Karloff meets Susan Hart at a Bobby Fuller dance.
American International Pictures had worked their *Beach Party* cast members into such household names by the mid-'60s that they were able to get away with murder (like this). *The Ghost in the Invisible Bikini* presents the sci-fi goofiness of *Pajama Party* kicked into a chamber of horrors. The incidental music is *Pet Sounds* meets *Psycho*, and that in itself is more of a highlight than the rest of the movie. The sick monsters and sets are particularly groovy and gruesome, but A.I.P.'s sometimes negligent presentation of rock'n'roll acts begins to stink.

The best musical number is the girl-group raver by Nancy Sinatra (pre-"Boots") singing "Geronimo." Everybody can laugh at the cute Italian import Piccola Pupa attempting to sing and dance to "Stand Up and Fight." But the greatest atrocity is the way the legendary Bobby Fuller Four are handled. They look confused trying to bop to songs they've never heard. Even worse for the guys (who played Fender equipment) is that they're forced to play hated Vox stuff here because of an A.I.P./Vox plugola contract. (Luckily, real footage of the group exists in *Where the Action Is.*) *The Ghost in the Invisible Bikini* inspired a special promotional episode of "Shindig" as well. Later. A.I.P. took this format to new depths with *Dr. Goldfoot and the Bikini Machine* and *Dr. Goldfoot and the Girl Bombs.* The best moments in any of these post-beach clunkers are the Donna Loren scenes in *Sgt. Deadhead*, in which she performs "How Can You Tell" and "Two Timin' Angel." (DP)

Geronimo (Nancy Sinatra); *Swing-a My Thing, Make the Music Pretty* (Bobby Fuller Four); *Don't Try to Fight It* (Quinn O'Hara); *Stand Up and Fight* (Piccola Pupa)   **SONGS**

THE GHOST OF DRAGSTRIP HOLLOW (1959)

CAST: Jody Fair, Martin Braddock, Russ Bender, Leon Tyler, Elaine Dupont, Henry McCann; DIR: William Hole Jr.; PROD: Lou Rusoff; SCREENPLAY: Lou Rusoff; STUDIO: American International; 65 min., b/w (no video release)

MUSIC ★★★★
ATTITUDE ★★★
FUN ★★★★

Haunted hot rods.
An amiable B comedy much like *Hot Rod Gang, The Ghost of Dragstrip Hollow* features a swell bunch of misunderstood hot rodders who say things like "He's got static in his attic—completely zonked!" and "Will somebody get this bag of bacteria lost?" Evicted from their clubhouse, they move to a haunted mansion, where they throw a monster ball. A sympathetic journalist covering their story unmasks a rubbersuited monster trying to scare the gang out. "I thought I'd seen you before!" the journalist says. "Of course you've seen me before!" the meek-voiced man in the suit replies. "I scared you to death in *The Day the World Ended.* You shivered when you saw me in *The She Creature.*" The timid, phony monster is played by Paul Blaisdell, creator of bug-eyed creatures for many A.I.P. classics.

The dance music at the kids' soda shop hangout is provided by the Renegades, who crank out some hot instrumentals. (The group's lineup included Bruce Johnston, Richard Podolor, Nik Venet, and Sandy Nelson.) Occasionally, hiccuping vocals are added by girlfriends from the car club. One number is punctuated by pistol shots and shouts of "Geronimo!" from the piano player. Later, at a slumber party, someone says, "Look, the club combo made a record of 'Geronimo'!" (There's a close-up of the beautiful American International Records label on the soundtrack 45.)

At the monster hop, there's more good rockin' from the Renegades, plus the awful "Tongue Tied", sung by the film's musical director ("Hey, a special treat! Jimmy Maddin's gonna sing one of his hit records!"). When a real ghost walks through the room, a wisecracking parrot comments, "He won't be back—the rock'n'roll jam got rid of him!" (JS)

LINES Female lead teenager on walking into the creepy mansion: "This place is loaded with ectoplasm, isn't it?" Male lead teenager: "Looks like a nightmare factory!"

SONGS *Geronimo, He's My Guy, I Promise You, Charge, Ghost Train* (Renegades); *Tongue Tied* (Jimmy Maddin)

GI BLUES (1960)

MUSIC	★★★
ATTITUDE	★★
FUN	★★★★

CAST: Elvis Presley, Juliet Prowse, Robert Ivers, James Douglas, Sigrid Maier, Leticia Roman; DIR: Norman Taurog; PROD: Hal B. Wallis; SCREENPLAY: Edmund Beloin, Henry Garson; STUDIO: Paramount; 104 min., color (Key)

He's in the army now.

Elvis got out of the army in 1960, and Paramount wasted no time taking advantage of the situation. Buddy Holly was dead, Chuck Berry was in jail, Little Richard had forsaken rock for the ministry, and Jerry Lee Lewis's career had been undone by his marriage to a 13-year-old cousin. The first generation of untamed rockabilly had yielded to a sweeter, more standardized sound. Now Elvis had to be cleaned up and neutered into the puppyish pretty boy who would sleepwalk through his next 28 movies.

In *GI Blues*, Elvis plays Tulsa McClean, an army private who dreams of opening a nightclub back in Oklahoma when he's discharged. Tulsa needs money, so he reluctantly agrees to a bet that he can seduce Lily (Juliet Prowse), the beautiful but frosty nightclub star. Wooing her, he falls in love. Then she finds out about the bet, and he murders her to keep from losing. Just kidding. They make up, and everything's jake. Did you think Elvis got to make a real movie? (TM)

SCENES Elvis's impossibly big GI hair; Elvis playing live interrupted by someone playing "Blue Suede Shoes" on the jukebox (0:17)

SONGS *GI Blues, It's Not Good Enough for You, Frankfurt Special, I'm Gonna Stop Shoppin' Around, So Ripe for Love, I Don't Have a Wooden Heart, Daddy Big Boots, D'ya Ever Get One of Them Days* (Elvis Presley); *Gotta Pocket Full of Rainbows* (Elvis Presley, Juliet Prowse)

GIFT (1993)

CAST: Perry Farrell, Casey Niccoli; **DIR:** Perry Farrell, Casey Niccoli; **PROD:** Allan Wachs; 80 min., color (Warner Reprise)

MUSIC	★★★★
ATTITUDE	★★
FUN	★★★★

The needle and the damage done.
This movie is everthing you wanted to know about heroin addiction (and weren't sure you wanted to ask). The film's disclaimer notwithstanding, Perry Farrell and his girlfriend Casey Niccoli certainly seem to be playing themselves. So much so that it's hard to tell in *Gift*, the story of two drug-addicted losers, where reality ends and the drama begins. Perry and Casey buy drugs, then Casey buys some more drugs while Perry records in the studio. In his white pancake makeup, Farrell looks like death, but it's Casey who actually dies of an overdose about twenty minutes into the film. That said, *Gift* really has its moments. In fact, for the most part, it goes down quite easily, despite the obviously well-practiced shots of Perry and Casey fixing. After the dismal sequence in which he discovers Casey's corpse, Perry cleans and dresses her while flashing back to images of their Mexican wedding and happier days together. (Okay, there is *some* necrophilia, but it's really tastefully done.)

To give Farrell credit, *Gift* could easily have slopped over into self-indulgent pretension. It does teeter a bit but never quite goes over the edge. Perry, of course, is the star here, and his acting is generally excellent (if a bit dopey). The later scenes, mostly interior monologues, are intercut and overdubbed with the music of Jane's Addiction and a few performance clips. There's even an upbeat sequence featuring actual footage of Perry and Casey's (not legally binding) Santeria wedding, behind which the cheery "Classic Girl" throbs pleasantly (0:56). It seems odd to say this, but *Gift* manages to make heroin addiction seem reasonable. I guess junkies have feelings, too. (DR)

SCENES The provocative rap session with hospitalized junkies (0:43)

LINES Perry, wearing a dress, trying to score: "Do I look like the police?" Perry on Casey: "I felt the same attraction for her that gay men and women feel."

SONGS *Stop, Three Days, Ain't No Right, Classic Girl* (Jane's Addiction); *Don't Call Me Nigger Whitey* (Perry Farrell, Ice-T)

GIMME SHELTER (1970)

DIR: David Maysles, Albert Maysles, Charlotte Zwerin; PROD: Ronald Schneider; STUDIO: Maysles Films; 90 min., color (Abkco)

MUSIC ★★★★
ATTITUDE ★★★★★
FUN ★★★★

Woodstock West it wasn't.

In 1969, with the peace, love, and music vibe blowing in the wind, the Rolling Stones embarked on their first American tour in three years. Not to be left standing in the shadow of Woodstock, Jagger & Co. planned to hold their own free festival at the Altamont Speedway in northern California. *Gimme Shelter* documents that now-infamous road trip and the Altamont concert that ended it with the stabbing death of an audience member by a Hell's Angels "security guard."

The style, attitude, and dress of the late '60s Stones will continue to inspire rockers for generations to come, but no matter how much the youthful Jagger prances, this movie belongs to attorney Melvin Belli, who worked with the Stones to secure a northern California concert site. Ever on the speakerphone in his office full of clients, Belli is an indication of things to come in the music business, If the killing at Altamont signified the premature end of innocence for the Woodstock Generation, Belli is rock'n'roll moving off the streets and into the corporate boardrooms. In one scene, Mick and drummer Charlie Watts watch the raw film footage of the killing through the cutting room viewfinder. The Maysles' camera, in turn, watches them. One can't help wondering whether rock'n'roll history might have forever been altered had the Angels not been there. Would Mick have been the victim instead? (TP)

SCENES The Stones taking the stage at Altamont (1:08); the decisive fight breaking out as the Stones play "Under My Thumb" (1:23)

LINES Belli, whenever he's on the speakerphone: "I'm sitting here with..." Jagger at a press conference explaining the reason for a free concert: "[To create] a microcosmic society which sets an example to the rest of America as to how one can behave in large gatherings."

CAMEOS Jerry Garcia, Michael Shrieve, Phil Lesh, Jim Dickinson, Bobby Keyes

SONGS *Jumpin' Jack Flash, Satisfaction, You Gotta Move, Wild Horses, Brown Sugar, Love in Vain, Honky Tonk Women, Street Fighting Man, Sympathy for the Devil, Under My Thumb* (Rolling Stones); *I've Been Loving You Too Long* (Ike and Tina Turner); *Six Days on the Road* (Flying Burrito Brothers); *The Other Side of This Life* (Jefferson Airplane)

THE GIRL CAN'T HELP IT (1956)

CAST: Tom Ewell, Jayne Mansfield, Edmond O'Brien, Fats Domino, The Platters, Little Richard, Gene Vincent, The Treniers, Julie London, Eddie Cochran, Johnny Olenn, Eddie Fontaine; DIR: Frank Tashlin; PROD: Frank Tashlin; SCREENPLAY: Frank Tashlin, Herbert Baker; STUDIO: 20th Century-Fox; 99 min., color (CBS/Fox)

MUSIC ★★★★★
ATTITUDE ★★★★★
FUN ★★★★★

This movie IS Hollywood rock.

Somebody should write a biography of Frank Tashlin. As a contemporary of Tex Avery and Friz Freling, Tashlin directed some of the greatest cartoons of animation's golden age. Later, he brought his bizarre cartoonish approach to such live-action comedies as *Son of Paleface* (with Bob Hope) and *Rock-a-Bye Baby* (with Jerry Lewis). For my money, though, his greatest claim to fame is *The Girl Can't Help It*. This movie stands out among 1950s rock films as one that never insults

The Girl Can't Help It

the intelligence of its audience. It's also loaded with rock'n'roll stars, and it's still funny.

Here's the story: Marty Murdock, a vicious gangster (Edmond O'Brien), hires Tom Miller (Tom Ewell), a once-successful, hard-drinking talent agent, to transform his blond bombshell girlfriend (Jayne Mansfield) into a recording star. As the story unfolds, we get a hilarious look at the sleazy machinations of the jukebox and record businesses. And we see a staggering array of contemporary rock stars (with a couple of lame nonentities thrown in for balance). They all get a chance to be heard at length and seen in glorious Technicolor. Look out for the scene in which Miller, during an attack of the DTs, hallucinates Julie London posing seductively all over his furniture and taunting him with a scorching rendition of "Cry Me a River." (MC)

SCENES Gene Vincent and Co. shaking their caps loose to "Be Bop-a-Lula" (a personal message to the Rock'n'Roll Hall of Fame nominating committee: DUH?); Jayne Mansfield walking down the street: Men look at her, and their eyeglasses shatter. Milk bottles explode and froth over. Ice blocks spontaneously melt. Tex Avery couldn't have done it better.

SONGS *My Idea of Love, Ain't Gonna Cry* (Johnny Olenn); *Ready Teddy, The Girl Can't Help It, She's Got It* (Little Richard); *Cool It Baby* (Eddie Fontaine); *Cry Me a River* (Julie London); *Be Bop-a-Lula* (Gene Vincent); *Twenty Flight Rock* (Eddie Cochran); *Rockin' Is Our Business* (Treniers); *Blue Monday* (Fats Domino); *You'll Never Never Know* (Platters); *Rock Around the Rockpile* (Edmond O'Brien)

GIRL HAPPY   (1964)

MUSIC ★★★★
ATTITUDE ★★
FUN ★★★

CAST: Elvis Presley, Shelley Fabares, Gary Crosby, Mary Ann Mobley, Joby Baker, Nita Talbot; DIR: Boris Sagal; PROD: Joe Pasternak; SCREENPLAY: Harvey Bullock, R.S. Allen; STUDIO: MGM; 96 min., color (MGM/UA)

See Elvis clam on the beach.

In the year that *Meet the Beatles* came out, Elvis could be found sinking in a quicksand of adolescent B movies. *Girl Happy* stars Elvis as Rusty Wells, a member of a singing combo that travels to Fort Lauderdale to play music and play with the girls. As a condition of his trip, Rusty is forced to baby-sit Valerie (Shelley Fabares) by her overprotective mobster father. Valerie predictably gets into countless scrapes from which Rusty must extricate her. *Of course* there are competing love interests, "zany" escapades and dozens of misogynous one-liners, all played out against an almost surreal landscape of bikini-clad female body parts.

Despite this dreary set-up, *Girl Happy* has some bright spots. The pacing is fast, the '60s color palette is often glorious (check out the mustards and reds at the film's beginning), and many of the musical numbers are engaging, especially "Let's Party Tonight" and the now legendary dance "The Clam." (TM)

SCENES Elvis does "The Clam" (0:50); Elvis in drag—the King is queen for a day! (1:27)

LINES The straight line: "The beach is crowded today." The punch line: "Not as crowded as that bathing suit." Describing that "perfect" girl: "Not much upstairs, but what a staircase."

SONGS *Spring Fever* (Elvis Presley, Shelley Fabares); *I've Got News for You* (Nita Talbot); *Girl Happy, Courtesy of Fort Lauderdale Chamber of Commerce, Let's Party Tonight, Wolf Call, Do Not Disturb, Cross My Heart Hope to Die, She's Evil, Do the Clam, Puppet on a String, Gotta Find My Baby* (Elvis Presley)

GIRL ON A MOTORCYCLE   (1968)

ALTERNATE TITLE: *Naked Under Leather*
CAST: Marianne Faithfull, Alain Delon, Roger Mutton, Marius Goring; DIR: Jack Cardiff; PROD: William Sassoon; SCREENPLAY: Donald Duncan; STUDIO: Claridge; 91 min., color (Midatlantic/Ares)

MUSIC ★★
ATTITUDE ★★★★
FUN ★★★

The feel of steel.
Girl on a Motorcycle exists solely as a vehicle for the unique beauty of Marianne Faithfull. The dialogue is, for the most part, her train of thought as she parades through Germany, Switzerland, and France, digging the feel of a motorcycle's steel and power between her legs. Plotwise, the film tells the story of her romance with Daniel (Alain Delon), a German professor. He's distant, but Faithfull speeds across borders to reach him on the motorcycle he gave her as a wedding present. Her husband (Roger Mutton) gets scant attention, as does the rest of the plot. It's the scenes of Faithfull's racing solitude that hold up best. Moralizing on issues from a soldier's precious waste of life to tourists trashing the countryside, she explores ideals that seem lost in our own time. The dreams of the wanderer and the romantic seemed so logical in 1968. Today, *Girl on a Motorcycle* will appeal mostly to Rolling Stones fans, because Faithfull was dating Mick Jagger at the time. There's no music from Faithfull here (see *Made in U.S.A.* for that). (DP)

GIRLS! GIRLS! GIRLS!   (1962)

CAST: Elvis Presley, Stella Stevens, Jeremy Slate, Laurel Goodwin, Benson Fong, Robert Strauss; DIR: Norman Taurog; PROD: Hal B. Wallis; SCREENPLAY: Edward Anhalt, Allan Weiss; STUDIO: Paramount; 106 min., color (Key)

MUSIC ★★★
ATTITUDE ★★
FUN ★★★

Elvis does Hawaii II—by sea.
Elvis was rather popular during the filming of his 11th feature. So popular that he was regularly mobbed by rabid fans. He lost a diamond ring and a watch in one melee on the day he arrived in Hawaii. In this film, Elvis assumes the role of Ross Carpenter, a down-and-out tuna fisherman who's in danger of losing the *Westwind,* a boat he built with his late father. In fact, a more apt title for this film would have been *Boats! Boats! Boats!* But that wouldn't have been nearly as marketable, and there's definitely no shortage of female talent on board here. As usual Elvis's character is rather sexist, he gets involved in something of a love triangle, and he winds up having to deck a guy.

At its best, the sea scenery is reminiscent of Duran Duran's airy "Rio" video. At its worst Elvis pilots the boat with all the authenticity of Toonces the Driving Cat from the "Saturday Night Live" skit. This film actually features a cat named Kapoo that can predict the weather. There are also several scenes that look like stock footage from "Gilligan's Island." (MB)

Arguably the most mysterious scene in any Elvis movie involves Ross (Elvis) singing "Earth Boy" in tandem with the very young Ling Sisters in their little blue matching outfits and pigtails (0:39). First Elvis translates their Hawaiian lyrics into English, then he breaks into Hawaiian himself. Lots of goofy mugging and questionable dancing ensues. The most stupid scene: Ross belts out "The Walls Have Ears" in Laurel's apartment as the neighbors bang to the beat on the floor, ceiling, and walls (1:14).

Elvis's epiphany at the end: "You know something...I should win a medal." "For what?" "For being the world's biggest jackass." *LINES*

SONGS   *Girls! Girls! Girls!, I Don't Wanna Be Tied, We'll Be Together, A Boy Like Me a Girl Like You, Earth Boy, Return to Sender, Because of Love, Thanks to the Rolling Sea, Song of the Shrimp, The Walls Have Ears, We're Coming In Loaded, Dainty Little Moonbeams* (Elvis Presley); *Never Let Me Go, The Nearness of You, Baby Baby Baby* (lip-synched by Stella Stevens, sung by Gilda Maiken)

THE GIRLS ON THE BEACH   (1965)

MUSIC   ★★★★★
ATTITUDE ★★★★
FUN   ★★★★

CAST: Noreen Cochran, Martin West, Linda Marshall, Steven Rogers, Anna Capri, Aron Kincaid, Nancy Spry, Sheila Bromley, Lana Wood, Mary Mitchell, Gayle Gerber, Linda Saunders, Peter Brooks; DIR: William M. Whitney; PROD: Harvey Jacobson; SCREENPLAY: David Malcolm; STUDIO: Paramount; 80 min., color (no video release)

Fake Beatles girl group saves the day.

Just about every major movie studio rushed to cash in on the surfing craze of the early 1960s. Paramount finally got in the soup when the studio secured the Beach Boys. Few people knew that Brian Wilson and the gang had just bailed out from plans to star in their own film for A.I.P. (The deal blew up when A.I.P. insisted on the soundtrack rights.) This film is all we get, but it's kooky anyway. The plot involves some girls, who believe they've booked the Beatles for a benefit concert. When they find out they've been conned, they impersonate the Fab Four themselves. The girls bash out two girls-in-the-garage tunes with the vocals dubbed in by Carol Connors. The Crickers wail on "La Bamba," and the scenes featuring the Beach Boys and Lesley Gore are especially well handled, as plot interruptions and dialogue are kept to a minimum. The performance of "Little Honda" is so good

that it's been used in just about every Beach Boys profile since, but Brian Wilson's beach campfire scene really steals the show. (DP)

Girl to boy: "Ooh, look at those glassy waves." Boy to girl: "Yeah, I wonder if there are any good sermons today." *LINES*

The Girls on the Beach, Lonely Sea, Little Honda (Beach Boys); *La Bamba* (Crickets); *Leave Me Alone, It's Gotta Be You, I Don't Wanna Be a Loser* (Lesley Gore); *Why Do I Love You So, We Wanna Marry a Beatle* (Carol Connors) *SONGS*

GIRLS TOWN (1959)

ALTERNATE TITLE: *The Innocent and the Damned*
CAST: Mamie Van Doren, Mel Tormé, Ray Anthony, Maggie Hayes, Paul Anka, Cathy Crosby, The Platters; **DIR:** Charles Haas; **SCREENPLAY:** Robert Smith; **STUDIO:** MGM; 92 min., b/w (Republic)

MUSIC ★★★
ATTITUDE ★★★★★
FUN ★★★★★

Cool, crazy, fantabulous.
A classic '50s teen flick, except that all the teens appear to be in their mid-30s. No matter. A member of the Jaguar gang (guess what kind of cars they drive) takes a cliff dive when the girl he's putting the moves on puts the moves on him. He dies, and said girl is identified as one Silver Morgan (Mamie Van Doren)—the blondest, stackedest, slangin'est girl you've ever seen—by another Jaguar called Fred (Mel Tormé), who was in the fatal vicinity at the fatal time. But Silver has an alibi: She stood up the dead guy to attend a Dragon gang barbecue, and the Dragons all swear she was there "since this crazy weenie roast started." The dead—and rich—guy's father demands that she be charged with murder, but Silver ends up instead at nun-managed Girls Town. Typical reform school incidents follow, while Silver tries to clear her name. She's helped by the local singing god, Jimmy (Paul Anka), who always seems to turn up at the most appropriate time. *Girls Town* is totally predictable—you figured out who the murderer was during the first five minutes—but it's lots of silly fun, especially the dialogue. (KW)

"What's holy water?" Silver asks another inmate. "Plain ordinary tap water with the hell boiled out of it." *LINES*

Wish It Were Me (Platters); *Ave Maria, It's Time to Cry, Lonely Boy* (Paul Anka) *SONGS*

GIVE MY REGARDS TO BROADSTREET (1984)

CAST: Paul McCartney, Bryan Brown, Barbara Bach, Ringo Starr, Tracey Ullman, Ralph Richardson, Linda McCartney, George Martin; **DIR:** Peter Webb; **PROD:** Andros Eraminondas; **SCREENPLAY:** Paul McCartney; **STUDIO:** Thorne-EMI; 108 min., color (CBS/Fox)

MUSIC ★★★
ATTITUDE ★★
FUN ★★★

Give my regrets to Paul McCartney.
Few films in rock history can boast such a litany of grotesquely embarrassing scenes. Paul McCartney is a rock musician who heads a rock'n'roll empire so important that the theft of his latest recording could have earthshaking repercussions. Yeah, right.

Early on, McCartney assaults us with a mum-and-dad version of "Ballroom Dancing," while Dave Edmunds and his band can only look on and wait for the humiliation to pass. The enactment of "Silly Love Songs," featuring the band wearing frosted cat-suits and Mr. and Mrs. McCartney sitting at twin-facing

Ferrante & Teicher-type pianos, is enough to have the most fervent McCartney fan retching. Fortunately for McCartney and the cast, the fictional stolen tape is recovered, and the film finally ends. Unfortunately for the rest of the world, no one stole the master tape of this film. (AF)

S O N G S   *Band on the Run, Ballroom Dancing, Eleanor Rigby, For No One, Good Day Sunshine, Yesterday, Here There and Everywhere, More Lonely Nights, Not Such a Bad Boy, Silly Love Songs, So Bad, Wanderlust, The Long and Winding Road* (Paul McCartney and Wings)

GO GO MANIA   *(1965)*

MUSIC ★★★★
ATTITUDE ★★★★
FUN ★★★

ALTERNATE TITLE: *Pop Gear*
DIR: Frederick Goode; **PROD:** Harry Field; **STUDIO:** Associated British Pathé; 68 min., color (no video release)

Mime doesn't pay.
The bands in this performance anthology are definitely above par—especially the Animals, the Spencer Davis Group, and the Nashville Teens—but their lip-synched performances are fairly lame. Adding to the disappointment is the over-dubbed cheers, which are almost as annoying as the ramblings of the host, British DJ Jimmy Savile. The Beatles' two songs are badly edited from poor quality news-reel footage. However, Matt Munro handles the pop music chores well; his "Pop Gear" is a delightfully ludicrous name-dropping tribute to a type of music that Munro clearly does not understand. The picture was shot in CinemaScope, so the only way to see it properly (that is, with all the band members visible) is letter-boxed. Oddly enough, this was the sort of picture that cinematographer Geoffrey Unsworth busied himself with before moving on to such films as *2001: A Space Odyssey* and other Academy Award-caliber fare. (BE)

S O N G S   *She Loves You, Twist and Shout* (Beatles); *Little Children* (Billy J. Kramer and the Dakotas); *Juliet, Black Girl* (Four Pennies); *House of the Rising Sun, Don't Let Me Be Misunderstood* (Animals); *A Little Loving* (Fourmost); *He's in Town, What in the World's Come Over You* (Rockin' Berries); *Have I the Right, Eyes* (Honeycombs); *Rinky Dink, William Tell* (Sounds Incorporated); *A World Without Love* (Peter and Gordon); *I'm into Something Good* (Herman's Hermits); *Humpty Dumpty* (Tommy Quickly); *My Babe* (Spencer Davis Group); *Tobacco Road, Google Eye* (Nashville Teens); *Pop Gear* (Matt Munro)

GO, JOHNNY, GO   *(1958)*

MUSIC ★★★★
ATTITUDE ★★★★★
FUN ★★★★

CAST: Jimmy Clanton, Alan Freed, Chuck Berry, Sandy Stewart, Herb Vigran, Frank Wilcox, Barbara Woodell, Milton Frome; **DIR:** Paul Landres; **PROD:** Alan Freed; **SCREENPLAY:** Gary Alexander; **STUDIO:** Hal Roach; 75 min., b/w (Video Treasures)

Alan Freed's final rock movie is his best.
There's rock'n'roll from the git-go with Chuck Berry playing "Johnny B. Goode" over the titles and neat performances by Jackie Wilson, Eddie Cochran, and Ritchie Valens (doing his rockingest song, "Ooh My Head," which was later sam-pled by Led Zeppelin in "Boogie with Stu"). Even the boy-girl part has more integrity than usual because Louisiana-born star Jimmy Clanton has a touch of blues in his soul. And in a major switch for one of these movies, a normally staid band—the balladizing Flamingos—turns in a wild "Shout"-like performance on "Jump, Children." Actingwise, Chuck Berry puts in a good, low-key performance as Freed's partner. In one irony-laden dressing room scene, when Clanton says he

doesn't mind paying taxes, Berry replies that he's taking things one day at a time. (Of course, in the '70s, Berry went to jail for tax evasion.) (AF)

CAMEOS   Joe Flynn

SONGS   *Angel Face, It Takes a Long Long Time, My Love Is Strong, Now the Day Is Over, Once Again, Ship on a Stormy Sea* (Jimmy Clanton); *Don't Be Afraid of Love* (Harvey); *Heavenly Father, Playmates* (Sandy Stewart); *Jay Walker, Please Mr. Johnson* (Cadillacs); *Jump Children* (Flamingos); *Little Queenie, Memphis Tennessee* (Chuck Berry); *Mama Can I Go Out* (Jo Ann Campbell); *Ooh My Head* (Ritchie Valens); *Teenage Heaven* (Eddie Cochran); *You Better Know It* (Jackie Wilson); *You Done Me Wrong* (Jimmy Clanton, Sandy Stewart)

GO-GO BIG BEAT   (1964)

DIR: Frank Gilpin; PROD: Harold Baim; STUDIO: Eldorado; 55 min., color (Rhino)

MUSIC ★★★
ATTITUDE ★
FUN ★★

Brit-beat's lamest.
Go-Go Big Beat was originally put together from three separate shorts and features: *Swinging U.K., U.K. Swings Again,* and *Mods and Rockers.* The first two are still part of this video, but the third has been dropped for reasons that become obvious once you see it. *Mods and Rockers* depicted the battles between the two subcultures in the title (set to songs by the Beatles), but as a modern dance showcase, it was quite homoerotic and thus *outre.* Unfortunately, the performance clips that remain are enormously dull, consisting mostly of bands awkwardly miming their finished recordings. There's not even any inventive camera work here. Only the Animals, Lulu, and the Hollies look remotely enthusiastic, but it is interesting to watch some of the other early Brit-beat acts: Ska pioneer Millie Small (her "My Boy Lollipop" was Island Records' first hit single in 1963), the Applejacks (doing a Lennon-McCartney song), the Merseybeats, and failed soft-jazz retreads like the Migil Five. Much of the lesser-known material is too soft to be of interest, however, and the color in Rhino's source print for *Go-Go Big Beat* has deteriorated to red, taking most of the detail with it. (BE)

SONGS   *Happy Tomorrow* (Cockneys); *Do You Love Me, Someone* (Brian Poole and the Tremoloes); *My Boy Lollipop, Oh Henry* (Millie Small); *Love or Money* (Wackers); *Fools Like Me, Don't Turn Around* (Merseybeats); *Mockingbird Hill, Long Tall Sally* (Migil Five); *Juliet, Running Scared* (Four Pennies); *Globetrotter* (Tornadoes); *Baby Let Me Take You Home* (Animals); *Here I Go Again, Baby That's All* (Hollies); *You're No Good, Don't Worry About Me* (Swinging Blue Jeans); *Like Dreamers Do* (Applejacks); *Shout* (Lulu and the Luvvers)

THE GOLDEN DISC   (1958)

Cast: Lee Patterson, Mary Steele, Terry Dene, Sonny Stewart Skiffle Group, Nancy Whiskey; DIR: Don Sharp; PROD: W.G. Chalmers; SCREENPLAY: Don Nichol, Don Sharp; STUDIO: Butcher's Films; 78 min., b/w (no video release)

MUSIC ★★
ATTITUDE ★★★
FUN ★★★

A glimpse of the '50s British coffee bar scene.
In terms of budget and finesse, this picture makes *The Tommy Steele Story* look like *Gone with the Wind.* The acting in *The Golden Disc* is truly awful, the script reads as though it was written over lunch (a quick one), and the music scarcely rocks at all. What *The Golden Disc* does offer is a peek at the coffee bar scene as it existed in England during the late 1950s. It also features the odd mix of skiffle and quasi-rock'n'roll that was popular at the time, as well as some insight into failed teen idol Terry Dene, who later suffered a breakdown and reemerged as an evangelist. (BE)

SONGS   *C'mon and Be Loved, Charm, In-Between Age, Johnny O* (Terry Dene)

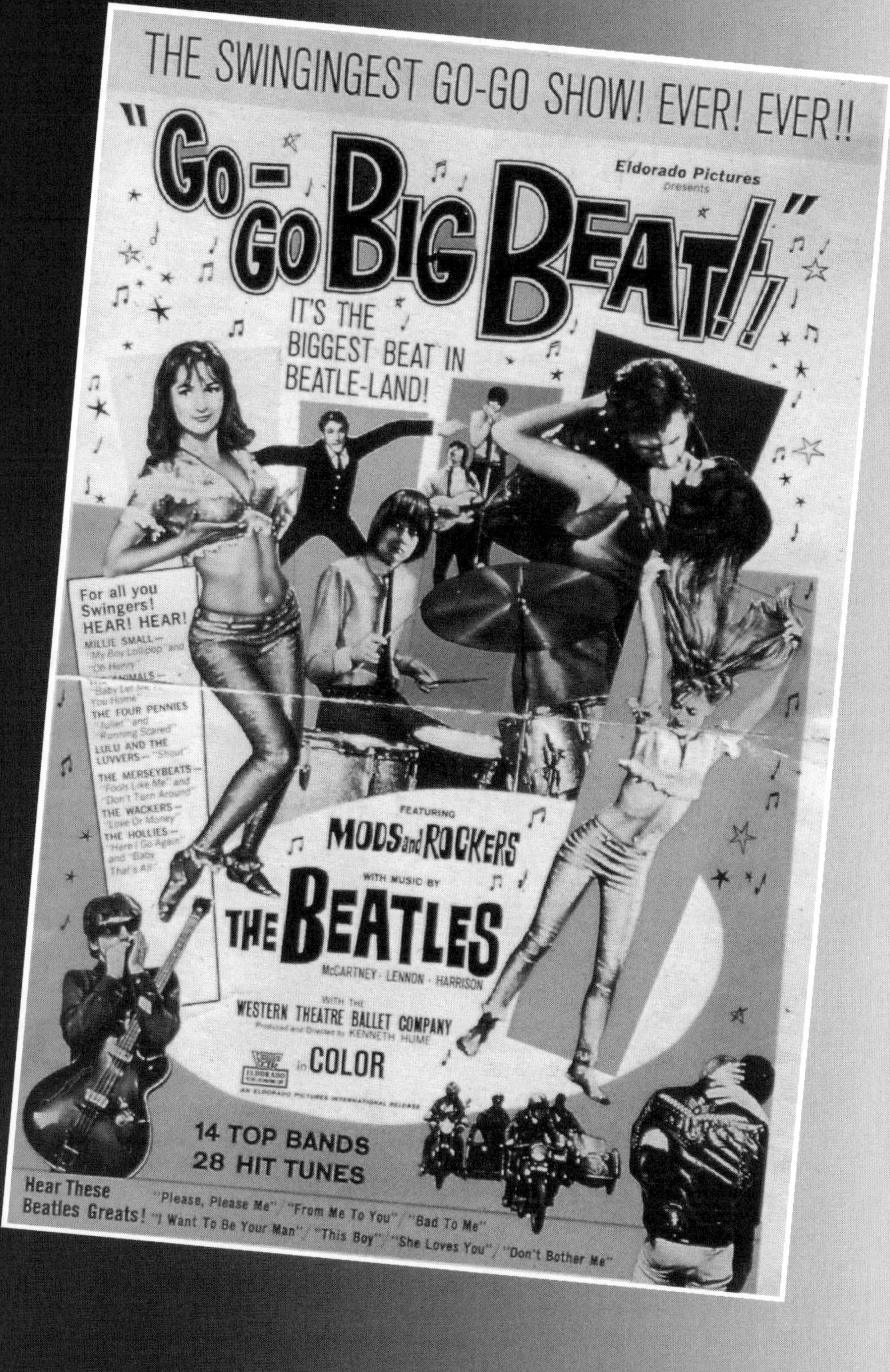
THE SWINGINGEST GO-GO SHOW! EVER! EVER!!
"GO-GO BIG BEAT!!"
Eldorado Pictures
presents
IT'S THE
BIGGEST BEAT IN
BEATLE-LAND!
For all you
Swingers!
HEAR! HEAR!
MILLIE SMALL—
"My Boy Lollipop" and
"Oh Henry"
THE FOUR PENNIES
"Juliet" and
"Running Scared"
LULU AND THE
LUVVERS—"Shout"
THE MERSEYBEATS—
"Fools Like Me" and
"Don't Turn Around"
THE WACKERS—
"Love Or Money"
THE HOLLIES—
"Here I Go Again"
and "Baby
That's All"
FEATURING
MODS and ROCKERS
WITH MUSIC BY
THE BEATLES
McCARTNEY · LENNON · HARRISON
WITH THE
WESTERN THEATRE BALLET COMPANY
Produced and Directed by KENNETH HUME
in COLOR
14 TOP BANDS
28 HIT TUNES
Hear These
Beatles Greats!
"Please, Please Me" / "From Me To You" / "Bad To Me"
"I Want To Be Your Man" / "This Boy" / "She Loves You" / "Don't Bother Me"

GONKS GO BEAT (1965)

MUSIC ★★★
ATTITUDE ★
FUN ★★

CAST: Kenneth Connor, Frank Thornton, Terry Scott, Jerry Desmonde; DIR: Robert Hartford-Davis; PROD: Peter Newbrook, Robert Hartford-Davis; SCREENPLAY: Jimmy Watson, Robert Hartford-Davis; STUDIO: Anglo-Amalgamated; 92 min., color (no video release)

Gonks get bonked!
Gonks Go Beat is a clear and favorite entry in the sweepstakes for stupidest rock'n'roll movie of all time: An alien visitor comes to Earth and arranges a competition between Beatland and Balladisle (shades of *Yellow Submarine*), featuring the Nashville Teens, Lulu and the Luvvers, the Graham Bond Organization, and the Troles. The music, such as it is, is third-rate considering the talent involved, and the sheer ludicrousness of the plot and settings is enough to make the Beatles' *Help!* look like a Eugene O'Neill adaptation. (BE)

GOOD TIMES (1967)

MUSIC ★★★
ATTITUDE ★★★
FUN ★★★

CAST: Sonny and Cher, George Sanders, Norman Alden, Larry Duran; DIR: William Friedkin; PROD: Lindsley Parsons; SCREENPLAY: Tony Barrett; STUDIO: Columbia; 92 min., color (Columbia)

Sonny and Cher. . .that's all!
This slickly produced if minimally plotted adventure captures the pre-nose job Sonny and Cher at the height of their reign as Hollywood's hippest couple. A pop music version of Fairbanks and Pickford, the bell-bottomed duo were riding high with hits like "The Beat Goes On," but it was *Good Times* that best showcased the natural comedic charm that would lead (several years later) to their popular TV show.

For Sonny and Cher, at least, there must have been a lot of pressure as to what their first big-screen vehicle would be like, and *Good Times* wound up being a spoof about just that. They play themselves, newly cast in a movie and pondering different story ideas. Sonny daydreams that they are in various parodies of standard Hollywood genres (western, spy, and jungle films), all the while avoiding the tired script being forced on them by the nasty studio bigwig Mordicus. Besides the amiable though overlong movie send-ups, there are of course plenty of Sonny and Cher songs, including a rather laid-back "I Got You Babe."

Good Times was the first film directed by William Friedkin, who would find greater success with *The French Connection* and *The Exorcist.* In a self-penned article in a 1967 issue of teen mag *16's Summer Spec*, Friedkin recalled telling Sonny the movie should be "a cross between *Bambi* and *The Wizard Of Oz*, as it might be played by W.C. Fields and Peter Sellers....You should do everything in it that you yourselves would like to see." In a 1991 interview, Friedkin would only say of *Good Times* that "I wish all prints of that film could be burned." *Good Times* may seem slight and slow-moving to nondevotees, but this colorful, modest effort remains required viewing for all S & C fans.

A final note: Distinguished screen veteran George Sanders gave one of his final performances as the evil studio head. The cynical Sanders—whose own autobiography was called *Memoirs of a Professional Cad*—would commit suicide five years later, citing boredom as the main reason. Hmmmmm. And look closely for Russ Meyer starlet Edy Williams. (JS)

SONGS *It's the Little Things, Ride on Your Merry-Go-Round, Trust Me, Don't Talk to Strangers Baby, Just a Name, I Got You Babe* (Sonny and Cher)

THE GOSPEL ACCORDING TO AL GREEN (1984)

MUSIC ★★★★★
ATTITUDE ★★★★
FUN ★★★★

DIR: Robert Mugge; PROD: Robert Mugge; SCREENPLAY: Robert Mugge; STUDIO: Film Four/Channel Four International; 94 min., color (Magnum)

And now for something uplifting.

In churches all over the country, people still wrestle with the conflict between spiritual and secular, or "worldly," music. At one extreme of this debate is the Full Gospel Tabernacle on Hale Road in Memphis, Tennessee. There, the Reverend Al Green has served as pastor since 1977. Before entering the ministry, Green made a name for himself as one of the greatest rhythm-and-blues singers of the early 1970's. His records from that remarkable period in R&B remain spellbinding.

In this film (originally produced as a documentary for England's Channel Four), Green describes the dramatic events that caused him to leave the world of pop stardom and embark instead on a search for the truth within himself. (No Cat Stevens jokes, please.) Here we see the Reverend Green in concert (at the Bolling Air Force Base Non-Commissioned Officers' Club), leading a service at the Full Gospel Tabernacle, and being interviewed. During his extensive chats with the filmmakers, Al is loose, thoughtful, and articulate. He has lived through a lot, and his story is a compelling one. Also interviewed at length is Willie Mitchell, the great Memphis-based record producer who discovered Green. Together, they created a sound that used to stop people in their tracks and is still as powerful as ever. This film is highly recommended, especially if you're an Al Green fan (i.e., not a bonehead). (MC)

SCENES   Green telling the harrowing story of his involvement with Mary Woodson, who allegedly committed suicide in Green's house after assaulting him with boiling grits; Willie Mitchell (in his office with "Let's Stay Together" on the stereo) speaking of Al's decision to record only gospel music, thus ending their partnership

SONGS   *What Am I Going to Do with Myself, Tired of Being Alone, People Get Ready, Let's Stay Together, Free at Last, Do Not Pass Me By, Amazing Grace/Nearer My God to Thee, The Lord Will Make a Way, Straighten Out Your Life* (Al Green)

THE GRADUATE   (1967)

MUSIC ★★★★★
ATTITUDE ★★★★★
FUN ★★★★★

CAST: Dustin Hoffman, Anne Bancroft, Katharine Ross, Murray Hamilton; DIR: Mike Nichols; PROD: Lawrence Turman; SCREENPLAY: Buck Henry, Calder Willingham; STUDIO: Embassy; 105 min., color (Embassy)

Confused college graduate woos mother, runs off with daughter.

This film's impact in 1967 was immense: Ben's evident bewilderment and helplessness in the face of adulthood (and adultery!) spoke to many Baby Boomers. Like *Blackboard Jungle,* the music was intrinsic, not featured, and propelled Simon and Garfunkel into superstardom. The harpsichord-laden soundtrack was the last gasp of the folk era before psychedelia set in. There's musical excitement in the race-to-Elaine finale as the chords to "Mrs. Robinson" are played percussively on strings apparently flattened with paper (shades of Johnny Cash!). "Sounds of Silence" was an eerily concrete choice as the movie's recurring theme. (AF)

CAMEOS   Richard Dreyfuss, Mike Farrell, Buck Henry

GRAFFITI BRIDGE   (1990)

CAST: Prince, Morris Day, Jerome Benton, Jill Jones, Ingrid Chavez, Mavis Staples, Robin Power, Tevin Campbell, T.C. Ellis; DIR: Prince; PROD: Arnold Stiefel, Randy Phillips; SCREENPLAY: Prince; STUDIO: Warner; 91 min., color (Warner)

MUSIC ★★★★
ATTITUDE ★★★
FUN ★★★

This silly smear campaign still sounds good.

A vague sequel to *Purple Rain*, *Graffiti Bridge* is less a feature film than a collection of flashy music videos strung together by the merest threads of plot and character. It seems that the dearly departed Billy has bequeathed the Glam Slam club to two rival bandleaders, Prince (with his New Power Generation) and Morris Day (with the Time, who regrouped for this movie and an unsuccessful album). Their limp threats and witless insults boil down to an old-fashioned battle of the bands: The Time whip out a tuneless turkey called "Shake!", then Prince and the NPG respond with the equally lame "Tick Tick Bang." But just when it looks as though Morris will carry the day, Prince triumphs with "Still Would Stand All Time," a fairly galvanizing spiritual that recalls the earlier film's anthem, "Purple Rain." Between musical sequences, Prince rides his motorcycle, writes letters to his dead father, and stares dreamily into space. As in *Under the Cherry Moon*, Prince's romance with the female lead—a talentless "poet" named Aura (Ingrid Chavez)—is an on-again, off-again thing that ends with her untimely and meaningless death. (AS)

George Clinton   *CAMEOS*

New Power Generation, Tick Tick Bang, Thieves in the Temple, Still Would Stand All Time, Joy in   *SONGS*
Repetition (Prince and the New Power Generation); *Release It, Love Machine, Shake!* (Time); *Round and Round* (Tevin Campbell); *Melody Cool* (Mavis Staples)

THE GRATEFUL DEAD MOVIE   (1977)

DIR: Jerry Garcia, Leon Gast; PROD: Edward Washington; STUDIO: Monarch-Noteworthy; 131 min., color (Monterey Home Video)

MUSIC ★★
ATTITUDE ★
FUN ★★

Take two tabs and call me in the morning.

They say there's nothing like a Grateful Dead concert. Maybe so, but this isn't it. The band is lethargic, and the music sounds as though somebody forgot to check the sound levels. The concert shown here was filmed during the band's middle age, when Keith Godchaux played keyboards, having replaced the late Ron "Pig Pen" McKernan. (Godchaux himself died in 1980, and his replacement, Brent Mydland, ten years later. Draw your own conclusions.)

The movie has got some curiosity value, though. For example, through the miracle of video, nouveau Deadheads can actually see what Jerry, Bob, and Phil looked like as youngish men. There's also a fabulous five-minute retrospective of the band's days in the Haight during the Summer of Love (1:01). Watching this montage of still photographs set against cuts from the 1969 *Live Dead* album makes you wish that Mr. Peabody had set his Way Back Machine for 1967 instead of 1976. (DR)

The films opens with animation by Gary Gutierrez (in the style of S.F. poster   *SCENES*
artists Mouse & Kelly and Rick Griffin). It's mesmerizing in that Dead sort of way. Some nice colors. Watch it with the lights out.

LINES   An anonymous Deadhead outside the auditorium: "I'm just trying to get my space together so I can go into the show."

CAMEOS   Bill Graham

SONGS   *U.S. Blues, One More Saturday Night, Going Down the Road, Truckin', Eyes of the World, Sugar Magnolia, Playing in the Band, Stella Blue, Casey Jones, Morning Dew* (Grateful Dead)

GREASE   (1978)

MUSIC   ★
ATTITUDE   ★
FUN   ★

CAST: John Travolta, Olivia Newton-John, Stockard Channing, Jeff Conaway, Barry Pearl, Eve Arden, Frankie Avalon, Edd Byrnes, Sid Caesar; DIR: Randal Kleiser; PROD: Robert Stigwood, Allan Carr; SCREENPLAY: Bronte Woodard; STUDIO: Paramount; 100 min., color (Paramount)

Almost as bad as Hair.

Grease is a must-watch for those kids who think that "Rock Around the Clock" was written as the theme song for "Happy Days." Everyone else, stay clear. What can be said about a movie that is actually a waste of Frankie Avalon's *talent?* As Sandy, the high school ingenue, Olivia Newton-John doesn't look a day over 31, and John Travolta (as Danny) makes his "Welcome Back, Kotter" turn as Vinnie Barbarino seem like Stanley Kowalski in comparison. Throw in appearances by Sid Caesar, Eve Arden, and Edd "Kookie" Byrnes, and what do you get? An experience that is (to borrow a phrase from Orson Welles) *very unrewarding.* (BV)

SONGS   *Grease* (Frankie Valli); *Summer Nights, You're the One That I Want, We Go Together* (John Travolta, Olivia Newton-John); *Hopelessly Devoted to You* (Olivia Newton-John); *Sandy* (John Travolta); *Beauty School Dropout* (Frankie Avalon); *Look at Me I'm Sandra Dee, There Are Worse Things I Could Do* (Stockard Channing); *Greased Lightnin'* (John Travolta, Jeff Conaway)

GREAT BALLS OF FIRE   (1989)

MUSIC   ★★★★
ATTITUDE   ★★★★
FUN   ★★★★

CAST: Dennis Quaid, Winona Ryder, John Doe, Alec Baldwin, Stephen Tobolowsky, Lisa Blount; DIR: Jim McBride; PROD: Adam Fields; SCREENPLAY: Jack Baran, Jim McBride; STUDIO: Orion; 108 min., color (Orion)

A movie as quick and fulfilling as the premarriage stage of Lewis's career.

Jerry Lee Lewis had the songs and presence to be the King. He also took his 13-year-old cousin as his wife, thus temporarily ending his career. *Great Balls of Fire* succeeds in condensing and simplifying a potentially complex tale by recognizing that today Lewis's marriage is just a rock'n'roll footnote. As a result, the story moves along at a quick pace. And unlike Lewis's lifestyle, it's also balanced. The Killer's rise is treated with the same time and respect as his fall. Even with a screenplay based on Myra Lewis's account of their marriage, Jerry Lee never comes off as a '50s Joey Buttafuoco. Lewis does seem cocky, abrasive, and uncalculating, but these traits combine to make him a rock'n'roller, not a scumbag. The re-recordings that Lewis supplied for Quaid's lip-synched performances perfectly finish the portrait. And Winona Ryder's Myra Lewis is so convincing that you can't fault Lewis for falling in love with her. (ALa)

SCENES   Upon meeting him for the first time, Sun records founder Sam Phillips tells Lewis, "You take a white right hand and a black left hand and what do you get? Son, you get rock and roll. Jerry, I got big plans for those hands." Lewis replies, "Mr. Phillips, these hands can heal the sick, raise the dead, and make the little girls talk right out of their heads."

Mojo Nixon, Jimmie Vaughan, Joe Bob Briggs, Steve Allen **CAMEOS**

Crazy Arms, I'm Throwing Rice at the Girl That I Love, Breathless, Whole Lotta Shakin' Goin' On, **SONGS**
Great Balls of Fire, High School Confidential, I'm on Fire, Real Wild Child (Jerry Lee Lewis)

THE GREAT ROCK'N'ROLL SWINDLE (1980)

CAST: Sid Vicious, Johnny Rotten, Steve Jones, Paul Cook, Malcolm McLaren, Ronnie Biggs, Liz Fraser, Jess Conrad, Tenpole Tudor, Irene Handl; **DIR:** Julian Temple; **PROD:** Jeremy Thomas, Don Boyd; **SCREENPLAY:** Julian Temple; **STUDIO:** Boyd's Co./Virgin; 104 min., color (Warner)

MUSIC ★★★★★
ATTITUDE ★★★★
FUN ★★★

A Svengali's guide to fooling the music industry, media, and record-buying public.
Often annoyingly scrambled and silly, *The Great Rock'n'Roll Swindle* describes the formation of the Sex Pistols by impresario Malcolm McLaren. Throughout the film, McLaren offers pearls of wisdom on how to build a musical phenomenon. You can't beat advice like "A band that can't play is better than a band that can play." Or "Cultivate hatred. It is your greatest asset. Force the public to hate you." Thus McLaren explains how he and the Pistols managed to "swindle" the recording industry out of £695,000 (about $1,000,000) by the time their ride was all over.

Swindle starts out as a fairly entertaining exercise (good footage of the band performing and interesting newsreel clips) but following the demise of the Pistols the film seems to keep going with no ultimate destination or purpose in mind. But really, are you surprised? Sid Vicious fans will get a thrill watching the bass player deliver his inimitable version of "Something Else" clad only in his skivvies. (EC)

"Ever get the feeling you've been cheated?" asks Johnny Rotten, on stage for what **LINES** would be his last show (Winterland, San Francisco) with the Pistols, just before being kicked out of the band.

The Great Rock'n'Roll Swindle, Anarchy in the U.K., God Save the Queen, Pretty Vacant, Johnny B. **SONGS**
Goode/Road Runner, Belsen Was a Gas, Silly Thing (Sex Pistols); *My Way, Something Else, C'mon Everybody* (Sid Vicious); *Lonely Boy* (Steve Jones); *You Need Hands* (Malcolm McLaren); *Anarchy in the U.K./God Save the Queen/Pretty Vacant/No One Is Innocent* (Black Arabs); *No One Is Innocent* (Ronnie Biggs); *Who Killed Bambi?* (Tenpole Tudor)

Great Balls of Fire

EXCELLENT...STUNNING and **UNFORGETTABLE** portrait of the lost ones—hard-bitten whores, teeny-boppers, girl-next-door lovelies, neurotics and near-psychopaths caught up in the drug and rock scene."

— Judith Crist, New York Magazine

groupies

the film

Starring
Miss Harlow, Cynthia P. Caster, Goldie Glitter
Andrea Whips, Patti Cakes, Lixie & Katy
and
Joe Cocker and The Grease Band
Ten Years After featuring Alvin Lee & Co.
Spooky Tooth   Terry Reid

Released by MARON FILMS LIMITED

GROUPIES *(1970)*

DIR: Ron Dorfman, Peter Nevard; PROD: Joseph Cates; STUDIO: Maron; 90 min., color (no video release)

MUSIC ★
ATTITUDE ★★
FUN ★

They're with the band.

If you've always wanted to know what the atmosphere was like on the hippie ballroom circuit circa 1969, look no further than this cinema verité exercise. *Groupies* focuses on a handful of bands (mostly forgotten today) who were considered up-and-coming at the time. There's also plenty about the kids whose lives revolved around getting stoned and hanging out where these bands played. Particular attention is paid to a certain group of girls and boys who devote themselves to knowing individual band members (so to speak) on an intimate basis. Most of the groupies are dull, shallow types, except for the Plaster Casters, who indulge their obsession by making plaster casts of musicians' "love guns." It's sort of like Sid Graumann (of Graumann's Chinese footprint fame), only different. Here the girls discuss technique as well as the artistic merits of their craft. According to producer Joseph Cates, the filmmakers actually captured one casting session on film (he doesn't recall now who the subject was), but for some reason they decided not to include it in the movie. Oh well. (MC)

"I'm gonna be so hip when I'm 22."   **LINES**

Pamela Des Barres   **CAMEOS**

Delta Lady (Joe Cocker); *Good Morning Little Schoolgirl, Help Me Baby* (Ten Years After); *Mr. Sun* (Dry Creek Road); *Super Lungs, Bang Bang* (Terry Reid)   **SONGS**

HAIR *(1979)*

CAST: John Savage, Treat Williams, Beverly D'Angelo, Annie Golden, Dorsey Wright, Don Dacus, Cheryl Barnes, Miles Chapin; DIR: Milos Forman; PROD: Lester Persky, Michael Butler; SCREENPLAY: Michael Weller; STUDIO: United Artists; 121 min., color (MGM/UA)

MUSIC ★★
ATTITUDE ★
FUN ★★★

A disco-era hippie musical.

Hair is not the 1960s, but an incredible simulation—an Epcot ride past silly draft-dodgers, quaint student protesters, and neat-o acid casualties. This adaptation of the Rado/Ragni/MacDermot musical is messy, facile, and at least five years too late to be anything other than a sugarcoated flashback. It's not that screenwriter Michael Weller has reconstructed the story around a radically mutated character (John Savage as army grunt-to-be Claude Hooper Bukowski), transforming the ending into an identity-switch prank gone bad. Hollywood tinkering is not unusual. And it's not that the musical numbers are frequently abrupt non sequiturs that neither further nor enhance the narrative. You can say that about most musicals. It's not even the toothless music and detumescent acting from such luminaries as former Chicago guitarist Don Dacus (playing Woof). Nope, the real problem is director Milos Forman's unfocused, sanitized portrayal of a vanguard moment in American history. In the No Free Speech '90s, *Hair*'s treatment of drugs, sex, and race seems revolutionary, but viewed in general, by more objective standards, its politics are simplistic, and its statement about the '60s nonexistent. (JC)

Berger crashing high society to the tune of "I Got Life" (0:32); "Hair" as a prison riot (0:42); the acid trip as a slick production number (0:50); the hilarious ode to "White Boys/Black Boys" (1:08)   **SCENES**

CAMEOS Nicholas Ray, Charlotte Rae, Michael Jeter, Nell Carter, Leata Galloway, Ellen Foley, Melba Moore, Ronnie Dyson, Johnny Maestro

HAIRSPRAY (1988)

CAST: Sonny Bono, Ruth Brown, Divine, Colleen Fitzpatrick, Michael St. Gerard, Debbie Harry, Ricki Lake, Leslie Ann Powers, Jerry Stiller, Mink Stole, Pia Zadora, Ric Ocasek; DIR: John Waters; PROD: Rachel Talalay; SCREENPLAY: John Waters; STUDIO: New Line; 96 min., color (RCA/Columbia)

Trash film guru John Waters takes on the Great Dance Craze.

Playing a menacing psychiatrist, John Waters asks a teenager, "Getting in touch with your anger?" Of course, nobody touches his teenage anger like Waters. In this nonstop catharsis of music and hilarity, the director of *Pink Flamingos* and *Polyester* recaptures all the joys and injustices of being a teenager in 1963. He renders the attitudes, the hairstyles, and the angst of the period all with breathtaking accuracy. The plot focuses on a TV dance show run by a local Baltimore DJ, the cornball but conscientious Corny Collins (played brilliantly by Shawn Thompson). Sonny Bono and Debbie Harry appear as the bad parents of the spoiled girl who rules the show's dance council. Jerry Stiller and Divine shine as the parents of Ricki Lake, who wants to integrate the dance show. Cameos abound, the most memorable being those of Pia Zadora and Ric Ocasek (of the Cars) as beatniks—Ocasek whips out bongos and hollers, "day-o." Ruth Brown also appears as the activist DJ Motormouth Mabel. The incredible Divine, who dominates the film, makes a rare appearance at the end as a man.

The ambient music here is both brilliant and insidious. Drawn from contemporary Baltimore charts, the songs are unfamiliar and thus fresh. (You don't hear Bunker Hill's "Hide and Go Seek" much on oldies radio!) Highlights include many authentic pre-Beatles dances, especially a mass performance of "The Madison" (for its attitude, the greatest dance sequence in movie history). In another stunning dance scene, the black kids grind *very* sexually to the Ikettes' "I'm Blue." (AF)

SCENES Toussaint McCall lip-synching "Nothing Takes the Place of You"

LINES "The council will now meet in private and debate your personality flaws."

A HARD DAY'S NIGHT (1964)

CAST: John Lennon, Paul McCartney, George Harrison, Ringo Starr, Wilfrid Brambell, Norman Rossington, John Junkin, Anna Quayle, Kenneth Haigh, Allison Seebohm, Victor Spinetti; DIR: Richard Lester; PROD: Walter Shenson; SCREENPLAY: Alun Owen; STUDIO: United Artists/Proscenium; 90 min., b/w (MPI)

The Beatles' debut.

The Beatles' first movie was also the first rock'n'roll movie to matter to people who didn't like rock'n'roll. Andrew Sarris called *A Hard Day's Night* "the *Citizen Kane* of jukebox movies," and he sold it short. The Beatles, immediately after their first U.S. appearance, play themselves enjoying and chafing under the constraints of fame as they prepare for a British television appearance. In the process, they manage to turn the television industry, the local police force, and the railway system upside down without once showing any self-consciousness. The mix of music and plot is so beguiling and effortless that the movie ends up having a pseudo-documentary style that anticipates such films as *Don't Look Back*. It's easy to forget that virtually the entire movie was scripted.

The comedy is some of the most inspired ever committed to the screen, and parts of it—such as George's misadventure in the producer's office—are astoundingly subtle and complex. The music is all first-rate (natch). If the concert sequence at the end seems especially inspired, it's because the director chose to mix the real, live sound of the screaming audience (the sound man was told to turn on his equipment and get out, and cinematographer Gilbert Taylor's hearing was damaged) with the studio recordings at full volume. He thus created the most realistic fake film concert ever shot. (BE)

"I fought the war for your sort," says Richard Vernon playing a stuffy railway passenger. "Bet you're sorry you won," replies Ringo.   **LINES**

*I'll Cry Instead, A Hard Day's Night, I Should've Known Better, I Wanna Be Your Man/Don't Bother   **SONGS**
Me/All My Loving, If I Fell, Can't Buy Me Love, And I Love Her, I'm Happy Just to Dance with You,
Tell Me Why, She Loves You* (Beatles)

A Hard Day's Night   HDN #5 (1459)

THE HARDER THEY COME   (1973)

CAST: Jimmy Cliff, Carl Bradshaw, Janet Bartley, Ras Daniel Hartman, Prince Buster; DIR: Perry Henzell; PROD: Perry Henzell; SCREENPLAY: Perry Henzell, Trevor D. Rhone; STUDIO: International; 98 min., color (Island Visual Arts)

MUSIC ★★★★★
ATTITUDE ★★★★★
FUN ★★★★★

The film that spawned a reggae revolution.
One of the few films to explore the reggae subculture, *The Harder They Come* made singer Jimmy Cliff (as Ivan) a huge star and helped to popularize reggae in the United States. A fierce coming-of-age and coming-to-grips story, *The Harder They Come* is gritty, often violent (who can forget the slashing knife as one of Ivan's adversaries warns, "Don't you be fucking with me, mon"), passionate, and

true to life. *The Harder they Come* is Jimmy Cliff's autobiography: poor boy comes to the big city in search of a dollar and a dream and struggles to maintain his heart and integrity in a cruel, hard world.

Throughout the '70s, *The Harder They Come* was a mainstay on the midnight movie circuit, and it remains one of the most powerful films ever made about the promised land of the music business and the cold, punishing slap-in-the-face reality that awaits those who can't tough it out. It's also a funky, soulful testimony to the power of faith and belief. (ALi)

SONGS   *Pressure Drop* (Toots and the Maytals); *The Harder They Come* (Jimmy Cliff)

HARUM SCARUM   (1965)

MUSIC ★★
ATTITUDE ★★
FUN ★★★★

CAST: Elvis Presley, Mary Ann Mobley, Fran Jeffries, Michael Ansara, Theo Marcuse, Jay Novello, Billy Barty; DIR: Gene Nelson; PROD: Sam Katzman; SCREENPLAY: Gerald Drayson Adams; STUDIO: MGM; 85 min., color (MGM/UA)

Elvis is abducted in the Middle East.
Submitted for your approval: American goodwill ambassador Johnny Tyrone (Elvis Presley) is kidnapped by Sinan (Theo Marcuse), chief of the Assassins terrorist sect, who wants to recruit him. Johnny escapes but must run a gauntlet of stereotypes that include a beautiful princess, a comical midget, thieves, bellydancers, a treacherous nobleman, and an adorable orphaned slavegirl.

Rocking the Casbah with the ripest dialogue this side of *What's Up, Tiger Lily?* ("Infidel pig!"; "Toranshah, you live!"), the movie offers one delirious interlude after another. How about Elvis growling the pedophile anthem "Hey Little Girl" to a hip-gyrating prepubescent? Or ponder the implications of El's historic encounter with Sinan, who as the actual 12th-century leader of the Assassins utters the immortal Presleyan slogan, "Nothing is true; everything is permitted." It's almost as though the entire movie has been made in code, with each moment of blissful obliviousness concealing a separate, impenetrable double meaning of its own. (HH)

LINES   Elvis: "I'm in love with your daughter. How could I assassinate you?"

SONGS   *My Desert Serenade, Go East Young Man, Mirage, Kismet, Shake That Tambourine, Hey Little Girl, Golden Coins, So Close Yet So Far, Harem Holiday* (Elvis Presley)

HATED: G.G. ALLIN AND THE MURDER JUNKIES   (1993)

MUSIC ★★★★★
ATTITUDE ★★★★★
FUN ★★★★★

DIR: Todd Phillips; PROD: Todd Phillips; STUDIO: Film Threat; 57 min., color (Film Threat)

Bring the kids! Fun for the entire family!
"Make no mistake, behind what he does is a brain." That's how serial killer John Wayne Gacy describes punk rock deathwish icon G.G. Allin. Whatever you might think about Allin—whether you consider his life's work a real show or just shit—the bottom line is that he was pretty much a pathetic idiot. Be prepared to enter a fast-paced freakshow world of hate, violence, obsession, self-mutilation, nudity, blood, scatology, vomit, drugs, alcohol, sex, screaming, and death. This documentary captures it all—the shit literally hits the fans as the suicidal punker from Concord, Vermont, and his band, the Murder Junkies, attempt to take the world by storm. Through interviews and performance footage, Todd Phillips probes the life and mind of the guy who annually planned to kill himself at a mythical Halloween performance.

On July 28th, 1993, Allin's rollercoaster of perversity jumped the tracks after an afternoon gig/riot at Manhattan's Gas Station on scenic Avenue B. No goin' out in that fabled blaze of glory—the rocker simply curled up on the floor of his pal Johnny Puke's apartment and overdosed. A hero to some and a fool to others, Allin will indeed be remembered. No need for any "Rest in Peace" plaques. The guy just wouldn't have wanted it that way. (MB)

Allin stuffs a banana up his ass at New York University's Loeb Student Center. He throws the juicy fruit into the audience. The cops interrupt (0:13). A generous young lady urinates into Allin's mouth. The rocker seems to enjoy drinking the bodily beverage, stopping only briefly to vomit (0:32). **SCENES**

Allin on "Geraldo": "My flushed blood and body fluids are a communion to the people—whether they like it or not." **LINES**

Geraldo Rivera, Dee Dee Ramone **CAMEOS**

Die When You Die, Snakeman's Dance, Fuck Authority, I Wanna Kill You, Bite It You Scum, Gypsy Motherfucker, When I Die, Carmelita, Suck My Ass It Smells (Murder Junkies) **SONGS**

HAVING A WILD WEEKEND (1965)

CAST: The Dave Clark Five, Barbara Ferris, David Lodge, Yootha Joyce, Julian Holloway; **DIR:** John Boorman; **PROD:** David Deutch; **STUDIO:** Anglo-Amalgamated; 91 min., b/w (no video release)

MUSIC ★★★★
ATTITUDE ★★★★★
FUN ★★★★

John Boorman's debut features the Dave Clark Five.
This Dave Clark romp is no *Hard Day's Night*, but it comes surprisingly close. It's a real movie, in which rock music plays just a small, but important, part. John Boorman's directorial style is more graceful than Richard Lester's was in the Beatles' film, and there is less reliance on quick cuts and short takes. This is understandable because Dave Clark, who made his living as a stuntman when he wasn't playing music, is a natural in front of the camera. Not that he's any actor, but between him and the cast of seasoned performers surrounding him, Boorman was able to build a real story. Barbara Ferris plays a budding television star who rebels against the grueling pace of her career by running off with Dave and the band. Her manager and producer follow in hot pursuit. The story and characterizations are surprisingly downbeat, and in that regard *Having a Wild Weekend* (originally called *Catch Us If You Can*) is a sobering answer to *A Hard Day's Night*, showing a seldom-seen dark side of Swinging London and its denizens. (BE)

Catch Us If You Can, Having a Wild Weekend, On the Move, Sweet Memories, Time, Move On, When Ol' Sol, I Can't Stand It (Dave Clark Five) **SONGS**

HEAD (1968)

CAST: The Monkees, Timothy Carey; **DIR:** Bob Rafelson; **PROD:** Bob Rafelson, Jack Nicholson; **SCREENPLAY:** Bob Rafelson, Jack Nicholson; **STUDIO:** Columbia; 85 min., color (Columbia Tristar)

MUSIC ★★★★
ATTITUDE ★★★★
FUN ★★★

We're the young generation, and we've got something to say.
In 1967, the Monkees were the top pop stars of the day, selling more records than the Beatles and the Rolling Stones combined. Still, the four young actor/musicians felt frustrated by a lack of input into their carefully packaged, teenybopper-safe TV

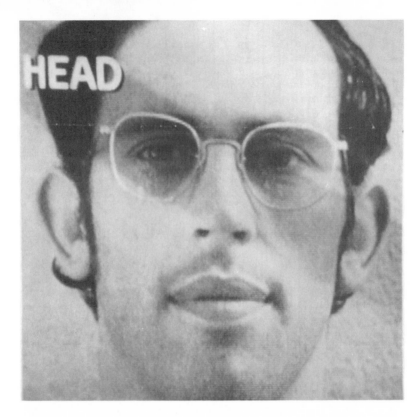

show (although they had just won a hard-fought battle for control of their music). When it came time to make a movie, the Monkees welcomed the chance to expand their audience and assert their truly heavy natures. One weekend, the group joined director Bob Rafelson and Jack Nicholson (yes, *him*) at the mountain resort of Ojai, California. They went with a tape recorder and a bag of Acapulco Gold. They came back with the screenplay for *Head.* No one knew then that this movie would essentially end the Monkees. (However, the scene in which the boys dive off a bridge into a psychedelic sea to the swirling sounds of "The Porpoise Song" could be interpreted as the symbolic death of their bubblegum selves.)

This plotless, triplike movie, which resembles a big-budget episode of "Laugh-In" for dopers, is filled with constant reminders that everyone involved was aware of the plastic, preconceived nature of the Monkees. Even the movie's title was a stoned wink to the underground, showing how groovy Mickey Dolenz, Davy Jones, Michael Nesmith, and Peter Tork *really* were. The film's surreal episodes include these four guys soul-kissing a sultry temptress, laughing at Tim Carey as a crippled villain, slipping in some timely antiwar sentiments, and walking through Victor Mature's hair. At one point, a waitress (actually a man) recognizes the band: "If it isn't God's gift to eight-year-olds! Changing your image, darlings? And while you're at it, why don't you have them write you some talent?" *Head*'s savaging of the Monkees' TV image (and fan base), combined with its minimal ad campaign (which didn't even mention the stars), ensured its failure at the box office. The film closed in most cities within a few days. (JS)

SCENES Frank Zappa as the Critic, giving a sober lecture to Davy Jones: "You've been working on your dancing...doesn't leave much time for your music. You should work on your music because the youth of America depends on you to show them the way." Davy: "Yeah?" Zappa: "Yeah."

Annette Funicello, Sonny Liston, Carol Doda, Frank Zappa, Teri Garr, Victor Mature · **CAMEOS**

The Porpoise Song, Circle Sky, Can You Dig It, Long Title: Do I Have to Do This All Over Again, Daddy's Song, As We Go Along (Monkees) · **SONGS**

HEARTBREAK HOTEL (1988)

CAST: David Keith, Tuesday Weld, Charlie Schlatter, Angela Goethals; DIR: Chris Columbus; PROD: Lynda Hill, Debra Obst; SCREENPLAY: Chris Columbus; STUDIO: Touchstone; 101 min., color (Touchstone)

MUSIC ★★★
ATTITUDE ★★★★
FUN ★★★★

A 1988 movie about a 1972 Elvis recapturing his 1956 youth.
Actually, the only baffling thing about *Heartbreak Hotel* is that it's an overlooked charmer instead of a household hit. When teenage guitarist Johnny Wolfe (Charlie Schlatter) presents a kidnapped Presley (David Keith) to his depressed El-crazed single mother (Tuesday Weld), both a reluctant Presley and the surprised mom rediscover their inner selves. David Keith is able to capture Elvis's charm without looking much like him, and director Chris Columbus's cliches are so good they seem original. The 1972 setting is an ingenious premise, which helps to make Presley's unplanned weekend getaway seem realistic—the King was down then, but not yet out. That Columbus did his homework is obvious. He uses flashbacks from real Elvis movies and concocts a mistaken-identity plot to play off Elvis's Oedipus complex. Even credited help from the Presley estate doesn't turn this film into propaganda. As proof consider the enlightening debate between Wolfe and Presley as to whether Elvis is really washed up. It's a great scene but a moot point, because with films like this, the King may never be dethroned. (ALa)

Elvis and Wolfe arguing over the King's downfall (0:46); Elvis helping Wolfe's band perform a hard-rock version of "Heartbreak Hotel" at a high school talent show (1:28) · **SCENES**

Elvis: "I never said my movies had anything to do with rock'n'roll." · **LINES**

HEARTS OF FIRE (1987)

CAST: Fiona, Rupert Everett, Bob Dylan, Richie Havens; DIR: Richard Marquand; PROD: Richard Marquand, Gerald Abrams, Jennifer Alward, Jennifer Miller; SCREENPLAY: Scott Richardson, Joe Eszterhas; STUDIO: Warner; 95 min., color (Warner)

MUSIC ★
ATTITUDE ★
FUN ★★

Possibly Dylan's greatest artistic gaffe—and that's saying something!
So abysmal that it was never released in the U.S., *Hearts of Fire* is an unwatchable cliche, noteworthy only for Bob Dylan's wonderfully inept performance. Rock's greatest poet was dumb enough to try his hand at acting again—opposite an even more dubious thespian, the talentless rock diva Fiona. The plot features Molly Maguire (Fiona) wasting away in a dying steel town, playing classic rock covers and dreaming of fame. Eventually, thanks to the largesse of retired legend Billy Parker (Dylan) and hearthrob synth-popper James Colt (Rupert Everett), she makes it. Of course, she discovers fame isn't all it's cracked up to be, and gets

caught between the two men romantically, losing both. Then, at her triumphant hometown gig, *both stars take the stage with her!* Cue rock video. Roll credits.

It's hard to decide which is more awful—watching Dylan try to emote or hearing a dozen of Fiona's Bonnie Tyler-meets-Pat Benatar rockers. The hackneyed flatness of Joe (*Basic Instinct*) Eszterhas's dramatic scenes make them quite hilarious, but it's the same joke over and over again. Even the state of Pennsylvania should be embarrassed that it's in this movie. (JC)

SCENES   Dylan-as-Billy demonstrating what it's really like to be a rock star by trashing the shit out of his room, TV-through-the-window and all (0:56)

LINES   Molly at her most articulate: "What the fuck, James?" and "You know what you are? You're a dip." James mooning over Billy's self-imposed exile: "You don't believe in magic anymore, do you?"

CAMEOS   Ian Dury, Tony Rosato, Ron Wood

SONGS   *Proud Mary, Cinnamon Girl, Hair of the Dog That Bit You, I'm In It for You, Let the Good Times Roll, The Nights We Spent on Earth, Tainted Love, Hearts of Fire* (Fiona); *The Usual, Couple More Years* (Bob Dylan); *Fear, Hate, Envy, Jealousy* (Richie Havens); *Had a Dream about You Baby* (Fiona, Bob Dylan); *The Other Side* (Rupert Everett)

HELLO DOWN THERE   (1969)

MUSIC ★★★★
ATTITUDE ★★
FUN ★★★

CAST: Tony Randall, Janet Leigh, Jim Backus, Ken Berry, Roddy McDowall, Charlotte Rae, Richard Dreyfuss, Kay Cole, Gary Tigerman, Lou Wagner, Arnold Stang, Harvey Lembeck, Merv Griffin, Lee Meredith, Bruce Gordon, Frank Schuller; **DIR:** Jack Arnold; **PROD:** Ivan Tors; **SCREENPLAY:** John McGreevey, Frank Telford; **STUDIO:** MGM; 98 min., color (no video release)

Garage band goes underground... and underwater.
One of Phil Spector's key writers, Jeff Barry, provides the songs for the proto-garage band in this film, which was produced around the time that Barry had a big success with the Archies' "Sugar Sugar." Don't scoff at these prefab bubblegum delights. They were among the best records released that year. For example, British sessions vocalist Tony Burrows sang both "Love Grows Where My Rosemary Goes" (Edison Lighthouse) and "Hitchin' a Ride" (Vanity Faire) using pseudonyms, and the Monkees were a made-up group, too, ya know. So dig, this film is an example of the stuff that filled the gap between mid-'60s garage punk and early-'70s pop like Badfinger, Big Star, and the Raspberries.

In *Hello Down There*, Richard Dreyfuss (what a crackup!) plays Harold, who rehearses his band, the Green Onion, in an experimental underwater home of the type displayed at the 1964 World's Fair. Playing his mother, Janet Leigh re-creates her scream from *Psycho*, and Tony Randall pulls off a great scene singing out of tune while the Green Onion back him up with pure out-of-tune trash-raunch. This ridiculous children's movie is a cross between *The Cool Ones, Flipper*, and *The Incredible Mr. Limpet*. Roddy McDowall reprises his *Cool Ones* role as a "tycoon of teen," but the attempt at humor is surprisingly dry for a film as silly as this one. Still, the hilarity does come out whenever the screenwriter tries to sound hip. The film's climax involves Roddy conning Merv Griffin into televising the band nationwide from its underwater pad. After the Green Onion conquer America, McDowall announces the opening of underwater nightclubs in Paris, London, Tokyo, and New York. (DP)

LINES   Merv Griffin introducing the band: "A brand new rock group called The Green

Onion.... And their manager, Nate Ashbury, tells me that he is *stoned* on these shouters, that they are mellow yellow, turned on and groovy, and the lead chick is so wigged out, she's out of sight."

Hello Down There (Jeff Barry); *Hey Little Goldfish, I Can Love You, Glub* (Green Onion); *Just One More Chance* (Tony Randall)   **SONGS**

HELP!   *(1965)*

CAST: John Lennon, Paul McCartney, George Harrison, Ringo Starr, Eleanor Bron, Leo McKern, Victor Spinetti, Roy Kinnear, Patrick Cargill, John Bluthal; DIR: Richard Lester; PROD: Walter Shenson; SCREENPLAY: Marc Behm; STUDIO: United Artists; 92 min., color (MPI)

MUSIC ★★★★
ATTITUDE ★★★
FUN ★★★

Helpless, hapless, and hopeless.
The Beatles' second film seemed disappointing at the time, and it hasn't aged well. Not willing to do another *Hard Day's Night*, director Richard Lester and the band opted for a script that mixed James Bond leftovers, about an Eastern cult trying to

117

retrieve a sacred ring from Ringo's finger, with a collection of songs that, except for "Ticket to Ride," failed to feature the group at its best—although Lennon's Dylanesque "You've Got to Hide Your Love Away" is pretty enough, and "Help!" has a good beat. The script is fairly flaccid, and the band members look very uncomfortable. By contrast, the character actors (especially Roy Kinnear) have a great time going through their eccentric comic bits. As a result, according to John Lennon, the Beatles felt (and often looked) "like extras in their own movie." *Help!* did play a key role in inspiring the Beatles to take control of their own creative affairs, and the video looks gorgeous. It was the first 1960's rock film to have its audio track remastered digitally, with great success. (BE)

SCENES Leo McKern (as the cult leader) trying to atttract John Lennon's attention: "Hey, Beatle—you shall have fun, eh?" "No, thanks," replies John, "I'm rhythm guitar and mouth organ."

SONGS *Help!, You're Gonna Lose That Girl, You've Got to Hide Your Love Away, Ticket to Ride, I Need You, The Night Before, She's a Woman, Another Girl* (Beatles)

HERE WE GO ROUND THE MULBERRY BUSH (1967)

MUSIC ★★★★★
ATTITUDE ★★★★★
FUN ★★★★★

CAST: Barry Evans, Judy Geeson, Angela Scoular, Adrienne Posta; DIR: Clive Donner; PROD: Larry Kramer, Clive Donner; SCREENPLAY: Hunter Davies, Larry Kramer; STUDIO: United Artists/Giant; 94 min., color (no video release)

Like a virgin.
Of all the "with-it" youth films of the 1960s, *Here We Go Round the Mulberry Bush* is the one that broke the most ground. Its take on of teenage sex was relatively honest, and it didn't pander. In some respects, *Here We Go Round the Mulberry Bush* seems like a British analog to *The Graduate*. It's all about teenage dropout Barry Evans and his desire to lose his virginity. His ardor leads to several awkward moments with various women—including Judy Geeson, Sheila White, and Adrienne Posta. Needless to say, complications ensue. However, unlike Mike Nichols's more celebrated movie, *Here We Go Round the Mulberry Bush* has a good hard-rock soundtrack. Both the post-Steve Winwood Spencer Davis Group and Traffic perform, and the former group can be glimpsed playing in a church dance sequence. (BE)

SONGS *Taking Out Time, Every Little Thing, Virgin's Dream, Picture of Her, Just Like Me, Waltz for Caroline* (Spencer Davis Group); *Here We Go Round the Mulberry Bush, Am I What I Was or Was I What I Am, Utterly Simple* (Traffic); *It's Been a Long Time* (Andy Ellison)

HEY, LET'S TWIST (1961)

MUSIC ★★★★
ATTITUDE ★★★★
FUN ★★★★★

CAST: Joey Dee, Teddy Randazzo, Zohra Lampert, Jo Ann Campbell, Kay Fern, Dino De Luca; DIR: Greg Garrison; PROD: Harry Romm; SCREENPLAY: Hal Halkady; STUDIO: Paramount; 80 min., b/w (no video release)

The birth of go-go as it really happened.
Everybody should see this movie. First of all, it's the only real explanation of the New York City, early '60s, greaseball culture from which go-go dancing, the Young Rascals and the Ronettes sprang. All of these crucial '60s idioms got rolling at the Peppermint Lounge via the Lounge's resident rock'n'roller, Joey Dee, a terribly misunderstood catalyst in the whole wazoo. In this film, we get to see some

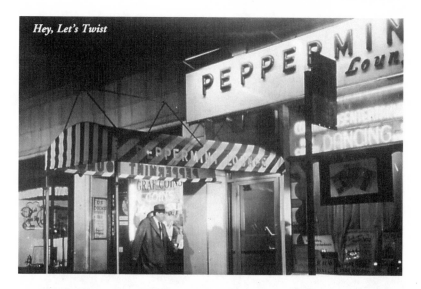

Hey, Let's Twist

real Italian family culture and the transformation of Joey from wild Latin kid to Ivy League student to nightclub motivator supreme. Leftover '50s crooner Teddy Randazzo co-stars as Joey's brother, and he winds up delivering a lesson for all time with a surprising plot twist.

A high-society dame, who has stumbled into the club to escape a Manhattan traffic jam, flirts with Randazzo. Then she books Joey and the gang to play a tux-and-tiara ball, where they shake the place up. When the newspapers catch the story, the Peppermint Lounge becomes the toast of New York. Still, the basic truths of rock'n'roll are exposed when the now-successful club institutes a maitre d', a cover charge, and a five-dollar minimum. The life goes out of the place, and it soon bombs out. Almost ready to throw in the towel, Dee throws the maitre d' out instead, puts up a neon sign blaring "No Cover" to the street, and busts into a frantic rendition of "Shout!" Randazzo dumps the socialite and dissapears. The lesson: Rock'n'roll is, and should always be, low budget, for kids, and free of corporate enterprise. (DP)

Lounge patron to Sharon Cassidy as she "discovers" the twist: "Work out, Baby!"   **LINES**

Hey Let's Twist, Round and Round, Let Me Teach You How to Twist, Roly Poly, Peppermint Twist, **SONGS**
Shout! (Joey Dee and the Starlighters); *Let's Twist* (Mama); *Shake Me Baby* (Jo Ann Campbell)

HIGH SCHOOL CAESAR   (1960)

CAST John Ashley, Gary Vinson, Judy Nugent, Lowell Brown, Steve Stevens, Daria Massey; DIR: O'Dale Ireland; PROD: O'Dale Ireland; SCREENPLAY: Ethelmae Page, Robert Slaven; STUDIO: Film Group/Marathon; 72 min., b/w (Rhino)

MUSIC	★★★★
ATTITUDE	★★
FUN	★★★

A rich, troubled teen terrorizes his high school.
This late entry into the teen flick realm is pretty decent: The kids seem real (maybe because the film was shot in Missouri, not L.A.), the plot is plausible, and the car-race sequences are excellent. The film is generally well crafted, especially the ending, in which the school turns on the class heel, but the sound is appalling (the microphone was apparently mounted on the camera), and the rock'n'roll is seriously wanting. Yes, the film is peppered with rock'n'roll moments, but the

squares who produced it still reverted to swing-type music for the dancin' and romancin'. (AF)

SONGS   *High School Caesar* (Reggie Perkins); *I Fell for Your Line Baby* (Johnny Faire); *Lookin' Waitin' Searchin' Hopin'* (Reggie Olson)

High School Confidential

HIGH SCHOOL CONFIDENTIAL   (1958)

MUSIC ★★★★★
ATTITUDE ★★★★★
FUN ★★★★★

ALTERNATE TITLE: *The Young Hellions*
CAST: Russ Tamblyn, John Drew Barrymore, Diane Jergens, Jan Sterling, Jackie Coogan, Mamie Van Doren, Michael Landon, Phillipa Fallon, Charles Chaplin Jr., Jerry Lee Lewis; DIR: Jack Arnold; PROD: Albert Zugsmith; SCREENPLAY: Lewis Meltzer; STUDIO: MGM; 85 min., b/w (Republic)

Tune in, turn on...burn out.
American rock'n'roll movies never got much better than this collaboration of producer Albert Zugsmith and director Jack Arnold *(The Incredible Shrinking Man)*, who had a knack for making something out of nothing. The period slang alone is worth the price of ownership. High school delinquent Russ Tamblyn works his way into the local drug ring and puts the moves on teen-queen Diane Jergens, while fending off the advances of his frustrated "aunt," Mamie Van Doren. The beauty of this picture is the knowing archness of its players. Each line of dialogue carries an oh-so-subtle nudge in the ribs; each is delivered for the greatest ironic impact. Coupled with the overheated lust of the female characters, this is a dazzling piece of exploitation filmmaking. The best parts, however, are the opening, featuring Jerry Lee Lewis doing the title song from the back of a flatbed truck, and two pseudo-beat poems written by Mel Welles and delivered by Phillipa Fallon and John Drew Barrymore. (BE)

SCENES   John Drew Barrymore as J.I. Coleridge, gang leader and hipster raconteur, addressing a class in the absence of the teacher (0:10)

LINES   Russ Tamblyn to Diane Jergens: "Hiya, sexy, you look real cultured. Let's cut out to some drag-and-eat pad." Phillipa Fallon as a beat poetess: "Tomorrow is drag, pops—the future is a flake."

SONGS   *High School Confidential* (Jerry Lee Lewis)

HOLD ON (1966)

CAST: Peter Noone, Karl Green, Keith Hopwood, Derek Leckenby, Barry Whitwam, Shelley Fabares, Sue Ann Langdon, Herbert Anderson, Bernard Fox; **DIR:** Arthur Lubin; **PROD:** Sam Katzman; **SCREENPLAY:** James B. Gordon; **STUDIO:** MGM; 85 min., color (no video release)

MUSIC ★★
ATTITUDE ★
FUN ★★★

Hermit-ically sealed.

Rock'n'roll movies don't get much sillier than this one, in which Herman's Hermits play the familiar role of a British rock group on tour in the United States. Reality takes a holiday when NASA decides to name a space capsule after the boys, and they become the object of a government investigation. The whole thing was conceived by that beloved schlockmeister Sam Katzman (natch), the producer who brought you *Rock Around the Clock, Twist Around the Clock*, etc. Arthur Lubin's pacing is nearly brisk enough to make one forget the absurdity of this nonsense— which is pretty good work for the director of *Mr. Ed* and *Francis the Talking Mule*. (BE)

Hold On, A Must to Avoid, All the Things I Do for You Baby, Where Were You, Make Me Happy, The George and the Dragon, Got a Feeling, We Want You Herman, Wild Love, Gotta Get Away, Leaning on a Lamppost (Herman's Hermits)

SONGS

HOME BEFORE MIDNIGHT   (1978)

CAST: James Aubrey, Alison Elliot, Debbie Linden, Chris Jagger, Jigsaw, Richard Todd; DIR: Peter Walker; PROD: Peter Walker; SCREENPLAY: Murray Smith; STUDIO: Heritage; 92 min., color (Video Search of Miami)

Underrated, understated, and underage.

Fans of '70s lite rock may remember a smash hit called "Sky High" by Jigsaw. Well, Jigsaw is featured prominently in this fine film by British director Peter Walker. *Home Before Midnight* is the story of an up-and-coming young songwriter named Mike, who has recently masterminded the successful pop band Bad Accident. (Mick Jagger's brother Chris plays one of the band members.)

One morning, Mike picks up a beautiful hitchhiker named Ginny. After falling passionately in love with her, he makes the shocking discovery that she's only 14 years old! If this movie were set in Louisiana instead of England, there might have been a happy ending. Instead, Mike finds himself involved in a scandal. He's betrayed by everyone (including Bad Accident), spurned by his parents, eaten alive by the tabloid press—and that's only the beginning. The film never reaches a moral resolution, however. It's just a sad tale of a young man learning an extremely bitter lesson in life. (MC)

SONGS   *Home Before Midnight, Kick Me When I'm Down, The Way We Dance, Every Move You Make* (Jigsaw)

THE HORROR OF PARTY BEACH   (1963)

CAST: John Scott, Alice Lyon, Allan Laurel, Eulabelle Moore, Marilyn Clarke, Charter Oaks Motorcycle Club of Riverside, Connecticut; DIR: Del Tenney; PROD: Del Tenney, Alan V. Iselin; SCREENPLAY: Richard Hilliard; STUDIO: Prism; 72 min., b/w (Prism)

Nobody surfs in Stamford.

This may be the only *Beach Party*-type movie that warns of the dangers of nuclear waste mismanagement. Dead bodies floating along the Atlantic coast are transformed into grotesque zombies by spilled radioactive waste. Sexy party girl Tina is the first to be killed by the monsters, while her friends are dancing to the Del-Aires and fighting with bikers. As the monsters go on a killing rampage, Tina's boyfriend (and aspiring scientist) Hank, her rival Elaine, and Elaine's scientist father Dr. Gavin discover that throwing sodium on the monsters will disintegrate them. So they get some sodium, throw it on the monsters, and that takes care of that. Reportedly filmed in and around Stamford, Connecticut, this movie didn't manage to cash in on the *Beach Party* craze. However, it does get shown frequently on late-night TV, enabling it to live on in glory. More to the point, New Jersey's Del-Aires, clad in striped shirts and flashing Fender Jaguars and Jazzmasters, lay down some blistering grooves. (MC)

SONGS   *Elaine, Just Wigglin' and Wobblin', Drag, Joyride, Zombie Stomp, You Are Not a Summer Love* (Del-Aires)

HOT ROD GANG   (1958)

CAST: John Ashley, Jody Fair, Gene Vincent; DIR: Lew Landers; PROD: Buddy Rogers; SCREENPLAY: Lou Rusoff; STUDIO: American International; 72 min., b/w (Embassy)

A preppy and his girlfriend lead double lives the A.I.P. way.

Rock movie fans of the '50s and '60s always knew that the American International Pictures logo meant a movie would be 100% Guaranteed Rock'n'Roll with none of that bogus sermonizing you could expect from the major studios. A.I.P. films always delivered the goods: fast cars, rock'n'roll, and postwar youths running completely amok. In *Hot Rod Gang*, John Ashley plays rich kid John Abernathy III. He's a rock'n'rollin' hot-rodder, but he conceals these passions from his legal guardians, two eccentric aunts. His girlfriend, Lois Cavendish, also leads a double life. When John's car club needs some money, Lois introduces him to her rock star friend Gene Vincent, who volunteers to do a benefit concert. Encouraged by

Vincent to keep singing, John changes his name, dons a false beard to fool his aunts, and releases a string of hit records. Rival gang members rat him out to the old ladies and plant stolen hubcaps in his trunk, but after a car chase and a couple of fistfights, the villains are thwarted. And thus ends *Hot Rod Gang*, an A.I.P. classic. But what really makes this a classic rock'n'roll movie is the presence of Vincent (in his only speaking role) and the Blue Caps, musically and visually one of the greatest and most exciting bands of all time. (MC)

SONGS   *Hit and Run Lover, Believe Me, Annie Laurie* (John Ashley); *Dance in the Street, Baby Blue, Dance to the Bop* (Gene Vincent)

THE HOURS AND TIMES (1992)

CAST: David Angus, Ian Hart, Stephanie Pack, Robin McDonald; DIR: Christopher Münch; 60 min., b/w (Fox Lorber)

Mop Top sexual psychodrama.

In his book *The Love You Make*, former Beatles aide Peter Brown suggested that Brian Epstein's long-suppressed love for John Lennon was consummated during a trip to Barcelona in April 1963. Brown claimed that Epstein, unable to keep such a juicy secret to himself, told him the story personally. Others, including Paul McCartney, have discounted Brown's information. Because both Epstein and Lennon are dead, we'll never know what might have occurred far away from the other Beatles and from John's wife, Cynthia, who had just given birth to their son Julian. But it may have looked like this.

At first, this hour-long, black-and-white saga seems like exploitative fluff, created mainly to appeal to dishy soap opera fans. The actor playing Lennon (David Angus) is not blessed with the greatest physical resemblance (although he looks a little like Julian at times), and Ian Hart's Epstein talks more like James Mason than the Beatles' manager. As the surprisingly complex script unfolds, however, it becomes clear that Münch and his actors put a lot of care into this film. The story is drawn from the well-documented lives of these two famous personalities: Lennon is arrogant and brooding, quickly bored and constantly searching for both intellectual and libidinous satisfaction. (It sounds cartoonish, but it's not.) Epstein is a more mysterious figure in musical history—uptight, unhip, and desperately lonely—in short, the stuff of which Rutles sketches are made. Epstein was obviously very intelligent, and this film does quite a bit to flesh out his persona and offer possible explanations for his motivations. As for the sex part, *The Hours and Times* shows some partial nudity and a bit of tentative grappling. But it avoids the big question, unless you care to interpret that gleam in Brian's eyes. (JS)

HOUSE PARTY (1990)

CAST: Kid'n'Play, Robin Harris, Martin Lawrence, Tisha Campbell, A.J. Johnson, Full Force; DIR: Reginald Hudlin; PROD: Warrington Hudlin; SCREENPLAY: Reginald Hudlin; STUDIO: New Line; 100 min., color (RCA/Columbia)

Risky Business *goes hip hop.*

Soon after the release of their 1988 album *2 Hype*, which was only limply received, Kid'n'Play (Christopher Reid, Christopher Martin) decided to hedge their bets by agreeing to star in *House Party*. It was a smart move. *2 Hype* was pabulum compared to the gangsta rap of contemporaries like N.W.A., and the pair were booed off the stage during a Madison Square Garden concert. On the other hand, this big, bright musical about respectably rebellious teens proved to be a much more suitable medium for their talents. *House Party* cost $2.5 million to make, but it grossed $27 million at the box office. As a result, Kid'n'Play became a Saturday morning cartoon show, a clothing line, and the stars of *House Party 2* (as well as guests on "Sesame Street") .

Set in the suburbs, *House Party* follows Kid for a day as he desperately tries to attend an illicit bash that night at Play's house. With his foot-high flattop-fade and E.T.-ish mien, Kid can be infectiously amusing. The movie is similarly likeable. Its normal teen heroes, just looking for a good time, run up against the predictable foes: hoodlums (expertly played by Full Force), cops, and parents. If it weren't for the constant profanity and a startlingly (for a movie that responsibly confronts problems like teen pregnancy and alcoholism) homophobic rap, *House Party* would make a great baby-sitter. (SBW)

A portrait of Ronald Reagan getting gooped with Jell-O during a cafeteria food fight (0:07)

S C E N E S

George Clinton

C A M E O S

HOW TO STUFF A WILD BIKINI   (1965)

CAST: Annette Funicello, Frankie Avalon, Mickey Rooney, Dwayne Hickman, Brian Donlevy, Harvey Lembeck, Beverly Adams, Jody McCrea, John Ashley, Timothy Carey, Marianna Guba, Len Lesse, Arthur Julian, Bobbi Shaw; DIR: William Asher; PROD: James H. Nicholson, Samuel Z. Arkoff; SCREENPLAY: William Asher, Leo Townsend; STUDIO: American International; 92 min., color (Warner)

MUSIC ★★★★
ATTITUDE ★★★
FUN ★★★★★

The great swimsuit issue.

In *How to Stuff a Wild Bikini*, the *Beach Party* gang takes on material that should have been a bad Broadway musical instead. Take, for example, the four times that each and every gang member's face crowds the screen to blurt out the chorus "stuff a wild bi-ki-ni...." They know it's stupid, but the joke's on you, pal. John (*High School Caesar*) Ashley does get to hold a guitar in this one, but it's all for show, which makes the scene both sublime *and* ridiculous. Frankie Avalon has been stationed on a tropical isle (with a tropical girl), but he still checks in on Annette (using the services of witch doctor Buster Keaton) to see whether she's remained faithful to him. Elizabeth Montgomery (Samantha on "Bewitched") makes a cameo as Keaton's witch daughter.

Only 10 minutes into the movie, you're already up to the third song, "How About Us," which features all the wonderful girls in the cast primping. Mickey Rooney and Brian Donlevy hack it up as ad men singing "Madison Avenue," while Harvey Lembeck, who gets more play here than in any other *Beach Party* flick. is a total joke singing "I Am My Ideal" and "I'm the Boy Next Door." Sure, Harvey, the boy next door really hangs out with the gruesome North Dakota Slim (played brilliantly by Timothy Carey) at a pool hall with a photo of Hitler on the wall. Annette Funicello gets three neat tunes, but her performance isn't nearly as memorable as Dwayne Hickman's Japanese make-out pad. The campfire singalong "After the Party" closes the haywire proceedings. The wildest moment features the Kingsmen shaking the whole gang up in their brash, Pacific Northwest style. (DP)

How to Stuff a Wild Bikini, How About Us, Healthy Girl, If It's Gonna Happen, After the Party (Cast); *Madison Avenue* (Mickey Rooney, Brian Donlevy); *Boy Next Door, Follow Your Leader* (Harvey Lembeck); *Give Her Lovin'* (Kingsmen); *Better Be Ready* (Annette Funicello)

S O N G S

HUMAN HIGHWAY **(1982)**

MUSIC ★★
ATTITUDE ★
FUN ★

CAST: Neil Young, Devo, Dean Stockwell, Sally Kirkland, Charlotte Stewart, Geralynne Baron, Dennis Hopper; DIR: Bernard Shakey [Neil Young], Dean Stockwell; PROD: L.A. Johnson; SCREENPLAY: Bernard Shakey [Neil Young], Jean Feld, Dean Stockwell, Russell Tamblyn; STUDIO: Shakey Pictures; 87 min., color (no video release)

Beware the grease monkey with the big wrench.

Ever wonder why you've never seen some of the films in this book? There's good reason. Caught at the crossroads—somewhere between his past, present, and future—Neil Young might have intended to give a *Wizard of Oz*-eye view of impending postmodern society, but the result was nothing more than a wacked-out, surreal stab at a low-budget Busby Berkeley musical. Made at a time when Young was putting down his acoustic guitar for a computer keyboard, when the nuclear threat was more real than at any time during his youth, and when dinosaur musicians of the '70s were bobbing in the wake of the punk New Wave, *Human Highway* is a litany of cliches. Small-town romance, survival, dreams, stardom, and a better way of life are all set against the ever-present threat of meltdown at ground zero. Luckily, Booji Boy saves the day.

Young plays Lionel, a dorky car mechanic working at the garage next to the town diner. He's got a crush on a waitress and a star on for singer Frankie Fontaine. When Fontaine drives up in a limousine to buy the diner, Lionel blacks out while working on the limo's differential. Devo, erstwhile engineers at the local nuclear power plant, enter Lionel's unconscious mind for the film's one redeeming moment: when Lionel and the Spud Boys rip it up on "My My Hey Hey (Out of the Blue)." As bad as the film is, this scene, like Young's best music, offers a glimpse into the redemptive power of rock'n'roll. (TP)

SCENES Lionel meeting Frankie, who is a blowtorch-wielding cross between Elvis and Robert Goulet (0:53); Lionel and Devo (1:02)

LINES Lionel: "I may not be Einstein, but it doesn't take a politician to know that anything is possible."

SONGS *It Takes a Worried Man, Come Back Jonee* (Devo); *Ride My Llama* (Neil Young); *My My Hey Hey* (Neil Young, Devo)

I WANNA HOLD YOUR HAND (1978)

CAST: Nancy Allen, Bobby DiCicco, Marc McCure, Susan Kendall Newman, Theresa Saldana, Wendy Jo Sperber, Eddie Deezen, Christian Juttner; **DIR:** Robert Zemeckis; **PROD:** Tamara Asseyeu, Alex Rose; **SCREENPLAY:** Robert Zemeckis, Bob Gale; **STUDIO:** Warner; 98 min., color (Warner)

MUSIC ★★★
ATTITUDE ★★★★
FUN ★★★★

Beatle-crazed Jersey teens run amok in Manhattan.
Before he became the big-ticket director of *Back to the Future* and *Who Framed Roger Rabbit?*, Robert Zemeckis piloted this predictable but winning Beatlemania comedy. On the day of the big Ed Sullivan show, suburban New Jersey teens Pam, Rosie, and Grace (Nancy Allen, Wendy Jo Sperber, Theresa Saldana) commandeer a funeral hearse (only limos can get to the hotel's door) and head for Manhattan. They're determined to meet, photograph, and/or marry the Beatles. Their male friends are not amused.

This is a lightweight film, with the predictable pratfalls and the obligatory happy ending, but Zemeckis and co-writer Bob Gale know their comedy formulas well, and they get the spirit right. Using 16 Beatles songs on the soundtrack, plus stock footage from the Sullivan program, *I Wanna Hold Your Hand* conjures up all the details of this crazy but very innocent cultural moment. There's the hysteria at the Plaza, a kid named Richard who's changed his name to "Ringo," and the frantic calls to Murray the K to answer trivia questions and win tickets. There's even a folkie-alternative type (Susan Kendall Newman), who turns up to protest the superficiality of the Beatles but converts instead when the power of pop music stops the cops from making an arrest. The Beatles, you see, are a force for good. (JC)

SCENES   Pam's glorious time alone in the Beatles' hotel room (0:38) cuts right to the real stuff of fandom: She fondles their clothes, lies in their bed, pulls stray hairs from brushes, and basically makes love to a guitar. She runs her fingers up and down the fretboard, pausing for lascivious little moans and cries of "Oh God," with ecstasy written all over her face.

LINES   Ed getting the crowd ready for the Fab Four: "I want you to be prepared for excessive screaming, hysteria, hyperventilation, fainting fits, seizures, spasmodic convulsions, even attempted suicides. It's all perfectly normal. It merely means that these youngsters are enjoying themselves."

CAMEOS   Murray the K, Will Jordan (as Ed Sullivan)

THE IDOLMAKER (1980)

MUSIC ★
ATTITUDE ★★★★
FUN ★★★

CAST: Ray Sharkey, Tovah Feldshuh, Peter Gallagher, Paul Land, Joe Pantoliano; DIR: Taylor Hackford; PROD: Gene Kirkwood, Howard Koch Jr.; SCREENPLAY: Edward DiLorenzo; STUDIO: United Artists; 118 min., color (MGM/UA)

Ray Sharkey creates Frankie Avalon and Fabian.
Ray Sharkey's brazen impersonation of a pop impresario (loosely based on producer/manager Bob Marcucci) neatly mirrors *The Idolmaker*'s premise: that Svengalis are cooler than Trilbys. Bronx boy Vinnie's a talented songwriter with budding marketing savvy, but his mug doesn't get the girls shrieking. So, with a little payola and the helping hand of teen mag editress Brenda (Tovah Feldshuh, basically playing *16*'s Gloria Stavers), he guides a couple of guys from Da Naybuhood to the top of the world of bandstands, sock hops, groupies, and teddy bears.

The proteges abandon their figurative father/lover/producer when they don't need him anymore, and Vinnie ends up at the Jersey dive where he began, performing his own songs with piano accompaniment. This is a movie about manipulative schlock that is itself manipulative schlock. (JC)

SCENES   The wildly homoerotic shaving cream fight between Vinnie and Tommy (0:25); Caesare's spontaneous transformation into a rock god (1:22)

CAMEOS   Olympia Dukakis, Maureen McCormick

SONGS   *Here Is My Love, Sweet Little Lover* (Jesse Fredericks); *A Boy and a Girl* (Sweet Inspirations, London Fog); *Baby, However Dark My Night, It's Never Been Tonight Before* (Peter Gallagher); *I Believe It Can Be Done* (Ray Sharkey)

IMAGINE (1971)

MUSIC ★★★★
ATTITUDE ★★★
FUN ★★★

DIR: John Lennon, Yoko Ono; PROD: John Lennon, Yoko Ono; SCREENPLAY: John Lennon, Yoko Ono; STUDIO: Joko; 55 min., color (Sony)

Give wealth a chance.
Blondie called their video disc *Eat to the Beat* the world's first "video album," but John Lennon did it about nine years before. Granted, *Imagine* wasn't available for home video consumption until much later, but the the film does feature performances of all 10 songs from the *Imagine* album. Most are nonsynchronous set pieces of John and Yoko inside their white, minimally furnished Tittenhurst Park mansion and the surrounding 74-acre estate. Essentially, *Imagine* is a collection of

home movies, albeit the most expensive home movies ever made, from one year in the life of John Lennon. After all, how many people can afford helicopter-made aerial shots? Of course, John Lennon can, and he includes one in the clip for "Jealous Guy." This segment also features the happy couple driving a large car across their rolling lawn, pulling up to their private lake, and taking a rowboat out to their own island, where they play chess in a miniature tea house. You'd be happy, too!

Just before this outing to the lake, you're treated to a scene with John sitting on the crapper before taking his breakfast on the veranda. Other clips are more conceptual: John playing billiards blindfolded, people in black bags walking around, a girl climbing on top of the house to view one of Yoko's art pieces. John plays the clown as Yoko plays sexpot, strutting around in a variety of braless outfits. Also included are two Yoko songs from her *Fly* album. *Imagine* will seem incredibly self-indulgent to anyone who doesn't love John Lennon...but don't we all? (JS)

Dick Cavett, George Harrison, Fred Astaire, Jack Palance, Jonas Mekas   **CAMEOS**

Imagine, Crippled Inside, Jealous Guy, It's So Hard, I Don't Wanna Be a Soldier Mama I Don't   **SONGS**
Wanna Die, Gimme Some Truth, Oh My Love, How?, How Do You Sleep?, Oh Yoko (John Lennon); *Don't Count the Waves, Mrs. Lennon* (Yoko Ono)

Imagine

IMAGINE: JOHN LENNON (1988)

MUSIC ★★★
ATTITUDE ★★
FUN ★★

DIR: Andrew Solt; **PROD:** Andrew Solt, David L. Wolper; **STUDIO:** Columbia; 103 min., color (RCA/Columbia)

Yoko Ono pulls a Geraldo, opening an empty Lennon vault.
In a battle of the mediums, this Yoko Ono-sanctioned bio-pic combats rock parasite Albert Goldman's book *The Lives of John Lennon.* Since Goldman's *Lives* lies, and Ono's stash appears about as valuable as Al Capone's, Lennon fans lose.

More documentary than rockumentary, *Imagine* is slow and, much of the time, an outright snoozer. The footage of Beatles concerts and post-Beatles live segments make for quality music, as they did the first hundred times (yawn) they were shown in TV specials, movies, and videos. The rarer Ono chats are even less interesting, considering the couple obviously kept the cameras rolling throughout their entire life together. The spurts of Lennon's old interviews that are used as narration seem out of place at times, but they glow in comparison to the sparse 1988 interviews with Ono, Sean Lennon, Julian Lennon, and Cynthia Lennon. Using Lennon's first wife is especially revealing—something the rest of the interviews aren't. Only when *Imagine* starts to examine the underpublicized part of Lennon's life—his musical withdrawal to concentrate on raising Sean—does the movie make you wish for more footage. But by then, Lennon's dead, and so is the possibility of *Imagine II*—a rockumentary to fill the middle ground between Goldman's dirt and Ono's propaganda. (ALa)

CAMEOS Andy Warhol, Ultraviolet, Dick Cavett, Jack Palance, Fred Astaire, Jonas Mekas, and George Harrison, all of whom visit the royal couple.

IT HAPPENED AT THE WORLD'S FAIR (1963)

MUSIC ★★
ATTITUDE ★
FUN ★

CAST: Elvis Presley, Joan O'Brien, Gary Lockwood, Vicky Tiu; **DIR:** Norman Taurog; **PROD:** Ted Richmond; **SCREENPLAY:** Si Rose, Seaman Jacobs; **STUDIO:** MGM; 105 min., color (MGM/UA)

Elvis visits the Seattle World's Fair.
Mike Edwards (Elvis Presley) is a charter airplane pilot in business with his friend Danny Burke (Gary Lockwood). When Danny's gambling debts force them to surrender their plane, the pair head for Seattle, hitching a ride with a Chinese produce driver and his charming seven-year-old niece Sue-Ling (Vicky Tiu). Seattle just happens to be hosting the World's Fair that year, with all its wonderful attractions. Beside the "Dream Car" exhibit and the Space Needle, Mike falls in love with a nurse (Joan O'Brien). Together they care for Sue-Ling, who has been mysteriously abandoned by her uncle, while the thoughtless Danny gets them all involved in smuggling. Except for travelogue shots of the World's Fair and Elvis's cool wardrobe, this film has little to offer. The plot is interchangeable with a dozen other Elvis films, the acting is uninspired, and the soundtrack (as usual) is flat and unimaginative. (TM)

SCENES Mike and Sue-Ling sing the duet "How Would You Like to Be," as he tries to cajole the depressed child into a better mood (1:20). Granted, it's not for the cynical, but you wouldn't be watching this movie if you were, would you?

LINES Mike (before he falls for the nurse) trying to make time with a buxom beauty: "Calm down, honey. You're like a fluttering bird. Racing that sweet little engine of yours on a warm day, that's bad."

IT'S A BIKINI WORLD (1967)

CAST: Tommy Kirk, Deborah Walley, Robert "Boris" Pickett, Suzie Kaye, Sid Haig; **DIR:** Stephanie Rothman; **PROD:** Charles S. Swartz; **SCREENPLAY:** Stephanie Rothman, Charles S. Swartz; **STUDIO:** Trans America: 86 min., color (No video release)

MUSIC ★★★★
ATTITUDE ★★
FUN ★★★

The death knell of the beach movie?
Beach-movie regulars Tommy Kirk (*Mars Needs Women*) and Deborah Walley (*Gidget Goes Hawaiian*) play Mike and Delilah, rivals in a multi-event athletic contest. The slightly feminist story is complicated (just a little) when Mike puts on glasses to pose as his nerdy twin brother, "Herbert," so he can appeal to Delilah's intellectual side. Presiding over the contest is cult hero Sid *Spider Baby* Haig, who plays Daddy, a beatnik surf/rock capitalist based loosely on Ed "Big Daddy" Roth. *It's a Bikini World* was the first feature for director Stephanie Rothman, who later gained exploitation-film notoriety with such Roger Corman productions as *The Student Nurses* and *The Velvet Vampire.*

So, another flimsy-plot-with-rock-bands-doing-songs movie? Yep, but look at the lineup of musical talent: Memphis frat geeks the Gentrys, featuring future pro wrestling personality Jimmy Hart; the Animals in their post-Alan Price lineup; girl-group one-hitters the Toys trying their best to follow up "A Lover's Concerto"; Minneapolis's finest, the Castaways, doing the *Nuggets* classic "Liar, Liar"; *and* then-obscure, garage-rockin' Pat and Lolly Vegas, who would later become famous as the all-Indian rock band Redbone. The great Mike Curb-penned main title theme is a pounding, reverby surf instrumental (oddly rare in beach movies) and much beloved by aficionados of the genre. (JS)

IT'S TRAD, DAD (1962)

ALTERNATE TITLE: *Ring-A-Ding Rhythm*
CAST: Craig Douglas, Helen Shapiro, Felix Felton, Arthur Mullard, Alan Freeman; **DIR:** Richard Lester; **PROD:** Milton Subotsky; **SCREENPLAY:** Milton Subotsky: **STUDIO:** Columbia; 78 min., b/w (no video release)

MUSIC ★★★★
ATTITUDE ★★★★★
FUN ★★★★★

Footloose in the early '60s.
Richard Lester's first movie is nearly as much fun as *A Hard Day's Night*, containing almost as many jokes per shot as his subsequent Beatles movie—as well as a lot of dazzling camera tricks, besides. The pacing is quick, the attitude is cynical, and not even the clunky acting of Craig Douglas and Helen Shapiro can slow down the proceedings. Douglas and Shapiro play teenagers who put on a pop-and-jazz show to prevent the banning of pop and jazz music in their town. Among the acts that can be glimpsed at the show, Del Shannon is by far the most important. The trad jazz performers—including Mr. Acker Bilk, Kenny Ball, and the Temperance Seven—are all worthwhile, but they don't exactly rock out. Check out Lester's camera work, a dry run for *A Hard Day's Night,* instead. (BE)

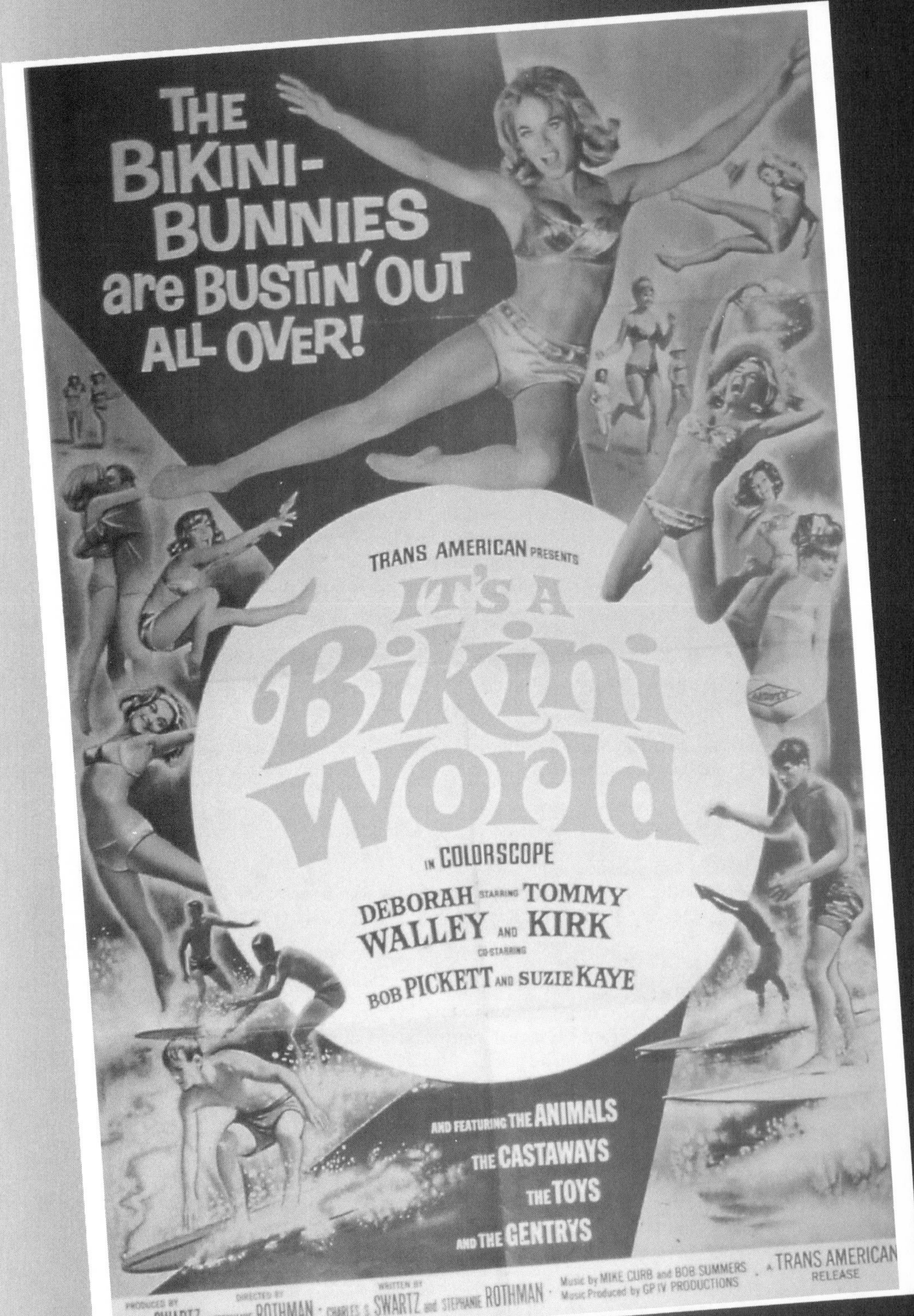
THE BIKINI-BUNNIES are BUSTIN' OUT ALL OVER!
TRANS AMERICAN PRESENTS
IT'S A Bikini World
IN COLORSCOPE
STARRING DEBORAH WALLEY AND TOMMY KIRK
CO-STARRING BOB PICKETT AND SUZIE KAYE
AND FEATURING THE ANIMALS
THE CASTAWAYS
THE TOYS
AND THE GENTRYS
PRODUCED BY CHARLES S. SWARTZ · DIRECTED BY STEPHANIE ROTHMAN · WRITTEN BY CHARLES S. SWARTZ and STEPHANIE ROTHMAN · Music by MIKE CURB and BOB SUMMERS Music Produced by GP IV PRODUCTIONS · A TRANS AMERICAN RELEASE

JAILHOUSE ROCK   (1957)

CAST: Elvis Presley, Judy Tyler, Mickey Shaughnessy, Dean Jones; DIR: Richard Thorpe; PROD: Pandro S. Berman; SCREENPLAY: Guy Trosper; STUDIO: MGM; 100 min., b/w (MGM/UA)

MUSIC ★★★
ATTITUDE ★★★★
FUN ★★

In which Elvis teaches us how to dress.

An early one, and it shows. Elvis was still a fresh face in Hollywood, and MGM hadn't quite worked out the kinks in his film persona yet. It may be difficult to imagine, but the Elvis in *Jailhouse Rock* is not a nice guy. Nor is he an innocent. Instead, Elvis plays a convict, serving a stretch of one-to-10 in the state pen for manslaughter. His big break comes when his cellmate (Mickey Shaughnessy), a former country-and-western star, features the kid in a prison revue. After he gets out, Elvis-the-country-singer flops. But Presley soon develops a new style, one with "some fire in it," that drives the local teenagers wild.

This Elvis vehicle is unusual in that it actually tries to make sense of both Presley's stardom and rock'n'roll's exciting, unexpected appeal. But *Jailhouse Rock* works best when it just lets the 23-year-old sensation do his thing. The tough guy Elvis plays probably owes more to the real-life Jerry Lee Lewis. But who other than Presley could have pulled off the often-imitated-but-never-duplicated "Jailhouse Rock" production number (1:10)? The boy had hips, and he knew how to use them. (DR)

Elvis's first on-screen haircut (0:10)   *SCENES*

Elvis grabs Judy Tyler, the prissy love interest, and kisses her. She pushes him *LINES*
away. "How do you think such cheap tactics would work on me?" she demands. "That ain't cheap tactics, honey," says Elvis. "That's the beast in me."

One More Day (Mickey Shaughnessy); *Young and Beautiful, I Wanna Be Free, Don't Leave Me*   *SONGS*
Now, Treat Me Nice, Jailhouse Rock, Baby I Don't Care (Elvis Presley)

JAMBOREE   (1957)

ALTERNATE TITLE: *Disc Jockey Jamboree*
CAST: Kay Medford, Robert Pastine, Freda Halloway, Paul Carr; DIR: Roy Lockwood; PROD: Max J. Rosenberg, Milton Subotsky; SCREENPLAY: Leonard Kantor; STUDIO: Warner; 71 min., b/w (no video release)

MUSIC ★★★
ATTITUDE ★★★
FUN ★★★★

A boy-girl singing team meets up with 16 other acts.

Why is this little-seen (and even less well known) exploitation film slightly better than its contemporaries? Partly because there's no message, and mainly because they booked two Sun acts. The irritating boy-girl duetting (Connie Francis ghost-sings the girl's parts) interrupts a forced mix of jazz (Count Basie), operatic-pop ("Toreador") rocking doo-wop (Louis Lymon, Frankie's little brother), and Fats Domino rock'n'roll ("Wait and See"). The Sun boys top it all off with some heavenly rockabilly. Carl Perkins turns in "Glad All Over"—NOT the Dave Clark Five song—and Jerry Lee Lewis performs an alternate take of "Great Balls of Fire." Sometime-rockers Buddy Knox, Jimmy Bowen, and Charlie Gracie don't fare as well here, and the so-called cameos in this movie are by 16 deejays from all over the globe. Warner Brothers must have thought their word-of-mouth would boost the picture. It didn't, but one of these record spinners, Joe Smith of WVDA in Boston, later became president of the Warner record label. (AF)

SONGS *A Broken Promise* (Four Coins); *Cool Baby* (Charlie Gracie); *Crazy to Care* (Mary Lou Harp); *Cross Over* (Jimmy Bowen); *For Children of All Ages, Siempre* (Connie Francis); *Glad All Over* (Carl Perkins); *Gone* (Louis Lymon and the Teenchords); *Great Balls of Fire* (Jerry Lee Lewis); *Hula Love* (Buddy Knox); *I Don't Like You No More* (Joe Williams); *If Not for You* (Paul Carr); *Jamboree, One O'Clock Jump* (Count Basie); *Record Hop Tonight* (Andy Martin); *Teacher's Pet* (Frankie Avalon, Rocco and the Saints); *Toreador* (Ron Colby); *Twenty Four Hours a Day, Who Are We to Say* (Paul Carr, Connie Francis); *Unchain My Heart* (Slim Whitman)

JANIS   (1975)

DIR: Howard Alk; PROD: Howard Alk, Seaton Findlay; STUDIO: Universal; 96 min., color (MCA)

MUSIC ★★★★
ATTITUDE ★★★
FUN ★★★

The best of Joplin's concert footage.

Back in 1975, in the days before *Hard Copy*, you didn't need a downfall theory to sell Janis Joplin's life story. In fact, you didn't even need a life story. All you needed was some good music, which is what *Janis* delivers. Forgoing such typical documentary elements as testimonial interviews and historical narration, *Janis* concentrates nearly exclusively on Joplin's emotional live performances. It's an approach that becomes more insightful each time Joplin moans and groans her way through one of the dozen songs included here. A *Cheap Thrills* recording session, her high school reunion, and clips from a European tour break up the live segments, but the best of the talk is delivered by Joplin on stage in deadly serious mid-song sermons on sex and work ethics. The 1970 clips suggest her poor health and upcoming demise, but producers Howard Alk and Seaton Findlay make no explicit reference to her slide from grace. Ultimately, the power and clarity of their portrait far outweighs any morbid speculation they might have offered on this count. (ALa)

SCENES Joplin's performance of "Move Over" on the Dick Cavett show and her witty couch chat with Dick (0:39); an argument between Joplin and Big Brother over the arrangement of "Summertime" (1:03)

LINES Cavett to Joplin: "You tore a muscle somewhere near Maryland?" Joplin: "It was a lot closer to home than that, honey!"

SONGS *Ball and Chain, Tell Mama, Kozmic Blues, Cry Baby, Try, Move Over, Comin' Home, Summertime, The Good Days, I Can't Turn You Loose, Me and Bobby McGee, Maybe, Piece of My Heart* (Janis Joplin)

JAZZ ON A SUMMER'S DAY   (1959)

DIR: Bert Stern; PROD: Bert Stern; SCREENPLAY: Arnold Perl, Albert D'Annidale; STUDIO: Raven/Galaxy Attractions; 85 min., color (New Yorker)

MUSIC ★★★★★
ATTITUDE ★★★★★
FUN ★★★★★

America the beautiful.

Jazz on a Summer's Day documents the 1958 Newport Jazz Festival (and, incidentally, the 1958 America's Cup trials). It's one of the most stylish, beautiful, and powerful musical films ever made, full of compelling moments and people who are cooler than Santa Claus. There are performances by R&B shouter Big Maybelle and Chuck Berry (our hero)—not to mention Mahalia Jackson, Dinah Washington, Anita O'Day, Louis Armstrong, and a dozen oother gods and goddesses of American culture. According to jazz historian Gary Giddins, Newport producers George Wein and John Hammond caught a lot of flak from purists for booking Berry. But Hammond rightly believed that Chuck was an absolutely unique stylist who was taking rhythm-and-blues in a brand new direction—combining the traditions of Muddy Waters, Louis Jordan, T-Bone Walker, and others in a way that smashed through stylistic and cultural barriers. (MC)

Janis

SCENES Chuck Berry has a longstanding reputation for treating pickup bands on the road like they don't exist (or barely deserve to). At this gig, he's got legends like Jo Jones and Jack Teagarden playing behind him, and nobody seems to know how to act. The hysterical, squeaking clarinet solo in the middle of "Sweet Little Sixteen" only twists things further out of shape.

All of Me (Dinah Washington); *Sweet Georgia Brown* (Anita O'Day); *Sweet Little Sixteen* (Chuck Berry); *Up a Lazy River, Tiger Rag* (Louis Armstrong); *Old Rockin' Chair, When the Saints* (Louis Armstrong, Jack Teagarden); *Didn't It Rain, The Lord's Prayer* (Mahalia Jackson)

JESUS CHRIST SUPERSTAR   (1973)

MUSIC ★
ATTITUDE ★★
FUN ★★

CAST: Ted Neeley, Carl Anderson, Yvonne Elliman, Barry Dennen, Joshua Mostel, Bob Bingham; DIR: Norman Jewison; PROD: Norman Jewison, Robert Stigwood; SCREENPLAY: Melvyn Bragg, Norman Jewison; STUDIO: Universal; 108 min., color (MCA)

It's a mixed-up world that embraced this thing and not Phil Spector's Christmas LP.
This picture (based on the "rock" opera by Tim Rice and Andrew Lloyd Webber) opens with a shot of ruins in the desert. A fuzz-tone guitar plays in the background—and thereafter, rock'n'roll is not heard from again. What proceeds is a stage musical—or opera, if your pretensions run that way. One argument for the "opera" tag is that there's no real dialogue here (although some songs are so wordy that they aren't really songs). It all comes down to Webber and Rice, who either please you or they don't. *Jesus Christ Superstar* is nice looking, certainly, and the bad guys conveniently wear black hats (so you can tell them from the good guys). But this biblical tale proves what Jerry Lee Lewis always suspected: that the devil has all the best tunes. (AF)

LINES "One thing I'll say for him, Jesus is cool."

JIMI HENDRIX   (1973)

MUSIC ★★★★
ATTITUDE ★★★★
FUN ★★★★

DIR: Gary Weis, Joe Boyd, John Head; PROD: Gary Weis, Joe Boyd, John Head; STUDIO: Warner; 102 min., color (Warner)

A documentary on the guitar maestro.
In this film, Pete Townshend says he and Eric Clapton first met and became friends because of their mutual admiration for Hendrix. Townshend also says that after Hendrix passed away, his friendship with Clapton faded, too. It's stories like this one that separate *Jimi Hendrix* from just about every artist-based rockumentary. *Jimi Hendrix* also features insightful commentary from people like the Allen twins (Arthur and Albert, the "Ghetto Fighters") and girlfriend/confidant Fayne Pridgeon, who knew Hendrix when he was scuffling and searching for his own identity. Released just three years after its subject's death, this film includes a wealth of interviews and over a dozen live clips, which serve to remind Hendrix diehards and newcomers alike that he reinvented the guitar each time he took the stage. Watching Hendrix prove it—as his friends and family ponder it all—is endlessly fascinating. Complete down to the still photographs that accompany the credits, *Jimi Hendrix* is truth in advertising—it delivers Jimi Hendrix. (ALa)

SCENES Townshend reveals that after an argument over who would follow whom at the Monterey Pop Festival (neither the Who nor Hendrix wanted to follow the other), Jimi vowed to "pull out all the stops." The rest is guitar-on-fire history (0:06).

Sax player Al Hendrix on his decision to keep making payments on his son's electric guitar: "I got behind on the sax and let it go because I knew he would do more with the guitar than I would with the sax."

Rock Me, Wild Thing, Voodoo Chile, Johnny B. Goode, Hey Joe, Purple Haze, Like a Rolling Stone, The Star-Spangled Banner, Machine Gun, Hear My Train a-Comin', Red House, In from the Storm (Jimi Hendrix)

JOEY (1985)

CAST: Neil Barry, James Quinn, Elisa Heinsohn, Ellen Hamill, Linda Thorson, Dan Grimaldi, Frankie Lanz; DIR: Joseph Ellison; PROD: Joseph Ellison; SCREENPLAY: Joseph Ellison; 97 min., color (Rock'n'Roll/Sartori)

MUSIC ★★★★
ATTITUDE ★★★★
FUN ★★★★

The Saturday Night Fever *of doo-wop.*
A washed-up doo-wop singer reunites with his son at a doo-wop revival—and steals the show. Doo-woppers, like Cajuns, are a hardy and isolated lot, little understood by outsiders. Likewise, this film, based on doo-wop, was a tough sell to a general audience, despite the inclusion of then-current New Wave music. But the film is a winner, with good acting, writing, and production. The music-fan filmmakers created *Joey* with an affection and commitment that speaks well for group harmony. (AF)

"Which Vito?"

The Boy from New York City (Ad Libs); *Daddy's Home* (Limelights); *Get a Job* (Silhouettes); *I Put a Spell on You* (Screamin' Jay Hawkins); *Little Star* (Elegants); *Why Do Fools Fall in Love?* (Teenagers); *Surfin' Bird* (Ramones); *Unchained Melody* (Vito Balsamo Group)

JOHNNY SUEDE (1991)

CAST: Brad Pitt, Catherine Keener, Calvin Levels, Alison Moir, Nick Cave, Tina Louise; DIR: Tom DiCillo; PROD: Yoram Mandel, Ruth Waldburger; SCREENPLAY: Tom DiCillo; STUDIO: Miramax; 97 min., color (Paramount)

MUSIC ★★★
ATTITUDE ★★
FUN ★★

Pompadours on parade.
Brad Pitt plays Johnny, a lovably naive daydreamer whose carefully cultivated '50s image includes retro clothing and an Esquerita-sized quiff. Johnny lives in a lonely hovel decorated with Ricky Nelson album jackets, bubble hair dryers, and other kitsch. Although his town looks a lot like New York, he laments that he can't find cool shoes anywhere—until one day when the perfect pair magically appears on the street. From then one, he calls himself... yep, Johnny Suede. In fantasies that follow, he delivers soliloquies on the fabric to fawning females: "Suede is a funny thing. It's rough, but it's soft. It's strong but quiet." In real life, while he avoids getting a job, he fronts a band that never seems to make it out of the rehearsal loft.

Then Johnny meets a spacey girl (Winona Ryder-lookalike Alison Moir), whose record-exec mom (Tina Louise, who played Ginger on "Gilligan's Island") expresses interest in his music. Alison only wonders why his tunes aren't more contemporary, like those of trendy, debauched rocker Freak Storm (expertly played by Nick Cave). Their affair quickly fizzles, leading Johnny to take up with a more normal woman, but his irresponsible ways and paranoid delusions mess up this relationship as well. In the end, Johnny finds himself alone, shoeless and band-less, with nobody to listen to such plaintive compositions as "I Ate a Carrot for Breakfast." The soundtrack includes "additional music" by Link Wray. (JS)

SCENES A disheveled Freak Storm regaling Johnny with a morbid ditty called "Freak's Mamma's Boy" before conning him out of $20 (presumedly for fix money)

SONGS *Never Girl, Midtown, Mamma's Boy* (Brad Pitt); *Freak's Mamma's Boy* (Nick Cave)

JOURNEY THROUGH THE PAST   (1973)

MUSIC ★★★★
ATTITUDE ★★★
FUN ★★

DIR: Bernard Shakey [Neil Young]; PROD: Frederic Underhill; STUDIO: New Line; 96 min., color (no video release)

Roll another number for the road.

The past must have seemed close behind him when Neil Young made this film, a series of concert clips loosely held together by pretentious narrative. With Crosby, Stills, and Nash over—and Crazy Horse on hold—Young found himself on his own, ready to live the hippie dream. In this film, the Stray Gators provide the musical net. Viewed two decades later, the film's concert footage is tremendous, documenting some amazingly understated performances in the wondrous career of this truly enigmatic performer. The rest of the time, life on the road clashes with the reality of life on the "journey." Interviews with Crosby, Stills, and Nash try to define the generation gap that was on everyone's mind at the time, but Young just plows through all the bullshit with his music. (TP)

SCENES CSN&Y performing "Southern Man" (0:23); Richard Nixon singing "God Bless America" (0:46); a guy taking his pickup truck for a walk on the beach as a troupe of masked crusaders, on horseback and carrying crosses, approach from behind the cliffs (1:03)

LINES Neil Young: "I don't do it for money; I get money for doing it." Stephen Stills: "We translate it into words in order to reassure ourselves. And someday the words, the reassurance by way of words, won't be necessary." Yeah.

SONGS *For What It's Worth, Mr. Soul, Rock and Roll Woman* (Buffalo Springfield); *Find the Cost of Freedom, Ohio, Southern Man* (Crosby, Stills, Nash, and Young); *Are You Ready for the Country, Alabama, Words, The Needle and the Damage Done* (Neil Young and the Stray Gators)

JUBILEE   (1978)

MUSIC ★★★
ATTITUDE ★★★★★
FUN ★★★★★

CAST: Jenny Runacre, Little Nell, Toyah Willcox, Adam Ant, Neil Kennedy, The Slits; DIR: Derek Jarman; SCREENPLAY: Derek Jarman; STUDIO: Whaley-Mailin; 101 min., color (Mystic Fire)

The picture that put Derek Jarman on the map.

Essentially a fantasy, *Jubilee* involves the teleportation of Queen Elizabeth I from Shakespearean times to Britain on the eve of Margaret Thatcher's election. Once in present-day England, Liz I encounters the anarchy, violence, and decadence of the period. We're not talking *Rock Around the Clock* here, but a fiercely inventive piece of filmmaking timed to coincide with Queen Elizabeth II's silver jubilee. Jarman's picture makes dazzling use of punk and early New Wave music in a series of nicely intercut performance clips. Suzi Pims's delivery of "Rule Brittania" is a stitch, but the most outrageous performance of them all is Wayne County's "Paranoia Paradise." Plot and continuity are occasionally disjointed, and *Jubilee's* lapses into lyricism can be even more jarring than its frantic anarchy. But overall, this may be the most sophisticated use ever made of the rock culture in a serious film setting. (BE)

Right to Work (Chelsea); *Paranoia Paradise* (Wayne County and the Electric Chairs); *Love in a Void* (Siouxsie and the Banshees); *Wargasm in Pornotopia* (Amilcar); *Jerusalem, Rule Brittania* (Suzi Pims)   **SONGS**

JUKE BOX RHYTHM   (1959)

Cast: Jack Jones, Susan Morrow, Brian Donlevy, Hans Conried, Marjorie Reynolds; DIR: Arthur Dreifuss; PROD: Sam Katzman; SCREENPLAY: Mary McCall Jr., Earl Baldwin; STUDIO: Columbia; 81 min., b/w (no video release)

Falling in love with rock'n'roll.
This is one of the most perfectly silly movies ever to come out of the Sam Katzman exploitation mill, primarily due to its ridiculous plot. Susan Morrow plays a princess visiting the Big Apple who falls for rock'n'roll and its personification, aspiring singer Jack Jones (you've been warned). Meanwhile, Jones is busy getting his father's stage show off the ground and his estranged parents back together again. If you can ignore Jones's awkward crooning, sit back and enjoy the Earl Grant Trio's smooth, polished R&B performances as well as the harder sounds of the Treniers and Johnny Otis. (BE)

Juke Box Rhythm, The Freeze, Make Room for Joy (Jack Jones); *I Feel It Right Here, Last Night* (Earl   **SONGS**
Grant Trio); *Willie and the Hand Jive* (Johnny Otis); *Get Out of the Car* (Treniers)

JUST FOR FUN   (1963)

CAST: Mark Wynter, Cherry Roland, Richard Vernon, Reginald Beckwith, Jeremy Lloyd, Jimmy Savile, Bobby Vee, The Crickets, The Springfields, Jet Harris, Tony Meehan, Joe Brown and the Bruvvers, The Tornadoes, Brian Poole and the Tremoloes. DIR: Gordon Fleming; PROD: Milton Subotsky; SCREENPLAY: Milton Subotsky; STUDIO: Columbia; 84 min., b/w (no video release)

Early-'60s British rockers rally 'round the flag.
This follow-up to director Richard Lester's *It's Trad, Dad* retains none of that film's care or pacing, nor are the performance clips half as clever. But *Just for Fun* does stuff in a lot of music—all rock this time, no jazz. The plot, such as it is, con-

cerns the upcoming parliamentary elections as the Conservatives ("We Never Had It So Good") and the Labor party ("We Never Had It") compete for the teenage vote. The twist is that the teens form their own political party (thus anticipating the plot of the much-better-known *Wild in the Streets*). The youth party's rallies provide the producers with the plot device they needed to load up on contemporary rock acts, some of which are pretty good here. The Springfields, featuring Dusty Springfield, perform a gorgeous, calypso-styled number called "Little Boat," while Joe Brown shines on "What's the Name of the Game," and the Crickets reprise both sides of their then-current British single. Also included are a host of pre-British invasion acts, including Karl Denver, the Tornadoes, and former Shadows Jet Harris and Tony Meehan. Unlike *It's Trad, Dad,* which was genuinely funny, *Just for Fun* relies entirely on music to keep the viewer engaged. The script has some good lines (one sketch involving a political pollster and a housewife is worthy of Monty Python), but director Fleming holds all of his shots just a beat too long, which blows the comedy out of the water. (BE)

SONGS *Just for Fun* (Cherry Roland); *Vote for Me, I'm Happy with You* (Mark Wynter); *Man from Nowhere* (Jet Harris and the Jet Blacks); *Sweet Boy* (Clodagh Rogers); *Let Her Go, What's the Name of the Game* (Joe Brown and the Bruvvers); *All on a Warm Summer Day* (Ketty Lester); *I Gotta Get Up Early in the Morning* (Freddie Cannon); *Touch Me, The Night Has a Thousand Eyes* (Bobby Vee); *Crazy Crazes, Monument* (Kenny Lynch); *Everybody but You* (Jimmy Powell); *Kisses Can Lie* (Lyn Cornell); *Go* (Sounds Incorporated); *Keep On Dancin'* (Brian Poole and the Tremoloes); *Lyin' to You* (Karl Denver); *Which Way the Wind Blows* (Louise Corday); *Little Boat* (Springfields); *Hully Gully* (Jet Harris, Tony Meehan); *Just Another Girl* (Vernon Girls); *All the Stars in the Sky* (Tornadoes); *My Bonnie Lies Over the Ocean* (Spotniks); *My Little Girl, Teardrops Fall Like Rain* (Crickets); *Just for Fun* (Mark Wynter, Cherry Roland)

KID GALAHAD   (1962)

MUSIC ★★★
ATTITUDE ★★★
FUN ★★★★

CAST: Elvis Presley, Gig Young, Lola Albright, Joan Blackman, Charles Bronson; **DIR:** Phil Karlson; **PROD:** Hall B. Wallis; **SCREENPLAY:** William Fay; **STUDIO:** Paramount.; 95 min., color (MGM/UA)

Elvis as a boxer.

This film, one of Elvis's more enduring efforts, employs a time-honored plot device—the underdog boxer—that has served actors well from James Garfield to Sylvester Stallone. In *Kid Galahad,* Elvis plays Walter Goolie, a recently discharged soldier who returns to his birthplace to discover his roots and make a new life for himself. Having left town after being orphaned in infancy, Walter comes back to Cream Valley, N.Y. with plans to open an auto repair ship. What he finds is a curious hodgepodge of ethnicities. Right next door to Leiberman's vacation lodge is the Gaelic Gardens, where fighters come to train for the ring.

Needing some money, Walter reluctantly agrees to box for the owner of the Gaelic Gardens (Gig Young), a gambling ne'er-do-well who's in deep trouble with some thugs. Despite the rigors of his training, Walter still finds time to fall in love with Willie's sister, fix everyone's car, sing a bunch of great pop songs, and earn the respect and love of the entire town with his chivalrous (hence the name Galahad) ways. The climax, of course, is the Big Fight, which Walter can't possibly win. Or can he? *Kid Galahad*'s subtext is about different cultures getting along, so it's unfortunate that Walter's opponent, Romero, has to be the "bad" immigrant who speaks a foreign language and is a little too dark. Still, Elvis charms in this warmhearted, simplistic story about melting-pot America. (TM)

SONGS *King of the Whole Wide World, This Is Living, Riding the Rainbow, Home Is Where the Heart Is, I Got Lucky, A Whistling Tune* (Elvis Presley)

THE KIDS ARE ALRIGHT   (1979)

DIR: Jeff Stein; PROD: Bill Curbishley, Tony Klinger; STUDIO: New World; 96 min., color (HBO)

MUSIC ★★★★★
ATTITUDE ★★★★★
FUN ★★★★

A Who fanzine on film.

Beginning in 1965, the Who were the most outrageous and unique band in rock'n'roll. Years ahead of the game in bringing violence, drama, and black humor to British rock, they sang songs about masturbation, crossdressing, drugs, revolution, and baked beans. About 1969, however, their hit singles began to dry up, so the band had to change with the times and adopt a more self-conscious, self-serious approach. It worked, and to this day, the Who are loved by millions (of Americans, mostly). The group never lost its sense of spectacle, and *The Kids Are Alright* testifies to that in recalling 14 years' worth of their greatest flops and triumphs. The film's entirely uncritical viewpoint is obviously that of a diehard fan, so some (perhaps more discriminating) Who fans will watch this with a finger on, or near, the fast-forward control. There's plenty of good music and excitement here, but there's also an underlying sense of melancholy: Keith Moon's decline is vividly on display here, and it's sad to see him devolve from an intensely alive force of nature (and drummer extraordinaire) to a ravaged, bloated burn-out case. It'll give you the blues. Keith, what happened? (MC)

Tommy Smothers, Ringo Starr, Steve Martin   CAMEOS

My Generation, Can't Explain, Shove and Shimmy, Baba O'Reilly, Young Man Blues, Pinball Wizard, Tommy Can You Hear Me, See Me Feel Me, Anyway Anyhow Anywhere, Success Story, Substitute, I'm a Boy, Heat Wave, Pictures of Lily, I Can See for Miles, Magic Bus, Happy Jack, A Quick One, Cobwebs Are Strange, Sparks, Barbara Ann, Roadrunner, Who Are You, Won't Get Fooled Again, Long Live Rock (Who)   SONGS

The Kids Are Alright

KING CREOLE (1958)

MUSIC ★★★★
ATTITUDE ★★★★
FUN ★★★★★

CAST: Elvis Presley, Carolyn Jones, Walter Matthau, Dean Jagger, Dolores Hart, Vic Morrow, Liliane Montevecchi; DIR: Michael Curtiz; PROD: Hal B. Wallis; SCREENPLAY: Herbert Baker, Michael Vincente Gazzo; STUDIO: Paramount; 151 min., b/w (Key)

Elvis is almost evil. What a shock!
From the King's opening duet ("Crawfish") with a street vendor, this early Elvis film offers a taste of the sensual playfulness that made him a rock'n'roll star. It's obvious that Elvis hasn't been "fixed" yet into the good-guy eunuch of his later films. In *King Creole*, he plays Danny Fisher, a rebellious high school dropout who's got problems with his wimpy father. Looking for a stronger role model, Danny gets involved with crooked nightclub owner Maxie Fields (Walter Matthau) and his beautiful "ruined" girlfriend. In order to help make Danny's delinquency credible, the script has him rip off a drugstore and participate in a mugging. He also tries to trick the good girl into sleeping with him, while his real emotional and sexual attachment is to the "wrong" girl. Predictably, Danny becomes a singer, foils Maxie's plot to ensnare him, reconciles with his father, and hooks up eventually with the virtuous damsel. For a few moments, though, it's fun to imagine how good a bad Elvis could have been. (TM)

SCENES Elvis playing a guitar in a drugstore while his partners rob the place (0:23); Presley singing "I'm Evil" at the Club Creole (0:51)

LINES Elvis: "God didn't give you those charms for what you're using them for." The bad girl: "That's funny, and I read the instructions so carefully."

SONGS *Crawfish* (Elvis Presley, Kitty White); *Let Me Be Your Lover Boy, I'm Evil, Itchy-Handed Rock, Young Dreams of Love, In New Orleans, Hard-Headed Woman, King Creole, Don't Ask Me Why, As Long as I Have You* (Elvis Presley)

KISS MEETS THE PHANTOM OF THE PARK (1978)

MUSIC ★★★★
ATTITUDE ★★
FUN ★★★

CAST: KISS, Anthony Zerbe; DIR: Gordon Hessler; PROD: Terry Morse Jr.; SCREENPLAY: Jan-Michael Sherman, Don Buday; STUDIO: Hanna-Barbera; 96 min., color (Goodtimes)

Star Wars *plus heavy metal plus Hanna-Barbera equals...*
When this made-for-TV feature was conceived, KISS were at their most platinum—having conquered records, live concerts, and even comic books. Taking a break from recording their solo albums, the band got together with Hanna-Barbera to make a silly, cheesy, and fun movie that's in every way a product of its time. The Kabuki-clad foursome make their entrance as flying, lightning bolt-hurling super beings who just happen to double as a rock band booked into a large amusement park (L.A.'s Magic Mountain). When the mad scientist who designed the park (Anthony Zerbe) gets fired, he creates evil-twin KISS robots, who replace the real band on stage in order to incite an apocalyptic riot.

This plot must have seemed juvenile even to the band's young fans, and the film's television origins are all too obvious (funky *Starsky and Hutch*-type music is played during the fight scenes). Still, *KISS Meets the Phantom* has a goofy charm. Although untrained, the band members (with their Noo Yawk accents intact) make earnest actors, and they play a number of songs, both hits and otherwise unavailable material. (A planned double soundtrack album never materialized.) Throughout the film, Peter Criss's speaking voice is actually that of an uncredited actor because Criss didn't bother to show up for the overdubbing sessions. (JS)

An entire audience in halter tops and T-shirts (the "KISS Army") is entranced by the hypnotizing lyrics of the bogus robot band. As the crowd chants along to "Rip and Destroy" (actually the KISS standard "Hotter Than Hell" with new lyrics), the real KISS members arrive just in time to defeat their lookalike foes. A victorious Paul Stanley asks triumphantly, "Are you ready for the real KISS? Are you READY TO ROCK'N'ROLL?" The ecstatic, now "normal" mob roars its approval—and looks scarier than ever.

SCENES

Wide-eyed girl: "What's that humming?" Gene Simmons: "It's a cosmic forcefield that protects our talisman." Girl: "Pretty mystical!"

LINES

Shout It Out Loud, I Stole Your Love, Beth, Rip and Destroy, Rock and Roll All Nite (KISS)

SONGS

KISSIN' COUSINS (1964)

CAST: Elvis Presley, Arthur O'Connell, Glenda Farrell, Jack Albertson, Pam Austin, Cynthia Pepper; DIR: Gene Nelson; PROD: Sam Katzman; SCREENPLAY: Gerald Drayson Adams; STUDIO: MGM; 96 min., color (MGM/UA)

MUSIC ★★★★
ATTITUDE ★★★★
FUN ★★★★★

Elvis fights heroically for a nuclear missile site.

Imagine a Tennessee mountain populated almost entirely by horny young ladies searching wildly for romance. What's missing from this picture? Elvis, of course. Actually, there are so many horny young ladies that two Elvises are required. *Kissin' Cousins* stars Elvis as army officer Josh Morgan, who's sent to the Smokey Mountains to negotiate with the local hillbillies for an ICBM base. Josh soon runs into his lookalike (but rather dense) cousin Jodie Tatum (also played by Elvis) in the lady-laden hills, where lots of fightin', drinkin', shootin', singin', and kissin' follow in rapid succession. Later, Pappy Tatum (Arthur O'Connell) and Captain Salbo (Jack Albertson from "Chico and the Man") match wits (sort of) over whether the army gets the lease to the land.

The humor is dumb, the gags are predictable, and the storyline is thin. But, hey, *Kissin' Cousins* has a certain nonnuclear charm all its own. In one scene, the army gives purdy underwear (bikinis) to all the mountain girls as a bribe to win them over. The girls try on the gifts right away and then flail around a lot. There's also a big blowout during which everybody gets hell-bent drunk on Pappy's moonshine, which he calls Mountain Maiden's Breath. "And you want me to give up this life for a miserable missile base?" Pappy slurs. Charm indeed. (MB)

"ICBM," says Josh, trying to describe the missile to Pappy. "You see B.M.?" says Pappy. "I don't see a thing,"

LINES

Maureen Reagan

CAMEOS

Kissin' Cousins, Smokey Mountain Boy, One Boy Two Little Girls, Catchin' On Fast, Tender Feeling, Barefoot Ballad, Once Is Enough, Pappy Won't You Please Come Home (Elvis Presley); *Kissin' Cousins* (Glenda Farrell)

SONGS

LA BAMBA (1987)

CAST: Lou Diamond Phillips, Esai Morales, Rosana De Soto, Elizabeth Pena, Danielle Von Zerneck; DIR: Luis Valdez; PROD: Taylor Hackford, Bill Borden; SCREENPLAY: Luis Valdez; STUDIO: Columbia; 103 min., color (RCA/Columbia)

MUSIC ★★★★
ATTITUDE ★★★
FUN ★★★★

La Bamba

What goes up must come down.
Ritchie Valens's eight-month professional career ended in the well-documented Buddy Holly plane crash. But during those eight months, Valens carved out a commercial and critical niche that has outlasted the "Chicano rock pioneer" tag. Certainly, there's more to Valens's catalogue than his reinterpretation of the Mexican folk classic "La Bamba," but Los Lobos' Number One cover did introduce Valens's work to a new audience almost 30 years after his death. Few biopictures tell a performer's story with the clarity and warmth of *La Bamba*. Its fine screenplay supports the career-making performances of Lou Diamond Phillips (in his motion-picture debut) as Ritchie and Esai Morales as Ritchie's alcoholic brother Bobby. The use screenwriter Luis Valdez makes of their sibling rivalry helps *La Bamba* escape the fetters of biopic into the land of real drama. (ALa)

CAMEOS Los Lobos, Brian Setzer, Marshall Crenshaw (as Buddy Holly)

SONGS *Rip It Up, Charlena, Oh Boy, Ooh My Head, Framed, The Paddywack Song, We Belong Together, Come On Let's Go, Donna, La Bamba* (Los Lobos)

LADIES AND GENTLEMEN, THE FABULOUS STAINS (1982)

CAST: Diane Lane, Ray Winstone, Laura Dern, Marin Kanter, Fee Waybill, Steve Jones, Paul Cook, Paul Simenon; DIR: Lou Adler; PROD: Joe Roth; SCREENPLAY: Rob Morton; STUDIO: Paramount; 87 min., color (no video release)

MUSIC ★★★
ATTITUDE ★★
FUN ★★★★

Diane Lane invents punk.
Here's an odd project! Diane Lane, Laura Dern and Marin Kanter play the Fabulous Stains, an all-girl rock trio that sounds like the Shaggs, minus drums, recorded by Rough Trade Records. They somehow wind up on tour with an aging hard-rock band, the Metal Corpses (fronted by Fee Waybill of the Tubes), and British punk band the Looters (portrayed by actor Ray Winstone, former Sex Pistols Steve Jones and Paul Cook, and Clash bassist Paul Simenon!). Playing Corinne Burns, the Stains' rebellious leader, Lane tries out a two-tone hairstyle as she taunts her unreceptive audiences with slogans like "We don't put out!" Given TV exposure by an ambitious anchorwoman, the Fab Stains become a hot new fad among disenfranchised teenage girls, who label themselves "skunks" and emulate Corinne's Siouxsie-meets-late-'70s-mall-teen fashion concepts. When the Looters' front man berates an arena full of skunks for being mindless consumers, the crowd turns angry and the Fabulous Stains' instant success comes crashing down. But the

problem is only temporary. A closing montage of magazine covers lets us know that the girls bounce right back to the top.

Ladies and Gentlemen, the Fabulous Stains includes some clever satire of TV magazine shows and happytalk news programs, but most of this rock movie rings hollow and false. Lane's female, Americanized Johnny Rotten character makes surly pronouncements that are cartoonishly simple and arrogant (although maybe that's the point), and a tantrum thrown by the band's mellow, Rastafarian bus driver (Don Letts inspired?) is unintentionally hilarious ("T'is bus is-a *my* ting, mon. Nobody know I come to dis country to play-a *reggae music*.... Jah! *Rastafari,* mon!"). Waybill steals the show as the burned-out heavy metal singer, while the real punk rockers mostly stay in the background, occasionally calling each other "wanker" or "you tosser!" (However, Cook and Jones did write all of the Looters' songs.) Director Lou Adler, who produced *The Rocky Horror Picture Show,* probably thought he had another cult hit on his hands. Actually, the movie made its debut on cable TV before playing briefly in art houses several years later. (JS)

SCENES L.A. punk band Black Randy and the Metrosquad (whose album was called *Pass the Dust, I Think I'm Bowie*) performing at an audition

SONGS *Join the Professionals, Conned Again* (Looters); *Road Map of My Tears* (Metal Corpses); *Waste of Time, Join the Professionals* (Fabulous Stains); *I Slept in an Arcade* (Black Randy and the Metrosquad)

THE LAST WALTZ   (1978)

DIR: Martin Scorsese; **PROD:** Robbie Robertson; **STUDIO:** United Artists; 117 min., color (MGM/UA)

MUSIC ★★★★★
ATTITUDE ★★
FUN ★★★

A Thanksgiving harvest of heavyweights
On Thanksgiving Day in 1976, the Band gave its farewell concert at San Francisco's Winterland ballroom. Director Martin Scorsese had agreed to film the show just six weeks before. The result was one of the greatest rock'n'roll documentaries to date. The directorial genius of Scorsese (who keyed his shooting script to the lyrics and chord changes of each song), the superb cinematography of Michael Chapman, and the sheer wealth of its musical talent enable *The Last Waltz* to sail over any weak spots. It's rewarding viewing, even for non-Band fans. The film alternates the songs of such guest stars as Neil Young, Bob Dylan, Ronnie Hawkins, and Van Morrison (each backed by the Band) with the group's own numbers. (The atmospheric studio performances of the Staple Singers and Emmylou Harris were filmed later.) Between musical sequences, Scorsese interviews Band members Robbie Robertson, Levon Helm, Rick Danko, Garth Hudson, and the late Richard Manuel (who committed suicide in 1986). Robertson, the film's producer, gets the most screen time. His bandmates seem bemused, reticent, pissed off, or simply stoned to the gills. (AS)

SCENES Robbie and Levon recalling their first trip to New York City (0:53) and an Arkansas encounter with Sonny Boy Williamson (1:05); Garth Hudson talking about how he countered his parents' objections to a rock'n'roll career by posing as the group's "music teacher" (1:27)

SONGS *Don't Do It, Up on Cripple Creek, The Shape I'm In, It Makes No Difference, Stage Fright, The Night They Drove Old Dixie Down, Ophelia* (Band); *Who Do You Love* (Ronnie Hawkins); *Such a Night* (Dr. John); *Helpless* (Neil Young); *The Weight* (Staples); *Dry Your Eyes* (Neil Diamond); *Coyote* (Joni Mitchell); *Mystery Train* (Paul Butterfield); *Manish Boy* (Muddy Waters); *Further On up the Road* (Eric Clapton); *Evangeline* (Emmylou Harris); *Caravan* (Van Morrison); *Forever Young, Baby Let Me Follow You Down* (Bob Dylan); *I Shall Be Released* (Ringo Starr, Ron Wood, Cast)

LIB

LET IT BE (1970)

MUSIC ★★★★★
ATTITUDE ★★★★★
FUN ★★★★★

CAST: Paul McCartney, John Lennon, George Harrison, Ringo Starr; DIR: Michael Lindsay-Hogg; PROD: Neil Aspinall; STUDIO: Apple; 80 min., color (Magnetic)

A sad piece of cinema verité about the final days of the Beatles.

Filmed on location at Apple and Twickenham Film Studios, *Let It Be* is rather hard to watch. It's obvious that things with the Beatles are strained at this point (witness the Paul McCartney/George Harrison creative squabble) and the enthusiasm and magic that propelled the band's career is somewhat dimmed. There are, however, still moments of absolute brilliance as the Fab Four bang out songs and reminisce. Yoko Ono is a cloying presence as John Lennon's silent, somewhat useless appendage throughout the film's entirety.

The final moments of film (starting at 0:59) are the band's legendary lunchtime performance on the roof of Apple. It was the first time the band had played together in three years and would also be the last. Things go along quite swimmingly until the chief officer of a nearby bank calls in the cops and has the impromptu performance shut down. Kind of makes you wonder if that guy ever had any idea what he put an end to. (EC)

SCENES John Lennon and Yoko Ono waltzing in the studio to "I, Me, Mine" (0:22); cool footage of people watching the rooftop performance, including a man in a bowler hat with a pipe climbing onto a nearby roof to watch (0:59)

LINES Paul on the Beatles' Maharishi entanglement: "What were we doing? I don't really remember, but we totally sort of put our own personalities over. We weren't sort of really very truthful there." John closing the band's rooftop performance: "I'd like to say thank you on behalf of the group and I hope we passed the audition."

CAMEOS Bill Wyman

SONGS *Don't Let Me Down, Maxwell's Silver Hammer, Two of Us, I've Got a Feeling, Oh Darling, The One After 909, Across the Universe, I Me Mine, For You Blue, Besame Mucho, Octopus's Garden, You Really Got a Hold on Me, The Long and Winding Road, Shake Rattle and Roll, Kansas City, Let It Be, Get Back, I Dig a Pony* (Beatles)

LET THE GOOD TIMES ROLL (1973)

MUSIC ★★★★★
ATTITUDE ★★★★★
FUN ★★★★★

DIR: Sid Levin & Robert Abel; PROD: Gerald I. Isenberg; STUDIO: Columbia; 98 min., color (Polygram)

One of the best concert movies ever made.

Let the Good Times Roll intercuts '50s documentary footage with latter-day performance clips. In 1973, Richard Nader brought together the greatest names in '50s rock for a reunion show in front of an extremely supportive New York audience. (As Fred Parris of the Five Satins exclaims tearfully, "This is just like 1956.") The result leaves the viewer stunned, drained, and speechless. It's Woodstock, only in reverse. Little Richard's nervous demand that his piano be moved forward ("I have to get close to the PEOPLE!"), the Five Satins singing blues backstage, Chuck Berry's nostalgic walk around his tour bus, and Bo Diddley's metal-mashing "Hey Bo Diddley" all make this indispensable viewing. Brutally, *Let the Good Times Roll* was released right on top of *American Graffiti*, which stole all its thunder. But the people who knew, knew. (AF)

Describing Bo Diddley: "If it wasn't for him, we'd be back listening to *LINES*
Beethoven!"

Rob Reiner (introducing the Coasters) *CAMEOS*

At the Hop (Danny and the Juniors); *Blueberry Hill, My Blue Heaven* (Fats Domino); *Charlie* *SONGS*
Brown, Poison Ivy (Coasters); *Everybody Loves a Lover, Soldier Boy* (Shirelles); *Good Golly Miss*
Molly, Lucille, Rip It Up (Little Richard); *Hey Bo Diddley, I'm a Man* (Bo Diddley); *I'll Be Seeing*
You, Save the Last Dance for Me/Sincerely/Earth Angel/In the Still of the Nite (Five Satins); *Let's*
Twist Again, Pony Time, The Twist (Chubby Checker); *Rock Around the Clock, Shake Rattle and*
Roll (Bill Haley and the Comets)

LET'S ROCK! (1958)

ALTERNATE TITLE: *Keep It Cool*
CAST: Julius La Rosa, Phyllis Newman, Conrad Janis, Julie Harmon; **DIR:** Harry Foster; **PROD:**
Harry Foster; **SCREENPLAY:** Hal Hackady; **STUDIO:** Columbia; 79 min., b/w (no video release)

MUSIC ★★★
ATTITUDE ★★★
FUN ★★★

An urban greaseball operetta.

Here's one more '50s rock movie with a non-rock lead, formulaic plot, and a
mixed bag of musical guests designed in a misguided attempt to appeal to movie-
goers of all ages. But despite all that, *Let's Rock!* exudes a certain greasy charm that
sets it apart. Its distinctive East Coast feel and generous location shots of
Manhattan support the film's appealingly schlocky yet street-smart talent roster.
Featured here are Danny and the Juniors, Roy Hamilton (doing a soundalike follow-up to "Don't Let Go"), a young and cocksure Paul Anka, and the fabulously
Brooklyn-accented Royal Teens (with future Four Season Bob Gaudio but not Al
Kooper, who hadn't joined yet). Payola notwithstanding, this movie gives a fairly
realistic look at the music biz as it operated during the late '50s.

Sinatra-imitator Julius La Rosa plays Tommy Adano, a singer of smooth ballads who finds his popularity plummeting thanks to the new craze for rock'n'roll.
Tommy's manager keeps trying to persuade him to try his hand at the rock game

Let's Rock

("There's gold in them thar triplets!"), but the proud crooner refuses. His stubbornness costs him the support of his record label, TV dance party host Wink Martindale, and his songwriter girlfriend (Phyllis Newman). Finally, Tommy relents and records "Crazy Crazy Party" with a performance that recalls Sinatra's own token rave-up, "Castle Rock." As usual, rock'n'roll saves the day. (JS)

SCENES   Modern-day grinning robot game-show host Wink Martindale (then a disc jockey) puts his all into singing the wild rockabilly number "All Love Broke Loose."

LINES   Tommy's manager giving him a prophetic lecture: "When you gonna come to the party? Rock'n'roll's been around a long time. It's gonna be around a lot longer."

SONGS   *Blast-Off* (Tyrones); *I'm Still Waiting for You* (Paul Anka); *Two Perfect Strangers, Casual, There Are Times, Crazy Crazy Party* (Julius La Rosa); *All Love Broke Loose* (Wink Martindale); *Here Comes Love, Pathway of Love* (Roy Hamilton); *Short Shorts* (Royal Teens); *At the Hop* (Danny and the Juniors); *Lonelyville* (Della Reese)

LIGHT OF DAY (1987)

MUSIC ★★
ATTITUDE ★★
FUN ★★★

CAST: Michael J. Fox, Gena Rowlands, Joan Jett, Michael McKean; DIR: Paul Schrader; PROD: Rob Cohen, Keith Barish; SCREENPLAY: Paul Schrader; STUDIO: Tri-Star; 107 min., color (Vestron)

Joan Jett and Michael J. Fox form a rock'n'roll band.
Light of Day is all about the relationship between a dying mother (Gena Rowlands) and her two aspiring rock star children (Michael J. Fox, Joan Jett). The kids' rock'n'roll hardships could have been an exciting point of conflict in this film, set in Cleveland. Instead, the rock'n'roll serves as little more than a convenient excuse to develop Jett's rebellious past. Perhaps it's just as well, because the fictional Barbusters make the same painful racket that we've come to expect from Fox whenever he picks up a guitar. There are some nice touches: the casting of Spinal Tap's Michael McKean as the Barbusters' bassist, a Bruce Springsteen-penned title song, some realistic low-budget tour sequences. But these rock trappings pale in comparison to the moving bedside performances of Fox and Jett. If only Oscar-winning screenwriter Paul (*Taxi Driver*) Schrader had left out the fake rock posing and instead used a simpler plot device, like athletics or drug addiction, this heartfelt project might have lived. (ALa)

CAMEOS   The Fabulous Thunderbirds, Trent Reznor.

SONGS   *Rude Mood, Doo Wah Diddy Diddy* (Michael J. Fox, Michael McKean, Paul Harkins); *This Means War, It's All Coming Down Tonight, Light of Day* (Barbusters); *Twist It Off* (Fabulous Thunderbirds); *Sweet Emotion* (Joan Jett); *Rescue Me* (Motion); *Rabbit's Got the Gun* (Joan Jett and the Hunzz); *True Love Ways* (Trent Reznor)

LIVE A LITTLE, LOVE A LITTLE (1968)

MUSIC ★★
ATTITUDE ★★
FUN ★★★★

CAST: Elvis Presley, Michele Carey, Don Porter, Rudy Vallee, Dick Sargent; DIR: Norman Taurog; PROD: Douglas Laurence; SCREENPLAY: Michael A. Hoey, Dan Greenburg; STUDIO: MGM; 89 min., color (MGM/UA)

The cinematography steals the show.
Veteran B-movie director Norman Taurog goes a bit crazy in this film—which is chock full of pans, dissolves, and odd camera sequences that relieve the plot's predictability, but not enough. Elvis stars as Greg Nolan, a dashing photographer

who meets a girl and her dog on the beach. As the girl who keeps changing her name, Michele Carey acts in a manner that's supposed to be whimsical and charming in a zany, '60s sort of way. But it's really annoying in every sort of way. At first, Greg is perplexed, and then—gosh—he's smitten by her. Greg's photography job allows Taurog to create some surprising visual mise-en-scènes, which is sometimes dated and trite but at other times quite elegant. Famed 1920s crooner Rudy Vallee appears as one of Greg's bosses, and it's amusing to see the two master songsters play against each other. Otherwise, Elvis does a terrible job with a god-awful script. He mugs unmercifully as the straight man for the fey Carey, and the songs he sings aren't much better. One of them has the following lyrics: "I'm on the edge of reality/That girl keeps tormenting me/The girl with the nameless name." Yeah, man. Crazy. (TM)

A very mod snapshot sequence of Elvis in the ocean (0:06); a great circular camera wipe that looks like a clock with Elvis in the middle (0:10); Elvis's dream in which the dog speaks to him (0:29)   **SCENES**

Rudy Vallee to Elvis: "You want to make it in advertising, right? Then you have to rise above personal problems. Personal appearance—that's what matters!"   **LINES**

Wonderful World, Edge of Reality, A Little Less Convention, Almost in Love (Elvis Presley)   **SONGS**

LIVE IT UP   (1963)

CAST: David Hemmings, Steve Marriott, Jennifer Moss, Veronica Hurst, Heinz Burt and the Tornadoes, Kenny Ball and his Jazzmen, Joan Newell, David Bauer, Patsy Ann Noble, Gene Vincent, Sounds Incorporated, The Outlaws, Andy Cavell and the Saints; DIR: Lance Comfort; PROD: Lance Comfort; SCREENPLAY: Lynn Fairhurst; STUDIO: Rank; 75 min., b/w (no video release)

MUSIC ★★★★
ATTITUDE ★★★★
FUN ★★★★

Brit-beat's peak.
David Hemmings plays an aspiring rock'n'roller whose band happens to include Tornadoes bassist Heinz Burt and future Small Faces guitarist Steve Marriott. Hemmings has only a month to succeed in rock'n'roll before his father forces him to take a "real" job. Despite a series of misadventures (including losing the demo tape of "Live It Up"), Hemmings manages to avoid real work when he makes good at an accidental audition. The film's plot is none too realistic, but its music (directed by Joe Meek) and the selection of bands that appear are superior. The Tornadoes provide most of the instrumental background tracks, and look out for the Outlaws with a young Ritchie Blackmore on lead guitar.

The missing link between two eras of British pop music, and a testament to Meek's insight, *Live It Up* captures the feel of the innocent (and somewhat prefabricated) world of '50s British pop without ignoring the changes that are already underway. Meek, who was Britain's first independent record producer, composed and produced nine of the 12 songs on the soundtrack, all of which feature his distinctive, haunting touch. Patsy Ann Noble delivers a performance that's a cut above the usual in her role as a Jo Ann Campbell-type singer. Even the costumes, provided by Swinging London designer Mary Quant, reflect the conscious youthful rebellion in the air. (BE)

Don't Take You Away from Me (Andy Cavell and the Saints); *Live It Up, Don't You Understand* (Heinz Burt and the Tornadoes); *Hand Me Down My Walking Shoes, Rondo* (Kenny Ball and his Jazzmen); *Sometimes I Wish* (Jennifer Moss); *Loving Me This Way* (Kim Roberts); *Keep It Moving* (Sounds Incorporated); *Law and Disorder* (Outlaws); *Accidents Will Happen* (Patsy Ann Noble); *Temptation Baby* (Gene Vincent)   **SONGS**

LOOK OUT SISTER (1948)

MUSIC ★★★★★
ATTITUDE ★★★★★
FUN ★★★★

CAST: Louis Jordan, Suzette Harbin, Monte Hawley, Bob Scott, Maceo Sheffield; DIR: Bud Pollard; PROD: Berle Adams; SCREENPLAY: John E. Gordon; STUDIO: Astor; 67 min., b/w (no video release)

Louis Jordan's cowboy picture.

People like Chuck Berry, Bill Haley, and James Brown have all cited Louis Jordan as a crucial, fundamental influence on their music. But, apart from its historical significance, Jordan's music is also great because it embodies an unbeatable combination of humor, depth, and butt-shaking rhythm. *Look Out Sister* was Jordan's third and final feature for Astor Pictures. Here, Louis checks into a hospital for a much-needed break from the road, while a mean promoter threatens to sue him because of the canceled bookings. In the hospital, Louis meets a little boy who loves cowboys (and cowboy movies). Then he takes a nap and has a dream about the Wild West. In the dream, Louis and his band (Two-Gun Jordan and his Jivin' Cowhands) are booked into a place called the Health and Happiness Ranch. The mean promoter appears in the dream as a scheming landowner, who wants to run the ranch out of business. When Louis wakes up, he calls his manager and tells him to "wire all the stars of stage, screen, and radio" and invite them to a benefit show. You see, Louis wants to open a place "where all the kids can go to have fun in the sun." Naturally, he wants to call it the Health and Happiness Ranch. At the film's climax, there's a Wild West-style furniture-smashing brawl. Unfortunately, the sound man neglected to dub in the punch sound effects, so this scene has a surreal quality. This is the wildest and most rocking of all the Louis Jordan films. (MC)

SONGS   *Jack You're Dead, Caldonia, Ten Gallon Hat, Don't Burn the Candle at Both Ends, Chicky-mo Craney Crow, We Can't Agree, Barnyard Boogie, You're Much Too Fat, Roamin' Blues, Early in the Morning, Look Out Sister, Let the Good Times Roll* (Louis Jordan)

LOVE ME TENDER (1956)

MUSIC ★★★
ATTITUDE ★★★
FUN ★★★★

CAST: Elvis Presley, Richard Egan, Debra Paget, Robert Middleton, William Campbell, Neville Brand; DIR: Robert D. Webb; PROD: David Weisbart; SCREENPLAY: Robert Buckner; STUDIO: 20th Century-Fox; 89 min., b/w (Key)

Elvis's first film—and an odd one, too.

Love Me Tender is a period potboiler set immediately after the Civil War. Everyone thinks Confederate raider Vance Reno (Richard Egan) is dead until he turns up one day alive. In his absence, his girl Kathy (Debra Paget) has married his younger brother Clint (Elvis). If that wasn't enough to irritate Vance, it turns out that he's got a posse on his tail because he and his buddies have recently robbed a government train.

By the time he made this movie, Elvis was a national star, having cut seven gold records in 1956 alone. But in *Love Me Tender*, the 21-year-old Presley seems unsure of himself. The acting skills he displays here are limited, to say the least, and he only gets four songs. His character verges on the dim-witted, except during those few scenes in which he offers up some anachronistic singing and dancing. This film is still a treasure, however—not for its aesthetics, but for the joy of seeing the boy legend on-screen for the first time, bad acting and all, on top of the world. (TM)

SCENES   Elvis's death scene, a must-watch for any fan (1:26)

Clint to his brother, who has just found out that Kathy has married Clint: **LINES**
"What's troublin' you, Vance?"

We're Gonna Move, Love Me Tender, Let Me (Elvis Presley); *Poor Boy* (Elvis Presley, Vera Matson) **SONGS**

LOVEDOLLS SUPERSTAR   (1986)

CAST: Jennifer Schwartz, Steve McDonald, Janet Housden, Cheeta Punkerton, Jeff McDonald; DIR:
David Markey; PROD: Jordan Schwartz; SCREENPLAY: David Markey, Jeff McDonald, Jennifer
Schwartz, Steve McDonald; STUDIO: We Got Power; 85 min., color (We Got Power)

MUSIC ★★★★
ATTITUDE ★★★★★
FUN ★★★★

Another backyard classic.
This Super-8 epic sequel picks up where *Desperate Teenage Lovedolls* left off. Ex-
rock goddess Kitty Karry-All (Jennifer Schwartz), now a homeless wino, bumps
into her old drummer Patch Kelly (Janet Housden), now a successful cult leader
under the name Patch Christ. Using Patch's zonked-out followers to do their bid-
ding, which includes murdering those who stand in their way, Kitty and Patch
reform the Lovedolls and record a hot version of the Brady Bunch classic "It's a
Sunshine Day." Meanwhile, Rainbow Tremaine (Steve McDonald)—the identical
twin but spiritual opposite of the Lovedolls' late, sleazy manager—comes to
Hollywood after studying peace and love at the Freedom School in New Mexico.
He eventually goes hardcore and joins "all-boy punk band" Anarchy Sixx, the
warm-up act for the Lovedolls. Once again the girls claw their way to the top, but
this time they get the blessings of the President (played by Jello Biafra), who offers
the services of NASA for the girls' intergalactic tour, provided they kill off their
troublemaking fan club.

Like its predecessor, *Lovedolls Superstar* features a cast of earnest amateurs and
L.A. punk musicians, no-budget special effects, and color processing by Thrifty
Mart. The cinematography showcases a Los Angeles that's trashed-out, sun-
bleached, and smoggy. While not as tightly paced as *Desperate Teenage Lovedolls*,
this movie still has plenty of good moments, including send-up/homages to *Billy
Jack*, Cheap Trick, Kim Fowley ("Slim Crowley"), KISS, and Jim Jones. The
soundtrack includes original incidental music by Gone, as well as songs by the
Meat Puppets, Sonic Youth, Redd Kross, and the Dead Kennedys. The filmmakers
even appropriate tracks from *The Monkees Songbook Played by the Golden Gate
Strings*. Director David Markey went on to make videos for such bands as Sonic
Youth, Firehose, Shonen Knife, and Gumball, plus the Sonic Youth concert film
1991: The Year That Punk Broke. (JS)

One of the Lovedolls' maniac fans dreams that he must assassinate Bruce **SCENES**
Springsteen, which he does in a hilarious scene patterned after the "Dancing in the
Dark" video.

Love Machine, It's a Sunshine Day, Now That I've Tasted Blood, I Wanna Be a Cholo Chick, Beer **SONGS**
and 'Ludes (Lovedolls); *Slam Spit* (Anarchy Sixx)

THE LOVE-INS   (1967)

CAST: Richard Todd, James MacArthur, Susan Oliver; DIR: Arthur Dreifuss; PROD: Sam Katzman;
SCREENPLAY: Hal Collins, Arthur Dreifuss; STUDIO: Columbia; 91 min., color (no video release)

MUSIC ★★
ATTITUDE ★★
FUN ★★★★

Hallucinatory hokum.
This time producer Sam Katzman's take on '60s youth culture centers on a
Timothy Leary-type college professor, Dr. Jonathan Barnett (Richard Todd), who

moves to Haight-Ashbury. There, the defrocked prof dons a toga and starts a messianic cult based on his teachings to "Be More, Sense More, Love More." The doc even promotes his cause on the Joe Pyne TV show. (Pyne was the original Morton Downey, Jr.) An earnest, young underground journalist named Larry (James MacArthur) at first supports Barnett but then loses faith as the Be More movement becomes larger (and more profitable). Finally, Larry assassinates Barnett at a giant stadium rally and then mutters, "I've created a martyr."

The centerpiece of *The Love-Ins* is an absurd LSD sequence experienced by Larry's girl, Pat (Susan Oliver), at one of the film's happenings. A psychedelic rock band grooves along as their slightly old, Gary Glitter-ish frontman starts to recite bits of *Alice in Wonderland.* When he pauses to command everyone to "make like a rabbit!", Pat hallucinates that he's grown rabbit ears and been joined onstage by other characters from the Lewis Carroll classic. Then Pat joins them in a bizarre ballet under strobe lights that flash to the chants of "Take the acid!" and "Mellow Yellow! Mellow Yellow!" Pat strips down to her lacy undies before Larry attempts to escort her back to reality. It's the Hollywood fogey version of the ultimate acid fantasy. Scattered throughout the rest of the film are teasing glimpses of the Chocolate Watch Band, all-girl band the U.F.O.'s, and some folks called the New Age Group. These bands are seen fleetingly at ballroom happenings, park be-ins, and on top of psychedelic schoolbuses. (JS)

LINES From a Columbia Pictures pressbook for *The Love-Ins:* "The Chocolate Watch Band got its name from a legendary musical organization that supposedly existed during King Arthur's Court. They were members of the Watch, a sort of police force of that period. As money was unknown at that time, legend says, the band was paid for their services in chocolate. Hence the name, Chocolate Watch Band." Sure.

CAMEOS Joe Pyne

SONGS *Are You Gonna Be There* (Chocolate Watch Band)

THE LOVELESS (1981)

MUSIC	★★★
ATTITUDE	★★★
FUN	★★

CAST: Willem Dafoe, Robert Gordon, Marin Kanter, J. Don Ferguson; **DIR:** Kathryn Bigelow, Monty Montgomery; **PROD:** Grafton Nunes, A. Kitman Ho; **SCREENPLAY:** Kathryn Bigelow, Monty Montgomery; **STUDIO:** Pioneer; 85 min., color (Media)

Comatose bikers descend on a small town.
The homoeroticism of *Scorpio Rising* meets the existential meaninglessness of *Two Lane Blacktop* in this, Willem Dafoe's first crack at quality time in front of a camera. (He debuted in *Heaven's Gate,* but nobody *saw* that.) Shame is, even in this one you'd never know Dafoe was a good actor because the script is so comatose. Vance (Dafoe) and Davis (played by neo-rockabilly singer Robert Gordon) are members of a disorganized motorcycle gang. On their way to Daytona, they get stuck in a small southern town. As they wait for one of their bikes to be repaired, Vance and Davis get the chance to slouch and sneer a lot, and the townsfolk get to act ignorant and narrow-minded, so everybody's happy (except for the chick who blows her own head off in the end, of course). The soundtrack (mostly by Robert Gordon with the help of John Lurie and Eddy Dixon) is passable fake-rockabilly and cool jazz, with an occasional recording actually made during the '50s thrown in for good measure. This works, because it's not exactly clear whether *The Loveless* takes place in the past or not. It's that existential. As for rocker Gordon's acting debut, I've seen worse. (BV)

Vance, in all seriousness, to his cronies: "We're goin' nowhere (pregnant pause)... **LINES** FAST!"

LOVING YOU (1957)

CASTP: Elvis Presley, Lizabeth Scott, Wendell Corey, Dolores Hart, James Gleason, Jana Lund, Yvonne Lime; **DIR:** Hal Kanter; **PROD:** Hal B. Wallis; **SCREENPLAY:** Herbert Baker, Hal Kanter; **STUDIO:** Paramount; 101 min., color (Warner)

MUSIC ★★★★
ATTITUDE ★★★★
FUN ★★★★

Elvis Presley at the peak of his form in blazing color.

In this film, Elvis, just 22, his hair dyed newly black, stuns you with his godlike presence. When he pulls up in his hot rod at the beginning of the picture, he's Brando, James Dean, and everyone else who's cool all rolled into one. Later, when he's shown from a low camera angle singing "Teddy Bear," he's closer to Zeus. The plot is simple, and while not crucial to the film, it's still enjoyable between the songs. Presley's musical numbers are close to what his early live shows were like—lots of shaking, bumping, grinding, and goofing. Good thing there are plenty of them. For trivia fans: The set for the final concert scene was the same one that Dean Martin and Jerry Lewis used a year earlier in *Hollywood or Bust*, which contained two other Elvis references. (AF)

At the end, when Elvis is singing "Got a Lot of Living to Do," he stops in front of **SCENES** a very large woman in a blue dress sitting on the aidle. It's his mother, Gladys. Devastated by her death in 1958, Elvis never viewed *Loving You* again.

"Hey you—sideburns." **LINES**

Skip Young **CAMEOS**

Party, Hot Dog, Lonesome Cowboy, Loving You, Mean Woman Blues, Got a Lot of Living to Do, **SONGS** *Teddy Bear* (Elvis Presley); *Detour, Candy Kisses, Dancing on a Dare* (Tex Warner's Rough Riding Ramblers)

MELANIE (1982)

CAST: Burton Cummings, Glynnis O'Connor, Paul Sorvino, Trudy Young, Don Johnson, Jamie Dick, Donnan Caven, Jodie Drake; DIR: Rex Bromfield; PROD: Peter Simpson; SCREENPLAY: Robert Guza Jr., Richard Paluck; STUDIO: Simcom; 109 min., color (no video release)

MUSIC ★★
ATTITUDE ★★★
FUN ★★

A hillbilly gal hooks up with a troubled L.A. rock star.

This film unfortunately chronicles ex-Guess Who singer Burton Cummings's output during 1978-79, when all of popular music fell under the malignant shadow of disco. Even his magnificent voice couldn't surpass the pleading, downbeat tone of this vanity effort. He plays Rick Manning, a downtrodden superstar living in a Hollywood Hills home, which may have been true of the real-life Cummings—or the image he wanted to project. Because Americans didn't know him that well (not nearly as well as Canadians did), it was up to Cummings to convince viewers of his character's status as a rock star—in a riotous concert sequence, for instance. But that scene never comes, and the picture becomes a dark, plodding dirge. Meek Glynnis O'Connor as a backwoods mom searching for her child can't find herself either in the title role, and 1973 Capitol recording artist Don Johnson (as the child-napping pop) likewise adds zilch to this funereal soap opera. (AF)

Mister Rock and Roll

MISTER ROCK AND ROLL (1957)

CAST: Alan Freed, Teddy Randazzo, Rocky Graziano, Lois O'Brien, Jay Barney; DIR: Charles Dubin; PROD: Ralph Serpe, Howard B. Kreitsek; SCREENPLAY: James Blumgarten; STUDIO: Paramount; 86 min., b/w (no video release)

MUSIC ★
ATTITUDE ★★
FUN ★★

Alan Freed rescues rock'n'roll from newspaper flak.

This film's title is a misnomer because its music, like that of so many '50s rock movies, is heartbreakingly tepid. Maybe theater owners, remembering the *Blackboard Jungle* riots, demanded unexciting material without any flavor. Such a conspiracy would dovetail well with the plot, which concerns a DJ (Alan Freed) who's trying to convince people that rock'n'roll does not cause juvenile delinquency. The acts featured here, most posed cheaply on bare soundstages, look uncomfortable. The gimmick songs performed by LaVern Baker and the Moonglows ("Barcelona Rock" has them in sombreros—just like in Spain!) would make you uncomfortable, too. Other lowlights include stiff lip-synchs by Frankie Lymon and Clyde McPhatter. Chuck Berry duckwalks, but through two of his weaker songs, "Oh Baby Doll" and "La Juanda." And even though Little Richard's "Lucille" is a standout, his performance is static compared to his fire-breathing live shows. Ferlin Husky's two lifeless country-pop songs, mislabeled as rockabilly, make him a fish out of water here, and as the movie's rock'n'roll lead, the handsome Teddy Randazzo croons what could best be described as "adult-conceived" rock. In short, this movie stinks. And though it may accurately reflect what movie companies wanted you to hear in 1957, the music in *Mister Rock and Roll* leaves a false impression of rock's earliest days. (AF)

SONGS *Barcelona Rock, Confess It to Your Heart* (Moonglows); *Drum Hi, Mister Rock and Roll, Hello Folks, Hey Poppa Rock, Star Rocket* (Lionel Hampton); *Fortunate Fella, Love Put Me Out of My Head* (Frankie Lymon and the Teenagers); *Get Acquainted Waltz, Pathway to Sin* (Shaye Cogan); *Humpty Dumpty Heart, Love Me Right* (LaVern Baker); *I Was the Last One to Know, I'll Stop Anytyhing I'm Doing, Kiddio, Perfect for Love* (Teddy Randazzo); *If I Had Only Known, Your Love Alone* (Brook Benton); *It's Simply Heavenly* (Lois O'Brien); *La Juanda, Oh Baby Doll* (Chuck Berry); *Lucille* (Little Richard); *Make Me Live Again, This Moment of Love* (Ferlin Husky); *Rock and Cry, You'll Be There* (Clyde McPhatter)

MONDO HOLLYWOOD   (1967)

ALTERNATIVE TITLES: *Hippie Hollywood, Images*
DIR: Carl Cohen; **PROD:** Carl Cohen; **SCREENPLAY:** Carl Cohen; **STUDIO:** Omega-Cyrano; 88 min., color (no video release)

MUSIC ★★★
ATTITUDE ★
FUN ★★★★

A film that's an excuse for a soundtrack.
No doubt inspired by the more widely successful (and accepted) *Mondo Cane*, the slightly more amateurish *Mondo Hollywood* followed a similar format, exposing the Hollywood scene of the mid-'60s. Photographed, directed, produced, and edited by Carl Cohen (who later rose to prominence with *Inside Red China, Inside East Germany*, and *Inside Castro's Cuba*), this 88-minute feature attempts to capture the happenings, feelings, and attitudes of the time. Among the unknowns, hipsters, celebrities, and wackos we meet are: Dr. Richard Alpert, who was dismissed from Harvard for experimenting with LSD; Rudi Gernreich, who sparked the topless fad; and sculptress Valerie Porter.

Culled from more than 120,000 feet of film shot over an 18-month period, *Mondo Hollywood's* offbeat images are appropriately matched by the cacophonous soundtrack produced by Mike Curb, who made a fortune then producing soundtracks for A.I.P. and other, smaller film companies. (For most of this work, Curb used personnel that he had under contract to his own Sidewalk record label.) Like the film itself, the music is a child of its time, perfectly matching the visuals. Cohen himself edited the tracks, co-writing a number of them with varying results. If you weren't there, this is your chance to see what Hollywood was like. If you were there, this is a good reason to forget! (SJM)

SONGS *Mondo Hollywood, Mondo Hollywood Freakout* (Mugwump Establishment); *The Magic Night* (Mike Clifford); *Moonfire* (Davie Allan and the Arrows); *Last Wave of the Day* (Riptides); *Vietnam* (Bobby Jameson); *Great God Pan* (God Pan); *You're Beautiful* (Darrell Dee); *Magic Night March* (18th Century Concepts); *Beast of Sunset Strip* (Teddy and Darrell)

MONDO MOD   (1967)

DIR: Peter Perry; PROD: Harry Novak, Peter Perry; SCREENPLAY: Sherman Greene; STUDIO: Box Office International; 73 min., color (Something Weird)

Mind rot on the Sunset Strip.

It's hard to believe that by 1967, this mesmerizingly senseless documentary of 1966 Hollywood already seemed dated, and even antiquated, with its greaser mods, beehived go-go girls, and distinctly pre-hippie disposition. Beginning with the title song, "It's a Mod Mod World" by the Gretschmen, *Mondo Mod* rambles uncertainly from discotheques to dirt bikes, taking in surfing, karate, go-carting, the Hell's Angels, political protests, pot parties and all the other trappings of the Now Generation. Along the way, we're treated to priceless footage of Pandora's Box, Gazzarri's, the Whisky A-Go-Go, the Fifth Estate, and countless other forgotten haunts of "the neon Neverland that the mod set calls home." Starring, according to the credits, "The Youth of the World," *Mondo Mod* features a pot-smoking, bongo-blasting finale during which these hipsters and flipsters start to strip down. It begins to makes sense only when you find out that this same cast and crew shot a soft-porn movie (*Pot Party Girls*) later that same night (after *Mondo Mod* was completed). What's even more astounding is that within a few years of *Mondo Mod*'s release, *both* of its cinematographers became world-famous: Laszlo Kovacs for *Easy Rider*, and Vilmos Szigmond for *Close Encounters of the Third Kind*. Meanwhile, the super-hip narrator Humble Harve landed in prison on a murder beef. Turn on, tune in, and drop dead. (JL)

SONGS *Mondo Mod/It's a Mod Mod World* (Gretschmen); *Mary Lou* (Sam the Soul and the Inspirations); *Feel a Whole Lot Better, Follow Me* (Group)

MONDO TEENO: THE TEENAGE REBELLION (1967)

DIR: Norman T. Herman; PROD: Norman T. Herman; SCREENPLAY: Norman T. Herman; STUDIO: Trans-American; 81 min., b/w (Something Weird)

Those crazy kids.

This quickie documentary, which was paired on a drive-in double bill with *Mondo Mod*, claims to provide the lowdown on crazy teenage goings-on around the globe. It gets off to a good start, showing glimpses of the Sunset Strip riots, the Paris student revolt, and English mods and rockers running wild in Brighton. However, narrator Burt Topper (who directed *I Was a High School Bride*) then launches a long-winded lecture that never ends in a serious, stentorian voice reminiscent of director Russ Meyer. Things soon wind down to such critical issues of the day as go-go dancing, striped hip huggers, bikers, and surfing, all of which seem to have been popular worldwide.

In London, we see Carnaby Street ("This is called a dolly-looking bird") and a mixed-race mod soul band (although the music heard is not them); in Japan, at a nightclub with electrified dragons hanging over the dance floor, one dancer strips down to her bra. Meanwhile, old clips of jitterbuggers and zoot suits are intercut to prove that 'twas ever so with youth. Reports on Swedish teen sex manuals were apparently inserted to wake up the dirty old men in all-night theaters who were probably the main audience for this film. We see make-out spots in Rome, drug use, unexplained mud wrestling, and teen hookers. "If loneliness drives some girls to prostitution, it drives some men in another direction," begins a look at the mod gay underworld. The cheesy soundtrack (written by Mike Curb and Bob

Summers) contains lots of Duane Eddyish guitar and shuffle beats, and there's a great garage/surf title song by the Glass Family. (JS)

"Across the country, every Friday and Saturday night, they gather in the temples to perform ceremonial dances to a rhythm that seems to reach back in time. It's called the beat." *LINES*

MONTEREY POP (1968)

DIR: D.A. Pennebaker; PROD: John Phillips, Lou Adler; STUDIO: Leacock/Pennebaker; 79 min., color (Sony)

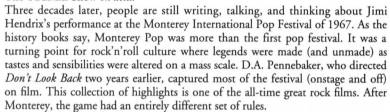

MUSIC ★★★★★
ATTITUDE ★★★★★
FUN ★★★★★

The T.A.M.I. Show *on acid.*
Three decades later, people are still writing, talking, and thinking about Jimi Hendrix's performance at the Monterey International Pop Festival of 1967. As the history books say, Monterey Pop was more than the first pop festival. It was a turning point for rock'n'roll culture where legends were made (and unmade) as tastes and sensibilities were altered on a mass scale. D.A. Pennebaker, who directed *Don't Look Back* two years earlier, captured most of the festival (onstage and off) on film. This collection of highlights is one of the all-time great rock films. After Monterey, the game had an entirely different set of rules.

Many of these new rules were written by the Jimi Hendrix Experience, who were making their American debut. The festival's other great star, Otis Redding, was backed by Booker T and the MGs, the best-dressed band at Monterey (long live Lansky Brothers of Beale Street!). LSD also played an important role, and Country Joe and the Fish obviously swallowed a big bunch of it before their appearance. The Who play an unintelligible version of "My Generation," then destroy all their borrowed equipment. (Of course, the real question is, how could anyone be stupid enough to loan equipment to the Who?) Jimi Hendrix closes his set with rock's crudest, crummiest, and perhaps greatest anthem, the Troggs' "Wild Thing." He plays it, to quote Dave Marsh, "with a mixture of malice and glee." Hendrix puts the Monterey Pop Festival (and this film) in his back pocket. To read about Monterey in depth, get *Monterey Pop* (Chronicle) by Joel Selvin and Jim Marshall. (MC)

California Dreamin', I've Got a Feeling (Mamas and the Papas); *Rollin' and Tumblin'* (Canned Heat); *59th Street Bridge Song* (Simon and Garfunkel); *Bajabula Bonke* (Hugh Masakela); *High Flying Bird, Today* (Jefferson Airplane); *Ball and Chain* (Big Brother and the Holding Company); *Paint It Black* (Eric Burdon and the Animals); *My Generation* (Who); *Section 43* (Country Joe and the Fish); *Shake, I've Been Loving You Too Long* (Otis Redding); *Wild Thing* (Jimi Hendrix Experience); *Raga Bhimpalasi* (Ravi Shankar) *SONGS*

MRS. BROWN, YOU'VE GOT A LOVELY DAUGHTER (1968)

CAST: Peter Noone, Karl Green, Keith Hopwood, Derek Lackenby, Barry Whitwam, Stanley Holloway, Sara Caldwell, Mona Washbourne, Sheila White; DIR: Saul Swimmer; PROD: Allen Klein; SCREENPLAY: Thaddeus Vane; STUDIO: MGM; 95 min., color (MGM/UA)

MUSIC ★★
ATTITUDE ★★
FUN ★★

Herman's Hermits lead a dog's life.
Before producing pictures with the likes of the Beatles and the Stones, Allen Klein had to settle for Herman's Hermits. The result was *Mrs. Brown, You've Got a Lovely Daughter.* Based on an old pop song, this innocuous film spins the story of a rock band (played by the Hermits) who inherit a racing dog. Meanwhile, lead singer Peter Noone pursues not one but *two* love interests. The musical numbers—which

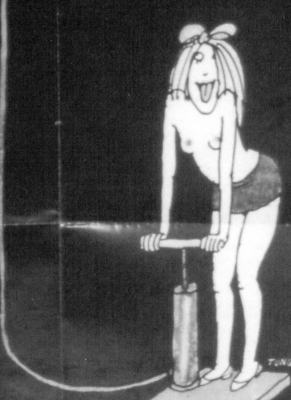

include two hits, the title track and "There's a Kind of Hush"—make for a movie that's pleasant, diverting fun in its own confused, empty-headed way. It's much more fun than Jean-Luc Godard's *Sympathy for the Devil*, for example, another Klein production. (BE)

It's Nice to Be Out in the Morning, Ooh She's Done It Again, Lemon and Lime, The World Is for the Young, Holiday Inn, The Most Beautiful Thing in My Life, Daisy Chain, Mrs. Brown You've Got a Lovely Daughter, There's a Kind of Hush (Herman's Hermits) **SONGS**

EL MUNDO LOCO DE LOS JOVENES   (1967)

ENGLISH TITLE: *The Crazy World of the Teenagers*
CAST: César Costa, Julissa de Llano; **DIR:** Fernandez Unsain; **PROD:** Aldolfo L. Grovas; **SCREEN-PLAY:** J.M. Fernandez Unsain; **STUDIO:** Klang/Columbia; 86 min., color (no video release)

MUSIC ★★★
ATTITUDE ★★★★
FUN ★★★★

A sexy, hard-to-get go-go singer in a world of hot-blooded teenage boys.
Filmed in Acapulco at Estudios Americana, this frantic teen pic features ultra-hip '60s sets, an op-art masked singer, and great dance scenes. The plot line focuses on four teenage boys doing everything they can to win the heart of pop singer Julianna. After several embarrassing failures, they enlist the aid of an old friend who has since become a famous singer. This is La Vóz Moscara (the Masked Voice), who lives in a wild '60s-stylized house complete with four go-go girl servants. La Vóz himself tries a number of ways to win Julianna's love, but all she wants is for him to remove his mask so that she can learn his true identity. When La Vóz finally does remove his mask in the film's neat conclusion, she falls madly in love with him. As for the teenage boys, they each get a go-go girl servant. Although there's music throughout the movie, none of the bands can rock the teenagers into a jerking frenzy any better than a garage outfit called T.J. y los Dug-Dugs. (TS)

Hazemé Feliz, Un Nuevo Sol (Julissa de Llano); *Tema Mi Corazon Tema el Despuro* (Chucho Ferrer); *Accurocadita* (Julio Brita); *Jornada Sentimental* (Green Homer Brown); *Yo Te Daré* (Francisca Angel Lovecchio); *Go-Go Music* (T.J. y los Dug-Dugs, Five Frenetics) **SONGS**

MUSCLE BEACH PARTY   (1964)

CAST: Frankie Avalon, Annette Funicello, Luciana Paluzzi, John Ashley, Don Rickles, Morey Amsterdam, Buddy Hackett, Jody McRea, Candy Johnson, Dick Dale and his Del-Tones, Rock Stevens; **DIR:** William Asher; **PROD:** James H. Nicholson, Robert Dillon; **SCREENPLAY:** Robert Dillon, William Asher; **STUDIO:** American International; 94 min., color (HBO)

MUSIC ★★★★★
ATTITUDE ★★★★★
FUN ★★★★★

Dick Dale and Brian Wilson freak with Stevie Wonder.
In *Muscle Beach Party*, all hell breaks loose with the beach-o-rama brigade. Essentially, it's an extension of the basics laid down in *Beach Party*, but in this one, the lunacy is full throttle. Because the Beach Boys were touring during the filming of *Beach Party*, Brian Wilson couldn't make an appearance. But he does turn up here with a bag of goodies—specially, six new tunes for the soundtrack. Dick Dale and his Del-Tones are back singing Brian's "My First Love," "Surfin' Woodie," "Muscle Beach Party," and "Muscle Bustle" (the last with Donna Loren). Frankie Avalon sings Brian's "Runnin' Wild," which easily ranks as Frankie's best recording, but it's the opening tune, "Surfer's Holiday," that really takes the cake. Frankie, Annette, and Dick Dale all sing a verse, while Dick delivers a blistering guitar break over Brian Wilson's track. Marvelous! If that isn't enough, Little Stevie Wonder ends this film with a rousing "Happy Street."

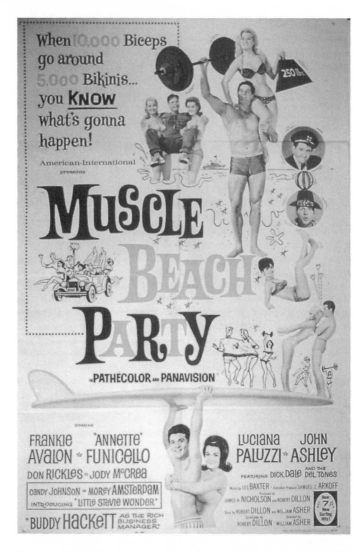

Muscle Beach Party is a pretty good watch, too. Morey Amsterdam (as the beatnik club owner Cappy) meets the genius of Buddy Hackett face-to-face—and outwails him! Later, Don Rickles rains on everyone's parade splendidly. Frankie Avalon manages to hold his own among these giants, delivering some of the best lines in the film. And even Annette gets to toss in a few sucker punches at the Frankie-stealing villain, Luciana Paluzzi. She's also featured in a cool scene singing "A Girl Needs a Boy" against the moonlit surf. Jody McRea grabs the honors as best supporting actor here, and Peter Lorre has a crucial cameo as Mr. Strangedour, king of the strongmen. Special kudos go to Candy Johnson's fantastic dance sequences, perhaps the best go-go dancing ever. All hail Gary Usher, Roger Christian, and Brian Wilson! (DP)

SONGS   *Surfer's Holiday* (Frankie Avalon, Annette Funicello, Dick Dale); *A Boy Needs a Girl, Runnin' Wild* (Frankie Avalon); *A Girl Needs a Boy* (Annette Funicello); *My First Love, Muscle Beach Party, Surfin' Woodie* (Dick Dale and his Del-Tones); *Muscle Bustle* (Dick Dale, Donna Loren); *Happy Street* (Little Stevie Wonder)

MYSTERY TRAIN   (1989)

CAST: Masatoshi Nagase, Youko Kudoh, Screamin' Jay Hawkins, Cinqué Lee, Nicoletta Braschi, Elizabeth Bracco, Joe Strummer, Rick Aviles, Steve Buscemi; DIR: Jim Jarmusch; PROD: Jim Stark; SCREENPLAY: Jim Jarmusch; STUDIO: Orion; 110 min., color (Orion)

MUSIC ★★★★★
ATTITUDE ★★★★★
FUN ★★★★

An encounter with the spirit of rock'n'roll.
If there are any sacred places left in modern America, Memphis must be one. The site of Elvis's Graceland and Sam Phillips's Sun Records, it's the birthplace of rock'n'roll. Jim Jarmusch's *Mystery Train* shows, during an overnight stay, how enchanting this once-blessed city can be. Three seperate tales come together at a seedy hotel on the outskirts of town. A pair of Japanese teenagers (Masatoshi Nagase, Youko Kudoh) stop over during their rock'n'roll tour of the States. An Italian widow (Nicoletta Braschi) seeks a night of refuge. An English thug (Joe Strummer of the Clash) dodges the police. Under the hovering spirit of the King, all three experience the preternatural energy of the place. The only character who remains unruffled is the hotel's manager, played grandly by Screamin' Jay Hawkins. Like all Jarmusch movies, *Mystery Train* is like going on a road trip with no destination. You're there just to enjoy the ride. But it does help that he tunes you into a great radio station playing rockabilly hits. (SBW)

Jun, the Japanese hipster, staring out of a hotel window, his pompadour ruffling in the breeze: "It feels cool... to be 18."   *LINES*

Rufus Thomas, Tom Waits   *CAMEOS*

THE NASTY RABBIT   (1964)

ALTERNATE TITLE: *Spies A-Go-Go*
CAST: Mischa Terr, Arch Hall Jr., William Watters, Melissa Morgan, Pat and Lolly Vegas, The Archers; DIR: James Landis; PROD: Nicholas Merriwether; SCREENPLAY: Arch Hall, Jim Critchfield; STUDIO: Fairway International; 85 min., color (Rhino)

MUSIC ★★
ATTITUDE ★
FUN ★

Yeccchh!
You probably thought you'd never see these words arranged together in a sentence, but here goes: This Arch Hall, Jr., movie is pure hell on film, impossible to enjoy. After writing the screenplay for the classic *Wild Guitar* and *Eegah* under the *nom de plume* Nicholas Merriwether, Arch Hall, Sr., chose (for some reason) to take credit under his real name for *The Nasty Rabbit*, a story about Russian spies, a dude ranch, chemical warfare, etc. Every possible Cold War-era comedy cliche is belabored to death in this movie. Arch, Jr., plays Brett Hunter, a rock'n'roll-singing FBI agent (could happen, I guess).

Skip this one and see the Two Arches' first film instead: In *The Choppers*, Arch, Jr., plays the leader of a gang of teenage car strippers who make their rounds in a chicken truck. He sings two great songs ("Kongo Joe" and "Monkeys in My Hatband"). *The Choppers* also stars the beautiful Marianne Gaba, who at one time was Ricky Nelson's girlfriend (on TV and in real life). (MC)

The only bearable thing in *The Nasty Rabbit* is the appearance of Pat and Lolly Vegas (who would later form the group Redbone and make a bunch of good records, including the 1974 classic "Come and Get Your Love"). Here they do an awesome dance tune called "The Robot Walk."   *SCENES*

The Spy Waltz, Jackie (Arch Hall, Jr.); *The Robot Walk* (Pat and Lolly Vegas)   *SONGS*

National Lampoon's Animal House

COLLEGE

NATIONAL LAMPOON'S ANIMAL HOUSE (1978)

MUSIC ★★★★★
ATTITUDE ★★★★★
FUN ★★★★★

CAST: John Belushi, Tim Matheson, John Vernon, Verna Bloom, Thomas Hulce, Cesare Danova, Peter Riegert, Stephen Furst, Donald Sutherland, Karen Allen, Sarah Holcomb, Kevin Bacon; DIR: John Landis; PROD: Matty Simmons, Ivan Reitman; SCREENPLAY: Harold Ramis, Douglas Kenney, Chris Miller; STUDIO: Universal; 109 min., color (MCA)

To-ga! To-ga!

This hilarious romp was the third important movie, after *Easy Rider* and *American Graffiti*, to use a rock'n'roll soundtrack to great effect. But where the first film fed paranoia and the second cooled people out, this film made it all right to be stupid—and imprinted an entire generation. Don't kid yourself—there is direct causality between this film and MTV, truck pulls, and Spuds the Dog. Of course, there are some anachronisms in this frat film set in 1962—the peace symbol on the prof's wall, the 1970 pic of Elvis in the dean's bedroom—but who cares? The truly troubling aspect of *Animal House* is its racism. When the frat boys stumble into a black bar, they assume they're in danger. (Perhaps to even out the racial stereotyping, the Italian mayor has mob connections.) The music, however, is quite effective. Playing this phenomenal stuff at movie-house volume worked profoundly well—especially Sam Cooke's "Twistin' the Night Away," which kicks off the toga party, and the film's recurring theme (some say the new national anthem) "Louie Louie." My one complaint is that when John Belushi breaks folksinger Stephen Bishop's guitar, it's not over his head. (AF)

LINES "Christ! Seven years of college down the drain!"

SONGS *Money* (John Belushi); *Shama Lama Ding Dong, Shout* (DeWayne Jessie)

1991: The Year That Punk Broke (1992)

CAST: Sonic Youth, Nirvana, Dinosaur Jr., Babes in Toyland, Gumball, The Ramones; **DIR:** Dave Markey; **STUDIO:** Sonic Life/We Got Power; 95 min., color (Geffen)

MUSIC ★★
ATTITUDE ★★★
FUN ★★

The year punk stunk.

It was a turning point, no doubt. Sonic Youth and their pals, all of whom had previously been playing club-level venues, go on a European summer tour of outdoor festivals and find themselves playing before tens of thousands of fans. They brought along a filmmaker (David Markey of the Lovedolls films), and now, according to the video box, we can "Witness the boredom! The cynicism!" for ever and ever. The end result is nicely shot and edited (and looks better than Super 8 should), but sure enough, *1991* makes hanging out on *this* rock tour seem like a very dull prospect.

The music doesn't help. Future generations may ponder why punk "broke" at a time when so many underground bands were emulating early-'70s hard rock moves. If punk equaled Black Sabbath, then did anything really change? Nirvana comes off as just another dumb rock band that throws food backstage, while Gumball and Babes in Toyland are virtually unlistenable. Only 10-year veterans Sonic Youth (and perhaps Dinosaur Jr.) show any class. Their Velvets/Television update shows their hearts are in the right place, but the endless rounds of feedback that end every song are ultimately tiresome. Even more disappointing is the much-vaunted sarcastic wit of frontman Thurston Moore. No one would mistake him for a member of the Algonquin Round Table—one thankfully underlit shot delivers a close-up of a turd floating in the bowl, as presumed creator Thurston gets in his best line, "Another work of art!" Famed Woman-In-Rock Kim Gordon mostly smiles and keeps quiet, which in retrospect isn't so bad. (JS)

SCENES At one backstage meal, we see several neatly tableclothed banquet tables set up with china and little placecards imprinted with "Nirvana," "Sonic Youth," and "Ramones." It's like a punk rock Bar Mitzvah.

CAMEOS Bob Mould, Mudhoney, Dave Kendall, Courtney Love

SONGS *Schizophrenia, Brother James, Teenage Riot, Dirty Boots, I Love Her All the Time, Mote, Kool Thing, Expressway to Yr Skull* (Sonic Youth); *Negative Creep, School, Endless Nameless, Smells Like Teen Spirit, Polly* (Nirvana); *Freak Scene, The Wagon* (Dinosaur, Jr.); *Dustcake Boy* (Babes in Toyland); *Pre* (Gumball); *Commando* (Ramones)

O Lucky Man! (1973)

CAST: Malcolm McDowell, Ralph Richardson, Rachel Roberts, Arthur Lowe, Helen Mirren, Randy Nichols, Mona Washbourne, Alan Price; **DIR:** Lindsay Anderson; **PROD:** Michael Medwin, Lindsay Anderson; **SCREENPLAY:** David Sherwin; **STUDIO:** Warner; 174 min., color (Warner)

MUSIC ★★★★
ATTITUDE ★★★★
FUN ★★★

A sprawling comic tour of England's decline.

Set to the ironic songs of Alan Price, *O Lucky Man!* presents the odyssey of young Mick Travis, played by Malcolm McDowell (reprising his character from *If...*). Starting out as a go-getting salesman for Imperial Coffee, Travis winds up being victimized by the same society in which he's been struggling madly to succeed. He's tortured by military intelligence, used as a guinea pig in some medical experiments, sent to prison, and attacked by a skid row mob. In the end, he finds himself up for the lead role in a new Lindsay Anderson film.

Meanwhile in this picture, Anderson uses Alan Price's intercut performance clips to comment on the dramatic action. Price's songs offer a jaunty, bittersweet counterpoint to Mick's willing degradation at the hands of the Establishment. A poor man's Ray Davies (he even has the same broad, knowing grin), ex-Animal Price is himself an affable but rather bland presence. But his music does indeed help to break up the inevitable monotony of this three-hour epic (an edited 148-minute version is also available). Despite the quasi-rock score, *O Lucky Man!* moves to the sleepwalk rhythms of a Marxist dirge. (HH)

SCENES　Mick's horrified vision of a man who has been turned into a sheep—literally (1:22)

SONGS　*O Lucky Man, Poor People, Keep That Smile On Your Face, On and On, There's Always Someone, Money/Justice, My Hometown, Everyone Changes* (Alan Price)

ONE MAN'S CHALLENGE　　　　(1962)

CAST: John Danglius, Roger Christian; DIR: Dale Smallin; PROD: Dale Smallin; STUDIO: Azusa Recreation Department; 24 min., b/w (no video release)

MUSIC ★★★★
ATTITUDE ★★★★
FUN ★★★★★

Teens get nightclub as Beach Boys stomp.
This is the only true document that exists of the teen surf explosion in Los Angeles circa 1962. We begin with a rare sight: juvenile-delinquent surfer kids roaming the streets (under palm trees) to the tune of "The Hitchhiker" by the Genteels. These guys are all wearing white T-shirts or Pendletons with Levis, and they've all got blond (or peroxided) hair. Then the film cuts to the office of John Danglius, the director of the Azusa Recreation Department, who has been "challenged" to create an acceptable form of social recreation for these kids. The rest of *One Man's Challenge* explores the step-by-step basics of forming a teen club—complete with a bamboo fence, thatch hut, surfboards, primitive arrows, and a huge tiki.

Each teen who joins the club (they can only be from a certain geographical area!) is given a set of rules and membership card. There are plenty of them, and they're shown doing the surfer stomp to a great (though unrecorded) garage surf band called the Raindrops. Just before the song ends, we see a close-up of two burger patties sizzlin' in a pan. Next we learn some details about the snack bar and how the patio is a great place for teen talk as they relax from the pace of dancing. The sound crew are shown spinning 45s while the audience slow-dances to a moody surf instrumental. Over at the bulletin board, other teens gaze at glossies of the bands that have appeared there...when a fight breaks out! Johnny Crawford signs autographs at a booth, and KFWB DJ Gene Weed takes the stage to introduce the Beach Boys—who also wear Pendletons, sport David Marks on rhythm guitar, and crunch out a primitive version of "Surfin' Safari." They look like gods in this scene. Later, a pre-"Wipe Out" incarnation of the Surfaris wails as the audience hits a feeding frenzy. Finally, the teen club takes a field trip to Disneyland. (DP)

SONGS　*The Hitchhiker* (Genteels); *Surfin' Safari* (Beach Boys); *Surf Bash* (Surfaris)

ONE-TRICK PONY　　　　(1980)

CAST: Paul Simon, Blair Brown, Rip Torn, Joan Hackett, Allen Goorwitz, Michael Pearlman, Lou Reed; DIR: Robert M. Young; PROD: Michael Tannen, Michael Hausman; SCREENPLAY: Paul Simon; STUDIO: Warner; 100 min., color (Warner)

MUSIC ★★★★
ATTITUDE ★★★
FUN ★★★

Paul Simon as film auteur.
Simon plays Jonah Levin, a '60s folksinger in his mid-30s who's lost in the world. He's separated from his wife (Blair Brown), who blames him for never growing up and never being around. Jonah spends most of his time on the road with his band

(Steve Gadd, Eric Gale, Tony Levin, Richard Tee), playing small clubs and waiting for his life to start happening again.

Simon wrote 10 new songs as well as the screenplay. Of course he's a better songwriter than screenwriter, but he does a creditable job going both ways here. The plot holds together, it ends effectively (often a problem these days), and there are more than a few well-written scenes. As for the acting, the supporting cast is full of pros, and Simon, if not brilliant, holds his own. Allen Goorwitz is memorable as a music business hack, the subject of a *Billboard* profile called "20 Years of AM Ears." Simon's portrait of the record business is so harsh and unrealistic that it comes off as bitter and unfair. However, as H.L. Mencken might have said, nobody ever lost any money overestimating the foulness of the music industry. (DR)

The Salute to the '60s Reunion with Sam and Dave and the Lovin' Spoonful (1:05)   *SCENES*

Jonah to his estranged wife: "I'm not dead; I'm in Cleveland."   *LINES*

Daniel Stern (as an airport Hare Krishna), Mare Winningham, Harry Shearer,   *CAMEOS* Tiny Tim, John Sebastian, David Sanborn

Late in the Evening, One-Trick Pony, How the Heart Approaches What It Yearns, God Bless the   *SONGS* *Absentee, Long Long Day, Ace in the Hole, Oh Marion, Soft Parachutes, That's Why God Made the Movies* (Paul Simon); *Rock Lobster* (B-52's); *Soul Man* (Sam and Dave); *Do You Believe in Magic?* (Lovin' Spoonful)

OUT OF SIGHT   *(1966)*

CAST: Jonathan Daly, Karen Jensen, Robert Pine, Carol Shelyne, The Out of Sight Girls, Wendy Wagner, Maggie Thrett, Deanna Lund, Rena Horton, Billy Curtis, Norman Grabowski; DIR: Lennie Weinrib; PROD: Bart Patton; SCREENPLAY: Larry Hovis; STUDIO: Universal; 87 min., color (no video release)

MUSIC ★★★★★
ATTITUDE ★★★
FUN ★★★★

Planet Earth is saved by the Girl with the Horn-Rimmed Glasses.
There's a lot of great music in *Out of Sight*, which is director Lennie Weinrib's follow-up to *Beach Ball* and *Wild Wild Winter*. But the star of this movie is the great George Barris custom hot rod. Most of the publicity for *Out of Sight* featured these wheels over names—except, that is, for the Turtles, the Knickerbockers, Dobie Gray, the Astronauts, Freddie and the Dreamers, and Gary Lewis and the Playboys, who perform the killer opening number, "Malibu Run." Most of the songs featured in this film are unique to its soundtrack, including the Turtles' "She'll Come Back," one of their best (and most) psychedelic tunes. The Astronauts also provide exciting music (again) with a punk-rock version of Them's "Baby Please Don't Go." The only bands who really disappoint are the usually awesome Knickerbockers, singing a campy version of "It's Not Unusual," and Freddie and the Dreamers, whose introduction (as "the big stars from England") says a lot about the nutball level of the rest of this film. It has a goofy, sci-fi plot about some scientist trying to blow up the world, which is saved in the end by Carol Shelyne (the "Girl with the Horn-Rimmed Glasses" from "Shindig"). In an obvious nudge of "The Man from U.N.C.L.E.," the sinister villains belong to the crime syndicate F.L.U.S.H. (DP)

Bob Eubanks   *CAMEOS*

Malibu Run (Gary Lewis and the Playboys); *It's Not Unusual* (Knickerbockers); *Baby Please Don't*   *SONGS* *Go* (Astronauts); *She'll Come Back* (Turtles); *Funny over You, A Love Like You* (Freddie and the Dreamers); *Out of Sight* (Dobie Gray)

PAJAMA PARTY   (1964)

CAST: Tommy Kirk, Annette Funicello, Elsa Lancester, Harvey Lembeck, Jesse White, Jody McRea, Ben Lessy, Donna Loren, Susan Hart, Dorothy Lamour, Bobbi Shaw, Candy Johnson, Buster Keaton, Lurie Holms; DIR: Don Weiss; PROD: James H. Nicholson, Samuel Z. Arkoff; SCREENPLAY: Louis M. Heyward; STUDIO: American International; 85 min., color (no video release)

MUSIC ★★★★
ATTITUDE ★★★
FUN ★★★★

The Beach Party *gang gets dressed for bedtime.*
After *Beach Blanket Bingo*, A.I.P. relied on format flips to keep its blockbuster *Beach Party* series going. In the meantime, the regular cast members became bona-fide rock'n'roll vehicles themselves. There's little doubt who provides the best rockin' moments in this shindig. Fans of the girl group sound can thrill to Donna Loren's "Among the Young" and Annette Funicello's title track. The latter is a fantastic moment during which only a deadbeat would stay in his or her seat. The humor rips off Moe, Larry, Curly, Groucho, Chico, Harpo, and even Bugs Bunny. One classic scene features Buster Keaton in a silent "perfume fight." Don Rickles and Frankie Avalon appear as interplanetary invaders, and Tommy Kirk plays alongside Annette (for variety's sake) as a fumbling martian teenager.

Still, it's the production numbers that really blow this movie through the roof. A.I.P. hired David Winters and Toni Basil to choreograph the proceedings, and for me, their work carries the rest of the picture over the top. Winters and Basil worked on all of the best go-go dancing of the '60s: *The T.A.M.I. Show*, *Hullaballoo*, *The Cool Ones*, and even *West Side Story*. They start the movie off with a bang as the gang enjoys some poolside dancing to an extended version of Annette's "It's That Kind of Day," one of the most positive song of the '60s. Japanese Lanterns bob, and Susan Hart explodes volcanoes with a slow hip sway. It's pure zeitgeist! Later, Dorthy Lamour sings at a pompous fashion show as girls break out into spontaneous go-go dancing. (DP)

Frankie Avalon, Don Rickles   *CAMEOS*

It's That Kind of Day, Stuffed Animal, Pajama Party (Annette Funicello); *Among the Young* (Donna   *SONGS*
Loren); *There Has to Be a Reason* (Annette Funicello, Tommy Kirk); *Where Did I Go Wrong?*
(Dorothy Lamour); *Beach Ball* (Nooney Rickett Four)

PARADISE HAWAIIAN STYLE   (1966)

CAST: Elvis Presley, Suzanna Leigh, James Shigeta, Donna Butterworth, Marianna Hill, Irene Tsu; DIR: D. Michael Moore; PROD: Hal B. Wallis; SCREENPLAY: Allan Weiss, Anthony Lawrence; STUDIO: Paramount; 91 min., color (Key)

MUSIC ★★★★
ATTITUDE ★★
FUN ★★★★

Elvis does Hawaii III—by air.
Elvis's 21st movie features the best scenery of his three Hawaiian adventures simply because a great deal of the action takes place in aircraft, making the luscious aerial photography a natural. *Paradise Hawaiian Style* also makes more sense than either *Blue Hawaii* or *Girls, Girls, Girls* did, probably because it repeats the *Girls, Girls, Girls* storyline, and screenwriter Allan Weiss did a better job this time around. (Elvis pilots planes here rather than boats.) *Paradise Hawaiian Style* also features Elvis at his womanizing peak. The film did okay at the box office, but then again the mid-'60s weren't exactly a high point in the King's career. Historical records show that the big "Drums of the Islands" number was marred by a fight among the native extras. It seems the canoe used in that scene was of Samoan origin, while the oarsmen were Tongan.

The plot here feature Elvis as Rick Richards, an out-of-work airline pilot who starts a charter business shuttling people around the islands in a helicopter. At one point, dogs being transported to a pet show get snarled up in the controls of the chopper. This encourages Rick to sing "A Dog's Life." The helicopter, which nearly crashes, buzzes the road just as the head of the Island Aviation Bureau is driving by with his wife. He's not very happy. On the whole, though, the charter business provides Elvis with many opportunities to meet girls and, inevitably, hit guys. When Elvis's hair gets wet, by the way, he doesn't look so hot. (TM)

LINES Elvis's catch phrase for every girl he meets and tries to use: "You scratch my back...I'll scratch yours." The great Elvis taunt: "Last one out of the water is a papaya picker!"

SONGS *Paradise Hawaiian Style, Queenie Wahini's Papaya, Scratch My Back , Drums of the Islands, A Dog's Life, Datin', House of Sand, Stop Where You Are, This Is My Heaven* (Elvis Presley); *Bill Bailey Won't You Please Come Home* (Donna Butterworth)

PAT GARRETT AND BILLY THE KID   (1973)

MUSIC ★★★
ATTITUDE ★★★★★
FUN ★★★

CAST: James Coburn, Kris Kristofferson, Richard Jaeckel, Katy Jurado, Chill Wills, Barry Sullivan, Bob Dylan; DIR: Sam Peckinpah; PROD: Gordon Carroll; SCREENPLAY: Rudy Wurlitzer; STUDIO: MGM; 121 min., color (MGM/UA)

Is Dylan an actor or just part of the scenery?
Bob Dylan is slovenly, gruff, and thoroughly respectable in his feature-film debut as Alias, a cowboy sidekick whose name serves as a metaphor for the character as well as Dylan's life (particularly his music and the never-ending travails of faith and spirituality). Dylan also wrote the soundtrack music, which includes "Knockin' on Heaven's Door." Sam Peckinpah biographer David Weddle says that the grizzled director was moved to tears at Bob's audition. Weddle also reports that Peckinpah sent a knife whizzing past the erstwhile actor's head when he screwed up a complicated scene.

Ultimately, though, Dylan's character is inconsequential. You get the feeling that Peckinpah placed him in frame so much because he's Bob Dylan, icon. But Dylan is no competition for the two title icons, played by James Coburn and Kris Kristofferson, respectively. Peckinpah's elegiac take on the legend posits Garrett as a rebel who sold out to the Man when he became sheriff and is unable to live with himself (or anyone else) after he kills his old friend. Coburn and Kristofferson are both supercool in an otherwise ponderous, anticlimactic film. MGM originally recut it over Peckinpah's objections, setting off the director's depressed and drunken artistic decline. Make sure to get the recently released director's cut, 16 minutes longer and much improved in tone and content. (JC)

SCENES The leisurely freeze-frame opening and the tense, sad mythic grandeur of the ending (1:50)—both classic Peckinpah sequences; Billy winning a duel by cheating the count before the other guy can (1:15)

LINES The utter strangeness of Dylan's most substantial dialogue, reading the labels of cans in a cupboard: "Beans. Spinach and beans. Baked Beans. Beans. Salmon. Beef Stew. Beans." This goes on for several minutes.

CAMEOS Jason Robards, Charlie Martin Smith, Harry Dean Stanton, R.G. Armstrong, Slim Pickens, Rita Coolidge, Rudy Wurlitzer

PERFORMANCE (1968)

CAST: James Fox, Mick Jagger, Anita Pallenberg, Michele Breton, Johnny Shannon, John Bindon; **DIR:** Nicolas Roeg; **PROD:** Sanford Lieberson; **SCREENPLAY:** Donald Cammell; **STUDIO:** Warner; 102 min., color (Warner)

MUSIC ★★★
ATTITUDE ★★★★
FUN ★★★

A thriller with a Jaggered edge.

After serving as a cinematographer on such pictures as *Live It Up*, Nicolas Roeg emerged during the late '60s as an important director. *Performance*, however, was probably a little too ambitious for him this early in his career. Certainly it was too much for Warner Brothers. The studio shelved the picture for two years after completion before it occured to someone that *any* picture starring Mick Jagger would make money. It didn't matter what the movie was about. And so *Performance* was finally released.

The story concerns the bizarre relationship that develops when a gangster moves in with a former pop star. Needless to say, the plot was hardly typical of rock star vehicles at the time. In fact, the project was as daring as anything Jagger ever did. It set the stage for David Bowie's later work in Roeg's *The Man Who Fell to Earth*. As in that sci-fi classic, Roeg's direction here is stylish, angular, and brimming with unnerving and unexpected edits. It's all strangely strange and oddly normal. (BE)

Gone Dead Train (Randy Newman); *Memo from Turner* (Mick Jagger); *Wake Up Niggers* (Last Poets); *Performance, Poor White Hound Dog* (Merry Clayton); *Dyed Dyed Red* (Buffy Sainte Marie)   **SONGS**

Performance

PHANTOM OF THE PARADISE (1974)

CAST: William Finley, Paul Williams, Jessica Harper, George Memmoli, Gerrit Graham, Harold Oblong, Jeffrey Comanor, Archie Hahn; **DIR:** Brian De Palma; **PROD:** Edward R. Pressman; **SCREENPLAY:** Brian De Palma; **STUDIO:** 20th Century-Fox; 92 min., color (Key)

MUSIC ★★★★
ATTITUDE ★★★★★
FUN ★★★★★

A rock parody of Phantom of the Opera.

Goons in the employ of the pop impresario Swan (Paul Williams), head of Death Records, steal the work of aspiring singer-songwriter Winslow Leach (William Finley), disfiguring Leach in the process. During the rest of the film, Leach (as the Phantom) terrorizes Swan's showcase theater, the Paradise, where he's redeemed by his love for a singer named Phoenix (Jessica Harper). In the end, he sacrifices his own life to save Phoenix from Swan.

Director Brian De Palma brings an almost visionary silliness to this multilayered pastiche of satire and slapstick melodrama. He skewers old horror movies, rock greed, decadence, androgyny, and even bad makeup—not to mention the legends of Phil Spector, Dick Clark, and Faust. Paul Williams's score isn't nearly as inspired as the direction, but it's still an effective conglomeration of received ideas, some of which are satirical even when they're not meant to be. The giddy running gags (e.g., the greasepainted band that's a 1973 KISS by way of the 1919 *Cabinet of Dr. Caligari*) may have doomed the film commercially, but you get the feeling that Gerrit Graham's fabulously overwrought Beef must have changed the course of Meatloaf's life forever. (HH)

SONGS *Died for Love* (Juicy Fruits); *Sell My Soul/Old Emotions, Come Together in Me* (William Finley); *What Life Is All About* (Beach Bums); *Once You Arrive, This Love* (Jessica Harper); *The Son Also Rises* (Undead); *Live at Last* (Gerrit Graham)

PINK FLOYD: THE WALL (1982)

CAST: Bob Geldof, Bob Hoskins; DIR: Alan Parker; PROD: Alan Marshall; SCREENPLAY: Roger Waters; STUDIO: MGM; 95 min., color (MGM/UA)

MUSIC ★★★★
ATTITUDE ★★
FUN ★★★

The death of the rock'n'roll dream as told by Roger Waters.

The stampeding of 11 teenagers at a Who concert in Cincinnati and the spread of ultraconservativism must have left their not-so-comfortably-numbing marks on Pink Floyd's resident visionary, Roger Waters. Since MTV had yet to be invented, what's a disillusioned concept artist to do but make a movie, of course. *The Wall* descends on its audience like a Lancaster bomber in a nose dive, dragging behind it a befuddling array of childhood trauma, teenage angst, and the sheer insanity of the rock lifestyle. It also leaves behind it a decidedly bitter aftertaste.

Burned-out rock star Pink (Bob Geldof) retreats into his inner hell in an L.A. hotel room and two film hours later emerges a fascist rock idol. A most humorless affair, *The Wall* gets its power from the late-era Floyd gems, some sophisticated animation by Gerald Scarfe, and the perfectly nightmarish vision of director Alan (*Midnight Express*) Parker. The hotel destruction scene, so popular in its day, looks nothing like the fun it must have been to create. But it's nicely amended by a meticulous reconstruction scene (echoes of the *Ummagumma* back cover?).

Audiovisual quotes from the Pink Floyd vocabulary appear everywhere, although their emergence in a narrative format makes them no more understandable. There are too many messages to keep up with. The film's stylish surrealism sets the stage for monsters everywhere: Teachers, women, and rock stars are just some of the cast of demons that lurk behind every scene. Young English kids, hired as extras during filming (and more in tune with punk than with rock dinosaurs Pink Floyd), booed the film crews, making them some of the edgiest extras in movie history. The emergence of neo-Nazism in Europe during the late '80s a few years later gives this film an added prophetic bite. Unlike *Quadrophenia*, which sidestepped philosophical musings, *The Wall* takes them on headfirst. It's a Nietzschean vision of the teenage wasteland. But rather than God dying, it's rock'n'roll that receives the last rites. (TR)

SCENES The animated dance of the two flowers to the tune of "Empty Spaces" (0:36)

SONGS *Another Brick in the Wall , Goodbye Blue Sky, Mother, Empty Spaces, Young Lust, Is There Anybody Out There?, Vera Lynn, Bring the Boys Back Home, Comfortably Numb, Run Like Hell, The Trial* (Pink Floyd)

PLAY IT COOL   (1962)

CAST: Billy Fury, Anna Palk, Michael Anderson Jr., Dennis Price, Richard Wattis; DIR: Michael Winner; PROD: David Deutch; SCREENPLAY: Jack Henry; STUDIO: Rank/Independent Artists; 81 min., b/w (no video release)

MUSIC ★★★★★
ATTITUDE ★★★★
FUN ★★★★★

Billy Fury's finest performance.
Billy Fury was the best British rock'n'roller before the Beatles came along, and this film shows why. *Play It Cool* is a low-budget but nicely produced drama about a struggling rock band involved with a runaway heiress. The band's safari through Soho in search of the girl's philandering fiancé gives the producers an excuse to program in performances of then-current rock acts. Fury is no actor, but he's sufficiently charismatic to pull off his role as the band leader. Much of the comedy is predictable, especially the running gag featuring Richard Wattis as a nervous airbus passenger, but the picture has a pleasing earthiness and a knowing cynicism about the music business that puts it several cuts above its American equivalents. For example, the script doesn't give the girl to the hero at the end. Perhaps prophetically, the songwriting credits include Dick Rowe, the Decca executive who turned down the Beatles. (BE)

A club owner to Fury and his band: "If you're good, you boys can come back and perform again for money—but not too much money!"   **L I N E S**

Play It Cool (Billy Fury); *Who Can Say* (Danny Williams); *It's Gonna Take Magic* (Shane Fenton and the Fentones); *Take It Easy* (Jimmy Crawford); *Who Can Say* (Bobby Vee); *Cry My Heart Out, But I Don't Care* (Helen Shapiro)   **S O N G S**

POLYESTER   (1981)

CAST: Divine, Tab Hunter, Edith Massey, David Samson, Mary Garlington, Ken King, Mink Stole, Joni Ruth White, Stiv Bators; DIR: John Waters; PROD: John Waters; SCREENPLAY: John Waters; STUDIO: New Line; 83 min., color (HBO)

MUSIC ★★★★
ATTITUDE ★★★★★
FUN ★★★★★

John Waters, rock superstar.
Most rock musicians are John Waters fans, and no tour-bus film library is complete without a couple of his movies. Waters makes comedies about the depravity that lurks just below the surface of suburbia, and he doesn't exaggerate much. Alongside the sick jokes and grotesque behavior in the average John Waters film, you'll also find a great rock'n'roll soundtrack, selected by Waters himself from the scratchy records in his own collection. His taste is superb. In *Pink Flamingos*, he uses "The Swag" by Link Wray as the opening theme and later employs a deranged version of "Wine Wine Wine" during the human barbecue sequence. Finally, Divine, the 300-pound drag queen who stars in most of Waters's films, delivers an incomparable tribute to Jayne Mansfield when he sashays down the street to the blasting strains of Little Richard's "The Girl Can't Help It."

Polyester, which could have been based on any number of Ramones songs, tells the story of the Fishpaw family: Elmer (David Samson), owner of a porn-movie theatre; Francine (Divine), his tormented and angst-ridden wife; LuLu (Joni Ruth White), their nymphomaniac daughter; and Dexter (Ken King), their sociopathic son. The cast also features '50s teen idol Tab Hunter as Todd Tomorrow and punk rocker Stiv Bators as LuLu's boyfriend. As a tribute to 1950s-gimmick-film auteur William Castle, *Polyester* was originally released to theaters in Odorama. Members of the audience received scratch'n'sniff cards so they could smell along

Polyester

with the story. (I still have mine.) John Waters's films are recommended to rock'n'roll fans and disenfranchised suburbanites everywhere. (MC)

LINES   Francine to her "rehabilitated" children: "We're a normal American family now." Bobo to Francine: "It was nice beating you, Mrs. Fishpaw."

SONGS   *Polyester* (Tab Hunter); *Be My Daddy Baby* (Michael Kamen); *TheBest Thing* (Bill Murray)

THE PRETTY THINGS (1966)

MUSIC ★★★★★
ATTITUDE ★★★★
FUN ★★★★

CAST: Phil May, Dick Taylor, John Stax, Brian Pendleton, Skip Alan; DIR: Caterina Avert, Anthony West; PROD: Anthony West, Bryan Morrison; SCREENPLAY: Caterina Avert; STUDIO: Amanda; 20 min., b/w (no video release)

They make the Rolling Stones look like squeaky-clean, preening pop stars.
The Pretty Things will always be tagged as the band that was louder, uglier, and wilder than the Rolling Stones. In fact, lead guitarist Dick Taylor was the Stones' original bass player. The Pretties' controversial image and their manic, uncompromising approach to R&B made an unforgettable impression when they first burst onto the British scene in 1964. In America, however, where the Pretties were less well known, they nevertheless inspired hundreds of teenage garage bands that aped every pound, snarl, and scream heard on their early Fontana sides. The energy level and sheer excitement of "Rosalyn," "Don't Bring Me Down," and "Come See Me" remain unequaled, and the Pretties continue to influence garage bands to this day.

The Pretty Things is a short promotional film, financed by the band's management, that was shot and released in 1966. Without any dialogue, the film relies on lively visual effects and the band's powerful music to keep it interesting. One intense scene shows the group in the studio powering through "Midnight-to-Six Man." From its swirling, psychedelic opening sequence through the Keystone Kops-type gimmickry of electronic bleeps and buzzes, and some *Hard Day's Night-*

inspired high jinks, this film typifies the vibrant, fast-paced style of mid-to-late-'60s London. Too bad the producers were too cheap to film this in color. (DP/MS)

Me Needing You, Midnight-to-Six Man, Can't Stand the Pain, L.S.D. (Pretty Things)

PRIVILEGE (1967)

CAST: Paul Jones, Jean Shrimpton, Mark Condon, Jeremy Child, Max Bacon, William Job; DIR: Peter Watkins; PROD: John Heyman, Peter Watkins; SCREENPLAY: Norman Boyner; STUDIO: Universal; 103 min., color (no video release)

MUSIC ★★★★★
ATTITUDE ★★★★★
FUN ★★★★★

A rock'n'roll martyr becomes cannon fodder.
Some people claim that *Privilege* is too murky and slow moving (what they really mean is too British), but the concert scenes are truly exciting, and the story of pop and politics is original. The new coalition government in Britain wants to keep the nation's youth off the streets and out of politics, but how? Well, how about employing a rebellious teen icon of the government's own making? Enter Steven Shorter (played by Paul Jones of Manfred Mann), who quickly becomes the biggest pop star of all time.

Jones is great as the perpetually pained and withdrawn Shorter. The film opens with Jones, wearing handcuffs, performing "Free Me." This production number, complete with a jail cell and club-wielding policemen, sends the teenage audience into a frenzy. Management types then drag Shorter from one function to another for the good of the cause ("Buy British!"). Supermodel Jean Shrimpton plays a chick (Vanessa) who has been commissioned to paint a portrait of Shorter. They get sort of friendly, but Shorter doesn't seem to be capable of much more since he looks like he's bleeding internally most of the time.

When Shorter's management and the government jointly decide that the rebellious martyr motif is just about played out, they switch gears. In conjunction with the church, they develop the "new" Shorter: a repentant rebel pleading to reenter society. The crusade kicks off with a stadium concert that resembles a Nazi rally as 40,000 youths devote themselves to God and country (all the while chanting "We will conform!"). With encouragement from Vanessa, Shorter decides he's had enough and delivers a banquet speech so disrespectful that he's banned from ever again making public appearances. Problem is he acted a little too late: The public is already brainwashed, and Shorter is never heard from again. (BV)

Free Me, I've Been a Bad Bad Boy (Paul Jones); *Onward Christian Soldiers, Jerusalem* (George Bean and the Bean Runners)

PSYCH-OUT (1968)

CAST: Susan Strasberg, Jack Nicholson, Dean Stockwell, Bruce Dern, Max Julien, Adam Roarke; DIR: Richard Rush; PROD: Dick Clark; SCREENPLAY: E. Hunter Willett, Betty Ulius; STUDIO: American International; 82 min., color (HBO)

MUSIC ★★★★
ATTITUDE ★★★
FUN ★★★★

Filmed entirely on location in hippie heaven.
Considering who produced it, *Psych-Out* is a surprisingly realistic slice of countercultural life, Haight-Ashbury style. Like the better American International films of the period, it was made quickly with little time for screenwriting, yet it shows authenticity and sincerity in its treatment of the hippie lifestyle. This was no doubt due to the care taken by the young, hip (and well-connected) cast and crew, almost all of whom would graduate to bigger things.

Susan Strasberg plays Jennie, a deaf runaway who has just arrived in San Francisco to find her long-lost brother, a mysterious bearded sculptor known around town as The Seeker (Bruce Dern). She falls in with a psychedelic rock band, Mumblin' Jim, whose members include Stony (a pony-tailed Jack Nicholson), Ben (Adam Roarke), and Elwood (Max Julien, later to star in the blaxploitation classic *The Mack*). They hide her from the fuzz in their crash pad, a Victorian house crowded with love beads and necking couples. Mumblin' Jim's truth-seeking friend Dave (Dean Stockwell) considers the band's pursuit of success "playing games," but he agrees to help Jennie anyway. The Seeker turns up at a concert, but he's chased by some right-wing thugs just as Jennie takes her first STP trip. This all leads to a tragic conclusion. Along the way are performances by the Strawberry Alarm Clock (who also contribute the great main title theme, "The Pretty Song from Psych-Out") and the Seeds, who play at a mock funeral happening. (JS)

SCENES The fuzzed-out instrumental that Nicholson and company pretend to play at a club is "Ashbury Wednesday," which according to the credits (and the Sidewalk soundtrack LP) was recorded by the Boenzee Cryque and written by *four* people. Actually, "Ashbury Wednesday" is a thinly disguised rewrite of "Purple Haze."

LINES Older, shorter-haired hippie: "The message is beads." Younger, fuzzy-haired hippie: "Beads." O.S.H.: "The message is...music. The message is staring at crystal." Y.F.H.: "You mean like, searching for the truth, wherever you may find it?" O.S.H.: "*No, maahnn.*"

CAMEOS Henry Jaglom as an artist with ridiculously large sideburns who freaks out on a bad trip and threatens people with power tools

SONGS *Rainy Day Mushroom Pillow* (Strawberry Alarm Clock); *Ashbury Wednesday* (Boenzee Cryque); *Two Fingers Pointing on You* (Seeds)

PUMP UP THE VOLUME (1990)

CAST: Christian Slater, Samantha Mathis, Mimi Kennedy, Scott Paulin, Cheryl Pollack, Anne Ross; DIR: Allan Moyle; PROD: Rupert Harvey, Sandy Stern; SCREENPLAY: Allan Moyle; STUDIO: New Line; 105 min., color (RCA/Columbia)

MUSIC ★★★★
ATTITUDE ★★★
FUN ★★★

How to steal the air while avoiding the FCC.
Hubert Humphrey High is a model school in the model suburb of Paradise Hills, Arizona. But the students have a new, somewhat-less-than-model hero. His name is Happy Harry Hard-On. He's a breath of fresh air in the desert who blows through every night at 10 on his own pirate radio station. Using shortwave and his own ingenuity, Harry plays music, talks hard, provokes, and muses. He even makes phone calls and fakes masturbation on the air. And he strikes a chord somewhere deep in the heart of every awkward, uncertain adolescent who hears him. A voice-distortion device hides his true identity, but we know he's shy, disaffected Mark (Christian Slater), whom nobody notices because he tries so hard to look like he's not there. The plot elements are predictable—evil principal, cool love interest. The kids get a cause, the cause gives them power, and in the end they seize the day. Or the night. Or the air. Still, the film touches on some serious issues along the way—pregnancy, suicide, sexuality, loneliness—which are handled with surprising maturity. This is no happy, hey-kids-let's-put-on-a-show deal, but for a teen flick, it's an unusually sensitive one. (KW)

The Popular Girl gathering up all her Popular Girl paraphernalia, stuffing it in the microwave, and nuking it (with half the kitchen as well) (0:27) *SCENES*

Harry: "There's nothing to do anymore. Everything decent has been done. All the great themes are used up." *LINES*

THE PUNK ROCK MOVIE (1978)

CAST: The Sex Pistols, The Clash, The Slits, Siouxsie and the Banshees, Generation X, The Heartbreakers; DIR: Don Letts; PROD: Peter Clifton; STUDIO: Cinematic Releasing; 80 min., color (Rhino)

MUSIC ★★★★
ATTITUDE ★★★★★
FUN ★★★

Postcard from the front.
Don Letts, who served as road manager for several British punk bands in the critical '76-'77 era (and later joined Big Audio Dynamite), made this simple but valuable chronicle of those glorious days, "photographed entirely on location in Super-8." Letts made full use of his total scene access, showing the hectic world of these young bands at rehearsal studios, on stage in tiny clubs, and on the road in their first tour buses. The talent roster includes outright legends (Pistols, Clash), future industry veterans (Siouxsie and the Banshees, Billy Idol), fondly remembered footnotes to history (X-Ray Spex, the Slits), and the completely forgotten (it's easy to forget that there was a time when Slaughter and the Dogs were considered state of the art).

Besides the Clash at their furious best, this movie also features some memorable opening credits under which a young Shane McGowan (future Nipple Erector/Nip/Pogue) madly pogos in his Union Jack coat and skinny tie while his punkette partner periodically flashes her breasts at the camera. (JS)

God Save the Queen, Seventeen, Liar, Pretty Vacant, New York (Sex Pistols); *Cranked Up Really High* (Slaughter and the Dogs); *Walking in the City* (Generation X); *White Riot, 1977* (Clash); *Why Don't You Shoot Me* (Subway Sect); *Fuck Off, Cream in My Jeans* (Wayne County and the Electric Chairs); *You* (Eater); *Bad Shape, Carcass* (Siouxsie and the Banshees); *Chinese Rocks, Born to Lose* (Heartbreakers); *Oh Bondage Up Yours* (X-Ray Spex) *SONGS*

PURPLE RAIN (1984)

MUSIC ★★★★★
ATTITUDE ★★
FUN ★★★

CAST: Prince, Apollonia Kotero, Morris Day, Clarence Williams III; DIR: Albert Magnoli; PROD: Robert Cavallo, Joseph Ruffalo, Steven Fargnoli; SCREENPLAY: Albert Magnoli, William Blinn; STUDIO: Warner; 111 min., color (Warner)

Prince at the pinnacle.

Prince's first feature, which has some of the naive charm of a big-budget home movie, also includes some outstanding performances by the Revolution, his best band to date. Unfortunately, *Purple Rain* has other problems—including sandbox misogyny, an aimless script, and some stiff, unconvincing acting. Prince plays the Kid, an aspiring musician out to conquer his hometown of Minneapolis. But first he must make a believer of a local club owner and subdue a rival band, the Time, led by the wisecracking and marcel-haired Morris Day. Prince romances femme lead Apollonia Kotero, but there's a nasty edge to his playful teasing. There's also some domestic violence relating to his parents' interracial marriage, but this conflict is never developed enough to really matter.

When Wendy Melvoin of the Revolution accuses Prince of being a paranoid control freak, the boundary between life and cinema seems to dissolve right before your eyes. However, all the minor dramas and complications are instantly subsumed by the musical action down at Glam Slam (actually a club called First Avenue; Prince opened his own Glam Slam in Minneapolis several years later). People obviously liked the music. *Purple Rain* won Academy Awards for Best Original Score and Best Song, and the soundtrack album held the top spot in the *Billboard* charts for a mindboggling 24 weeks, selling over 10 million copies. (AS)

SONGS *Let's Go Crazy, Take Me with U, The Beautiful Ones, When Doves Cry, Computer Blue, Little Nikki, Purple Rain* (Prince and the Revolution); *Sex Shooter* (Apollonia with Vanity 6); *Cool* (Time)

Purple Rain

Quadrophenia

QUADROPHENIA (1979)

CAST: Phil Daniels, Leslie Ash, Garry Cooper, Sting; DIR: Franc Roddam; PROD: Roy Baird, Bill Curbishley; SCREENPLAY: Dave Humphries, Franc Roddam, Martin Stellman; STUDIO: World-Northall; 120 min., color (RCA/Columbia)

MUSIC ★★★★★
ATTITUDE ★★★★★
FUN ★★★★★

The Who's second rock opera comes to the silver screen.

Quadrophenia is probably the best serious picture ever made from a rock concept work, not that its competition has been so great (Ken Russell's *Tommy* or *Pink Floyd: The Wall*, for instance). The action takes place in Britain during the mid-1960s, when mods and rockers used to riot in the surfside resort of Brighton whenever they got the chance. Phil Daniels plays Jimmy, a gawky, unhappy kid who becomes a mod in order to resolve his identity problems. He has no idea of the violence and disillusionment that awaits him.

   Quadrophenia is one of the bleakest, most honest, and most disheartening visions of youth ever put on celluloid—a cinematic *Catcher in the Rye* for the post-'60s generation. Franc Roddam's enormous directorial drive and energy manage to digest Pete Townshend's songs and raise them to a level that Townshend himself probably never imagined. *Quadrophenia* is a history lesson and a moral lesson all wrapped up in one. (BE)

RAINBOW BRIDGE (1971)

DIR: Chuck Wein; PROD: Barry de Prendergast; STUDIO: Alcyone; 74 min., color (Rhino)

MUSIC ★★★★★
ATTITUDE ★★★★★
FUN ★★

A short lesson in how to take lots of drugs and act like a totally cosmic geek.

Rest assured that *Rainbow Bridge* definitely captures the mood of an era. The late '60s really were silly, rambling, and impenetrable—just like this film, which also suffers from poor picture and sound quality. Viewing *Rainbow Bridge* with an altered state of mind, however, might change one's assessment. Pat Hartley makes a pilgrimage to the Rainbow Bridge Occult Meditation Center on Maui, where she meets some really spaced-out coolies. But Pat's not the reason we're watching. The real star of *Rainbow Bridge*, Jimi Hendrix, doesn't show up until 40 minutes into the film, but his short concert ("The Rainbow Bridge Laboratory Color Sound Experiment") is worth the wait. Despite its utterly disjointed form, *Rainbow Bridge* is something of a hoot thanks to groovy scenes of totally spaced-out hippieness. In one of these riotous episodes, a couple debates whether or not to make love and thus squander their precious "cosmic energy." (EC)

SONGS　*New Rising Sun/May I Come Along with You Baby, Foxy Lady, Get My Heart Back Together, Voodoo Chile, Purple Haze, Hear My Prayer* (Jimi Hendrix)

RAT PFINK A BOO-BOO　　　　(1965)

MUSIC ★★★★★
ATTITUDE ★★★★★
FUN ★★★★

CAST: Carolyn Brandt, Vin Saxon, Titus Moede, George Caldwell, Romeo Barrymore, Dean Danger; DIR: Ray Dennis Steckler; PROD: Ray Dennis Steckler; SCREENPLAY: Ronald Haydock, Ray Dennis Steckler; STUDIO: Morgan-Steckler; 72 min., b/w (Camp Video)

He looked like he could have been Gene Vincent's brother.
The star of this film, Ron Haydock (also known as Vin Saxon), enjoyed a brief recording career in Chicago with his band, the Boppers, before heading out to Hollywood. In Tinseltown, he wrote for and edited monster movie magazines, pornographic novels, and the occasional screenplay. He also acted, usually in Ray Dennis Steckler productions. He tried hard, but Haydock never came close to achieving his dreams of fame and fortune. He died on the night of August 13, 1977, when an 18-wheeler mowed him down as he wandered along Route 66 outside Victorville, California. Ouch!

　　Rat Pfink a Boo-Boo is Ron Haydock's testament, his ultimate gift to pop culture. He plays rock star Lonnie Lord, who doubles as a crime-fighting superhero named Rat Pfink. You could call this movie enigmatic, preposterous, bizarre, surreal, silly, and crazy. I just call it great. A footnote for the Ray Dennis Steckler fans out there: If you're ever in Vegas and you want to rent a video, try Mascot Video or the Video Exchange. Steckler owns both of them. (MC)

SCENES　Lonnie Lord standing outside the Capitol Tower signing autogaphs before heading down the Vine Street Walk of Fame (The first star to cross his path belongs to *guess who*? Who else? Gene Vincent!)

SONGS　*Runnin' Wild, You Is a Rat Pfink, I Stand Alone, Go Go Party* (Ron Haydock)

RECORD CITY　　　　　　　(1978)

MUSIC ★
ATTITUDE ★
FUN ★★★★

CAST: Dennis Bowen, Michael Callan, Joe Higgins, Maria Grimm; DIR: Dennis Steinmetz; PROD: James T. Aubrey; SCREENPLAY: Ron Friedman; STUDIO: American International; 90 min., color (no video release)

Total trash '70s-style.
How's this for an all-star cast: Ruth Buzzi, Jack Carter, Rick Dees, Alice Ghostley, Frank Gorshin, Ted Lange, Leonard Barr ("Dean Martin's uncle"), Ed Begley Jr., Harold "Oddjob" Sakata, Michael Callan, *and* the great Larry Storch?

All these TV has-beens in one movie? Somebody pinch me! How 'bout a rock'n'roll movie in which the big-deal musical guest is Kinky Friedman? Yes, it really happened.

This tacky mishmash was meant to be a lighthearted situation comedy in the style of the highly successful *Car Wash*. This time, the wacky fun takes place in a typical mid-'70s chain record store covered with posters of Cheap Trick and Blondie, where zany guys and gals make their livings selling double-live LPs. Caught between schlock-rock and disco (with no real evidence of the brewing punk revolution), *Record City* has little to offer beyond its creepy Bicentennial vibe. The tawdry gags and goofy characterizations offered up by Storch and the rest of the cast certainly don't help. This film may be conclusive proof that the mid-'70s were the low points for comedy *and* rock (until about 1989, anyway). In a cost-cutting move (to offset the expense of all the acting talent, perhaps?), *Record City* was shot on video and then transferred to film for its short-lived theatrical run. (JS)

REET, PETITE, AND GONE (1946)

CAST: Louis Jordan and his Tympany Five, June Richmond, Milton Woods, Bea Griffith; DIR: William Forest Crouch; PROD: William Forest Crouch; SCREENPLAY: Irwin Winehouse; STUDIO: Astor; 75 min., b/w (no video release)

MUSIC ★★★★★
ATTITUDE ★★★★★
FUN ★★★★

Louis Jordan gets real gone.

His innovative (and humorous) music made Louis Jordan the most popular black entertainer of the 1940s, as well as the widely acknowledged father of rock'n'roll. Over the years, he put down about 100 songs on film, scattered among various feature films and shorts. Like his other three (*Beware, Caldonia,* and *Look Out Sister*), this one is loaded down with performance clips that make up for the flimsy plot. The acting is better here than elsewhere, but *Reet, Petite, and Gone* is still no *Citizen Kane*. However, unlike today's rock videos, Jordan's performance clips are *hot*. He lip-synchs so well that you'd swear he was performing live. The songs, all bona-fide hits, were rerecorded especially for this movie. Two of them—"That Chick's Too Young to Fry" and "Ain't That Just Like a Woman"—are even better here than on record! (AF)

Rudy Toombs

CAMEOS

Caldonia, Texas & Pacific, All for the Love of Lil, Blues Ain't Nuthin', Green Grass, Wham Sam, I Know What You're Puttin' Down, Let the Good Times Roll, Reet Petite and Gone, That Chick's Too Young to Fry, If It's Love You Want, Baby That's Me (Louis Jordan)

SONGS

RENALDO AND CLARA (1978)

CAST: Bob Dylan, Joan Baez, Sara Dylan, Bob Neuwirth, Harry Dean Stanton, Sam Shepard; DIR: Bob Dylan; PROD: Mel Howard; SCREENPLAY: Bob Dylan; 240 min., color (no video release)

MUSIC ★★★★
ATTITUDE ★★★★★
FUN ★★★

Bob Dylan's directorial effort.

Dylan's prodigious canon makes it tempting to discount this hard-to-find film's history of negative reviews and bad word-of-mouth. It's all too easy to expect an insight that other critics have missed. Unfortuntately, the naysayers were right. *Renaldo and Clara* is not so much a bad film as a disappointing one. Form is rejected for mood, and the result is a mediocre student effort in need of a good edit. Certainly, were it not for Dylan's presence, this film would never have been released.

Dylan's general idea was to use the Rolling Thunder Revue as a backdrop to convey the fractured nature of a life spent on stage and on the road. There's no narrative per se, although several threads recur. Wearing a furry white coat and carrying a red rose, the Woman in White (Joan Baez) wanders through many dimly lit rooms until she finds Renaldo (Dylan) smooching with Clara (played by his real-life wife Sara). The trio sit around smoking cigarettes while the women complain that Bob—I mean, Renaldo—never gives a straight answer to anything. Bob responds, "But what is Truth?" Ba-dump-bump.

Bob Neuwirth, another longtime Dylan sidekick, appears several times playing pinball as he recounts their early days as folkies. Several scenes on a train lend a sense of conspiracy to the film. Meanwhile, Allen Ginsberg makes several landings. Concert footage and some scenes of tour life—the bus, the stage being set up, backstage—round out the show. It's too bad that neither the sum nor the individual parts add up to anything more than a mood that has already been established well before the fourth hour. *Renaldo and Clara* seems fraught with implication, but there's actually very little to chew on. It's torpid, languid, and ponderous. Yet some part of me wants to watch it again. (RG)

SCENES   A socialite welcoming committee mistaking Ronnie Hawkins for Dylan (0:24); Neuwirth recounting the writing of "Blowin' in the Wind" (0:37); a shirtless Ginsberg mumbling unintelligibly to a woman in a red brassiere (2:31); Ginsberg and Dylan visiting Jack Kerouac's grave (2:43)

LINES   Dylan: "Evasiveness is all in the mind."

SONGS   *When I Paint My Masterpiece, A Hard Rain's a-Gonna Fall, It Ain't Me Babe, Knockin' on Heaven's Door, Hurricane, Romance in Durango, House of the Rising Sun, One More Cup of Coffee, Sara, Tangled Up in Blue, Just Like a Woman* (Bob Dylan); *Everything's Coming Up Roses, Diamonds and Rust* (Joan Baez); *Chestnut Mare* (Roger McGuinn)

RHYTHM-AND-BLUES REVUE   (1955)

DIR: Joseph Kohn; PROD: Ben Frye; SCREENPLAY: Leonard Reed, Ben Frye; STUDIO: Studio Films; 70 min., b/w (Matinee Classics)

MUSIC   ★★★★
ATTITUDE ★★★★★
FUN   ★★★★★

Good-time music with depth.

According to numerous fans and critics, rock'n'roll started sliding down the toilet right around 1954. By that time, the music was being geared more and more toward an ever-growing teenage "crossover" audience. This feature film and its companion, *Rock'n'Roll Revue*, were originally released in 1955 to cash in on this trend, but they actually contain performances shot before the "rot" set in. The two films cover black popular music during the decade after World War II. Bringing jazz, pop, and swing to the table are Duke Ellington, Lionel Hampton, Dinah Washington, Sarah Vaughan, and Nat King Cole, among others. The early rock'n'rollers include the Clovers ("Your Cash Ain't Nothing but Trash"), Big Joe Turner ("Shake, Rattle, and Roll"), and Ruth Brown ("Tears Keep Tumbling Down"). It's life-affirming stuff. (MC)

SCENES   R&B notable Amos Milburn (whose booze-and-sex songs included "Good Good Whiskey" and "One Bourbon, One Scotch, One Beer") doing his big hit "Bad Bad Whiskey"

RIDE·THE WILD SURF (1964)

CAST: Fabian, Shelley Fabares, Tab Hunter, Susan Hart, Peter Brown, Barbara Eden, Anthony Hayes, James Mitchum; DIR: Don Taylor; PROD: Jo Napoleon, Art Napoleon; SCREENPLAY: Jo Napoleon, Art Napoleon; STUDIO: Columbia; 101 min., color (no video release)

MUSIC ★★★★
ATTITUDE ★★★★★
FUN ★★★★

The Pipeline heavies are okay, but they can't match the savage surf at Waimea Bay.
This is the one beach exploitation picture that focuses on both surfing *and* surf music. Credit here should go to Stu Philips, the genius arranger responsible for the soundtrack. He rocked up "Blue Moon" for the Marcels in 1961, handled Shelley Fabares's Colpix records, and worked on "The Monkees" and "Gidget" TV shows as well as countless film scores. His "Main Theme from Ride the Wild Surf" is a great tune, and it made for a bitchin' record by the Astronauts, probably the only viable surf music that ever featured an orchestra. *Ride the Wild Surf* is also the film in which legendary Malibu surf ace Mickey Dora doubled for Fabian on the 25-foot waves (even though Dora had never surfed Waimea before!). Jan and Dean were slated to star in this flick, but at the last minute Columbia pulled them because a friend of Dean's had gotten involved in the kidnapping of Frank Sinatra, Jr.! All that remained of Jan and Dean was their dramatic title track, which Jan Berry wrote for the film with Brian Wilson and Roger Christian.

Instead of Jan and Dean, we get Fabian and Tab Hunter. Shelly Fabares co-stars as Fabian's girlfriend, and it's a shame that she doesn't sing here, because her best records were cut about this time ("He Don't Love Me" with Jan Berry and a couple more with P.F. Sloan). A lot hipper than most people think, Shelley's supported here by Barbara ("I Dream of Jeannie") Eden and Susan Hart, who contributes a splendid hula routine. We should be thankful that at least one beach movie bothered to get things right, so give Columbia Pictures credit. When it comes to the true surroundings of surf culture, *Ride the Wild Surf* is right on. Plus, the music is C-double-oh-L...COOL! (DP)

"To a lot of guys, this may look like a jet plane. But to surfers, man, it's a flying carpet to the promised land—Hawaii." *LINES*

RIOT ON SUNSET STRIP (1967)

CAST: Aldo Ray, Mimsy Farmer, Laurie Mock, Tim Rooney; DIR: Arthur Dreifuss; PROD: Sam Katzman; SCREENPLAY: Orville H. Hampton; STUDIO: American International; 87 min., color (no video release)

MUSIC ★★★★★
ATTITUDE ★★★
FUN ★★★★

The garage rock Nashville.
A.I.P producer Sam Katzman, ever watchful of trends, based this film on the Sunset Strip violence of 1966, following police harassment of the mobs of teenagers there. "The most shocking film of our generation" (according to the ads), *Riot on Sunset Strip* was supposed to blow the lid off the wild goings-on in Hollywood discotheques. Mimsy Farmer plays Andy, a troubled teenage girl who falls in with the wrong crowd at a local rock club. At a wild party, someone slips LSD into her diet soda, whereupon five boys take sexual advantage of her. The twist is, her father happens to be the previously tolerant chief of police (Aldo Ray). The chief's violent reaction to his daughter's rape triggers a massive youth demonstration.

As fun as this wild, acid-crazed youth business is, the best reason to see *Riot on Sunset Strip* is the great footage of garage-rock heroes in the nightclub scenes. The Standells (of "Dirty Water" near-fame) play the great title track and the otherwise unavailable "Get Away from Here" (even the soundtrack LP contains a different version). The Chocolate Watch Band dish up some scorching punk anthems, and the underrated Enemies also perform. (This last band left behind a few 45s on MGM before singer Cory Wells decided to reunite with Danny Hutton to form Three Dog Night.) (JS)

SCENES The acid-crazed Andy performing a wild, genuinely erotic dance; the Chocolate Watch Band, featuring genius Mick Jagger-imitator Dave Aguilar (now an astronomy professor) performing "Don't Need Your Lovin'" (a canny rewrite of "Milcow Blues"), which stands as the cinematic definition of punk rock—past, present, and future

SONGS *Riot on Sunset Strip, Get Away from Here* (Standells); *Jolene, I'm Leaving You* (Enemies); *Sitting There Standing, Don't Need Your Lovin'* (Chocolate Watch Band)

ROADIE (1980)

MUSIC ★★★★
ATTITUDE ★★★★
FUN ★★★

CAST: Meatloaf, Kaki Hunter, Art Carney, Alice Cooper, Blondie; **DIR:** Alan Rudolph; **PROD:** Carolyn Pfeiffer; **SCREENPLAY:** Big Boy Medlin, Michael Ventura; **STUDIO:** United Artists; 106 min., color (Wood-Knapp)

A stupid but valuable souvenir of '70s rock excess.

This is a textbook sex, drugs, and rock'n'roll movie. Produced in 1980 as a starring vehicle for the phenomenon that was Meatloaf, *Roadie* documents the decline and fall of '70s rock, seen here in its most decadent phase. Meatloaf plays Travis W. Redfish, a Texas beer truck driver. One day he fixes the Hank Williams, Jr., tour bus and—voila!—finds his true calling as the world's greatest roadie. He's so good that he can power a broken PA with just potatoes and manure. Touring as head roadie for a rock'n'roll circus, Travis encounters such cameo stars as Blondie, Asleep at the Wheel, and even Roy Orbison. He also falls in love with a 16-year-old groupie (Kaki Hunter) whose one goal in life is to lose her virginity to Alice Cooper. The dialogue here ("The bands make it rock; the roadies make it roll") does little to elevate *Roadie*, but this film does deliver the kind of mindless entertainment that was '70s rock. You know, it's stupid but honest. (ALa)

SCENES Hank Williams, Jr., and Roy Orbison stopping a barroom brawl at Austin's legendary Soap Creek venue with their "Eyes of Texas" duet (0:18)

LINES After being head-butted in a brawl, Redfish gets "brainlock" and begins asking random questions, the best of which is: "Who'd win a fight between Bo Diddley and Kate Smith?"

CAMEOS Alvin Crow, Asleep at the Wheel, Hank Williams Jr., Roy Orbison, Peter Frampton, the Blues Brothers

SONGS *Outlaw Women, Family Tradition* (Hank Williams Jr.); *The Eyes of Texas* (Hank Williams Jr., Roy Orbison); *Spittle* (Standing Waves); *Ring of Fire* (Blondie); *Beaumont Rag, Texas Me and You* (Asleep at the Wheel); *Only Women Bleed* (Alice Cooper); *Wedding Jig* (Alvin Crow)

ROCK AROUND THE CLOCK (1956)

MUSIC ★★★
ATTITUDE ★★★★
FUN ★★★★

CAST: Bill Haley and his Comets, Johnny Johnston, Alix Talton, Lisa Gaye, John Archer, Henry Slate, Earl Barton; **DIR:** Fred F. Sears; **PROD:** Sam Katzman; **SCREENPLAY:** Robert E. Kent, James B. Gordon; **STUDIO:** Columbia; 72 min., b/w (no video release)

IT'S THE WHOLE STORY OF ROCK AND ROLL!

BILL HALEY AND HIS COMETS

ROCK AROUND THE CLOCK

with

THE PLATTERS
ERNIE FREEMAN COMBO

TONY MARTINEZ
AND HIS BAND

FREDDIE BELL
AND HIS BELLBOYS

ALAN FREED

JOHNNY JOHNSTON

ALIX TALTON

LISA GAYE
EARL BARTON
HENRY SLATE
JOHN ARCHER

Story and Screen Play by
ROBERT E. KENT and JAMES B. GORDON
Produced by   Directed by
SAM KATZMAN · FRED F. SEARS
A CLOVER PRODUCTION
A COLUMBIA PICTURE

In which Hollywood cons Bill Haley fans into attending the theater.

In the wake of *Blackboard Jungle*'s success, Hollywood jumped on the rock'n'roll bandwagon, cranking out a string of forgettable rocksploitation flicks. This one caused a few riots in England, but it's hard to understand why. Because Bill Haley topped the charts in 1955 with "Rock Around the Clock" (it was *Blackboard Jungle*'s theme song), the title track is performed not once here but twice.

This rather silly film begins when Steve Hollis (Johnny Johnston), a big band manager, realizes that big band music is quickly becoming passé. He dumps the band he was handling and hits the road with his dumb sidekick, Corny LaSalle (Henry Slate). On their way to New York, they discover Haley, his band, and Johnston's love interest, Comets manager Lisa Johns (Lisa Gaye), who also happens to dance. In short order, Steve and Lisa fall in love, and everybody leaves the hick town of Strawberry Springs for the bright lights of New York. Steve gets Alan Freed to book the unknown rockers as a headliner, the kids go crazy, and the rest is history—or at least hysteria. Haley, pudgy and decidedly stiff, performs six of his hits, making it perfectly clear why he's considered by some to be a totally unlikely rock'n'roll star. (MG)

LINES   Corny to Steve as they witness rock'n'roll for the first time: "What is that outfit playing up there?" Steve: "I don't know. It isn't boogie, it isn't jive, and it isn't swing. It's kind of all of that."

SONGS   *See You Later Alligator, Rock-a-Beatin' Boogie, Razzle Dazzle, Rock Around the Clock, Rock Happy Baby, Rudy's Rock* (Bill Haley and his Comets); *Cubros, Mambo Capri, Sad and Lonely, Codfish and Potatoes* (Tony Martinez); *I'm Gonna Teach You How to Rock, Giddyup Dingdong* (Freddie Bell and his Bellboys); *Only You, The Great Pretender* (Platters)

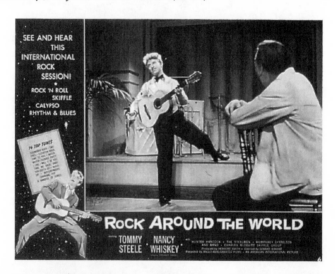

ROCK AROUND THE WORLD   (1957)

ALTERNATE TITLE: *The Tommy Steele Story*
CAST: Tommy Steele, Patrick Westwood, Hilda Fenemore, Chris O'Brien's Caribbeans, The Chas. McDevitt Skiffle Group, Humphrey Lyttleton; DIR: Gerard Bryant; PROD: Nat Cohen, Stuart Levy; SCREENPLAY: Norman Hudis; STUDIO: Insignia; 82 min., b/w (no video release)

MUSIC ★★★★
ATTITUDE ★★★
FUN ★★★★★

Britain's first rock'n'roll movie.

This picture doesn't really offer much in the way of style or musical content—or even acting—but it was a bit of fresh air that blew over the staid British pop culture of the time. Tommy Steele isn't Elvis, and this movie doesn't have the budget or slickness of the King's early movies, but Steele was a thoroughly ingratiating performer. And the movie does capture the odd blend of music hall, American R&B, and country music that helped spawn what passed for English rock'n'roll during the '50s. Pay no attention to the storyline. Just take in the Bill Haley-style tunes that Steele played so well. You might also like the calypso and trad jazz, too. (BE)

Calypso lyrics over the opening credits: "Our Tommy Steele/We are proud to reveal/How we lose control/When you are doing the rock'n'roll!" *LINES*

Take Me Back Baby, Butterfingers, I Like, Water Water, You Gotta Go, Elevator Rock, Teenage Party, Doomsday Rock (Tommy Steele) *SONGS*

ROCK YOU SINNERS   (1957)

CAST: Philip Gilbert, Colin Croft, Adrienne Scott, Jackie Collins; DIR: Denis Kavanaugh; PROD: B.C. Fancey; STUDIO: Small Films; 59 min., b/w (Video Yesteryear)

MUSIC ★★★
ATTITUDE ★★★★★
FUN ★★★★★

Cool Britannia.
This is the story of Johnny Lawrence (Philip Gilbert), a radio DJ who decides to produce a TV extravaganza featuring all the top British rock'n'roll acts. Along the way, he gets into a brief spot of trouble when his girlfriend spies him meeting songstress Joan Small in a coffee bar (strictly business). But soon the misunderstanding is resolved, the TV show is successful, and everybody ends up entirely happy.

So what is there to recommend this movie, apart from the wooden performances, numbingly dull dialogue, and storyline that barely exists? Lots. The musical numbers, filmed at real ballroom locations, capture some genuine excitement and great, frenzied dancing. As for the performers, they're either convincingly high-spirited (Rory Blackwell, Tony Crombie and his Rockets) or amusingly, endearingly inept (Don Sollash and his Rocking Horses, Curly Pat Barry). Look out for future novelist Jackie Collins, who wears lots of tight clothing, shakes her body wildly to the jams, and exudes star quality to spare. (MC)

Rockin' with Rory (Rory Blackwell); *Rock'n'Roll Blues* (Don Sollash and his Rocking Horses); *Let's You and I Rock, Brighton Rock* (Tony Crombie and his Rockets); *You Can't Say I Love You to a Rock'n'Roll Tune* (Joan Small); *Stop It I Like It* (Curly Pat Barry) *SONGS*

ROCK, BABY, ROCK IT   (1957)

CAST: Johnny Dobbs, Kay Wheeler, Joan Arnold, Bill Brookshire, Gayla Graves, Mike Biggs, Linda Moore, Lee Young, David Miller: DIR: Murray Douglas Sporup; PROD: J.G. Tiger: SCREENPLAY: Herbert Margolis, William Raynor; STUDIO: Freebar; 84 min., b/w (Rhino)

MUSIC ★★★★★
ATTITUDE ★★★★★
FUN ★★★★

Required viewing for every American.
The point of this 1956 masterpiece is that it has rock'n'roll in it. Tons of rock'n' roll. Never mind that the writing is mindless and the production values crude— that's how the best rock'n'roll records were made! From the opening salvo of "Hot Rock!" fired off by some middle-aged Bill Haleys and segueing into Johnny Carroll's version, the incredible music never stops. Made by amateur filmmakers

Rock, Baby, Rock It

in Dallas in late 1956, *Rock, Baby, Rock It* probably came in under its $29 budget, but what a lollapalooza it was! Crafted at the precise moment that rock'n'roll was boiling over, this clumsy, plotless cheapie contains an incredible swath of rock music: Fats Domino boogie from Preacher Smith; brilliant Texas doo-wop from the Five Stars; mad Memphis blues from Roscoe Gordon; and white vocal group stylings from Don Coats and the Bon-Aires. But wait, there's more—notably, the incredible Elvis-fueled rockabilly of 19-year-old Johnny "Hot Rock" Carroll and the otherworldly harmony of the Belew Twins. *Rock, Baby, Rock It* also features Kay Wheeler, the president of the Elvis Presley fan club and a hot-bopping kitten in her own right. The adult actors are wooden and lost, but the under-21ers are Dallas kids in their street clothes, whose awkwardness and sincerity make this one-of-a-kind document instantly loveable. (AF)

LINES   "And they thought us kids were going to the devil because we played pool!"

SONGS   *Bop It, Chicken in the Rough* (Roscoe Gordon and the Red Tops); *China Star, Love Never Forgets, Stop the World, Sugar Baby* (Don Coats and the Bon-Aires); *Crazy Crazy Lovin', Rock Baby Rock It, Rockin' Maybelle, Sugar Baby, Wild Wild Women* (Johnny Carroll and the Hot Rocks); *Eat Your Heart Out, Roogie Doogie* (Preacher Smith and the Deacons); *Hey Juanita, Your Love Is All I Need* (Five Stars); *Hot Rock, Lonesome, Love Me Baby* (Belew Twins); *Saints Come Rockin' In* (Cell Block 7)

ROCK, PRETTY BABY (1956)

CAST: Sal Mineo, John Saxon, Luana Patten, Edward C. Platt, Fay Wray, Rod McKuen; DIR: Richard Bartlett; PROD: Edmond Chevie; SCREENPLAY: Herbert Margolis, William Raynor; STUDIO: Universal; 89 min., b/w (no video release)

MUSIC   ★★
ATTITUDE   ★★
FUN   ★★

A teenage boy and his rock'n'roll band struggle for stardom.

During the 1950s, there were two sorts of teenage movies: the lousy and the extremely lousy. *Rock, Pretty Baby* is among the latter because we're concerned with music, and the music stinks. It was composed by one Hank Mancini, whose heart was clearly elsewhere (perhaps sailing along Moon River), while unknown studio hacks overdub the fictitious band Jimmy Daley and the Dingalings. The songs themselves are simply unbearable. Rod McKuen sings two of them, and if you remember "Happiness Is a Warm Gym Shoe," you'll also remember that he's no singer. Considered strictly as a movie, *Rock, Pretty Baby* is not a bad teen flick. But you've still got to work your way around John Saxon's moody, Brando-style performance. When his father criticizes him for buying a new guitar, Saxon looks like he's about to tear his heart out and stomp on it. (AF)

CAMEOS Shelley Fabares, George "Foghorn" Winslow, Douglas Fowley

SONGS *Big Band Rock'n'Roll, Dark Blue, Free and Easy, Hot Rod, Jukebox Rock, Kool Kid, Rockin' the Boogie, Teenage Bop, The Most, Young Love* (Henry Mancini); *Picnic by the Sea, Happy Is a Boy Named Me* (Rod McKuen); *Can I Steal a Little Love?, Rock Pretty Baby, Rockabye Lullabye Blues, What's It Gonna Be* (Jimmy Daley and the Dingalings)

Rock, Pretty Baby

ROCK, ROCK, ROCK (1956)

CAST: Alan Freed, Fran Manfred, Tuesday Weld, Teddy Randazzo, Jacqueline Kerr, The Moonglows, The Johnny Burnette Trio, Chuck Berry, LaVern Baker, Cirino and the Bowties, The Flamingos, Jimmy Cavallo and the Houserockers, Frankie Lymon and the Teenagers, Ivy Schulman; DIR: Will Price; PROD: Max J. Rosenberg, Milton Subotsky; SCREENPLAY: Milton Subotsky; STUDIO: DCA/Vanguard; 83 min., b/w (Goodtimes)

MUSIC ★★★★★
ATTITUDE ★★★★★
FUN ★★★★★

A gift from the patron saint of rock'n'roll.
A legend today, the late Alan Freed is generally recognized as a visionary champion of racial equality who almost single-handedly transformed America's musical taste during the early 1950s. In exchange, he got a totally raw deal (in his time) as the payola scandal made him a victim of 1950s-style phony morality. Freed merely wanted to entertain people, create some fun and excitement, and put some long green stuff in his pocket. He didn't deserve to be a sacrificial lamb.

To get an amazing tape of Alan Freed doing his radio show in 1955, write to the Aircheck Factory, Wildrose, Wisconsin 54984. To read about his career, get *Hit Men* (Random) by Frederick Dannen. To see what Freed's public persona was like, try this film or *Go, Johnny, Go. Rock, Rock, Rock* has a plot, but it's not worth discussing here. Musically, however, the film is a total feast for the eyes and ears. (MC)

SCENES   Chuck Berry, with his unstoppable charisma (and Gretsch guitar) lip-synching to "You Can't Catch Me"; the smirk on Frankie Lymon's face as he sings "I'm Not a Juvenile Delinquent"; four-year-old Ivy Schulman's performance of "Rock, Pretty Baby," which will have lovers of the truly inane in hog heaven; the blissful (for rockabilly fans) appearance of the Johnny Burnette Trio, featuring guitar hero Paul Burlison; Jimmy Cavallo and the House Rockers letting it rip with a blast of sax-driven thug rock

SONGS   *Rock Rock Rock, The Big Beat* (Jimmy Cavallo and the Houserockers); *I Never Had a Sweetheart, Little Blue Wren* (Connie Francis); *When It Comes to Love, Give Me One More Chance* (Teddy Randazzo); *Rock Pretty Baby* (Ivy Schulman, Cirino and the Bowties); *Rock'n'Roll Boogie* (Alan Freed); *I Knew from the Start, Over and Over Again* (Moonglows); *You Can't Catch Me* (Chuck Berry); *Would I Be Crying* (Flamingos); *Lonesome Train on a Lonesome Track* (Johnny Burnette Trio); *Tra La La* (LaVern Baker); *Ever Since I Can Remember* (Cirino and the Bowties); *Baby Baby, I'm Not a Juvenile Delinquent* (Frankie Lymon and the Teenagers)

ROCKIN' THE BLUES (1957)

CAST: Hal Jackson, Manton Moreland, Flournoy Miller, The Cuban Dancers; DIR: Arthur Rosenblum; PROD: Fritz Pollard; STUDIO: Austin; 68 min., b/w (no video release)

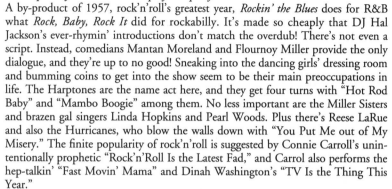

MUSIC ★★★★★
ATTITUDE ★★★★★
FUN ★★★★★

This is possibly the best movie to play at a party.

A by-product of 1957, rock'n'roll's greatest year, *Rockin' the Blues* does for R&B what *Rock, Baby, Rock It* did for rockabilly. It's made so cheaply that DJ Hal Jackson's ever-rhymin' introductions don't match the overdub! There's not even a script. Instead, comedians Mantan Moreland and Flournoy Miller provide the only dialogue, and they're up to no good! Sneaking into the dancing girls' dressing room and bumming coins to get into the show seem to be their main preoccupations in life. The Harptones are the name act here, and they get four turns with "Hot Rod Baby" and "Mambo Boogie" among them. No less important are the Miller Sisters and brazen gal singers Linda Hopkins and Pearl Woods. Plus there's Reese LaRue and also the Hurricanes, who blow the walls down with "You Put Me out of My Misery." The finite popularity of rock'n'roll is suggested by Connie Carroll's unintentionally prophetic "Rock'n'Roll Is the Latest Fad," and Carrol also performs the hep-talkin' "Fast Movin' Mama" and Dinah Washington's "TV Is the Thing This Year."

None of these groups are well known today, and it's doubtful that any stuck-in-the-'70s classic rock fan will ever care to hear their names again. But you'd be hard pressed to find many groups that rock this hot. *Rockin' the Blues* doesn't fool around with any bullshit: the pianos roll, the guitars crunch, the saxes wail, and there's great singing over the top! This is one of the few movies in which rock'n'roll and rhythm-and-blues are completely synomynous—different names for the same thing. And if you'd really like to see something special, dig out the 1955 Ed Sullivan show in which Ed gives Harlem DJ "Dr. Jive" 15 minutes to present live performances by Bo Diddley, LaVern Baker, the Five Keys, and Gator Tail Jackson. Then you'll be able to tell me in five words or less why the band Boston should be banned! (DP)

SONGS

Rock'n'Roll Is the Latest Fad, Fast Movin' Mama, TV Is the Thing This Year (Connie Carroll); *My Sweetie Pie* (Wanderers); *Everybody's Havin' a Ball, Do You Wanna Blow* (Miller Sisters); *I Got to Have You by Myself, They Raided the Joint* (Linda Hopkins); *First Last and Only Girl, Hot Rod Baby, Oowee Baby, Mambo Boogie* (Harptones); *Baby Don't Be That Way* (Reese LaRue); *You Put Me out of My Misery, That Army Life* (Hurricanes); *He's So Lazy, I Can't Wait Til You're Mine* (Pearl Woods)

ROCK'N'ROLL HIGH SCHOOL (1979)

CAST: Vince Van Patten, Grady Sutton, Mary Woronov, Paul Bartel, P.J. Soles, The Ramones, Dey Young, Dick Miller, Clint Howard; DIR: Allan Arkush; PROD: Roger Corman, Michael Finnell; SCREENPLAY: Richard Whitley, Russ Dvonch, Joseph McBride; STUDIO: New World; 94 min., color (Warner)

MUSIC ★★★★★
ATTITUDE ★★★★★
FUN ★★★★★

Don't be a dropout.

Despite what you might think, it is possible for human beings to achieve perfection. Take this movie: Every joke is funny, every song is fantastic, and every frame is shot according to God's will. The action takes place in and around Vince Lombardi High School, and if memory serves, high school students really do behave more or less in the cartoonish, absurd manner shown here. The film's about the classic confrontation between mindless authority and rebellious youth. In the end, the kids win and blow up the school.

Where do the Ramones fit in? Well, the film's main character, Riff Randle (P.J. Soles), is obsessed with them, and the entire school seems to be caught up in Ramones mania. Reportedly, Joey & Co. weren't the first choice for featured band in this movie. But without the wit and the spirit of the Ramones and their music, this movie would not be the classic that it is. The last laugh is theirs. (MC)

SCENES Riff Randle smoking some pot and hallucinating that the Ramones (singing "I Want You Around") are in her bedroom, her shower, and her backyard; Mr. McGree (Paul Bartel) dancing with Riff and tearing his clothes off to the beat of "High School" by the MC5; the Ramones making their entrance while eating chicken vindaloo in a Cadillac convertible with leopard-skin seats and license plate "NY-Gabba-Gabba-Hey"

CAMEOS Grady Sutton, Rodney Bingenheimer, director Allan Arkush

SONGS *Rock'n'Roll High School* (P.J. Soles); *I Just Wanna Have Somethin' to Do, I Want You Around, Blitzkrieg Bop, Teenage Lobotomy, California Sun, Pinhead, She's the One, Do You Wanna Dance, Rock'n'Roll High School* (Ramones)

ROCK'N'ROLL NIGHTMARE (1987)

MUSIC ★★
ATTITUDE ★★
FUN ★★★★

CAST: Jon-Mikl Thor, Paola Francescotto, Teresa Simson, Jesse D'Angelo, Dave Lane, Rusty Hamilton; DIR: John Fasano; PROD: Jon-Mikl Thor; SCREENPLAY: Jon-Mikl Thor; STUDIO: Shapiro Entertainment; 89 min., color (Academy)

Truer words were never spoken.

Take over an hour's worth of rock'n'roll cliches: from the geek manager to the dumb drummer with a bad British accent to the snotty girlfriend to the *sensitive* singer with dreadful hair. Combine them with a plot that has their band, the Tritonz, relocating to a remote Canadian farm to record its new album. Then add some action, such as being picked off one by one by demons and turned into zombies. (We never find out what happens to the band members after that: it might keep you up at night.) Toss in a surprise ending, add water, and throw this tape out the window. (KW)

SCENES Sensitive lead singer John (Jon-Mikl Thor) almost getitng it from a demon who's hiding in the refrigerator disguised as leftovers (0:35); the final showdown between John and a praying mantis-like demon he calls Bub

LINES "Rod, Max, Stig, let's tune our weapons."

SONGS *We Live to Rock, Energy, Edge of Hell, Danger, Live It Up, Steal Your Thunder, The Challenge, Heads Will Turn, Touch Me Feel Me, Maybe It's Love* (Thor and the Tritonz)

THE ROCKY HORROR PICTURE SHOW (1975)

MUSIC ★★★★★
ATTITUDE ★★★★★
FUN ★★★★★

CAST: Tim Curry, Susan Sarandon, Barry Bostwick, Richard O'Brien, Patricia Quinn, Little Nell; DIR: Jim Sharman; PROD: Lou Adler, Michael White; SCREENPLAY: Jim Sharman, Richard O'Brien; STUDIO: 20th Century-Fox; 100 min., color (CBS/Fox)

The queen of the midnight cult films.

Could Richard O'Brien have known what would happen to his musical play? After all, it was a hit on the stage in London and then in Los Angeles. But this business about the film—it's hard to believe that some people have seen it more than a

The Rocky Horror Picture Show

thousand times. Okay, those people are probably a bit strange, but this picture does seem to have an undeniably intoxicating effect on the pleasure center of the brain. O'Brien's extravaganza pays kinky tribute to the RKO science-fiction films of the '50s—classics like *The Day the Earth Stood Still, Forbidden Planet,* and *It Came from Outer Space.* But the real hook here is the joyous (and often hilarious) sexuality of the *Rocky Horror* production numbers.

This film is so packed with music that its songs easily overwhelm both the dialogue and the plot, which is just as well. On a dramatically stormy night on a lonely road, superstraight Brad Majors (Barry Bostwick) and his virgin fiancée, Janet Weiss (Susan Sarandon), have a flat tire near the castle of a mad alien scientist, Dr. Frank-N-Furter (Tim Curry), who's visiting us from the planet Transsexual. Curry's remarkable performance lifts the picture into orbit, while O'Brien's fantastically sneaky turn as the butler Riff Raff gives *Rocky Horror* just the right amount of conceited deceit. You know the movie's infectious when Curry sings "Don't dream it, be it," and you believe him. (DR)

Richard Nixon delivering his resignation speech on the car radio just before Brad and Janet's tire goes flat (0:12); a thin—well, thin*nish*—Meatloaf singing "Hot Patootie" (0:42) **SCENES**

Frank to Janet: "You're as sensual as a pencil." **LINES**

Meatloaf **CAMEOS**

Science Fiction Double Feature (Richard O'Brien); *Dammit Janet, Super Heroes* (Barry Bostwick, Susan Sarandon); *Over at the Frankenstein Place* (Barry Bostwick, Susan Sarandon, Richard O'Brien); *The Time Warp* (Richard O'Brien, Little Nell, Patricia Quinn); *Sweet Transvestite, I Can Make You a Man, Wise Up Janet Weiss, I'm Going Home* (Tim Curry); *Hot Patootie—Bless My Soul* (Meatloaf); *Touch-a Touch-a Touch Me* (Susan Sarandon); *Eddie* (Jonathan Adams); *Rose Tint My World* (Cast) **SONGS**

THE ROSE (1980)

MUSIC ★
ATTITUDE ★★★
FUN ★★★

CAST: Bette Midler, Alan Bates, Frederic Forrest; **DIR:** Mark Rydell; **PROD:** Martin Worth, Aaron Russo; **SCREENPLAY:** Bill Kerby, Bo Goodman; **STUDIO:** 20th Century-Fox; 134 min., color (CBS/Fox)

The horrors of superstardom.

Bette Midler plays the Rose, a Janis Joplin-like singer careening toward tragedy. She's got Joplin's torn-velvet voice and provincial past. She also explores bisexuality, consumes whiskey as though it were one of the primary food groups, and dies from a heroin overdose. But apart from these details, the Rose is a different creature than Joplin, driven by a different Thanatos. In one postcoital confession, Midler whispers to her lover (Frederic Forrest) that she once let her entire high school football team screw her. In other words, men have trashed her life. As a result, the only time she can really take control is when she's on stage. Although Midler bravely throws herself into her portrait of this pathetic character, it's misleading to suggest that Joplin herself was an out-of-control victim who happened to have a legendary voice. Like so many contemporary rock artists, Joplin was ruined by the primal excess of her times, not by her womanhood. (SBW)

SCENES Midler abruptly smashes a whiskey bottle in a hillbilly's face, showing us an unusually fast and effective way to stem sexual harassment (0:27).

CAMEOS Harry Dean Stanton

SONGS *Camellia, Stay with Me, Evil Lies, The Night We Said Goodbye, Sold My Soul to Rock'n'Roll, Keep On Rockin', Fire Down Below, Whose Side Are You On, When a Man Loves a Woman, Midnight in Memphis, Let Me Call You Sweetheart, I've Written a Letter to Daddy* (Bette Midler)

ROUSTABOUT (1964)

MUSIC ★
ATTITUDE ★★★
FUN ★★★

CAST: Elvis Presley, Barbara Stanwyck, Joan Freeman, Leif Ericson, Sue Ann Langdon, Pat Buttram, Jack Albertson; **DIR:** John Rich; **PROD:** Hal B. Wallis; **SCREENPLAY:** Anthony Lawrence, Allan Weiss; **STUDIO:** Paramount; 100 min., color (Key)

Elvis the troublemaker joins a carnival and reforms.

The King is refreshingly unsavory here in his role as the leather-jacketed biker Charlie Rogers. When an irate father runs him off the road early in the picture, Elvis is forced to hook up with a traveling carnival until his bike can be fixed. The carnival is run by a broken-down drunk (Leif Ericson), his tough old broad of a wife (Barbara Stanwyck), and their nubile daughter (Joan Freeman). Along the way, Elvis (who's got a chip on his shoulder about being an orphan) somehow learns about family values from this vaguely dysfunctional one.

Produced just before the deluge of lobotomized smirkfests that made Elvis films a genre, *Roustabout* is a slapdash but likeable enough B-movie. In fact, had anyone bothered, *Roustabout* might have been pretty good. As it turned out, the acting is relaxed, the plot unobtrusive, and the setting pleasant. Elvis is sexy and enjoyable early on, although he tends to go blank during those valuable life lessons. Joan Freeman makes a better-than-average love interest, and Pat Buttram makes hay as a scheming rival carny based on the legend of Colonel Tom Parker. (HH)

LINES Elvis to a frat rat who's taunting him about his Japanese two-wheeler: "You don't dig world trade, college boy?"

CAMEOS Raquel Welch's one-line screen debut

RUDE BOY (1980)

CAST: The Clash, Ray Gange, John Green, Barry Baker, Terry McQuade; DIR: Jack Hazan, David Mingay; PROD: Jack Hazan, David Mingay; SCREENPLAY: David Mingay, Ray Gange, Jack Hazan; STUDIO: Buzzy Enterprises; 120 min., color (Sony)

MUSIC ★★★★
ATTITUDE ★★★★★
FUN ★★★

Give 'em enough film.

When the Clash filmed *Rude Boy* around the time of their second album (*Give 'Em Enough Rope*), they were still making the awkward transition from radical outsiders to popular rock band. They had not yet broken in America, and while this independent feature is often muddled and unfocused, it provides an unflinchingly honest look at this once-great punk hope. Apparently a seamless blend of documentary, improvised, and scripted footage, the movie stars the improbably named Ray Gange (supposedly an actual Clash fan) as Ray, a Clash fan.

Ray lives in the same bleak British landscape that inspired a hundred punk songs. He wanders from his council block home, littered with racist graffiti, to a lonely job at an adult book store. He runs into Joe Strummer at a pub and shares his drunken views on politics, a subject that Ray thinks is all "bollocks." Ray then starts to hang out backstage at Clash shows, eventually gets hired as a roadie, and witnesses firsthand how dismal the rock world can be. He sees vicious bouncers pummeling fans, is shamed by band and crew alike, and poorly performs the tedious task of disassembling the drum hardware. The increasingly alcoholic Ray is gently let go from his duties, but he continues to follow the band on tour and in the studio, constantly trying and failing to connect with the band members on a more than superficial level (Mick Jones snarls, "I'm watching you!"). Intercut with Ray's story is lots of good live footage, and Strummer is shown laying down a vocal track to "All the Young Punks," hyperventilating between verses. (JS)

Joe Strummer patiently explaining why he wears a T-shirt commemorating an Italian terrorist group, sounding very informed and logical...Not!   **S C E N E S**

Mick Jones, letting his hair grow out and seeming especially comfortable with his new role as rock star, glaring at neophyte roadie Ray, who is trying to fix a guitar cord: "GET OFF THE FUCKING STAGE!!"   **L I N E S**

Caroline Coon, Jimmy Pursey   **C A M E O S**

Police and Thieves, Garageland, London's Burning, White Riot, White Man in Hammersmith Palais, I'm So Bored with the U.S.A., Janie Jones, The Prisoner, Tommy Gun, All the Young Punks, Stay Free, City of the Dead, Safe European Home, What's My Name, I Fought the Law (Clash)   **S O N G S**

RUST NEVER SLEEPS (1979)

DIR: Bernard Shakey [Neil Young]; PROD: Elliot Rabinowitz, L.A. Johnson; STUDIO: International Harmony; 113 min., color (Warner Reprise)

MUSIC ★★★★
ATTITUDE ★
FUN ★

Listen, he probably can't make a decent soufflé, either.

As long as Neil Young is singing, this concert film is tolerable. He plays a solo acoustic set and then an electric one with Crazy Horse. The song selection is classic, and the sound is even good. But a filmmaker, this guy is not. The movie opens with seven full minutes of little people—what are they, irradiated munchkins?—scrambling about in dim light on the stage. And if you think the opening sounds pointless (you're supposed to), they come back later! Do yourself a favor. Buy the CD (*Live Rust*), and skip the movie. If you do watch the film, you might want to stick around after the credits for the "surprise" encore. (DR)

SONGS *Sugar Mountain, I Am a Child, Comes a Time, After the Gold Rush, Thrasher, My My Hey Hey* (Neil Young); *When You Dance I Can Really Love, The Loner, Welfare Mothers, The Needle and the Damage Done, Lotta Love, Sedan Delivery, Powderfinger, Cortez the Killer, Cinnamon Girl, Like a Hurricane, Hey Hey My My, Tonight's the Night* (Neil Young and Crazy Horse)

SATISFACTION (1988)

CAST: Justin Bateman, Liam Neeson, Trini Alvarado, Scott Coffey, Britta Phillips, Julia Roberts; DIR: Joan Freeman; PROD: Aaron Spelling, Alan Greisman; SCREENPLAY: Charles Purpura; STUDIO: 20th Century-Fox; 92 min., color (CBS/Fox)

MUSIC ★
ATTITUDE ★
FUN ★★

The flimsy saga of an all-girl band.
If someone were to make a movie today about an all-girl rock band just out of high school, the band would probably posture like riot grrrls and sound something like L7. But *Satisfaction* was made way back in 1988 in Hollywood, so Jennie Lee and the Mystery sound instead like a nightmare cross between Patty Smyth's Scandal and a more rockin' Wilson Phillips. Justine Bateman plays Jennie, supported by Britta Phillips, Trini Alvarado, and Julia Roberts as the band. (Roberts has the smallest part as the bass player.)

From the beginning, *Satisfaction* makes very little sense—like, why do bad girl Mooch (Alvarado) and junkie Billie (Phillips) hang out with valedictorian Jennie in the first place? Then, loading up on clichéd dramatic situations, the movie descends into a *Flamingo Kid*-style class struggle between the poor rocker girls and their rich resort audiences. In case that one's not enough, there's also the lonely girl who's opened up by the sensitive boy piano player, and the retired songwriting legend (well played by Liam Neeson) whose love for Jennie enables him to begin writing again. The music is truly awful, the comedy utterly witless, and I dare you to find a single instance of emotion, energy, or meaning in the entire film. At one point, Bateman announces, "We can either get out there and make the kind of noise that's going to wake this world from its stagnant slumber, or we can bloat ourselves on the synthetic pap sucked from the techno tit." Too bad they picked option number two. (JC)

CAMEOS Debbie Harry, Steve Cropper

SONGS *Satisfaction, Knock on Wood, Iko Iko, C'mon Everybody, Mr. Big Stuff, Mystery Dance, Lies* (Jennie Lee and the Mystery); *Loving You* (Blow Fish); *God Bless the Child* (Britta Phillips); *Dedicated to the One I Love, Talk to Me* (Jennie Lee)

SATURDAY NIGHT FEVER (1977)

CAST: John Travolta, Donna Pescow, Karen Lynn Gorney; DIR: John Badham; PROD: Robert Stigwood; SCREENPLAY: Norman Wexler; STUDIO: Paramount; 112 min., color (Paramount)

MUSIC ★★★
ATTITUDE ★★★★★
FUN ★★★★

Disco, bread, and circuses.
Although Van McCoy's hit "The Hustle" freed disco from the subterranean dance laboratories of Manhattan, it was this film that infected the nation. Released in

1977, years after disco dancing had been refined in private Harlem clubs, *Saturday Night Fever* gave white, straight America a visual guide. The sales of platform shoes and gold medallions skyrocketed, and the soundtrack album, featuring the Bee Gees, became the top-selling soundtrack ever.

The plot of *Saturday Night Fever* revolves around Tony (John Travolta), the 20-year-old disco king of Bay Ridge, Brooklyn. He slogs through each week working at a paint store and being abused by his dysfunctional parents. But on Saturday nights, he sets the local discotheque on fire. From Travolta's electrifying opening strut through the gray streets of Bay Ridge, it's clear that this role marks the peak of his career. His dancing scenes are thrilling, and somehow he makes his blow-styled hair and white polyester suit look cool and sexy. Travolta's brilliance lies in his seriousness. Despite the Bee Gees' kitschy music, the outrageous choreography, and the cheesy polyester fashion, Travolta never allows his character to become a parody. Through his sober boogying, *Saturday Night Fever* re-creates the fantasy universe that was disco. (SBW)

SCENES

Tony terrorizing his grandmother, chanting "Attica, Attica!" in black bikini underpants (0:24); Tony—clad in a Quiana shirt and tight, salmon-pink bell-bottoms—taking over the discotheque floor (0:58)

Saturday Night Fever

THE SAVAGE SEVEN (1968)

CAST: Robert Walker, Adam Roarke, Larry Bishop, Duane Eddy, Penny Marshall, Joanna Frank, Susannah Darrow; DIR: Richard Rush; PROD: Dick Clark; SCREENPLAY: Michael Fisher; STUDIO: American International; 96 min., color (no video release)

MUSIC ★★★
ATTITUDE ★★
FUN ★★★

Only a bad attitude will do.

The two major forces in this A.I.P. exercise are a biker gang and an odd assortment of American Indians led by Johnnie Little Hawk (Robert Walker). At various times these two groups are adversaries and allies. Based on a story by Rosalind Ross, this film was structured along the lines of a western with the bikers as modern-day cowboys. Among the cast members, you'll find a lot of biker-film regulars, particularly gang leader Adam Roarke, as well as guitar hero (and longtime Dick Clark associate) Duane Eddy. Roger Corman veteran Beach Dickerson plays Fat Jack, and future *Laverne and Shirley* co-star Penny Marshall is Tina in a role that she probably wants to forget. As an example of the biker-film genre, *The Savage*

Seven certainly lives up to its name, grossly exploiting sex and violence in its total disregard for the established order.

Much of the music for this film was provided by Mike Curb, who later had a brief political career as the lieutenant governor of California. *The Savage Seven* soundtrack was one of many biker-film scores this young music-business huckster produced between 1966 and 1970. Curiously enough, Curb's work on these films led to his political downfall. A political rival made them into a campaign issue, claiming that the pictures were antisocial and had a damaging effect on developing teenage minds. These attacks severely damaged Curb's until-then squeaky-clean Republican image. (SJM)

S O N G S   *Anyone for Tennis* (Cream); *Maria's Theme* (Barbara Kelly and the Morning Good); *Iron Butterfly Theme, Unconscious Power* (Iron Butterfly); *Ballad of the Savage Seven* (American Revolution)

SEASIDE SWINGERS (1964)

MUSIC ★★
ATTITUDE ★
FUN ★

ALTERNATE TITLE: *Every Day's a Holiday*
CAST: John Leyton, Mike Sarne, Freddie and the Dreamers, Ron Moody, Liz Fraser, The Mojos; DIR: James Hill; PROD: Ronald J. Kahn, Maurice J. Wilson; SCREENPLAY: James Hill, Jeri Matos, Anthony Marriot; STUDIO: Embassy; 94 min., color (no video release)

Freddie and the Dreamers have a nightmare.

This is a fairly abysmal effort even for a quickie cash-in. The point was to piggy-back the successes of the Beatles and Gerry and the Pacemakers, but all we get are Freddie and the Dreamers preparing for a talent show at a seaside resort. If only they could have drowned somehow during the first reel. Singer/actor John Leyton had already appeared in *The Great Escape*, so this film must have been an even bigger embarrassment for him than it was for the rest of the ensemble (although Liz Fraser is appealing in that mid-'60s dolly-bird sort of way). Really, *Seaside Swingers* shouldn't have been this bad. James Hill went on to direct *Born Free*, and cinematographer Nicolas Roeg went on to direct *Performance*, *The Man Who Fell to Earth* , and—oh, yes—*Walkabout*. (BE)

S O N G S   *What's Cooking, Don't Do That to Me* (Freddie and the Dreamers); *Crazy Horse Saloon, All I Want Is You* (John Leyton)

SEE MY MUSIC TALKING (1969)

MUSIC ★★★★★
ATTITUDE ★★★★★
FUN ★★★★★

ALTERNATE TITLE: *Experience*
DIR: Peter Neal; PROD: Austin John Marshall; STUDIO: Pomegranate; 29 min., color (no video release)

Color, attitudes, music—with Jimi Hendrix as the main primary.

This is the only film that Jimi Hendrix made in his own time. Very forward in its presentation, it's representative of the pop art movement in England at the time. Sharp interviews with Hendrix emphasize his Indian background and experience as a paratrooper. The film also features the famous white-background acoustic guitar performance of "Hear My Train a-Comin'," and in general, Hendrix's music and raps are more pertinent here in their original setting. Mitch Mitchell and Noel Redding ask the questions in *See My Music Talking*, parodying the paparazzi who mobbed Jimi at the time. Interesting film montages accompany "Foxy Lady" and "Castles Made of Sand," while live versions of "Purple Haze" and "Wild Thing" are thrown in for good measure.

What's most important about *See My Music Talking* is its sense of immediacy. It's been very difficult since his death to grasp the impact of Jimi Hendrix first-hand. Most Hendrix documentaries have a dulled and careful sense of '70s retrospect. Jimi's style was the '60s pop art scene of the Who and the Creation taken to the hilt, and the many bands who tried to extract "influence" from Jimi were just a cheap and stale rehash. For both black and white kids, Hendrix was the same: no secrets, all sharing and openness, with everyone grooving to a tumultuous, revolutionary vibe. *See My Music Talking* is the only artifact from that infinitely lost moment. (DP)

LINES

Hendrix; "Yeh, I never did want to go to the moon too much. I always wanted to go to Saturn or Venus or something like that. Something that could show me some kind of scenery."

SONGS

Purple Haze, Foxy Lady, Castles Made of Sand, May This Be Love, Wild Thing (Jimi Hendrix Experience)

SERIOUS CHARGE (1959)

CAST: Anthony Quayle, Andrew Ray, Sarah Churchill, Irene Ray, Cliff Richard, Percy Herbert; DIR: Terence Young; PROD: Mickey Delamar; SCREENPLAY: Guy Elmes, Mickey Delamar; STUDIO: Alva; 99 min., b/w (no video release)

MUSIC	★★★
ATTITUDE	★★★★
FUN	★★★★

A gritty, British-made tale of delinquency.
This little-known feature is one of the most serious juvenile delinquency dramas ever filmed. Although the rock'n'roll is generally kept in the background, it's still never too far from view. As the new vicar of a small village, Anthony Quayle incurs the wrath of local teen gang leader Andrew Ray. When Ray's girlfriend dies as a result of complications during pregnancy, the thug tries to divert attention from himself by claiming that Quayle attempted to sexually molest him. Cliff Richard, England's first home-grown rock star, had no prior acting experience when he made *Serious Charge*, so he's given only a small role here as Ray's younger brother. Cliff does perform three songs, however, including a superior, rocked-up version of his soft pop hit "Living Doll." Director Terence Young, who went on to direct the first two James Bond movies, elevated *Serious Charge* into an intense little picture driven by still-topical subject matter. Some of the drama seems stagy today, but the grittiness and harshness of the plot runs rings around most American rock'n'roll vehicles. (BE)

No Turning Back, Mad, Living Doll (Cliff Richard)

SONGS

SEXTETTE (1978)

CAST: Mae West, Timothy Dalton, Ringo Starr, George Hamilton, Tony Curtis, Alice Cooper, Dom DeLuise; DIR: Ken Hughes; PROD: Daniel Briggs, Robert Sullivan; STUDIO: Crown International; 91 min., color (Media)

MUSIC	★
ATTITUDE	★
FUN	★

Precious moments wasted.
Words like "atrocious," "preposterous," and "grotesque" don't come close to describing what a horror-show this film is. *Sextette* features Mae West doing the same naughty schtick that titillated and shocked people back in the '30s. Only here, she's 80 years old. This film is unique. It's worthy of mention here due to the presence of Ringo Starr, Alice Cooper, and Keith Moon. Keith demonstrates that if he hadn't been so busy dying young (and drumming for the Who) he might

have become a great film comedian (like Norman Wisdom, whom he resembles). Ringo rises to the occasion as well. (MC)

CAMEOS   Keith Moon, Keith Allison, Van McCoy

SONGS   *Baby Face, After You've Gone* (Mae West); *Marlo* (Van McCoy); *Next Next* (Alice Cooper)

SGT. PEPPER'S LONELY HEARTS CLUB BAND (1978)

MUSIC ★
ATTITUDE ★
FUN ★

CAST: Peter Frampton, The Bee Gees, Frankie Howard, Paul Nicholas, Donald Pleasence, Sandy Farina, George Burns; DIR: Michael Schultz; PROD: Robert Stigwood, Dee Anthony; SCREENPLAY: Henry Edwards; STUDIO: Universal; 111 min., color (MCA)

The infamous Beatles-inspired atrocity.

Many careers were terminated as a result of the artistic and commercial failure of this film, based on the Beatles' 1967 concept album. One person who somehow managed to escape with his reputation intact was George Martin, who was drafted into the project in order to give producer Robert Stigwood's fiasco some air of authenticity and authority. In the end, this movie is about as entertaining as a Pet Rock, and watching it is like watching human life descend several rungs on the evolutionary ladder. (DR)

SONGS   *Sgt. Pepper's Lonely Hearts Club Band, A Day in the Life* (Bee Gees); *A Little Help from My Friends, Golden Slumbers* (Peter Frampton); *Fixing a Hole* (George Burns); *I Want You* (Cast); *Here Comes the Sun* (Sandy Farina); *Nowhere Man, Oh Darling, Getting Better, Being for the Benefit of Mr. Kite* (Bee Gees, Peter Frampton); *Maxwell's Silver Hammer* (Steve Martin); *Because* (Alice Cooper); *Got to Get You into My Life* (Earth, Wind and Fire); *Come Together* (Aerosmith); *Get Back* (Billy Preston)

Sgt. Pepper's Lonely Hearts Club Band

SHAKE, RATTLE, AND ROCK (1956)

CAST: Mike Connors, Sterling Holloway, Lisa Gaye, Fats Domino, Big Joe Turner; DIR: Edward L. Cahn; PROD: James H. Nicholson; SCREENPLAY: Lou Rusoff; STUDIO: American International; 75 min., b/w (RCA/Columbia)

MUSIC ★★★★
ATTITUDE ★★★
FUN ★★

Not the worst rock'n'roll movie ever made.

A citizens' group wants to have the rock'n'roll TV show "Roll, Rock, and Shake" taken off the air, and its host Gary Nelson (Mike Connors of "Mannix") put in jail. The rockers and fogies face each other down in a phony trial, during which Nelson convinces everyone that rock'n'roll is really an art form. The entire movie appears to have been shot using only five sets, but there are a few redeeming touches: Sterling Holloway's performance as Axe McAllister, who only speaks in '50s slang, and some great rock'n'roll from Fats Domino and Big Joe Turner. The grown-ups are portrayed as dotty, fun-hating nincompoops who can't be taken seriously, but Margaret Dumont and Percy Helton are their usual superb selves. (MG)

When Axe is cross-examined, the judge can't understand his slang and calls for an interpreter. Subtitles appear as Axe continues to deliver his hipster jive (1:05).

SCENES

A TV executive to Nelson: "Rock'n'roll is a gimmick to sell Shadrock shoes as far as I'm concerned!"

LINES

Honey Chile, Ain't That a Shame, I'm in Love Again (Fats Domino); *Rockin' on Saturday Night* (Annita Ray); *Feelin' Happy, Lipstick Powder and Paint* (Joe Turner); *Sweet Love on My Mind* (Tommy Charles)

SONGS

SID AND NANCY (1986)

CAST: Gary Oldman, Chloe Webb, David Hayman, Tenpole Tudor, Courtney Love, Iggy Pop; DIR: Alex Cox; PROD: Eric Fellner; SCREENPLAY: Abbe Wool, Alex Cox; STUDIO: Nelson; 111 min., color (Embassy)

MUSIC ★
ATTITUDE ★★★★★
FUN ★★★★★

The needle and the damage filmed.

For the most part, the movie biz has failed miserably when it cames to portraying the ethos and mentality of punk. For those of us who lived through and dove into this particularly charming period of American pop culture, *Sid and Nancy* is a demented, Dilaudid-ed home movie that manages to make the late Sid Vicious, bassist of the Sex Pistols, sympathetic without lionizing his pathetic existence.

This is the true life, love, and death story of Vicious and Nancy Spungen, the original rock'n'roll suicide fun couple. It is to director Alex Cox's credit that he pulls off what is essentially a horrifying and totally depressing story. The flash in the zeitgeist that was the Sex Pistols is almost secondary to the sad, often touching, and ultimately tragic tale of love gone sour and then blue.

Now a major star, Gary Oldman was still unknown when he made this film, and he gives what may be his finest performance as the wasted Sidney. Using a classic method style, Oldman transforms himself into the rock legend. Equally awesome and somewhat lost in the critical shuffle is Chloe Webb as the less like-able harridan, Nancy. In what must be one of the finest portrayals of the junkie mindset, Nancy harangues Sid over using dope and in the same breath whines, "And you didn't save me any!" To rank this film in terms of enjoyability is point-less; it's a tough, unflinching gaze through half-closed eyes at a lifestyle that kids

20th Century-Fox presents

TOMMY SANDS

LILI GENTLE

SING BOY SING

CO-STARRING
EDMOND O'BRIEN · John McINTYRE

CINEMASCOPE

Produced and Directed by
HENRY EPHRON · Screenplay by
CLAUDE BINYON

should definitely not try at home. But taking that in mind, *Sid and Nancy* is a brilliant film. (ALi)

Stepping Stone, Anarchy in the U.K., No Feelings, Holiday in the Sun, Pretty Vacant, Problems (Fake Sex Pistols); *My Way, Something Else, I Wanna Be Your Dog* (Sid Vicious)   **S O N G S**

SING, BOY, SING   (1958)

CAST: Tommy Sands, Edmond O'Brien, Nick Adams, Lili Gentle; DIR: Henry Ephron; PROD: Henry Ephron; SCREENPLAY: Claude Binyon; STUDIO: 20th Century-Fox; 90 min., b/w (no video release)

MUSIC ★
ATTITUDE ★
FUN ★★

A period piece with Ampex 350 decks, 1957 Mercurys, and RCA ribbon microphones. Adapted from a TV drama, *Sing, Boy, Sing* stars Tommy Sands as Virgil Walker, America's Number One teenage singing idol. Its plot is cobbled together from *The Jazz Singer, Loving You, Jailhouse Rock*, and Elvis's 1956 TV Guide interview (in which he bares his soul about being lonely and overwhelmed). Virgil—raised by his grandfather, a tent-show preacher—finds himself torn between religious fundamentalism and worldly temptation. He's also lonely at the top and anguished over several moral crises. The rest of the time, he sings really, really awful rock'n'roll songs like "Soda Pop Pop."

Tommy Sands once made a genuinely classic rock'n'roll record called "The Worrying Kind" and an okay one called "Teenage Crush," but they were both too good for inclusion in this film. Edmond O'Brien is great as Virgil's iron-fisted Svengali manager, and Nick Adams is well cast as Virgil's dumb-as-a-dog sidekick. But it's still a crummy movie. (MC)

Gonna Walk and Talk, With My Lord, Who Baby Who, Soda Pop Pop, Sing Boy Sing, Crazy Crazy, A Little Love, Rock of Ages (Tommy Sands)   **S O N G S**

SINGLES   (1992)

CAST: Bridget Fonda, Campbell Scott, Kyra Sedgwick, Sheila Kelley, Jim True, Bill Pullman, Matt Dillon; DIR: Cameron Crowe; PROD: Cameron Crowe, Richard Hashimoto; SCREENPLAY: Cameron Crowe; STUDIO: Warner; 100 min., color (Warner)

MUSIC ★★★★
ATTITUDE ★★★
FUN ★★★★

The dating game.
If Rolling Stone alumnus Cameron Crowe hadn't been in the right place at the right time—Seattle during grunge's national emergence—we might have waited another year before Hollywood's first attempt at a grunge cash-in. Luckily, *Singles* makes other Seattle movies unnecessary, because Crowe's knowledge of the grunge scene is encyclopedic. From an opening shot that highlights graffiti about seminal Seattleites Mother Love Bone to extended Pearl Jam cameos (shot way before the band's first video), Crowe avoids an updated *Spinal Tap* by centering his film not on a band, but on a relationship-plagued apartment building full of frustrated twentysomethings. Imagine *When Harry Met Sally* at *Melrose Place*, and you'll have some idea of the mind games about love that these characters play. As one pair of romantic leads, Kyra Sedgwick and Campbell Scott think that second-guessing relationships is about as important as picking out the right flannel for a Soundgarden show—in other words, very. The inept, bumbling courtship of Bridget Fonda by hilariously stupid grunge frontman Matt Dillon gets a similar treatment. With pacing that's fast yet far from MTV-trendy, *Singles* is both a dark tribute to a confused mood and a "date" movie so insightful that it will either strengthen a good relationship or kill a bad one. (ALa)

SCENES A Campbell Scott childhood flashback to confusing '70s sex education (0:10); Alice in Chains in a classic Seattle bar (0:16); the fictional Citizen Dick (Pearl Jam and Dillon) reading a critical trashing in a typical Seattle coffee house (0:49)

LINES The neurotic Sedgwick character on her love affair with a Spanish exchange student: "If I marry him, he could live in this country, and I'd always have someone to go out with." The airheaded Cliff Poncier (Dillon) asked by an interviewer about the growth of the "Seattle scene": "I just don't like to reduce us to the Seattle scene.... We're huge in Europe right now."

CAMEOS Pearl Jam, Chris Cornell, Soundgarden, Alice in Chains, Tad, Peter Horton, Pat DiNizio, Bruce Pabitt, Cameron Crowe, Xavier McDaniel

SONGS *It Ain't Like That* (Alice in Chains); *Birth Ritual* (Soundgarden)

THE SIX-FIVE SPECIAL (1957)

MUSIC ★★
ATTITUDE ★
FUN ★★★

CAST: Diane Todd, Avril Leslie, Lonnie Donegan, The John Barry Five, Jim Dale, Petula Clark, Cleo Laine, John Dankworth, Victor Soverall, Jimmy Lloyd, Finlay Currie; DIR: Alfred Shaunessy; PROD: Nat Cohen, Stuart Levy; SCREENPLAY: Norman Hudis; STUDIO: Anglo-Amalgamated; 85 min., b/w (no video release)

Teen lives in '50s Britain.
Two teenage girls (Diane Todd, Avril Leslie) travel to London in search of stardom and, natch, end up with the stars of *The Six-Five Special* (then England's biggest TV music showcase). That's the plot, and the acting—apart from veteran character actor Finlay Currie, who appears as himself—is nonexistent. Ditto the production values. Most of the acts appearing in *The Six-Five Special* have more to do with light jazz, pop music, and calypso than with rock'n'roll, but it's a good representation of what British youth had to listen to during the mid-'50s. There is actually some good rock sandwiched in the midst of it: Lonnie Donegan's set is energetic and boasts some fierce playing by lead guitarist Denny Wright, future James Bond and *Dances with Wolves* composer John Barry really cooks in his spot as well, nd seeing future *Barnum* star Jim Dale doing "Train Kept a-Rolling" is a kick. (BE)

SONGS *You Are My Favorite Dream* (Diane Todd); *Train Kept a-Rolling, Sugar Time* (Jim Dale); *Midgets* (Desmond Lane); *Gypsy in My Soul* (Ken-Tones); *Train Gang* (John Dankworth); *What Am I Going to Tell Them Tonight?* (Cleo Laine with John Dankworth); *I'll Close My Eyes* (Joan Regan); *Say Goodbye Now* (Victor Soverall); *Ever Since I Met Lucy* (Jimmy Lloyd); *Baby Lover* (Petula Clark); *I Had a Dream* (Russ Hamilton); *Every Which Way* (John Barry); *Hand Me Down My Walking Cane, Six-Five Jive* (King Brothers); *King of Dixieland, Come To My Arms* (Dickie Valentine); *Grand Coolie Dam, Jack O' Diamonds* (Lonnie Donegan)

SKI PARTY (1965)

MUSIC ★★★★★
ATTITUDE ★★★
FUN ★★★★

CAST: Frankie Avalon, Dwayne Hickman, Deborah Walley, Yvonne Craig, Robert Q. Lewis, Aron Kincaid, Bobbi Shaw, Patti Chandler, Mary Hughes; DIR: Alan Rafkin; PROD: Gene Corman; SCREENPLAY: Robert Kaufman; STUDIO: American International; 90 min., color (no video release)

Surfers hit the slopes.
Ski Party may not have reaped the box-office harvest of A.I.P.'s beach movies, but it's still a knockout. For one thing, Alan Rafkin directs this time, adding some sick twists to scenes that would otherwise have been standard. The camera work is

also pretty weird on the shaking bikinis as Frankie Avalon sings "Lots Lots More." Subtle pleasures like this pop up all the time. When Deborah Walley reveals the secret of femininity to a cross-dressed Dwayne ("Dobie Gillis") Hickman, a voice-over proclaims, "In order to comply with the government's request to keep the population explosion going at full blast, the sound will be turned off for the next few moments." Annette Funicello makes a cameo here as a 35-year-old college professor necking in a hot rod. At one point, Hickman intones to the theater audience, "Look, have a Coke or something. Nothing's gonna happen for at least ten minutes."

The soundtrack, produced by Gary Usher, is the best in any A.I.P. beacher. The most amazing example of Usher's skill is the guitar sound he gets on the Hondells' "The Gasser." It's a great song with a driving beat, one of the best musical moments in any film. But it's surrounded here by some pretty formidable stuff. James Brown and the Famous Flames appear in their prime performing "I Got You" by the fireplace in ski sweaters. Another happy moment occurs during the bus ride to the mountain resort as Lesley Gore gets the whole gang (including Yvonne Craig) singing along to "Sunshine, Lollipops, and Rainbows." In the end, the cast ditches their skis, and the Hondells rock Santa Monica beach. Old habits sure die hard, I guess. (DP)

C A M E O S   Annette Funicello

S O N G S   *Sunshine Lollipops and Rainbows* (Lesley Gore); *Ski Party, Lots Lots More, Paintin' the Town* (Frankie Avalon); *I Got You* (James Brown and the Famous Flames); *We'll Never Change Them* (Deborah Walley); *The Gasser, Ski Party* (Hondells)

SMASHING TIME   (1967)

CAST: Lynn Redgrave, Rita Tushingham, Michael York; DIR: Desmond Davis; PROD: Carlo Ponti, Roy Millichip; SCREENPLAY: George Melly; STUDIO: Paramount; 96 min., color (no video release)

MUSIC ★★
ATTITUDE ★★★★★
FUN ★★★★★

Searching for stardom in Swinging London.
This is the story of two teenage girls from the north of England: Yvonne (Lynn Redgrave), who is conceited and self-obsessed, moves to London to chase down her dreams of fame and glory. Steadfast and pure-of-heart Brenda (Rita Tushingham) gets dragged along for the ride. Once in London, they both have many hilarious misadventures. Grasping for stardom, Yvonne ends up swindled, exploited, and humiliated. Meanwhile, Brenda becomes the girlfriend and protégé of an eminent fashion photographer, who makes hers a household face. Everything's jolly until Brenda becomes disillusioned with the coldheartedness of the big city and decides to rescue Yvonne. In the end, they leave the trendmongers, leeches, and charlatans behind and head back home arm in arm.

Fans of 1960s British pop culture will no doubt swoon over this movie's sanitized yet vivid look at Swinging London, especially screenwriter George Melly's satirical digs. My favorites are Yvonne's song "I'm So Young" and a TV ad for "Direct Action" perfume. (MC)

S C E N E S   The pie-fight sequence, during which the psychedelic band Tomorrow (featuring guitarist Steve Howe) makes a cameo appearance

S O N G S   *Smashing Time Theme, Your Fault, Sunshine Day* (Lynn Redgrave, Rita Tushingham); *Carnaby Street, I'm So Young* (Lynn Redgrave); *Waiting for a Friend, New Clothes* (Rita Tushingham)

SMITHEREENS   (1982)

CAST: Susan Berman, Brad Rinn, Richard Hell; DIR: Susan Seidelman; PROD: Susan Seidelman; SCREENPLAY: Ron Nyswaner, Peter Askin; 93 min., color (Media)

MUSIC ★★★
ATTITUDE ★★★
FUN ★

Self-absorbed downtown losers pretend they have a life.
One of the first punk dramas, Susan Seidelman's debut feature is the kind of marginal mediocrity that gives indie filmmaking a bad name. Its "experimental" touches include excessive fade-outs, dodgy acting, quirky settings, and a low-bud-

get, no-edit watching-paint-dry pace. On the surface, *Smithereens* is an infatuated portrait of Downtown Cool, with the Peppermint Lounge as a backdrop and a lead performance by Richard Hell, from whom Malcolm McLaren stole his fashion ideas. But it's actually an unsympathetic deglamorization of club-rat mores that, despite Seidelman's knowing eye, is as empty and predictably structured as a big-budget studio flick. Screenwriter Ron Nyswaner jumped to Hollywood easily, most recently penning Jonathan Demme's *Philadelphia*.

Smithereens features a not-quite love triangle, New Wave style, with narcissist and aspiring pseudo-celebrity Wren (Susan Berman) vying for the affections of punk-rock cad Eric (Hell, who can't act, but sure looks cool) and Montana naif Paul (Brad Rinn). Of course, Wren only visits Paul when the much more happening Eric isn't accessible. Seidelman's take on Wren's vicarious life and materialist soul teeters on the edge of contempt, leaving her pathetic, unlikeable and, by the film's end, on the verge of whoredom. *Smithereens'* only charge comes from its soundtrack (by Glenn Mercer and Bill Million of the Feelies), but even that's just their *Crazy Rhythms* LP sans vocals. (JC)

Eric puts beer in his hair for 'do maintenance (0:14). When a woman smiles at Eric and asks for a light, the nihilistic rocker simply throws the book of matches at her (1:11).	*SCENES*
"I'm on the guest list."	*LINES*
Cookie Mueller, Chris Noth, Tom Cherwin	*CAMEOS*
I Never Fell (Nitecaps)	*SONGS*

SOMETHING WILD (1986)

CAST: Jeff Daniels, Melanie Griffith, Ray Liotta; DIR: Jonathan Demme; PROD: Jonathan Demme, Kenneth Utt; SCREENPLAY: E. Max Frye; STUDIO: Orion; 112 min., color (HBO Cannon)

MUSIC	★★★★
ATTITUDE	★★★★★
FUN	★★★★

All dressed up like an Elvis from hell.

Although music and musicians aren't central to this story, Jonathan Demme's *Something Wild* qualifies for inclusion here for several reasons. First, the movie's theme is quintessentially rock'n'roll: Ray, a demonic working-class figure played to perfection by Ray Liotta, threatens to shatter the bourgeois happiness shared by carefree adventurers Lulu (Melanie Griffith) and Charlie (Jeff Daniels). The movie's best extended sequence is a bizarre but believable high school reunion, where the Feelies perform three great songs: the Monkees' "I'm A Believer," David Bowie's "Fame," and Freddy Fender's "Before the Next Teardrop Falls." Finally, *Something Wild* contains nearly 50 songs, including on-screen performances by the Feelies and reggae star Sister Carol. There's also an original score by Laurie Anderson and John Cale and tunes (in whole or in part) by David Byrne, X, New Order, Jimmy Cliff, UB40, and Oingo Boingo. In fact, there's a little *too much* music in this film, detracting from the tension and drama in some scenes. (AS)

The Class of '76 reunion (0:38); Ray robbing the convenience store (1:00); Ray returning for a final paroxysm of violence (1:35)	*SCENES*
John Waters, John Sayles, Su Tissue	*CAMEOS*
I'm a Believer, Before the Next Teardrop Falls, Fame (Feelies); *Wild Thing* (Sister Carol)	*SONGS*

The Song Remains the Same

THE SONG REMAINS THE SAME   (1976)

MUSIC ★★★★
ATTITUDE ★★★
FUN ★★★★

DIR: Peter Clifton, Joe Massot; PROD: Peter Grant; STUDIO: Columbia; 137 min., color (Warner)

Forever and ever, amen.

If only Jonathan Demme had gotten ahold of Led Zeppelin on one of their great nights in 1975! Alas, all that Zeppelin fans have to sustain them now is *The Song Remains the Same*, a piecemeal documentary featuring footage shot during the final three nights of the band's 1973 U.S. tour. Zeppelin was, by their own admission, in a rather road-weary shape at the time, but some of the band's live charisma does come through on numbers like "Dazed and Confused" and "No Quarter." When Jimmy Page takes a violin bow to his Les Paul, there's still a power and mystique that even *Spinal Tap* hasn't diminished.

The film is not entirely without a sense of humor (casting manager Peter Grant as a '20s-style mobster), but *The Song Remains the Same* works best when it simply lets the band rock. While the film showcases the onstage chemistry between Robert Plant and Jimmy Page, the most refreshing and least pretentious moments feature bassist/keyboardist John Paul Jones and drummer John Bonham. The profile of Bonham, whose 1980 death sealed the group's fate, is particularly appealing. There's none of the Arthurian lore that pollutes the other band-member profiles. Instead, we see Bonham riding a tractor on his farm, hanging out at his local pub, playing with his infant son behind a drum kit, and racing dragsters to the tune of his showcase drum solo in "Moby Dick." The Bonham piece concludes onstage with John hitting a gong that's been set on fire, a sequence that's hard to top for sheer attitude and impact. Appropriately, it concludes the film.

There's no denying the shortcomings here: the film lacks a strong directorial vision (Joe Massot was fired and replaced by Peter Clifton midway), and the concert footage was shot too late in the tour to catch the band's best performances. When the group was forced to cancel its 1976 tour due to Robert Plant's car accident, Grant dusted off the old footage and hurriedly completed *The Song Remains the Same* so that the film could be released to eager fans in lieu of the band. (TR)

SCENES   John Bonham, in muddy rubber boots, trying to get a stubborn ox to move (he looks like Michael Palin of Monty Python)

SONGS   *Autumn Lake, Bron-Y-Aur, Rock'n'Roll, Black Dog, Since I've Been Loving You, No Quarter, The Song Remains the Same, The Rain Song, Dazed and Confused, Stairway to Heaven, Moby Dick, Whole Lotta Love* (Led Zeppelin)

SOUL HUSTLER   (1975)

MUSIC ★★
ATTITUDE ★★
FUN ★★★

ALTERNATE TITLE: *The Day the Lord Got Busted*
CAST: Fabian Forte, Nai Bonet, Tony Russel, Casey Kasem; DIR: Burt Topper; PROD: Burt Topper; SCREENPLAY: Burt Topper; STUDIO: American; 81 min., color (Monterey)

Behind the saintly image was a man of earthly desires.

Fabian Forte, star of *Hound Dog Man* and *Maryjane*, gives a decent performance in this slightly sordid tale made at the height of the "Jesus freak" movement (but before the advent of contemporary Christian rock). He plays Matthew Crowe, a whoring, pot-smoking, wandering singer who teams up with a tent-show preacher. The preacher recognizes Matthew's charisma, and together they collect big donations delivering sermons with rocking gospel songs. Soon enough, Matthew lands a record deal, and the older man becomes the manager of Crowe's new act: Matthew,

Son of Jesus. They hire a backup group of mustachioed rock musicians, who play in brown monks' robes, in contrast to Matthew's white robe and sandals.

When the debut album by Matthew and the People, *The Lovin' Man*, becomes a huge hit, a sleazy promoter in a paisley jacket and sideburns (Casey Kasem!) helps the band book bigger dates. Meanwhile, Matthew becomes a junkie, getting his limo driver to score for him until the driver OD's. Freaking out from withdrawal and the bad vibes he gets from his manager (who now yells at him with venomous disgust at every meeting), Matthew runs away, finding solace with a Hispanic woman who takes him in. Crowe returns for his biggest show yet (actually filmed at the L.A. Forum) and plans to go straight, but in a paranoid moment, he suddenly drives his truck off a cliff. *Soul Hustler* was made by Burt Topper, narrator of *Mondo Teeno: The Teenage Rebellion*. The songs were written by Harley Hatcher, who helped make rock soundtracks for many '60s drive-in classics including *Satan's Sadists* and *Dr. Goldfoot and the Girl Bombs*. (JS)

Matthew to his manager: "All this talk about bread is great. Meanwhile, give me a hundred so I can get laid!" **LINES**

The Lovin' Man, Listen and Believe, Send Me a Friend, I Get High on Jesus, All God's Children, Back with My People, Set Me Free (Matthew and the People) **SONGS**

SOUL TO SOUL (1971)

DIR: Denis Sanders; PROD: Richard Bock, Tom Mosk; STUDIO: Cinerama; 95 min., color (Atlantic)

MUSIC ★★★★★
ATTITUDE ★★★★
FUN ★★★★★

A concert to celebrate Ghanian independence.
To celebrate the anniversary of Ghana's independence, Atlantic Records put together a concert package featuring some of its leading R&B and jazz artists with supporting acts "borrowed" from other companies. Director Denis Sanders documented their trip to Ghana as well as the "Soul to Soul" concert. The American stars are seen here sampling African cuisine, shopping in the open markets, and engaging in some surprisingly frank dialogue with their native guides about the history of the West African slave trade. The film also captures performances by a variety of Ghanian choirs, dance troupes, and percussion ensembles. Some of these indigenous acts seem like slick tourist shows, while others have the quality of an organic village celebration. The Soul to Soul concert footage is excellent. The sound and cinematography are of uneven quality, but the occasion has brought out the best in the performers. Ike Turner's frenzied double-time break on "I Smell Trouble" must be one of the 10 greatest guitar solos on film. (AS)

Les McCann and Eddie Harris "beat boxing," a decade before Biz Markie and Doug E. Fresh (0:05); Tina Turner getting a lesson in the Ashanti language (0:25); the Voices of East Harlem in a spontaneous a capella jam in a public square (0:27) **SCENES**

Soul to Soul, Ooh Poo Pah Doo, River Deep Mountain High, I Smell Trouble (Ike and Tina Turner); *In the Midnight Hour, Land of 1,000 Dances* (Wilson Pickett); *Run Shaker Life* (Voices of East Harlem); *Jingo* (Santana, Willie Bobo); *Black Magic Woman/Gypsy Queen* (Santana); *Heyjorler* (Les McCann, Eddie Harris); *Trying Times* (Roberta Flack); *When Will We Be Paid?, Are You Sure?* (Staple Singers) **SONGS**

SPARKLE (1975)

CAST: Irene Cara, Philip Michael Thomas, Lonette McKee, Dawn Smith; DIR: Sam O'Steen; PROD: Howard Rosenman; SCREENPLAY: Joel Schumaker; STUDIO: Warner; 100 min., color (Warner)

MUSIC ★★★★
ATTITUDE ★★★★★
FUN ★★★★★

A 1950s girl group seen through a 1970s lens.

Our story takes place in Harlem circa 1958, where a group of (mostly good) kids form a singing group. As they pursue their dream of fame, they find themselves drawn into a vortex of violence, drugs, corruption, and death. This movie starts out as the story of a prototypical girl group but goes on to tell a much larger story about ghetto life and the hardness of the world. Having already written "Mama Didn't Lie" and "Freddie's Dead," Curtis Mayfield was a great choice for musical director of *Sparkle,* and we've all heard the great hit song from this movie, "Something He Can Feel." The version here isn't as powerful as Aretha Franklin's (or En Vogue's), but then what is? (MC)

SONGS   *Jump, What Can I Do with This Feeling, Something He Can Feel, Givin' Up* (Cast); *Take My Hand Precious Lord, Lovin' You Baby* (Irene Cara); *Look into Your Heart* (Irene Cara, Philip Michael Thomas)

SPEEDWAY   (1968)

MUSIC ★★
ATTITUDE ★★
FUN ★★★

CAST: Elvis Presley, Nancy Sinatra, Bill Bixby, Gale Gordon, William Schallert; DIR: Norman Taurog; PROD: Douglas Laurence; SCREENPLAY: Phillip Shuken; STUDIO: MGM; 94 min., color (MGM/UA)

Elvis puts the drag into drag racing.

The King gets together with fast cars and Nancy Sinatra in this romantic comedy about the exciting worlds of drag racing and tax evasion. In *Speedway,* Elvis plays Steve Grayson, a successful race car driver who's generous to a fault. Bill Bixby plays the girl-chasing manager/best friend who gambles away all their winnings. Nancy plays Susan, an IRS agent who's assigned to collect the astronomical taxes that have accrued. But the fun never begins.

Speedway came out a year after Nancy's Number One hit "Something Stupid," a duet with her famous dad Frank. But this film's attempt to pair her with Elvis fails miserably. Nancy's parched personality and juiceless acting make Elvis look like Brando. And there should have been more than enough cinematic proof by this point that drag racing never looks interesting on the big screen. It's hard to believe that this rather passive Elvis is on the verge of making his celebrated '68 comeback. (TM)

SCENES   Nancy mustering up some feeling for the surprisingly cool "Your Groovy Self" (0:26); Elvis's terrible "love-trap" trailer—equipped with recordings of wild animals, fake radio announcements, and a remote-controlled clock to assist him technologically in his merry pursuit of what we now call date rape (0:31)

SONGS   *Speedway, Let Yourself Go, Your Time Hasn't Come, He's Your Uncle, Who We Are, There Ain't Nothing Like a Song* (Elvis Presley); *Your Groovy Self* (Nancy Sinatra)

SPINOUT   (1966)

MUSIC ★
ATTITUDE ★
FUN ★

CAST: Elvis Presley, Shelley Fabares, Carl Betz, Deborah Walley, Diane McBain, Warren Berlinger; DIR: Norman Taurog; PROD: Joe Pasternak; SCREENPLAY: Theodore J. Flicker, George Kirgo; STUDIO: MGM; 93 min., color (MGM/UA)

Elvis sinks in another sitcom quagmire.

As Mike McCoy, Elvis once again plays a singing race car driver. His task this time out is to disentangle himself from three marriage-minded females and (what else?) win the big race. Even as Elvis vehicles go, this one is unconscionably vacuous.

Donna Reed refugees Carl Betz and Shelley Fabares play a wholesomely creepy father-and-daughter team out to snare El. One wants him for a driver, the other for a husband. Once you get bored enough, you'll start to imagine *Spinout* as a musical version of *Lolita*, which at least adds a smirking touch of irony to such vanilla swill as "Adam and Evil" and "I'll Be Back." (HH)

Providing an early clue to his postmortem plans, Elvis sings "I'm comin' back" to his apostles (1:30). **SCENES**

Stop Look Listen, Adam and Evil, Because of You, Never Say Yes, Am I Ready?, Beach Shack, Spinout, Smorgasbord, I'll Be Back (Elvis Presley) **SONGS**

SPIRIT OF '76 (1991)

CAST: David Cassidy, Olivia d'Abo, Geoff Hoyle, Jeff McDonald, Steve McDonald, Leif Garrett; DIR: Lucas Reiner; PROD: Susie Landau; SCREENPLAY: Lucas Reiner; STUDIO: Castle Rock; 82 min., color (SVS/Triumph)

MUSIC ★★★★
ATTITUDE ★★★★
FUN ★★★★

Bicentennial baroque.

This time-travel comedy in the style of *Bill and Ted's Excellent Adventure* concerns future beings who travel back to the 1970s and try to make sense of that wacky decade. The loveably dopey '70s teenagers are expertly played by Steve and Jeff McDonald, the creative nucleus of Redd Kross, who have have been poking fun at '70s trash culture since long before the *Have a Nice Day* CDs came out (see the *Desperate Teenage Lovedolls* review). This movie was made by the offspring of various Hollywood folks, explaining the presence of some of their elders in cameo roles. Other parts are played by musical celebrities and more '70s icons.

The movie opens in a gray, post-apocalyptic future, where scientists have decided to travel back in time to 1776. Wanting to learn about the birth of democracy (and retrieve the Constitution), they recruit time-machine mechanic Adam 11 (David Cassidy) to help them. Unfortunately, his ship malfunctions, sending them 200 years off-course and depositing them in the suburban backyard of Chris and Tommy (the McDonald brothers). The boys hop off their Sting Ray bikes and serve as tour guides to this strange world, hiding the scientists from the government until Adam 11 can get his machine working again. In the meantime, the visitors from the future get to learn about head shops, EST-type groups (featuring Rob Reiner in a scene directly stolen from *Semi-Tough*), junk food, exploding Pintos, and disco.

Ironically, in the year of the Bicentennial, with stars and stripes everywhere, nobody seems to care much about the Constitution. *Spirit of '76* played an extremely limited theatrical run. If it had come out about two years later, a lot more people would have gotten the joke, but then the producers would have had to pay a lot more for the rights to the nonstop soundtrack of now-trendy, embarrassing hits by the likes of B.T.O., Peter Frampton, Sweet, the Starland Vocal Band, and many more. (JS)

As the scientists inspect Chris's typical teenage bedroom, one of them inadvertently bumps into his stereo system, turning it on and frightening the others with the thunderous roar of Grand Funk. Chris: "Haven't you ever seen an eight-track before?" Tommy: "Yeah, don't they have *those* in the future?" **SCENES**

Devo, Carl Reiner, Moon Unit Zappa, Tommy Chong, Julie Brown, Rob Reiner, Barbara Bain, Don Novello, Iron Eyes Cody **CAMEOS**

STAMPING GROUND (1971)

MUSIC ★★★★★
ATTITUDE ★★★★★
FUN ★★★★★

ALTERNATE TITLE: *Love and Music*
DIR: Jason Pohland; PROD: Wolf Schmidt, Sam Waynberg; STUDIO: Cine 3-Planet; 101 min., color (no video release)

A Dutch version of Monterey Pop.
An exceptionally well-directed and well-edited documentary, this little-known feature, shot at the 1970 Rotterdam Pop Festival, feaures a few acts left over from Woodstock, plus some others that one doesn't normally associate with festivals (Al Stewart and It's a Beautiful Day, for instance). The music is well played and recorded, and the camera work is lively enough to make this entertaining even on the small screen (where it probably works better than *Woodstock* ever will). The variety of acts is also a big plus. Watch for the Byrds, albeit the Clarence White edition. (BE)

SONGS   *Zero She Flies* (Al Stewart); *Human Condition* (Canned Heat); *White Rabbit* (Jefferson Airplane); *Western Union Blues* (It's a Beautiful Day); *Old Blue* (Byrds); *Saucerful of Secrets* (Pink Floyd); *Mardi Gras Day* (Dr. John); *Pavilions of the Sun* (T. Rex); *Big Bird* (Flock); *Gumbo* (Santana)

STARDUST (1974)

MUSIC ★★★★
ATTITUDE ★★★★★
FUN ★★★

CAST: David Essex, Adam Faith, Larry Hagman, Edd Byrnes, Marty Wilde, Keith Moon, Dave Edmunds; DIR: Michael Apted; PROD: David Puttnam, Sandy Lieberson; SCREENPLAY: Ray Connolly; STUDIO: Columbia; 111 min., color (no video release)

The decline and fall of a rock'n'roll star.
This sequel to *That'll Be the Day* traces the rise to international rock superstardom and eventual decline of Jim MacLaine (David Essex), amid drug use and decadence. There's hardly a scene or shot in this parable that isn't depressing in the extreme, both about the late '60s and the music it produced. The "Dea Sancta" number here is a stand-in for all those arty late-Beatles projects, and it's as empty and motionless as MacLaine. The presence of Dave Edmunds and his group (called the Stray Cats in the film, a name later picked up by the Long Island rockabilly outfit) is a major musical plus, but most people bought the soundtrack album simply because it had a lot of mid-'60s oldies on it. (BE)

SONGS   *When Will I Be Loved, A Shot of Rhythm and Blues, Some Other Guy, Make Me Good, C'mon Little Dixie* (Dave Edmunds and the Stray Cats); *You Keep Me Waiting, Stardust, Americana Stray Cat Blues, Dea Sancta* (David Essex)

STARSTRUCK (1982)

MUSIC ★★★★★
ATTITUDE ★★★★★
FUN ★★★★★

CAST: Jo Kennedy, Ross O'Donovan, Margo Lee, Max Cullen, Pat Evison, John O'May, Ned Lander, The Swingers; DIR: Gillian Armstrong; PROD: David Elfick, Richard Brennan; SCREENPLAY: Stephen MacLean; STUDIO: Cinecom; 95 min., color (Embassy)

The New Wave equivalent of Andy Hardy.
Starstruck's surface is all hot pink hair and postpunk pop, but the heart of this wonderful rock'n'roll comedy belongs to the classic Hollywood musical. You know, the kind in which Judy Garland and Mickey Rooney used to sing and

dance their way to romance, fame, and enough money to save the family business. As played by the deliciously wry Jo Kennedy, cheeky star-in-the-making Jackie makes every move as though she were onstage. Director Gillian Armstrong helps her out with concert scenes that are lavishly designed set pieces, crossing avant rock-video moves with old-fashioned musical storytelling. *Starstruck* subverts and advances old conventions even as it pays tribute to them. The unapologetically corny finale is a tour de force. The music, sung by Kennedy and largely written by Oz-rockers Phil Judd and the Swingers, is a fab collection of high-tech pop that can stand proudly among the real New Wave of the time. (JC)

Jackie's nude highwire act (0:28); dancing on countertops at the family pub (0:37); **SCENES** Angus starring in his very own New Wave video, "I Want to Live in a House" (0:52)

Jackie on her ambitions: "I want a band. I want amplifiers. I want, I want, I want." **LINES** Mocking her bandmate/suitor: "[My cousin Angus] reckons that guitars are like *phallic symbols*. And guitarists *masturbate* for a living. So God knows why you need me."

Gimme Love, Starstruck (Swingers); *Temper Temper, Surfside Tango, Body and Soul, My Belief in* **SONGS** *You, It's Not Enough, Monkey in Me, Starstruck* (Jo Kennedy); *I Wanna Live in a House* (Ross O'Donovan); *Tough* (John O'May, Jo Kennedy); *Tournaround* (Tournaround)

STAY AWAY JOE   (1968)

CAST: Elvis Presley, Burgess Meredith, Joan Blondell, Katy Jurado, Thomas Gomez, Henry Jones; DIR: Peter Tewksbury; PROD: Douglas Lawrence; SCREENPLAY: Michael A. Hoey; STUDIO: MGM; 102 min., color (MGM/UA)

MUSIC	★★
ATTITUDE	★★★★
FUN	★★★

Elvis at home on the range.
Joe Lightcloud (Elvis) is a famous rebel cowboy who returns to his Indian home-land to watch over a herd of cattle that the government has given his poor, imbe-cilic father (Burgess Meredith). Unfortunately, on his first night back, Joe and his pals get drunk and slaughter the herd's only bull. "Elvis goes West... and the West goes wild!" was the catch phrase used to advertise this film, the King's 26th. Elvis comes across here as a party-hardy James Dean type—good for heavy drinking, hardcore girl-chasing, and not much else. Of course, the guy has a heart of gold, and by the end he proves it without even singing too many songs. Joe's attempt to find a replacement bull turns up a steer that's more interested in sleep than sex. Then there's Joe's sister (Susan Trustman), who's about to marry into a very well-to-do family. Both situations lead to a lot of slapstick between the sexes. There's lots of weird male bonding, too. Number 26, huh? (MB)

The finale (1:41), in which Elvis fights all the men whose women he has stolen, **SCENES** ends with the destruction of the entire Lightcloud house. "Man, that's what I call one hell of a fight," Elvis says as the roof comes crashing down. The entire cast laughs hysterically.

Elvis on seeing an attractive babe: "She can chew on my moccasins anytime she **LINES** wants to."

Stay Away, Stay Away Joe, Lovely Mamie, Dominick, All I Needed Was the Rain (Elvis Presley) **SONGS**

THE STONES IN THE PARK (1969)

MUSIC ★★★★
ATTITUDE ★★★★★
FUN ★★

ALTERNATE TITLE: *The Stones in Hyde Park*
STUDIO: Granada TV; 45 min., color (no video release)

The Rolling Stones play Hyde and seek.
The Rolling Stones' gig in Hyde Park on July 5, 1969, was the band's first concert in more than two years and the first with Mick Taylor, who replaced the late Brian Jones. Unfortunately, the concert wasn't so great, and the film is worse. The group sounds much too loose, lacking the muscle of its subsequent U.S. tour—and there are simply too many close-ups of Jagger, while the rest of the band is ignored. The band's subpar performance can be explained away by its untested new sound and lineup, but it makes this film far less interesting and satisfying than *Gimme Shelter*, which includes performance clips from the American tour. Curiously, this Hyde Park bill also featured the original King Crimson in one of their earliest major gigs. (BE)

SONGS   *I'm Yours She's Mine, Jumpin' Jack Flash, No Expectations, Mercy Mercy, Stray Cat Blues, I'm Free, Downtown Girl, Love in Vain, Loving Cup, Midnight Rambler, Satisfaction, Honky Tonk Women, Street Fighting Man, Sympathy for the Devil* (Rolling Stones)

Stop Making Sense

STOP MAKING SENSE (1984)

MUSIC ★★★★★
ATTITUDE ★★
FUN ★★★★

DIR: Jonathan Demme; PROD: Gary Goetzman; SCREENPLAY: David Byrne; STUDIO: Cinecon/Island Alive; 99 min., color (RCA/Columbia)

The Talking Heads do it their own way. As usual.
With very little fanfare, a pair of immaculate white sneakers walks out onto a bare stage. This, we assume, is David Byrne, and of course it is. He sets down a cassette deck, hits play, and with a click track and an acoustic guitar, he rips through "Psycho Killer." Then bassist Tina Weymouth joins him—now we have bass, gui-

tar, and vocals—and they play "Heaven" while the drum riser is set up behind them. Drummer Chris Frantz adds the beat to "Thank You" as ever more equipment is rolled onstage. Finally, Jerry Harrison appears to complete the combo, although by the fifth song, they've added two backup singers, a percussionist, and a second guitarist. Kind of like connect the dots: The more dots you connect, the more picture you see. By the time the band gets to "Making Flippy Floppy," you've got a full-on performance on your hands with costumes, backdrops—it's a rock'n'roll extravaganza. But like everything else this band has ever done, this picture feels just a little bit tongue-in-cheek, as though it were a surrealist joke that you didn't really understand, You wonder whether anyone really does. Or is it all just nonsense? You'll never know for sure. (KW)

The performance of "Life During Wartime" (0:30) *SCENES*

"I have a tape I want to play for you," says Byrne. His other monologue is some- *LINES*
thing like, "Thank you. Good night."

Psycho Killer, Heaven, Thank You for Sending Me an Angel, Found a Job, Slippery People, Cities, *SONGS*
Burning Down the House, Life During Wartime, Making Flippy Floppy, Swamp, What a Day That
Was, Naive Melody, Once in a Lifetime, Big Business/I Zimbra, Genius of Love, Girlfriend Is Better,
Take Me to the River, Cross Eyed and Painless (Talking Heads)

STRAIGHT TO HELL   (1987)

CAST: Sy Richardson, Joe Strummer, Dick Rude, Courtney Love, Zander Schloss; DIR: Alex Cox; PROD: Eric Fellner; SCREENPLAY: Dick Rude, Alex Cox; STUDIO: Island; 86 min., color (Key)

MUSIC ★★
ATTITUDE ★
FUN ★★

Punk rockers playing cowboy.
With the offbeat cult hit *Repo Man* and the much-publicized *Sid and Nancy*, young British director Alex Cox won serious recognition from mainstream film critics and got to hang out with the hipster elite of punk rock and independent filmmaking. Say what you like about his directing skills, as a friend Cox seems to have been very good indeed. He apparently cast every last one of his new pals in his next film, *Straight to Hell.* In the grand tradition of such improvised works as *Beat the Devil* and *The Last Movie,* Cox quickly assembled a crew, flew off to an exotic location, and made up the "script" as he went along, while spending someone else's money on a budget that must have certainly included a generous amount for liquid refreshment. (The credits include special thanks to "all the bars in southern Spain.")

    While *Straight to Hell* is clearly intended to be a parody of spaghetti westerns, its action is confusingly set in the present. Sy Richardson, Joe Strummer, and Cox regular Dick Rude play desperadoes on the run after a bungled contract hit and bank robbery. Traveling with them are a load of cash and Richardson's screechy, pregnant girlfriend (the now-famous Courtney Love). They hole up in a desolate town (Tabernas, Spain) mostly populated by the violent and inarticulate MacMahon gang, played by the Pogues. After a few tense days of drinking coffee, espousing nonsensical dialogue, and coveting their neighbors' wives, everyone starts shooting each other. That's essentially the plot. If the sights of Strummer combing his hair with gasoline and Elvis Costello meekly pouring coffee strike you as amusing, then you might have the right frame of mind to enjoy this expensive home movie. (JS)

Elvis Costello, Jim Jarmusch, Dennis Hopper, Grace Jones, the Pogues, Edward *CAMEOS*
Tudorpole (alias Tenpole Tudor)

217

STREETS OF FIRE (1984)

MUSIC ★★★
ATTITUDE ★
FUN ★★

CAST: Michael Paré, Diane Lane, Rick Moranis, Amy Madigan, Willem Dafoe, Bill Paxton; DIR: Walter Hill; PROD: Lawrnce Gordon, Joel Silver; SCREENPLAY: Walter Hill, Larry Gross; STUDIO: Universal; 93 min., color (MCA)

Somebody shoulda kidnapped the screenwriter.
Because director Walter Hill has a reputation for cinematic reality, it's difficult to imagine what he was thinking when he created New Wave/disco singer Ellen Aim (Diane Lane). Her phoniness alone undermines this movie's musical credibility, which otherwise might have been pulled out of the historical muck in which it's mired. The plot is pretty facile: In a *Bladerunner*-style L.A., rock star Aim is kidnapped. Michael Paré plays the moody soldier-of-fortune, an ex-boyfriend, who's hired by manager Rick Moranis to find her.

The most noteworthy music on Ry Cooder's soundtrack is turned in by the Blasters, who perform the little-known Leiber-Stoller song "One Bad Stud" and "Blue Shadows." The Blasters were a bit off in their choice of films, however: They turned down *48 Hours* to do this one. Lee Ving, lead singer of the L.A. punk-type band Fear, plays a small role, and *Flashdance* fans can savor the fully lit appearance of Marine Jahan, who did the silhouetted dance numbers for Jennifer Beals in that film. A final note: Lane's co-star, Amy Madigan, once fronted a band called Jelly, which toured with Bread (honest). Lane herself starred in *Ladies and Gentlemen, the Fabulous Stains.* (AF)

CAMEOS   Robert Townsend, Ed Begley Jr., The Blasters, Lee Ving

SONGS   *Blue Shadows, One Bad Stud* (Blasters); *Countdown to Love* (Winston Ford); *Never Be You, Sorcerer* (Laurie Sargent)

Streets of Fire

SUMMER HOLIDAY (1963)

CAST: Cliff Richard and the Shadows, Laurie Peters, Melvyn Hayes; **DIR:** Peter Yates; **PROD:** Kenneth Harper; **SCREENPLAY:** Peter Myers, Ronald Cass; **STUDIO:** Associated British-Pathé; 109 min., color (no video release)

MUSIC ★★
ATTITUDE
FUN ★★★

A lightweight Cliff Richard comic caper.
Cliff and the Shadows are back, this time running a shuttle bus service to Europe and getting involved with a runaway pop star. The story is innocuous enough, and the color photography makes Europe easy on the eyes. The score, too, is quite pleasant, as was most of Richard's post-*Young Ones* music. It's very soft. So is the movie. Watch it if you're in the mood. (BE)

Bachelor Boy, All at Once, A Stranger in Town, A Swinging Affair, Dancing Shoes, Foot Tapper, **SONGS**
Summer Holiday (Cliff Richard and the Shadows)

SURF PARTY (1963)

CAST: Bobby Vinton, Patricia Morrow, Jackie DeShannon, Kenny Miller, Lory Patrick, Richard Crane, Jerry Summers, Martha Stewart, Mickey Dora, John Fain, Pam Colbert, Donna Russell, Lloyd Kino; **DIR:** Maury Dexter; **PROD:** Maury Dexter; **SCREENPLAY:** Harry Spalding; **STUDIO:** 20th Century-Fox; 68 min., b/w (no video release)

MUSIC ★★★★
ATTITUDE ★
FUN ★★★

Beach boys meet surf sweeties.
This film premiered close on the heels of American International Pictures' *Beach Party,* but it was a poor substitute for the original. An obvious (and I mean *obvious*) attempt to pick up some of the beach action, *Surf Party* was constructed in much the same fashion as *The Young Swingers* (1964), another Maury Dexter film. The basic idea was to provide a vehicle for popular recording artists to peddle their wares. The stars of this contrived film are, ironically, a contrived band called the Routers (pronounced ROOT-ers on the West Coast and ROUT-ers on the East Coast). Unlike the real surf instrumental groups of the period, the Routers were professional (and largely black) studio musicians. (The band members shown performing "Crack Up" are just extras.)

Surf Party recounts the tale of three girls from the Midwest who travel to Malibu in search of their lost brother. Amazingly filmed in black-and-white (when its rival was shot in beautiful Pathécolor), this film lacks all the nuance and panache of *Beach Party* and, as a result, fared poorly at the box office. Pop crooner Bobby Vinton receives top billing here. Vinton's agent had been hounding A.I.P.'s Lou Rusoff to use Vinton as the lead in *Beach Party,* but the studio settled instead on Frankie Avalon because (being Italian) he looked better with Annette Funicello. Let's all be grateful for small mercies! (SJM)

If I Were an Artist, Pearly Shells (Kenny Miller); *That's What Love Is* (Patricia Morrow); *Never* **SONGS**
Comin' Back, Glory Wave (Jackie DeShannon, Patricia Morrow, Lory Patrick); *Firewater, Surf Party* (Astronauts); *Symphony for Sorrow, The Big Wheel, Racing Wild* (Jimmie Haskell); *Great White Water, Crack Up* (Routers)

SWEET TORONTO (1970)

ALTERNATE TITLE: *Keep On Rockin'*
DIR: D.A. Pennebaker, Chris Hegedus; **PROD:** D.A. Pennebaker, Chris Hegedus; **STUDIO:** Pennebaker; 102 min., color (no video release)

MUSIC ★★★★
ATTITUDE ★★★★
FUN ★★★★★

Jerry Lee shows them who's really king.

On September 13, 1969, the Toronto Peace Festival celebrated the end of the '60s by putting together a bill featuring the greatest acts of the '50s. For a headliner, the promoters snagged John Lennon (recently of the Beatles) and his new Plastic Ono Band (with Eric Clapton sitting in). Finally, D.A. Pennebaker (*Don't Look Back, Monterey Pop*) was invited to record the event, which also happened to be Lennon's debut as a solo performer. The result was released as *Sweet Toronto* in 1970, then pulled for legal reasons, edited, and rereleased as *Keep On Rockin'* in 1972. Pennebaker had to delete the Lennon footage, replacing it with clips of Jimi Hendrix and Janis Joplin from *Monterey Pop*.

A straightforward performance film, *Sweet Toronto* features Pennebaker's trademark handheld camera shots as well as lots of footage of the audience. The film is consistently entertaining, if largely unremarkable. There's no complete copy available commercially on video (the cassette called *Sweet Toronto* [1988] includes only the Lennon set), but you can find the rest of the music on separate Little Richard, Chuck Berry, and Jerry Lee Lewis tapes. (KHB)

SCENES Jerry Lee shows them all up with a set composed mostly of Elvis's tunes. On "Mystery Train," the Killer plays guitar instead of piano. Hot stuff!

SONGS *Hey Bo Diddley, Bo Diddley* (Bo Diddley); *Mystery Train, Don't Be Cruel, Hound Dog, Mean Woman Blues, Great Balls of Fire, Whole Lotta Shakin' Goin' On, Jailhouse Rock* (Jerry Lee Lewis); *Rock'n'Roll Music, No Particular Place to Go, Johnny B. Goode, Hoochie Coochie Man, Sweet Little Sixteen* (Chuck Berry); *Lucille, Good Golly Miss Molly, Rip It Up, Tutti Frutti, Hound Dog, Jenny Jenny, Long Tall Sally* (Little Richard); *Blue Suede Shoes, Money, Dizzy Miss Lizzie, Yer Blues, Cold Turkey, Give Peace a Chance* (John Lennon and the Plastic Ono Band); *Don't Worry Kyoko, John John* (Yoko Ono and the Plastic Ono Band)

A SWINGIN' SUMMER (1965)

MUSIC ★★★★★
ATTITUDE ★★★★☆
FUN ★★★★☆

CAST: James Stacy, William Wellman Jr., Raquel Welch, Quinn O'Hara, Bob Blair; **DIR:** Robert Sparr; **PROD:** Reno Carell; **SCREENPLAY:** Leigh Chapman; **STUDIO:** United Screen Arts; 85 min., color (no video release)

We'll watusi all night—Gary Lewis is in town.

A Swingin' Summer was United Screen Arts' one stab at the *Beach Party* tidal wave. Luckily, the studio managed to ride in on the whitewater. Strangely, the producers decided to leave the Pacific behind, moving the plot to the mountains—Lake Arrowhead, specifically. It was a brilliant move, one of the best things about the movie, because that swingin' teenage area was a really cool hangout back then (it was later destroyed in a fire). Gary Lewis and the Playboys don't perform any of their hits, but they nevertheless "swing" the place out of control. The instrumentals they do have a lot of juice, and they hold up well under the threat of high-volume speakers. The Playboys also back up the Righteous Brothers in the film's blazing closer, "Justine." It's one of the hottest moments in any beach movie.

Bruce Johnston and Terry Melcher (a future Beach Boy and Byrds/Paul Revere producer) can be heard singing "Red Hot Roadster" on the audio track, although it's the "road" Rip Chords onstage, of course! More fun occurs (unintentional, this time) when Donnie Brooks is introduced as "Mr. Personality," and he kicks off his number with a cornball "hey gang" rap before busting into "Penny the Poo" (rhymes with "She knows exactly what to do," right?). One shudders to think that Bob Dylan was probably completing the final mixdown of "Subterranean Homesick Blues" at the very same time! A familiar angle, the "chicken" race, is given a *Beach Party* twist on water skis! The sleeper in this cinematic escapade is

the soundtrack album, wherein Carol Connors sings her self-penned title track (Jody Miller sings it on the film). As with most of her work (Teddy Bears, Carol and Cheryl, etc.), she delivers a smooth-rollin' blast. This is also the film debut of Raquel Welch, who attempts to sing "Ready to Groove." Some great rock'n'roll lies within this somber but swell change of pace. (DP)

Gypsy Boots

CAMEOS

A Swingin' Summer (Jody Miller); *Nitro, Out to Lunch* (Gary Lewis and the Playboys); *Red Hot Roadster* (Rip Chords); *Penny the Poo* (Donnie Brooks); *Ready to Groove* (Raquel Welch); *Justine* (Righteous Brothers)

SONGS

SYMPATHY FOR THE DEVIL　　(1968)

MUSIC ★★
ATTITUDE ★★
FUN ★★

ALTERNATE TITLE: *One Plus One*
DIR: Jean-Luc Godard; PROD: Michael Pearson, Ian Quarrier; SCREENPLAY: Jean-Luc Godard; STUDIO: New Line; 100 min., color (no video release)

Maybe the devil is God in exile?

The cross-pollination of revolutionary politics and rock'n'roll? Neither is *that* connected to the other in this movie, except for the lurking presence of the devil in Mr. Jagger's song and the omnipresence of revolution in stormy 1968. The initial focus of this film may have been on the Rolling Stones, but it doesn't linger there. We see Jagger & Co. in the studio recording "Sympathy for the Devil," taking an almost honky-tonk demo and transforming it into the fearful jungle symmetry of the final version. But Godard has much more to say about the world in 1968 than about the world's greatest rock'n'roll band. The great one interviews black revolutionaries, Trotskyites, fashion models, and all the other icons of the 1960s underground. He confronts racism, sexism, and totalitarianism. But the only conclusion he can reach is that making a revolution can be every bit as tedious as making a record album. (TP)

SCENES　The Stones finally get the song right (0:47).

LINES　"Orgasm is the only moment when you can't cheat life."

CAMEOS　Jean-Luc Godard

SONGS　*Sympathy for the Devil* (Rolling Stones)

THE T.A.M.I. SHOW　　(1964)

MUSIC ★★★★★
ATTITUDE ★★★★★
FUN ★★★★★

DIR: Steve Binder; PROD: William Sargent Jr., Lee Savin; STUDIO: Screen Entertainment; 96 min., b/w (no video release)

An event that deserves a book unto itself.

This concert film from late 1964 perfectly captures a particularly brilliant and explosive moment in rock history. Every element of that year's diverse and innovative scene is represented here. Virtually every significant chart act of the day (except for the Beatles and the Four Seasons) appears in this film, all performing as though their lives depended on it.

The show opens with hosts Jan and Dean introducing Chuck Berry, who's paired onstage with Liverpool's Gerry and the Pacemakers. Chuck does a half-minute version of "Nadine." Gerry responds with "I Like It," one of his Tin Pan Alley throwaways. Then Chuck does "Sweet Little Sixteen," and Gerry answers with "How Do You Do It?" The kids love it and go totally nuts. Lesley Gore performs some of the songs that have made her a gay-culture icon (including the anthemic "You Don't Own Me").

The Supremes, wearing massive hairdos and tight dresses, deliver a brief but scorching set of hits, near-hits, and non-hits. The close-ups of Diana Ross's mouth are among the film's highlights. Then from Brian Epstein's management stable comes arch-geek Billy J. Kramer mouthing the best Lennon and McCartney songs that the Beatles never sang. Representing garage rock is the film's token unknown act (somebody obviously owed somebody a favor), the Barbarians, who feature a one-handed drummer named Moulty. During the next year, the Barbarians would

score a minor hit with the pre-punk classic "Are You a Boy or Are You a Girl?" Representing what Paul Le Mat called (in *American Graffiti*) "that surfin' shit," the Beach Boys show up in their striped shirts and tear the already hysterical audience to shreds. But for some mysterious reason, their performance is missing from most prints of this movie.

James Brown wanted to close *The T.A.M.I. Show*, but the producers insisted on the Rolling Stones. Rock Film fans often refer to these back-to-back sets as The Battle of the Century. Both acts were at career crossroads: The Stones had been causing riots in England for a year but hadn't yet scored a significant U.S. hit single. James Brown was the biggest star in R&B, but he hadn't yet found consistent crossover success. James's set is a breathtaking spectacle of bodies in motion and balls-out musical excitement. On the other hand, in 1964, the Stones were playing what every bar band in America was playing: Chuck Berry covers and recent R&B hits. But they did have charisma and a mystique that no other group could match. Their relentless attack here drives the audience past the point of hysteria. Who wins The Battle? Everybody. Who loses? Only those who don't watch.

A footnote: Sometime during the early 1980s, highlights from *The T.A.M.I. Show* and *The Big TNT Show* were edited together for a home video called *That Was Rock*. It's a hatchet job and a piece of garbage, so why did I buy it? (MC)

SONGS *Here They Come, The Little Old Lady from Pasadena, Sidewalk Surfin'* (Jan and Dean); *Johnny B. Goode, Sweet Little Sixteen, Nadine* (Chuck Berry); *Maybellene* (Chuck Berry, Gerry and the Pacemakers); *Don't Let the Sun Catch You Crying, It's Gonna Be Alright, How Do You Do It?, I Like It* (Gerry and the Pacemakers); *That's What Love Is Made Of, You Really Got a Hold On Me, Mickey's Monkey* (Smokey Robinson and the Miracles); *Stubborn Kind of Fellow, Pride and Joy, Can I Get a Witness, Hitchhike* (Marvin Gaye with the Blossoms); *Maybe I Know, You Don't Own Me, It's My Party, Judy's Turn to Cry* (Lesley Gore); *Little Children, I'll Keep You Satisfied, Bad to Me, From a Window* (Billy J. Kramer and the Dakotas); *When the Lovelight Starts Shining Through His Eyes, Run Run Run, Baby Love, Where Did Our Love Go* (Supremes); *My Little Girl* (Barbarians); *Out of Sight, Prisoner of Love, Please Please Please, Night Train* (James Brown and the Famous Flames); *Around and Around, Off the Hook, Time Is on My Side, It's All Over Now, It's All Right* (Rolling Stones); *Surfin' U.S.A., Surfer Girl, Dance Dance Dance, I Get Around* (Beach Boys)

TEENAGE CRUISERS (1977)

MUSIC ★★★
ATTITUDE ★★
FUN ★★

CAST: Tony Conn, Johnny Legend, Colin Winksi, Jerry Sikorski, Lynne Margulies, Serena; DIR: Johnny Legend; PROD: Johnny Legend; SCREENPLAY: Johnny Legend; STUDIO: Raunchy Tonk; 84 min., color (Weird World)

Porn-again cruisin'.

Teenage Cruisers may be assembled with slightly more wit than the average flesh fantasy, but the movie is basically a hard-core porn flick with a storyline whose only purpose is to connect various scenes of fucking and sucking. The one remarkable thing about this crudely made, ill-photographed effort is the music. Strewn throughout are rockabilly songs from Rollin' Rock Records artists Billy Zoom, Ray Campi, Tony Conn (a character in the film), Mac Curtis, and Alvis Wayne. (The Blasters' "Marie Marie" is on the Rhino-released soundtrack album but does not appear in the film.) Film deejay Mambo Remus is in (semi-)real life Johnny Legend, wrestling manager and rockabilly Rasputin. Other rockabilly heroes doing cameos are Rollin' Colin Winksi and Jumpin' Jerry Sikorski, both of whom were in the Rockin' Rebels, who played behind Ray Campi and opened some shows for the Clash. Also, you get to see John Holmes, the famous wad guy. In the end, Babs the nuthouse nympho apparently gets satisfied, Serena the porn star gets glue or something all over her, and Tony Conn, the lonely lead, either kills himself or takes a swim at the end. (AF)

LINES "Read all about it! Nuthouse Nympho ravages city, then disappears."

SONGS *Are You Hep to It, Hot Rock* (Johnny Legend); *Bad Boy, Crazy Crazy Lovin', Don't Teach Me, Say When* (Billy Zoom); *Bip BobBoom* (Chuck Higgins); *Birmingham Mama* (Tony Conn); *Eager Boy* (Ray Campi); *Hungry Hill* (Jackie Lee Waukeen Cochran); *I Wanna Eat Your Puddin'* (Alvis Wayne); *Red Hot Mama* (Colin Winksi); *Slippin' In* (Mac Curtis); *That Certain Female* (Charlie Feathers); *Wail Baby* (Kid Thomas)

TEENAGE MILLIONAIRE (1961)

MUSIC ★
ATTITUDE ★
FUN ★★

CAST: Jimmy Clanton, ZaSu Pitts, Rocky Graziano, Maurice Gosfield, Diane Jergens, Sid Gould; DIR: Lawrence Doheny; PROD: Howard B. Kreitsek; SCREENPLAY: H.B. Cross; STUDIO: United Artists; 84 min., b/w (no video release)

The attempted murder of rock'n'roll.

Teenager Jimmy Clanton (he looks about 28 here) inherits a fortune. Thereafter, Rocky Graziano becomes his chaperon. As a rule, if you see Graziano's name in the credits for a rock movie, run. The producers of this film are probably on the run, too, because there's no statute of limitations on crimes like this. With all the conspiracy theories around these days, it's surprising how little attention has been paid to the attempted murder of rock'n'roll in 1960. With Buddy Holly dead, Chuck Berry behind bars, Little Richard in the ministry, Jerry Lee Lewis banned, and Elvis's brain destroyed by army drugs, the Establishment flooded the teen market with violin-drenched pop in the hopes of killing rock'n'roll forever. Of course, the music survived, even in *Teenage Millionaire*, which features two performance clips of the Bill Black Combo, three of Jackie Wilson, and string-laden songs by Vicki Spencer that are actually okay. But the sloblike appearance of Maurice Gosfield ("Doberman" on "The Phil Silvers Show") has more to do with rock'n'roll than anything else in this film. A final note: The music sequences in this film were shot in Musicolor, a short-lived duotone process that substituted blue-and-white (or brown-and-white, etc.) stock for the usual black-and-white film. (AF)

THAT'LL BE THE DAY (1973)

MUSIC ★★★★★
ATTITUDE ★★★★★
FUN ★★★★★

CAST: David Essex, Ringo Starr, Rosemary Leach, James Booth, Billy Fury, Keith Moon, Rosalind Ayres; DIR: Claude Whatham; PROD: David Puttnam, Sanford Lieberson; SCREENPLAY: Ray Connolly; STUDIO: EMI; 90 min., color (HBO)

'50s rock'n'roll with Essex appeal.

That'll Be the Day is a truly great rock'n'roll movie—really a much superior, grittier successor to *Expresso Bongo*. In a role loosely based on the early life of John Lennon (and producer David Puttnam himself), David Essex plays Jim MacLaine, a 1958 dropout who drifts around with his buddy Ringo Starr (in the best performance of his career), lives in squalor, has lots of sex, gets married, and eventually drifts into rock'n'roll. The music performances are first-rate, which is no surprise since, in addition to playing a part in the film, Keith Moon served as musical director with veteran Beatles alumnus Neil Aspinall. The background soundtrack is chock'full of a dazzlingly perfect selection of oldies by Bill Justis, the Everly Brothers, Dion, Jerry Lee Lewis, Del Shannon, the Paris Sisters, and Johnny and the Hurricanes. Plus you get on-screen performances by Billy Fury (as Stormy Tempest, a loving reprise of his pre-Beatles rock star career) and Eugene Wallace. The story is downbeat but honest, and the movie helped foster a major revival of interest in '50s British rock. (BE)

SONGS   A Thousand Stars, Long Live Rock, What'd I Say, Get Yourself Together, That's All Right, What in the World (Billy Fury); *Slow Down* (Eugene Wallace); *Rock On* (David Essex)

THAT'S THE WAY OF THE WORLD (1974)

MUSIC ★★★★★
ATTITUDE ★★★★★
FUN ★★★★★

CAST: Harvey Keitel, Ed Nelson, Bert Parks, Cynthia Bostick, Jimmy Boyd, Earth Wind and Fire; DIR: Sig Shore; PROD: Sig Shore; SCREENPLAY: Robert Lipsyte; STUDIO: United Artists; 100 min., color (U.S.A.)

'70s R&B forever!

A "wholesome" family vocal group that's really a pack of degenerates. Gangsters as record company powerbrokers. Racism, graft, and corruption in the music business. Just what is going on here? A documentary? No, it's *That's the Way of the World*, a great movie starring Harvey Keitel and Earth, Wind, and Fire, written by journalist Robert Lipsyte, and directed and produced by Sig Shore of "Superfly" fame. Keitel plays Coleman Buckmaster, the son of a famous jazz pianist. As a hot young staff producer, he's the creative backbone of A-Chord Records, but the new company president is putting the squeeze on him. He's being forced to work with the Pages, a family singing group from Orlando. Coleman thinks they're "bullshit whitebread bubblegum" and resents having to take time and energy away from his pet project, the Group (Earth, Wind, and Fire). Much double-dealing and scamming ensues. This film's soundtrack album is a classic and (YES!!) is still in print. (MC)

SCENES   Visiting his father at dad's day gig, a piano factory, Coleman takes him a small gift, a stash of cocaine.

LINES   The Pages' lead singer, Velour, drinking a toast to Janis Joplin: "She was ugly on the outside and beautiful on the inside. I'm just the opposite."

CAMEOS   Frankie Crocker, Murray the K, Doris Troy

THIS IS ELVIS (1981)

DIR: Malcolm Leo, Andrew Solt; PROD: David L. Wolper; SCREENPLAY: Malcolm Leo, Andrew Solt; STUDIO: Warner; 144 min., color (Warner)

MUSIC ★★
ATTITUDE ★★
FUN ★★★

The authorized docudrama.

This Elvis fest could have been a lot worse. Instead, producer David Wolper, the impresario who masterminded *Roots*, bought off Graceland, Colonel Tom Parker, and the Memphis Mafia to make his version of Elvis for Beginners. The result is some generally palatable Presleyana. As we are reminded, no footage of Elvis exists before he turned 21, so scenes of his childhood in Tupelo and his adolescence in Memphis are re-created here (with reasonable accuracy) for your viewing pleasure. After that, the film relies primarily on excerpts from Presley's movies and his television appearances. The selection of clips is blandly predictable—Elvis singing "Hound Dog" to a real live pooch on the Steve Allen show; his gyrations on Milton Berle that caused such a fuss; the familiar home movies from Graceland; the usual crewcut suspects condemning rock'n'roll. But Elvis impersonator Ral Donner does a fine job narrating the King's story in Presley's own voice, if not his own words. And if your kids haven't seen Elvis's appearance on Ed Sullivan or his 1968 comeback special, *This Is Elvis* will get them caught up real fast. (DR)

The movies opens with a reenactment of the morning that Presley died. Elvis con- **S C E N E S**
fidant Joe Esposito, who was there, plays himself (badly). Take a close look at the King's bedroom and adjoining bathroom. The Graceland folks don't let you up there on the tour.

A fan outside Graceland on the day Presley died: "I'm just glad that Elvis died here **L I N E S**
in Graceland instead of on the road just like any other rock'n'roll singer."

THIS IS SPINAL TAP (1984)

CAST: Christopher Guest, Michael McKean, Harry Shearer, Rob Reiner, Tony Hendra; DIR: Rob Reiner; PROD: Karen Murphy; SCREENPLAY: Christopher Guest, Michael McKean, Harry Shearer, Rob Reiner; STUDO: Embassy; 88 min., color (Embassy)

MUSIC ★★★
ATTITUDE ★★★★★
FUN ★★★★★

The ultimate rock parody. Or is it a tribute?

This Is Spinal Tap is so well-crafted and on-target that many preview audiences didn't realize it was a joke. To rock musicians and others in the biz, however, *Spinal Tap* instantly became a cultural landmark against which reality could be measured. Rob Reiner plays veteran director Marty DiBergi ("the commercial with the dogs chasing the chuck wagon was mine"), who sets out to record for posterity the hapless American tour of "one of England's loudest bands." Guest and McKean score massively as Tap's egregiously stoopid lead and rhythm guitarists, Nigel Tufnel and David St. Hubbins. In one of his many precious moments (0:23), Nigel shows Marty a custom-made amp. While most amps dial up to 10, Nigel explains carefully, *his* goes up to 11. It's *one* louder, you see. (DR)

Paul Shaffer's cameo as fey Artie Fufkin, head of Midwest promotion for Polymer **S C E N E S**
Records (0:45); the Stonehenge production number (0:54)

This Is Spinal Tap

LINES David St. Hubbins on the cover art for *Smell the Glove*: "It's such a fine line between stupid and clever." Explaining the basis for his unique creative viewpoint: "I believe virtually everything I read."

CAMEOS Fran Drescher, Dana Carvey, Billy Crystal, Bruno Kirby, Ed Begley Jr., Danny Kortchmar, Paul Benedict, Howard Hesseman, Paul Shaffer, Anjelica Huston, Fred Willard

SONGS *Tonight I'm Gonna Rock You, Big Bottom, Hell Hole, Listen to What the Flower People Say, Rock'n'Roll Creation, Heavy Duty Rock'n'Roll, Stonehenge, Sex Farm* (Spinal Tap); *Gimme Some Money* (Thamesmen)

TICKLE ME (1965)

MUSIC ★★
ATTITUDE ★
FUN ★★

CAST: Elvis Presley, Julie Adams, Jocelyn Lane, Jack Mullaney; Merry Anders; DIR: Norman Taurog; PROD: Ben Schwalb; SCREENPLAY: Elwood Ullman, Edward Bernds; STUDIO: Allied Artists; 90 min., color (Key)

You won't get a laugh any other way.

Elvis stars as Lonnie Beals, an out-of-work rodeo star who gets a job at a health ranch where women go to slim down. While there, he gets involved with Pam (Jocelyn Lane), a feisty dance instructor who's trying to find her dead grandfather's hidden mining treasure. She's being mysteriously harassed, and Lonnie helps out when he's not fighting off the inevitable hordes of horny women. *Tickle Me* is a crazy quilt of music, mystery, romance, and comedy. Plus, in an attempt to re-create the phenomenally successful Dean Martin/Jerry Lewis comedy team, Elvis is paired with Stanley (Jack Mullaney), an awkward geek who's continuously shutting doors on and otherwise tripping up the Dean-like Elvis. All these elements make for an awkwardly paced and rather pallid film (even for an Elvis picture). Elvis's songs are mostly dull and fade out very artificially on the soundtrack. Cheap, cheap, cheap. (TM)

The western saloon scene in which Elvis plays a milk-drinking tough guy (0:36)   *S C E N E S*

Pam to Lonnie: "I know your type. Just a sagebrush Lothario looking for a good   *L I N E S* thing."

Just Keep Movin' Down the Line, If It Feels So Right, Such an Easy Question, Dirty Feelin', Put the   *S O N G S* *Blame on Me, I'm Yours, Night Rider, I've Loved You Forever, Slowly but Surely* (Elvis Presley)

THE TIGERS (1968)

CAST: The Tigers, Kaori Kumi, Lumi Koyama; DIR: Kunihiko Yamamoto; PROD: Susumu Watanabe, Naoto Gumyo; SCREENPLAY: Yasuaki Tanami; STUDIO: Tokyo Developing; 88 min., color (Toho)

MUSIC ★★★★
ATTITUDE ★★★
FUN ★★★★

Discovering the Japananese Monkees.

The Tigers, a Japanese rock band armed with Teisco guitars and *Revolver* haircuts, are usually referred to as "the Japanese Monkees" by knowledgeable Jap-rock collectors. They made a few albums and got to star in this *Help!*-style feature—in which they clown around, look cool, and play songs that are an acceptable mixture of generic '60s beat music and eastern melodies. If you look through enough ethnic video shops, you might be able to locate this letter-boxed, unsubtitled tape. Here's what seems to happen (I don't know Japanese): After some nice closeups of their exotic guitars, we get our first look at the Tigers, who sing an upbeat theme song behind the credits that is repeated occasionally throughout the movie—sometimes in orchestrated, George Martin-style snippets. Then the music suddenly stops, and one member of the groups runs off to a room labeled "W.C." He soon returns, and they finish the song. (Bathroom jokes are a major part of Japanese humor.) In the next scene, the Tigers miss a school roll call, but some girls yell the Japanese word for "here" in deep voices to cover their absence. Where are the Tigers? Jumping around in fields, wearing matching black turtlenecks and Beatles boots, and eating rice dishes.

From then on, the Tigers run around town, meeting girls and playing impromptu songs. Several times they're shown in nightclubs or standing next to buses inexplicably plastered with photos of the *real* Monkees. In one scene, they set up their equipment in an abandoned building and tap into a power line, enabling them to play a cool, punkish song until the transformer fries. The police come and throw them in jail, where they all bow to their cellmate, a black trumpet player who shows them how to draw guitars and drums on the walls that magically make sound. Then the small cell dissolves into a facsimile of the famous *Jailhouse Rock* production number. In a field of flowers, they play on pieces of machinery that turn into their actual equipment, as their parents look on proudly. This cuts to a montage of the band in concert on a giant stage, a printed backdrop announcing "JAPAN POPS NEW—THE YM WORLD." The crowd cheers wildly as the picture freezes on one last Richard Lester leap. (JS)

TIMES SQUARE (1980)

CAST: Tim Curry, Trini Alvarado, Robin Johnson; DIR: Alan Moyle; PROD: Robert Stigwood, Jacob Brackman; SCREENPLAY: Jacob Brackman; STUDIO: RSO; 111 min., color (Thorn-EMI)

MUSIC ★
ATTITUDE ★
FUN ★★

Even the worst critics of punk couldn't have dreamed up this one.

Even mentioning this movie seems to dignify it unnecessarily. Apparently, disco guru Robert Stigwood thought he could cash in on punk rock. Consequently, the

Times Square soundtrack features the Talking Heads and the Ramones, but even they don't help much because the picture itself has no credibility. Even if *Times Square's* teenage rebellion plot does suggest punk's raison d'être, the film's deadly serious treatment of its heroines, two runaway teenage girls who become punk sensations, negates whatever impact it might have had. Filled with boring scenes and two painfully bad live music segments, *Times Square* is big and stupid. Punk may have been stupid, too, but at least there was some life to it, you know? (ALa)

SONGS *Flowers in the City, Your Daughter Is One* (Robin Johnson)

TO SIR, WITH LOVE   (1966)

MUSIC ★★
ATTITUDE ★★★★
FUN ★★★★

CAST: Sidney Poitier, Judy Geeson, Christian Roberts, Suzy Kendall, Lulu; DIR: James Clavell; PROD: James Clavell; SCREENPLAY: James Clavell; STUDIO: Columbia; 105 min., color (RCA/Columbia)

London's East End spawns its own Blackboard Jungle.

After searching unsuccessfully for work as an engineer, Thackeray (Sidney Poitier) accepts a teaching job at a rough, East End high school. His colleagues warn him about the impossible brutes he will encounter there, but still he enters his classroom unprepared for their horrible defiance. *To Sir, with Love* is a classic portrayal of teen angst. These impoverished, battered kids, who have turned out just awful, are determined to torture everyone around them. The teachers let them dance between classes to vent some of their aggressive energy, but they still treat the classroom as though it were an unsupervised sandbox. With transcendent dignity, Thackeray tames them and teaches them self-respect. As corny as the plot may be, the kids' transition is touching, and Poitier is as cool and classy as ever. (SBW)

SCENES Thackeray's students try to out-slack each other when answering roll call (0:13); the groovy photo montage shot at the Victoria and Albert Museum (0:48)

LINES Thackeray admonishing the girls: "No man likes a slut for long, and only the worst kind marries one."

SONGS *To Sir with Love* (Lulu); *Stealing My Love from Me, Off and Running, It's Getting Harder All the Time* (Mindbenders)

TOMMY   (1975)

MUSIC ★
ATTITUDE ★
FUN ★

CAST: Roger Daltrey, Ann-Margret, Oliver Reed; DIR: Ken Russell; PROD: Ken Russell, Robert Stigwood; SCREENPLAY: Ken Russell; STUDIO: Columbia; 111 min., color (RCA/Columbia)

Pete Townshend's rock opera goes video.

Ken Russell really drops the ball on this one. Amazingly, there seems to be even less plot here than in the Who's original album about a deaf, dumb, and blind boy. If you think MTV can get monotonous, just try two hours of Russell's mindless, meandering vignettes. With the single exception of Elton John, all the musical talent here is wasted. And whose brilliant idea was it to let Ann-Margret and Oliver Reed *sing*, anyway? The proof that Russell's self-indulgence really messed things up is *Quadrophenia*, which confirms that Townshend's writing can indeed work on the big screen. (DR)

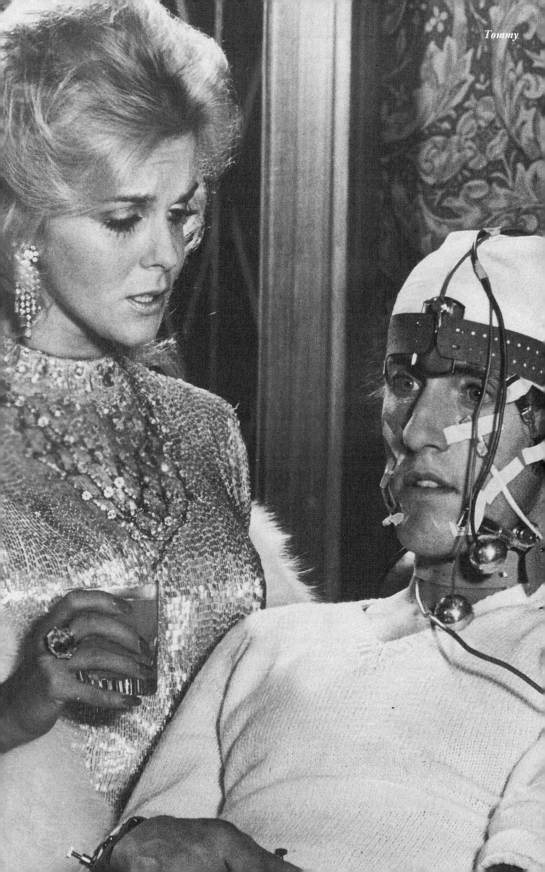

SCENES   Elton John playing the Pinball Wizard at the height of Elton's glitter period, when he really knew how to accessorize (0:54)

CAMEOS   Pete Townshend, John Entwistle, Eric Clapton, Tina Turner, Keith Moon, Elton John, Jack Nicholson

SONGS   *Amazing Journey, Sally Simpson* (Pete Townshend); *Eyesight to the Blind* (Eric Clapton); *Acid Queen* (Tina Turner); *Cousin Kevin* (Paul Nicholas); *Fiddle About* (Keith Moon); *Sparks* (Who); *Pinball Wizard* (Elton John); *I'm Free, Sensation, We're Not Gonna Take It* (Roger Daltrey)

TONITE LET'S ALL MAKE LOVE IN LONDON (1967)

MUSIC ★★★★
ATTITUDE ★★★★
FUN ★★★

CAST: Mick Jagger, Andrew Loog Oldham, Julie Christie, Michael Caine, Lee Marvin, David Hockney, Alan Aldridge; DIR: Peter Whitehead; PROD: Peter Whitehead; STUDIO: Lorrimer; 72 min., color (no video release)

An excellent portrait of Swinging London.
Peter Whitehead's disjointed Swinging London documentary, subtitled "A Pop Concerto," comprises a number of different "movements," each depicting a different theme underscored by music: An early version of Pink Floyd's "Interstellar Overdrive" plays behind some arty nightclub scenes, while Chris Farlowe's rendition of the Stones' "Out of Time" accompanies a young woman's description of London nightlife and the vacuousness of her own existence. In another segment, the Marquess of Kensington (ex-Kinks manager Robert Wace) croons the nostalgic "Changing of the Guard" to shots of Buckingham Palace's changing of the guard, and Immediate Records act Vashti are seen at work in the studio. Sandwiched between are clips of Mick Jagger (discussing revolution), Andrew Loog Oldham (discussing his future)—and Julie Christie, Michael Caine, Lee Marvin, and novelist Edna O'Brien (each discussing sex). There's also a much-too-long talk with painter David Hockney about art. The best part is footage of the riot that interrupted the Stones' October 12, 1966, Royal Albert Hall concert. Close behind are the clips of artist Alan Aldridge body-painting a nude model to "Paint It Black," performed by Farlowe, and footage of the arrival of London's first Playboy bunnies, scored to the Small Faces' "Here Comes the Nice." (BE)

SONGS   *Interstellar Overdrive* (Pink Floyd); *Changing of the Guard* (Marquess of Kensington); *Night Time Girl* (Twice as Much); *Out of Time, Paint It Black* (Chris Farlowe); *Winter Is Blue* (Vashti); *When I Was Young* (Eric Burdon and the Animals); *Here Comes the Nice* (Small Faces)

TOUGHER THAN LEATHER   (1988)

MUSIC ★★★★★
ATTITUDE ★★★★
FUN ★★★

CAST: Joseph [Run] Simmons, Darryl [DMC] McDaniels, Jason (Jam Master Jay) Mizell, Rick Rubin, Richard Edson, Jenny Lumet, Lois Ayres, The Beastie Boys; DIR: Rick Rubin; PROD: Vincent Giordano; SCREENPLAY: Ric Menello, Rick Rubin; STUDIO: New Line; 92 min., color (RCA/Columbia)

Run-DMC avenge a friend's death.
Crooked record producer Vic (Rick Rubin) signs the unwitting Run-DMC to his record label, which is really a front for mob money-laundering. After Vic kills a friend of theirs, Run, DMC, and Jam Master Jay team up to administer some street justice, wrecking Vic's operation in between performances. Unfortunately, the visceral kick of Run-DMC's music doesn't help this movie's clumsy passes at action. The violence here looks like kids playing with water pistols. And when the stars aren't onstage, they seem withdrawn, smaller than life. Nevertheless, as flat as

the script and direction are, two members of the oddball supporting cast deserve mention: Richard Edson as the last word in low-life suck-ups and porn goddess Lois Ayres as a venomous platinum sex object. And yes, as the sleazeball egomaniac Vic, Rick Rubin is perfectly cast as the B-movie heavy (playing perhaps only a minimally exaggerated version of himself). Rapper Slick Rick's cameo performance of "Treat Her Like a Prostitute" sums up this film's sexual politics. (HH)

Beats to the Rhyme, Mary Mary, Run's House (Run-DMC); *Desperado* (Beastie Boys); *Sardines* (Junkyard Band); *Treat Her Like a Prostitute* (Slick Rick)   **S O N G S**

THE TROUBLE WITH GIRLS   (1969)

CAST: Elvis Presley, Marlyn Mason, Nicole Jaffe, Sheree North, Edward Andrews, John Carradine, Dabney Coleman; DIR: Peter Tewksbury; PROD: Lester Welch; SCREENPLAY: Arnold Peyser, Lois Peyser; STUDIO: MGM; 97 min., color (MGM/UA)

MUSIC ★★
ATTITUDE ★★
FUN ★

The trouble with Elvis.
Paired with the Japanese flick *The Green Slime* when it was first released to the-atres, *The Trouble with Girls* doesn't live up to its name. There ain't too many girls; there ain't that much trouble. Elvis plays Walter Hale, the leader of a 1927 Lollapalooza-like traveling show called the Chautauqua. Glenn Ford was originally supposed to play Hale, and then Dick Van Dyke. But when Elvis got involved with the picture, the original title, *Chautauqua*, was changed to suit the King's image a little better. The only interesting thing that happens in the movie is the murder of a womanizing ass named Harrison Wilby (Dabney Coleman). Joyce Van Patten turns in an amusing performance as a famous swimmer lecturing with the Chautauqua who discovers the dead body. After he figures out the killer's identity, Elvis craftily advertises that the murderer of Wilby will be revealed at the musical show. The whole thing is rather low-key, but there's one cool performance scene with Elvis that uses weird camera angles, blurs, and fast cuts in the same way "The Monkees" TV show did. All in all, a pretty dull effort. Maybe *The Green Slime* was better. (MB)

Creeping toward a blunt sexual proposition, Hale inadvertently throws a cigar into **S C E N E S** a huge box of fireworks, extinguishing his crass pass in a fiery blaze of glory (0:47).

A roadie: "The cannibals are complaining that their mattresses are too lumpy." **L I N E S** Elvis: "I told them to quit eating 'em."

Anissa Jones, Vincent Price, Frank Welker, the Jordanaires   **C A M E O S**

Swing Low Sweet Chariot, The Whiffenpoof Song, Violet, Clean Up Your Own Backyard, Sign of the **S O N G S** *Zodiac* (Elvis Presley); *The Darktown Strutters' Ball* (Anissa Jones, Pepe Brown); *Susan Brown* (Farmhand Trio); *Toot Toot Tootsie* (Linda Sue Risk)

TRUTH OR DARE   (1991)

DIR: Alex Keshishian; PROD: Jay Roewe, Time Clawson; STUDIO: Miramax; 118 min., color (Live)

MUSIC ★★★★★
ATTITUDE ★★★★
FUN ★★★

Madonna's tempest in a D-cup.
Not content to wait for time itself to resolve her place in history's annals, the ever-plucky Mizz Ciccone went out and created her own documentary, originally enti-tled *In Bed with Madonna*. That she paid for this shindig sorta undermines its objectivity, but that's also sorta beside the point. This is pure exhibitionism by the

woman who put the *B* back in *Blatant*. How much you dig this of course depends on how much Madonna you can stomach. But the concert sequences alone are quite something.

Sure, she can't sing, but who cares? Watch as Madonna finks out her drug-addict brother. Gasp as Madonna emotionally coldcocks a childhood gal pal. Thrill as Madonna and then-beau Warren Beatty attend premieres. Smirk as Madonna gets dissed by Antonio Banderas, proving that even she can't get laid on demand. Featuring the now legendary Evian bottle head scene and the equally boss gag-me-with-a-spoon Kevin Costner intro, *Truth or Dare* is megalomania with a capital *Me*, just like the lady in charge. At the end, one is left with an overwhelming feeling of sorrow for the poor little rich girl. She may have a body to die for, as well as a cadre of gay boys who worship her, but judging by this flick, Madonna Ciccone ain't such a happy camper. (ALi)

CAMEOS   Warren Beatty, Sandra Bernhard

SONGS   *Express Yourself, Oh Father, Like a Virgin, Like a Prayer, Holiday, Live to Tell, Vogue, Commotion, Keep It Together* (Madonna)

THE TWIST   (1993)

DIR: Ron Mann; PROD: Ron Mann; STUDIO: Alliance; 77 min., color

MUSIC ★★★
ATTITUDE ★★★
FUN ★★★★

Twisted values.

Made up almost entirely of archival footage, this history of the greatest rock'n'roll dance craze has been pieced together with obvious affection. The film, which is divided into seven "lessons," gives proper credit to Hank Ballard, who wrote the song, but tries too hard to portray him as a victim. It may be true that Ballard was used by the Philadelphia music machine that manufactured Chubby Checker, but half-a-lifetime's worth of royalty checks must count for something. Joey Dee, whose "Peppermint Twist" helped ignite the fad, is also featured, along with "American Bandstand," whose influence then was unquestionable, like MTV's today. Interviews with former Bandstand dancers reveal there really was a "council" like the one parodied in *Hairspray*. Clips of "square" dance lessons from the early '50s intercut with dances from the '60s help makes this film a fun, informative look at a fleeting, and ultimately trivial, moment in rock history. (AF)

TWIST AROUND THE CLOCK   (1961)

CAST: John Cronin, Maura McGiveny, Alvy Moore, Tom Middleton, Mary Mitchell, Tol Avery, Lenny Kent, Jeff Parker, John Bryant; DIR: Oscar Rudolph; PROD: Sam Katzman; SCREENPLAY: James B. Gordon; STUDIO: Columbia; 86 min., b/w (no video release)

MUSIC ★★★★
ATTITUDE ★★
FUN ★★★

Rock'n'roll is dead, so the Twist is IT.

After Chuck hit jail, Jerry Lee was slandered, Little Richard got religion, Elvis got drafted, and Buddy crashed, the reactionary power of mainstream culture was able to bring its ersatz adaptation of the big beat to the masses. Like all the "latest fads," it worked, yet brewing underneath the tame surface of the Twist lurked the still-wild spirit of rock'n'roll. Case in point: The ostensible star of *Twist Around the Clock* is Chubby Checker, who announces the arrival of this breaking new craze. But the real star is Clay Cole, who doesn't even sing. All he does is grunt, act obnoxious, and get everybody worked up. The Marcels are also wonderfully stupid singing "Merry Twistmas" (in a scene that really makes you think

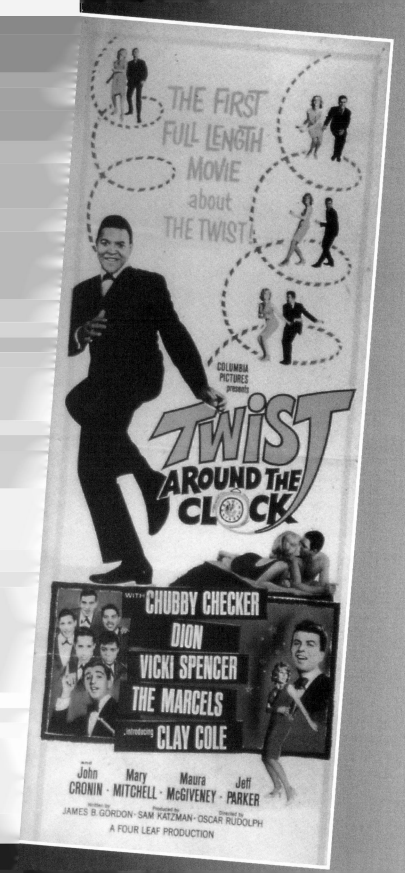

rock'n'roll was dead). Yet it's Dion's segments that outlives them all. His three tunes represent the New York hood artist's best work on celluloid. It's Sam Katzman's genius at work again, making something out of nothing for the moment's sake, that really gives this film life (despite the cloak of decency). Katzman proves once again that his eye for hot rockin' new talent never failed him, despite the faddish goop that most of his pictures represented. Soon enough, the Twist broke loose into a frantic go-go frenzy in no time flat, and the peak of the 1960s was still to come. (DP)

SCENES Talent agent Mitch Mason to canceled act Joe Cook and his Kooks: "Rock'n'roll has had it, daddy-o. There aren't enough rock'n'rollers left in this country to keep you in tight pants and suede shoes. So either change the style of the band or go back to being a busboy."

SONGS *Twist Around the Clock, The Twist Is Here to Stay, Don't Twist with Anyone Else but Me, Here There and Everywhere* (Clay Cole); *The Wanderer, The Majestic, Runaround Sue* (Dion); *Twistin' U.S.A., Your Lips and Mine, Twist Along* (Chubby Checker); *Too Many Boyfriends, He's So Sweet* (Vickie Spencer); *Merry Twistmas* (Marcels)

200 MOTELS   (1971)

MUSIC ★★★★
ATTITUDE ★★★★★
FUN ★★★★

CAST: Ringo Starr, Theodore Bikel, Frank Zappa, Mark Volman, Howard Kaylan, Ian Underwood, Aynsley Dunbar, George Duke; **DIR:** Frank Zappa; **PROD:** Jerry Good, Herb Cohn; **SCREENPLAY:** Frank Zappa; **STUDIO:** United Artists; 100 min., color (MGM/UA)

Frank Zappa's artistic wizardry.
How much brilliance and cheesiness can fit on the head of a pin? Answer: all of the above! Frank Zappa's organizational genius and vigorous exploration of expressive possibilities make this film an early tour de force. There's even a story-line here, albeit a simple vehicle for knitting together the dizzying array of performers and situations. The film opens with the road-weary Mothers of Invention arriving in allegorical Centerville, U.S.A., where they proceed to take in the local color.

Zappa, who composed the score for *200 Motels* while touring with the Mothers, shot video footage first and later had it transferred onto film stock. Zappa then edited the footage himself in a tiny editing room in a matter of weeks. As a result, the finished product has the feel and texture of a '70s sitcom from a parallel universe. Casting Ringo Starr as himself, Zappa appears only briefly. Instead, Mark Volman and Howard Kaylan (otherwise known as Flo and Eddie) are the most visible characters.

But this movie isn't about character. The kaleidoscopic layering of television camp, orchestral music, and rock'n'roll idioms, as well as the sheer beauty of early video effects (that predate MTV by 10 years and still look good), make *200 Motels* a pioneering effort, though exhausting to watch at times. The movie's commercial failure can perhaps be attributed to the fact that most Americans have never appreciated this film's absurd beauty. (TR)

SCENES Who drummer Keith Moon literally stumbling across members of the Royal Philharmonic Orchestra while wearing a nun's habit

LINES Keyboardist George Duke: "I bought a copy of *Downbeat* so I could carry it around and look like I know what's happening."

CAMEOS Keith Moon

UNDER THE CHERRY MOON (1986)

CAST: Prince, Jerome Benton, Kristin Scott-Thomas, Steven Berkoff; DIR: Prince; PROD: Robert Cavallo, Joseph Ruffalo, Steven Fargnoli; SCREENPLAY: Becky Johnson; STUDIO: Warner; 98 min., b/w (Warner)

MUSIC ★★★★
ATTITUDE ★★★
FUN ★★★

Who's moonin' who?

Prince stars as Christopher Tracy, a cabaret pianist and singer on the French Riviera. He wears several thousand dollars' worth of designer threads and jewelry while tooling around in a cherry `64 Buick convertible. Still, he can't afford to pay the rent on the flat he shares with soul brother and general factotum Jerome Benton. The two men spend considerable screen time comparing wardrobes, lounging around bare-chested, and mocking each other (and the supporting cast of honky aristocrats) in high-pitched "Miss Thing" voices. Sure, Prince romances wealthy Euro-babe Mary Sharon (Kristin Scott-Thomas) despite the opposition of her mean old dad (Steven Berkoff). But there's virtually no chemistry between these lovers compared to the warmth, wit, and affection shared by Prince and Benton. When Prince stands up Jerome for a tryst with Mary, the two men have what can only be described as a lovers' quarrel and abruptly break off what Benton calls their "partnership." *Under the Cherry Moon* climaxes with Prince's death, but it's Jerome who weeps and wails while Mary just stares (un)soulfully. The music of Prince and the Revolution is first rate (available on their Warners album *Parade*), but it's nearly all in the background. Prince performs "Girls and Boys" and "Mountains" in two rock-video sequences, and in a surprisingly moving scene sings along while his car radio plays "Kiss." (AS)

When a (white) suitor sings a tuneless "Happy Birthday" to Mary, Prince sneers: "Billy Eckstine he ain't, baby!" Later, Jerome Benton avers: "I'm my own man— just like Liberace!"   *LINES*

Girls and Boys, Mountains, Kiss (Prince)   *SONGS*

THE UNHEARD MUSIC (1986)

DIR: W.T. Morgan; PROD: Christopher Blakely, Everette Greaton; SCREENPLAY: W.T. Morgan; STUDIO: Skouras; 86 min., color (CBS/Fox)

MUSIC ★★★★★
ATTITUDE ★★★★★
FUN ★★★★

A great band at its peak.

The pioneering L.A. band X began its long journey to the top of the underground in 1978. Along the way, the group recorded four excellent albums, carrying with them the hopes and dreams of fans and critics for the salvation of American rock'n'roll. That's a heavy load for any one band to carry, and their fifth LP— *Ain't Love Grand*, a failed attempt at mainstream airplay—left many believers feeling betrayed. However, independent filmmaker W.T. Morgan put X's story on film while the group was still at their peak, and *The Unheard Music* is the best cinematic explanation of a rock band since *A Hard Day's Night*.

Morgan's film moves and dazzles with the frenzied pulse of its subject. The excitement of the nascent L.A. punk scene is vividly conveyed through quick editing and still-photo montages, while X themselves are seen hard at work and play in home baby movies and their own 8mm footage. Early interviews present a band on the rise as record execs, both hip and square, philosophize on why they signed/passed on X. Later, the group communes with fans at a record store. Individual bits with the four members reveal serious musicians and whimsical artists. Billy Zoom's smirk notwithstanding, X never claimed to be the world's greatest rock band. John Doe and Exene Cervenka, modern Venice beatniks whose frustrations and rocky marriage inspired some of X's best songs, just wanted some truth and in return offered all they had. There's a lot of that truth in *The Unheard Music.* (JS)

SCENES The amazing video for "Because I Do" brilliantly re-creates a German Expressionist silent movie. Exene's unorthodox beauty—she's a punk Gloria Swanson— fits the style perfectly.

CAMEOS Ray Manzarek, Jello Biafra, Rodney Bingenheimer

SONGS *The Unheard Music, Los Angeles, Year One, Riding, Because I Do, Beyond and Back, Soul Kitchen, Real Child of Hell, The World's a Mess, It's in My Kiss* (X)

UNION CITY (1981)

MUSIC ★
ATTITUDE ★★★★
FUN ★★★

CAST: Dennis Lipscomb, Deborah Harry, Irina Maleeva, Everett McGill, Pat Benatar; DIR: Mark Reichert; PROD: Graham Belin; SCREENPLAY: Mark Reichert; STUDIO: Tuxedo; 84 min., color (RCA/Columbia)

Murder and spilt milk in New Jersey.
Despite the presence of Blondie's Deborah Harry in a big supporting role and rocker Pat Benatar in a smaller one, not a song is to be heard in this oddball melodrama set in repressed, pre-rock 1953. *Union City* tells the story of how accountant Dennis Lipscomb's obsession with a milk thief leads to murder, insanity, and suicide. This would-be cult movie, which never found its following, also features Everett McGill, who eventually became a regular on "Twin Peaks." In fact, much of *Union City* looks like an apartment-bound prequel to the deadpan dementia of David Lynch's TV show. Debbie Harry is pretty bad as a drab, miserable hausfrau (she proved far more at home as the zonked thrill junkie in *Videodrome*), but Benatar is fun in her quick bit as a newlywed (grinning like a dirty-minded chipmunk). The score, by Blondie's Chris Stein, is an atrocious stew of blowsy film noir cues, but Lipscomb's clammy, disintegrating CPA almost holds the movie together. He's such a mass of rage and guilty fixations that he sucks you right underneath his crawling skin, and strands you there. (HH)

U2: RATTLE AND HUM (1988)

MUSIC ★★★★★
ATTITUDE ★★★
FUN ★★★★

DIR: Phil Joanou; PROD: Paul McGuinness, Michael Hamlyn; STUDIO: Paramount; 99 min., color (Paramount)

Hum-baby.
Part concert footage and part see-the-band-look-thoughtful stuff, *U2: Rattle and Hum* attempts to accomplish two things at once, but only one works. What works is the way American director Phil Joanou is able to capture a distinctly European fascination with Americana. That fascination—part awe, part contempt—is utterly engaged here as the band sings with a Harlem gospel choir, visits Graceland, records at Sun Studios, watches the Mississippi roll by at twilight, and defaces the Embarcadero in San Francisco. The only scenes really missing are trips to the Grand Canyon and Mount Rushmore. To an outsider, America is brash, adolescent, and dangerous, and that's the way we see the country here. What *Rattle and*

Hum fails to do is establish the band members as individual personalities, or even personalities at all. That said, the movie is a quite enjoyable, slightly nostalgic look back at a band that has moved on since 1988. (KW)

U2 performing "Still Haven't Found What I'm Looking For" in Harlem with the Voices of Freedom (0:16)   **SCENES**

An interviewer: "So what is the film about?" Bassist Adam Clayton: "We just wanted to capture the band ... aw, fuck, I don't know."   **LINES**

Helter Skelter, Van Diemen's Land, Desire, Exit, Still Haven't Found What I'm Looking For, Silver and Gold, Angel of Harlem, All Along the Watchtower, In God's Country, When Love Comes to Town, Heartland, Bad, Where the Streets Have No Name, Milk, With or Without You, Bullet the Blue Sky, Running to Stand Still, Sunday Bloody Sunday, Pride, All I Want Is You (U2)   **SONGS**

VALLEY GIRL (1983)

CAST: Deborah Foreman, Nicholas Cage, Elizabeth Daily, Michael Bowen; **DIR:** Martha Coolidge; **PROD:** Wayne Crawford, Andrew Lane; **STUDIO:** Atlantic; 107 min., color (Vestron)

MUSIC	★★★★
ATTITUDE	★★★★
FUN	★★★★

An improbable love flourishes in the San Fernando Valley.
Released a year after Moon Unit Zappa made the charts with her novelty record "Valley Girl," this movie sums up the national nanosecond that was California mall-surf culture. The story is standard: Boy gets Valley girl, boy loses Valley girl, boy gets Valley girl back again. As the aforementioned Val-gal, perky Julie (Elizabeth Daily) falls for a Hollywood New Waver named Randy (Nicolas Cage). In doing so, she disturbs the balance of her entire high school. But more interestingly, this movie is a time capsule of Val-speak, skinny leather ties, Devo posters, and the music of Bananarama, the Jam, Men at Work, the Psychedelic Furs, and Modern English. For anyone who was a teen in the mid-'80s, *Valley Girl* offers a nostalgic look back, whether you thought that Valley thing was bitchin' or it gagged you with a spoon. (SBW)

A spaced-out Valley mom preparing mountains of sushi for her daughter's party (0:10)   **SCENES**

A Valley girl ruminating on life: "It's like a total bummer when you're young and don't know why you're here."   **LINES**

A Million Miles Away, Everywhere at Once, Oldest Story in the World (Plimsouls); *He Could Be the One, School Is In, Johnny Are You Queer* (Josie Cotton)   **SONGS**

VELVET REDUX (1993)

DIR: Declan Lowney; **PROD:** David Heffernan; **STUDIO:** Warner; 90 min., color (Warner)

MUSIC	★★★★
ATTITUDE	★★★★
FUN	★★★

They're not underground anymore.
It's difficult to imagine that the members of the Velvet Underground—on one of those long. strung-out mid-'60s nights after a weird, violent gig at the Cafe Bizarre—ever thought about a 1993 reunion, or even about living that long. Surprise! *Velvet Redux* documents the Paris segment of their 25th-reunion tour, proving that rock stars are destined neither to die young nor to disappear.

However, Lou Reed, John Cale, Maureen Tucker, and Sterling Morrison succeed here mostly by eschewing their former selves.

Shot in a blue light so cool that you expect to see the band's breath, the Velvets accelerate through 14 of their most popular songs and encore with a new one for good luck. Reed plows over the old melodies with some angry poetic to-ing and fro-ing, while Cale camps it up as a composer of Serious Music. That Reed and Cale dominate should come as no surprise, because their careers were the ones that took off after the Velvets' breakup in 1972. Once in a while, Morrison shows off some fancy finger work and even cracks a smile, but Tucker generally looks as though she'd be more comfortable baking bread than pounding drums. The concert peaks with "Hey Mr. Rain," a fifteen-minute tour-de-force jam between Cale and Reed. Ironically, this used to be one of the band's most misunderstood pieces. Even more ironic are the dewy, scrubbed faces of the young Parisians, who innocently mouth the nasty lyrics to "Heroin" and "Venus in Furs." How far we all have come. (SBW)

S O N G S   *Venus in Furs, White Light/White Heat, Beginning to See the Light, Some Kind of Love, Femme Fatale, Hey Mr. Rain, I'm Sticking with You, I Heard Her Call My Name, I'll Be Your Mirror, Rock'n'Roll, Sweet Jane, I'm Waiting for the Man, Heroin, Pale Blue Eyes, Coyote* (Velvet Underground)

VILLAGE OF THE GIANTS   (1965)

MUSIC ★★★★
ATTITUDE ★★★★★
FUN ★★★★★

CAST: Tommy Kirk, Johnny Crawford, Ron Howard, Beau Bridges, Chris Noel, Joy Harmon, Bob Random, Gail Gilmore, Tisha Sterling, Tim Rooney, Kevin O'Neal, Charla Doherty, Toni Basil; DIR: Bert I. Gordon; PROD: Bert I. Gordon; SCREENPLAY: Allen Caillou; STUDIO: Embassy; 90 min., color (no video release)

Gargantuan teens invade the Whisky a Go-Go.
Jack Nitzsche's music shakes up this monster-teen sci-fi masterpiece based on H.G. Wells's *The Food of the Gods*. So does Toni Basil's go-go-cage frenzy, whipped up to the beat of the Beau Brummels. Famous for "Laugh Laugh" and "Just a Little," San Francisco's premier band performs "When It Comes to Your Love" and "Woman" here. In addition, you get Freddie Cannon at a backyard party, fresh from singing the theme to *Where the Action Is*, and Mike Clifford sings "Maryann" over a lush Nitzsche track. Chris Noel returns from her escapades in a bunch of beach movies, and Tommy Kirk stars, extending the "science fair" side of his personality that he exhibited in *The Monkey's Uncle* and *Pajama Party*. Johnny Crawford is also pretty funny in a supporting role.

Ron Howard gets his best role ever as a crazy laboratory kid in a basement who invents some goo that makes living things grow king-sized. The "good" teenagers view the discovery as a boon to science until a visiting group of "bad" kids (led by Beau Bridges) steal the goo and grow king-sized in order to terrorize all authority. *Village of the Giants* features lots of classic dialogue, and the entire movie reads like a textbook on '60s punk humanity. Jack Nitzsche's theme song thunders throughout the proceedings, typifying what is—beyond any doubt—the most dramatic soundtrack I've encountered in a rock'n'roll film. Originally pressed a year earlier as a 45 called "The Last Race," this song is the cinematic equivalent of a sonic boom. (DP)

S O N G S   *Village of the Giants Theme [The Last Race], Make-Out Theme* (Jack Nitzsche); *When It Comes to Your Love, Woman* (Beau Brummels); *Little Bitty Corrina* (Freddie Cannon); *Maryann* (Mike Clifford)

VIVA LAS VEGAS   (1963)

CAST: Elvis Presley, Ann-Margret, Cesare Danova, William Demarest, Nicky Blair; DIR: George Sidney; SCREENPLAY: Sally Benson; STUDIO: MGM; 85 min., color (MGM/UA)

MUSIC   ★★★
ATTITUDE ★★★★
FUN   ★★★★★

An American wet dream: Elvis and Ann-Margret do Vegas.

The apotheosis of Elvis-cinema, *Viva Las Vegas* raises mindlessness to an art form. Presley plays Lucky Jackson, an impoverished racing car driver who's forced to compete with Count Mancini (Cesare Danova), a blueblooded speedster, for the hand of hardworking Rusty (Ann-Margret). The setting is the City of Spectacle, a fitting backdrop for this mating dance between two Easter Island-sized sexual icons. In a charming and weirdly poetic way, Elvis and Ann-Margret seem suspended beyond time, as though they were merely a floating tableau of carnal longing. Elvis's performance of "What'd I Say" in a crowded nightclub is both a reverie and an orgy, and Ann-Margret contributes her own synthesis of the conventional and the irrational with her performance of "Appreciation" (the missing link between Marilyn and Madonna). The closing race sequence is as thrilling as it is surreal. Here as nowhere else, Elvis and Ann-Margret present a sunny map of the American psyche: innocence, lust, flawless beauty, easy money, flesh. (For the deviant attractions on that map, see Ann-Margret's *Kitten with a Whip*, made that same year, in which she plays nihilist jailbait who brings a middle-aged politician to his knees.) (HH)

The Yellow Rose of Texas/The Eyes of Texas, C'mon Everybody, You'll Always Be, What'd I Say, **SONGS**
Santa Lucia/If You Think I Don't Need You, Viva Las Vegas, I Need Somebody to Lean On (Elvis Presley); *The Lady Loves Me* (Elvis Presley, Ann-Margret); *Appreciation, My Rival* (Ann-Margret)

Viva Las Vegas

WAYNE'S WORLD (1992)

MUSIC ★★★
ATTITUDE ★★★★★
FUN ★★★★★

CAST: Mike Meyers, Dana Carvey, Tia Carrere, Rob Lowe, Donna Dixon, Alice Cooper, Ed O'Neil, Lara Flynn Boyle, Brian Doyle-Murray; DIR: Penelope Spheeris; PROD: Lorne Michaels; SCREEN-PLAY: Mike Meyers, Bonnie Turner, Terry Turner; STUDIO: Paramount; 95 min., color (Paramount)

Bill and Ted to the nth degree.
Stupidity deserves its place in the sun, and to the rescue come Mike Meyers and Dana Carvey with the film version of their "Saturday Night Live" skit. Directed by teen angst B-movie diva Penelope Spheeris (*Dudes, Suburbia*), *Wayne's World* brought the lexicon of suburban homeboys to the free world ("Party on!"), and became one of the year's biggest grossing cinematic experiences in the time-honored tradition of going light on the plot and heavy on the gags.

Wayne and Garth's cable TV show oeuvre is fleshed out for this wonderfully disposable comedy, which celebrates white male teenage heavy metal boneheaded obsessiveness and elevates it to high art. Featuring a suitably oily Rob Lowe as the dastardly playboy who wants to exploit our heroes (and naturally get the girl) and wickedly mental Ed O'Neil ("Married with Children") as a diner owner who forgot to take his medication, the plot revolves around Wayne and Garth's pursuit of their dream (the cable show) and their dream girls. Tia Carrere is Cassandra, an Asian Lita Ford who rocks Wayne's world, while Donna Dixon cameos as Garth's unattainable dream babe. Spoofing rock'n'roll, "Laverne and Shirley," '70s trash culture (check out the "Dream Weaver" montage) and suburbia in general, *Wayne's World* is a one-trick pony with frisky legs. In the film's best-known scene, the now-infamous "Bohemian Rhapsody" singalong, *Wayne's World* captures the delightful inanity of teen male bonding with precision and glee. (ALi)

SONGS   *Fire, Touch Me, Why You Wanna Break My Heart, Ballroom Blitz* (Tia Carrere)

WEEKEND REBELLION (1970)

MUSIC ★★★★
ATTITUDE ★★★★
FUN ★★★★

ALTERNATE TITLE: *Mondo Daytona*
DIR: Frank Willard, Barry Mahon; PROD: Bill Packham, Gordon Craddock; SCREENPLAY: Joe Packham; STUDIO: Cinetron; 80 min., color (no video release)

Beach music, beer, and...Grand Funk?
When it was first released as *Mondo Daytona* in 1967, this film featured documentary-style footage of clean-cut teens romping in the sun and lip-synched performances by the Tams and the Swingin' Medallions, plus a few songs and some narration by Billy Joe Royal. Then, in 1970, the producers took this Daytona Beach travelogue ("Where the sun is hot, but the action is hotter") and spliced in two painfully long promo clips of Grand Funk Railroad. They also added a bunch of cheap-looking psychedelic segues that are about as out of place as you can get. Not that the original film was such a great piece of art, but who wouldn't prefer the wacky Swingin' Medallions swimming fully clothed in a motel pool compared to Grand Funk's Mark Farner playing shirtless while he swings his hair all over the place. (Hmmm, sounds like MTV.) The good news is that, thankfully, nothing was cut to make room for him. (BV)

SCENES   The Swingin' Medallions trying to keep up with their lip-synching when somebody accidentally accelerates the speed of the record player

From Billy Joe Royal's narration: "It's a new day. A new beat. After a good, cold *LINES* bottle of breakfast, here we go again!"

On Time, Paranoid (Grand Funk Railroad); *She Drives Me Outa My Mind, Double Shot of My* *SONGS* *Baby's Love, Hush, These Are Not My People* (Swingin' Medallions); *Down in the Boondocks* (Billy Joe Royal); *What Kind of Fool* (Tams); *Backfield in Motion* (Joe South)

WHAT A CRAZY WORLD   (1963)

CAST: Joe Brown and the Bruvvers, Susan Maughan, Marty Wilde, Harry H. Corbett, Freddie and the Dreamers; DIR: Michael Carreras; PROD: Michael Carreras; SCREENPLAY: Alan Klein, Michael Carreras; STUDIO: Warner; 88 min., b/w (no video release)

MUSIC ★★★★
ATTITUDE ★★★★★
FUN ★★★★

But Joe Brown makes it bearable.
Paul McCartney and George Harrison were both fans of Joe Brown, one of the top guitar players of the pre-Beatles era. *What a Crazy World* was Brown's best film vehicle. It's an unpretentious drama about a young Cockney lad from a working-class background who tries to make it as a musician. The plot is somewhat predictable, but the feel, language, and manner of the film give it a bracing effect, somewhat reminiscent of Val Guest's earthy Cliff Richard vehicle *Expresso Bongo*. The songs are slightly less than first-rate, but overall the film is a must-see for its honesty. It was one of the very last vehicles of its kind. The success of *A Hard Day's Night* a year later put big dollar signs in the eyes of would-be producers of this sort of movie, and seriousness went out the window. Brown, however, later enjoyed a great deal of success on the British stage. (BE)

What a Crazy World We're Living In, Layabout's Lament, I Sure Know a Lot about Love, Bruvvers, *SONGS* *Just You Wait and See* (Joe Brown and the Bruvvers)

WHAT'S LOVE GOT TO DO WITH IT   (1993)

CAST: Angela Bassett, Lawrence Fishburne, Venessa Bell Calloway, Jenifer Lewis, Rob LaBelle; DIR: Brian Gibson; PROD: Doug Chapin, Barry Krost; SCREENPLAY: Kate Lanier; STUDIO: Touchstone; 80 min., color (Buena Vista)

MUSIC ★★★★★
ATTITUDE ★★★
FUN ★★★★★

Rockin' blood-and-guts version of the Tina Turner story.
Like most rock stars' biopics (*La Bamba, The Buddy Holly Story*), this one falls a little flat as a film. We already know the story, which begins when Ike Turner (Lawrence Fishburne) discovers Annie Mae Bullock (Angela Bassett) at a St. Louis nightclub. The plot then follows their personal and professional ups and downs until Tina finally leaves Ike after 20 years to become an even bigger star on her own. What makes this film a real treat are the knockout performances by Bassett and Fishburne.

Some of their scenes are painfully violent, particularly one in which Ike simultaneously chokes and rapes Tina and another in which he beats her after she unwisely tells him that all his songs "sound the same." Fishburne is simply amazing as Ike. He's hip, stylish, and appealing for the first half of the film. Then, once drugs get a grip, he unravels. Playing opposite Fishburne, Bassett *is* Tina: sexy, vulnerable, girlish, and ultimately strong as a steel bar. Helpfully, director Brian Gibson succeeds at evoking the style and feel of the various time periods in which the action takes place. A hint: Watch the hair. You can see Ike's greasy pomp transform first into Beatle bangs and then into an Afro. (MG)

SCENES A loving re-creation of the historic recording session in which Phil Spector produced "River Deep Mountain High"; Tina and a former Ikette mimicking Ike ("Fine your ass!")

LINES A coked-out Ike admonishes a hanger-on: "It' ain't cool 'til I say it's cool."

SONGS *A Fool in Love, Rock Me Baby, It's Gonna Work Out Fine, Proud Mary, Shake a Tail Feather, Nutbush City Limits, Disco Inferno, I Might Have Been Queen, Why Must We Wait Until Tonight, I Don't Wanna Fight, What's Love Got to Do with It* (Tina Turner); *Rocket 88* (Larry Fishburne); *You Know I Love You* (Tina Turner, Larry Fishburne); *River Deep Mountain High* (Ike and Tina Turner)

WHEN THE BOYS MEET THE GIRLS   (1965)

MUSIC ★★★★
ATTITUDE ★★★
FUN ★★

CAST: Connie Francis, Harve Presnell, Sue Ann Langdon, Fred Clark, Joby Baker, Frank Faylon, Davis and Reese; DIR: Alvin Ganzer; PROD: Sam Katzman; SCREENPLAY: Robert E. Kent; STUDIO: MGM; 97 min., color (no video release)

Gershwin's Girl Crazy *with a British invasion flavor.*
Connie Francis and Harve Presnell star as romantic leads in this *Girl Crazy* remake, which still includes a number of the original Gershwin tunes. Producer Sam Katzman tried to spice things up with some gratuitous pop performances by Sam the Sham, Louis Armstrong, Liberace, and Herman's Hermits, but the net result is a film that doesn't really make it. Following a contemporary trend, Katzman cast a number of actors from popular TV sitcoms, but their jokes—routine mid-'60s schtick—sound like they were copped from the set of an Elvis movie. That said, this picture does include about 15 minutes' worth of choice bits, reaching its climax with an extensively choreographed production number of Gershwin's "I Got Rhythm." (KHB)

SCENES The opening scene, in which Sam the Sham performs at the film's fictional college while two jocks go-go dance in drag dressed as showgirls

CAMEOS Peter Noone

SONGS *When the Boys Meet the Girls, But Not for Me* (Connie Francis); *Monkey See Monkey Do* (Sam the Sham and the Pharaohs); *Embraceable You* (Harve Presnell); *Throw It Out of Your Mind* (Louis Armstrong); *Listen People, Bidin' My Time* (Herman's Hermits); *I Got Rhythm* (Connie Francis, Harve Presnell); *Aruba Liberace* (Liberace); *Treat Me Rough* (Sue Ann Langdon)

WHITE STAR   (1981)

MUSIC ★
ATTITUDE ★★
FUN ★★★

ALTERNATE TITLE: *Let It Rock*
CAST: Dennis Hopper, Terrance Robay, Ramona Sweeney, David Hess; DIR: Roland Klick; PROD: Roland Klick; SCREENPLAY: Roland Klick; 75 min., color (Media)

Reich'n'roll with Dennis Hopper.
After *Apocalypse Now* and *Out of the Blue*, and well before his return to prominence with *Blue Velvet*, Dennis Hopper gave yet another crazed, high-energy performance in this German-made (but English-language) obscurity. Hopper plays Kenneth Barlow, the super-hustling manager of New Wave musician Moody Moodinsky (Terrance Robay). Barlow hypes Moody's minimalist techno rock as "the Future," renaming him "White Star." Barlow then arranges for a bunch of

METRO-GOLDWYN-MAYER
presents

The Boys... The Girls...
and THAT WILD, WAY-OUT, WICKED, WONDERFUL BEAT!

HERMAN'S HERMITS
"Listen People" "Bidin' My Time"

SAM the SHAM and the PHARAOHS
"Monkey See"

Harve Presnell
That "Molly Brown" Boy

Connie Francis
When The Boys Meet The Girls
"Mail Call"

Liberace
"Andre Liberace"

Louis Armstrong
"Throw It Out Of Your Mind"

It makes the old young and the young scream when these song-belting stars and frug-frantic dolls get together in one great big wig-flipping bowl of a jamboree!

WHEN the BOYS meet the GIRLS

CONNIE FRANCIS
HARVE PRESNELL
SAM the SHAM and the PHARAOHS
LIBERACE
LOUIS ARMSTRONG

co-starring SUE ANE LANGDON · FRED CLARK · FRANK FAYLEN · JOBY BAKER

and featuring HERMAN'S HERMITS

SCREEN PLAY BY ROBERT E. KENT · DIRECTED BY ALVIN GANZER · PRODUCED BY SAM KATZMAN

A FOUR LEAF PRODUCTION IN PANAVISION AND METROCOLOR

Original Sound Track Album On MGM Records

punk thugs to start a riot at a White Star concert that destroys four city blocks but generates massive publicity. Barlow's unscrupulous methods carry him and his reluctant client close to the top, but the desperate scheme eventually backfires.

The plot here is as thin as White Star's sparse synth music (which, interestingly, is barely heard), and the music world trappings seem inauthentic. Even though "the Future" (as a New Wave marketing theme) was already pretty tired by 1981, Barlow screams the phrase over and over as sort of a punk rock mantra. Still, *White Star* is worth watching if only for Hopper's wired performance. He's viscerally entertaining as always yet more believable than in some of his more famous roles. The foreign atmosphere is often striking in this very violent movie, which presents the German punk scene as an extremely scary place. The video release (retitled *Let It Rock*) adds a clip from *Suburbia* of TSOL performing "Wash Away" that's dropped into the middle of a nightclub scene. (It's funny how all stages look alike.) (JS)

LINES   Barlow, thinking out loud: "Marketing, promotion—it's dirty, it's dishonest. It takes a genius to make it work. It's a bitch. But when it works, it's a beautiful bitch."

THE WILD ANGELS   (1966)

MUSIC ★★
ATTITUDE ★★
FUN ★★★

CAST: Peter Fonda, Nancy Sinatra, Bruce Dern, Diane Ladd; DIR: Roger Corman; PROD: James H. Nicholson, Samuel Z. Arkoff, Roger Corman; SCREENPLAY: Charles B. Griffith; STUDIO: American International; 84 min., color (Embassy)

Roger Corman introduces America to the Hell's Angels.
In 1966, this film could have been a bold statement. Hippies hadn't yet had time to grow their hair very long, Nixon was still retired, and (as we hear from a brief radio blurb) the war in Vietnam was still escalating. America was ready to be shocked, but director Roger Corman, despite the obvious presence of the zeitgeist, fails to deliver a good story here or even any real feeling. *The Wild Angels* is more a mood piece, reveling in its depiction of bikers doing biker things. Set in Southern California and accompanied by good Mexican-tinged surf R&B, Corman's film has lots of long, lingering shots of choppers riding through the desert and authentic Angels being tough, as well as one quick but particularly strong piece of editing in which Blues (Peter Fonda) starts his bike. Unfortunately, *The Wild Angels* tries a little too hard to prove that it really is an inside look at the real Hell's Angels.

Fonda plays president of a Hell's Angels chapter, while Bruce Dern (as Loser) is his best pal. When they botch their attempt to retrieve a stolen bike, Loser ends up in the hospital. The Angels bust him out, he dies, and they bury him. Nancy Sinatra co-stars as the forlorn puppy who annoyingly snips at the heels of big dog Blues. Imitating real life, Diane Ladd plays Loser's wife, looking exactly like their daughter, Laura Dern. The plot is basically a buildup to the last half-hour in which Loser's funeral becomes another wild party. (RG)

SCENES   A canyon party that features scantily clad femmes splashing around a pool, bikers chasing a rabbit, and lots of fighting (0:21); Loser's fatal toke (0:44); the funeral party (1:01)

LINES   A cop to an Angel: "Where do you think you're going?" The Angel, poorly aping Brando in *The Wild One*: "Anywhere but here, man." Blues to Mike (Sinatra): "You think I should go up there?" Mike, very believably: "I don't think." Blues telling an enquiring preacher what the Angels want: "We want to be free—to ride our machines without being hassled by the Man. And we want to get loaded."

WILD GUITAR (1962)

CAST: Arch Hall Jr., Nancy Czar, William Watters, Cash Flagg; DIR: Ray Dennis Steckler; PROD: Nicholas Merriwether; SCREENPLAY: Nicholas Merriwether, Bob Wheling; STUDIO: Fairway International; 92 min., b/w (Rhino)

MUSIC ★★★★★
ATTITUDE ★★★★★
FUN ★★★★

Record racket exposed!!!
Bud Eagle (Arch Hall, Jr.) of Spearfish, South Dakota, heads for Hollywood with his heart set on fame as a rock'n'roll star. At his first stop in town (the Coffee Cup Cafe), he meets the love of his life, Vicki (former Olympic ice skater Nancy Czar), who's a go-go dancer on the Hal Kenton TV Show. She gets Bud a spot on the show that very same day, and he's immediately discovered by Mike McCauley, a successful and powerful impresario (played by "William Watters," who's actually Arch Hall, Sr.). Contracts are signed that night, after which Bud finds out that McCauley plans to control him mind, body, and soul on a 24-hour-a-day basis. Tensions soon develop.

Art imitates life in *Wild Guitar.* According to an article in that superb journal of American culture, *KICKS* magazine, Arch Hall, Jr.'s movie career was master-minded by his dad. *Wild Guitar* is one of six films produced by Arch, Sr.'s company, Fairway International, that star the young blond bombshell. The script for *Wild Guitar* (co-written by Arch, Sr., using another pseudonym, "Nicholas Merriwether") has many bizarre twists and turns that defy rational judgment. But rational judgments aside, I love this movie. I think it's better than *Gone with the Wind.* A footnote: Speaking of pseudonyms, "Cash Flagg" is actually Ray Dennis Steckler. (MC)

SCENES

McCauley demands that Bud stop seeing Vicki, but the lovers eventually reunite and head straight for an ice-skating rink. For about five minutes, we see them skating together in a long shot, accompanied by delicate music. This scene is very artfully done, thanks to Ray Dennis Steckler (who made his directorial debut in this film) and future Oscar-winning cinematographer William Szigmond.

SONGS

Yes I Will, I'm Growing Taller Every Day, Vicki, Twist Fever (Arch Hall, Jr.)

WILD IN THE COUNTRY (1961)

CAST: Elvis Presley, Hope Lange, Tuesday Weld, Millie Perkins, Rafer Johnson, John Ireland; DIR: Philip Dunne; PROD: Jerry Wald; SCREENPLAY: Clifford Odets; STUDIO: 20th Century-Fox; 114 min., color (Key)

MUSIC ★
ATTITUDE ★★★
FUN ★★

Elvis does the Oedipus thing.
Even though this was already his seventh film, Elvis still had a lot to learn about acting. He seems to have memorized his part one line at a time, and he blurts the words out as quickly as possible before he forgets them. But his star power does make this draggy Shakespearean soap opera at least passably entertaining. Elvis plays Glenn Tyler, a misunderstood young rebel on probation who winds up falling for his parole officer (Hope Lange). Things get extremely complicated (a rarity in an Elvis movie), but by the film's conclusion (after many fights, kisses, alcoholic indulgences, and an accidental murder), Glenn is headed off to college, having discovered that he's really a talented writer. Director Philip Dunne shot two endings, but advance screenings indicated that the sadder one (in which Glenn's sweetheart kicks the bucket) had to be nixed. Incidentally, rumor has it that during the making of this movie, the King had to seek treatment for several troubling boils on his butt. (MB)

LINES Betty Lee describing Glenn: "You're wild and unsettled—like a porcupine that can't be held."

CAMEOS Christina Crawford

SONGS *Wild in the Country, I Slipped I Stumbled I Fell, In My Way, Husky Dusky Day* (Elvis Presley)

WILD IN THE STREETS (1968)

MUSIC ★★★
ATTITUDE ★★★
FUN ★★★★

CAST: Christopher George, Shelley Winters, Diane Varsi, Hal Holbrook, Millie Perkins, Richard Pryor, Bert Freed, Kevin Coughlin, Ed Begley; DIR: Barry Shear; PROD: Samuel Z. Arkoff, James Nicholson; SCREENPLAY: Robert Thom; STUDIO: American International; 97 min., color (HBO)

Jack Webb's worst nightmare.
Shelley Winters outdoes herself here as the mother of rock star Max Frost, who's sort of a cross between Jim Morrison and Bobby Sherman. During the course of *Wild in the Streets*, Max leads his millions of fans in a full-scale revolution. He even becomes president once junior high school students get the vote. Next thing you know, everyone over 35 (including Max's mom) gets shipped off to internment camps, where they are given LSD as a round-the-clock pacifier. Good idea! Despite the few unfortunate moments during which the movie tries to make serious sociopolitical statements, *Wild in the Streets* is a total, definitive trash classic. (MC)

SCENES After tearing up the living room furniture, smashing the house to pieces, and writing "Mama Papa Screw Off" on his mother's mirror in red lipstick, Max says good-bye to the family bulldog, blows up his dad's car with homemade dynamite, and leaves home.

CAMEOS Walter Winchell, Dick Clark

SONGS *Free Lovin', Fifty-Two Percent, Just Listen to the Music, Fourteen or Fight, Sally LeRoy, The Shape of Things to Come* (Max Frost and the Troopers)

WILD ON THE BEACH (1965)

MUSIC ★★★★
ATTITUDE ★★★★
FUN ★★★★

CAST: Frankie Randall, Sherry Jackson, Russ Bender, Booth Coleman, Justin Smith, Robert Golden, Larry Gust, Jerry Grayson, Marc Seaton; DIR: Maury Dexter; PROD: Maury Dexter; SCREENPLAY: Harry Spalding; STUDIO: 20th Century-Fox; 77 min b/w (no video release)

Beach tre-ja vu.
The third (and last) of Maury Dexter's *Beach Party* ripoffs, *Wild on the Beach* is so third rate and low-budget (it's even shot in black-and-white) that an unintentional sense of "realism" creeps into it. Given so little to work with in the way of situation and dialogue, the actors talk like real people instead. As a result, when Sonny and Cher perform "It's Gonna Rain" at a teen nightclub, you feel like you're actually there, because the movie's sense of artifice has been removed. Three numbers by the hot, vital, and often-overlooked Astronauts give the shakes. A rare appearance by drum lord Sandy Nelson ("Teen Beat," "Let There Be Drums") also cools out the scene, but the funny part is girl group obscurity Cindy Malone, who sings "Run Away from Him" while a hokey scientist tries to demonstrate a new invention that creates a wild echo. Well, real life can be pretty hokey, too! By the time

ELLAS ALQUILARON UNA
CABANA EN LA PLAYA...

Y ELLOS ALQUILARON
LA MISMA CABANA...

-y
ahora
hay

FRENESI
A
Go-Go

(Wild on the Beach)

Los jóvenes se
divierten con
ritmos impetuosos
y fogosos

Protagonistas
FRANKIE RANDALL · SHERRY JACKSON
coprotagonistas
JACKIE & GAYLE · SONNY & CHER · THE ASTRONAUTS · CINDY MALONE · SANDY NELSON
Escrita por HARRY SPALDING · Producida y Dirigida por MAURY DEXTER · De un Argumento Original de HANK TANI · Una Producción Lippert Inc.
Distribuida por 20th Century-Fox

the movie ends, you feel as though you've gotten to know all the actors personally, and the bands have been playing in your living room all night. It's a little frustrating that you can't walk right in, dance with the girls, and hang out for a spell. (DP)

SONGS   *The House on the Beach, The Gods of Love* (Frankie Randall); *Rock the World, Pyramid, Snap It, Little Speedy Gonzalez* (Astronauts); *Run Away from Him* (Cindy Malone); *It's Gonna Rain* (Sonny and Cher); *Yellow-Haired Woman* (Russ Bender); *Drum Dance* (Sandy Nelson); *Winter Nocturne* (Jackie and Gayle)

WILD WHEELS   (1969)

CAST: Don Eppson, Bruce Kimble, Casey Kasem, 13th Committee, Robert Dix, Terry Stafford, Billie & Blie, Three of August, Saturday Revue; **DIR:** Kent Osborne; **PROD:** Bud Dell; **SCREENPLAY:** Kent Osborne, Ralph Luce; **STUDIO:** Fanfare; 64 min., color (Video Gems)

MUSIC ★★★
ATTITUDE ★★★★
FUN ★★★★

West Side Story *with sand flies.*
Ostensibly the tale of rival gangs of surfers and bikers, this fabulously cheesy *über* B movie is an excuse to get as many shots of groovy chicks and cool dudes fruggin' the night away as humanly possible. The acting is strictly from hunger, as are the cinematography (hitherto known as aiming the camera), script, and music. Yet in some way, the horrible equals the transcendent, and *Wild Wheels* becomes a rip-snorting hoot.

Worth mentioning is the romance between a snarly biker dude and his swinging but chaste surfer gal, who holds on to her virginity with a fervor that would make her mother proud. Of course they fall madly and deeply in love, as Biker Dude learns to respect a girl who won't knock boots on the first date. There is a subplot (and I use that term loosely) about country rock crooner Reb who bursts into song from time to time. The soundtrack features groups who lip-synched their way into oblivion. All in all, there's more attitude here than the law should allow. (ALi)

LINES   In what may rank as one of the all-time classic lines in film, a gal politely demurs an offer of marijuana with "I gave all that up when I left California." Yeah!

SONGS   *I Hear Music* (13th Committee); *I Fell for You* (Reb Smith); *Holiday Right Here* (Saturday Revue)

WILD WILD WINTER   (1966)

CAST: Chris Noel, Gary Clarke, Steve Franken, Jay and the Americans, The Beau Brummels, Dick and Dee Dee, The Astronauts, Jackie and Gayle; **DIR:** Lennie Weinrib; **PROD:** Bart Patton; **SCREENPLAY:** David Malcolm; **STUDIO:** Universal; 80 min., color (no video release)

MUSIC ★★★★★
ATTITUDE ★★★★
FUN ★★★★

One for the Steve Franken fans.
Billed as a "Surfin' Snow Ball," *Wild Wild Winter* is a collegiate escapade that replaces snow with California sand. Fresh from her starring role in *Beach Ball* (also a Weinrib-Patton collaboration), Chris Noel stars here as professional goody-goody Susan Benchley, the romantic object of Ronnie Duke (Gary Clarke from "The Virginian"). The film also features Steve Franken as Clarke's romantic rival, the obnoxious John Harris, who's not that different from the role of Chatsworth Osborne, Jr., that Franken played on "The Many Loves of Dobie Gillis." Intertwined among these romantic escapades is the threatened takeover of Alpine College by some shadowy underworld characters. After an intercollegiate ski race

(similar to that held in A.I.P.'s *Ski Party*) resolves all the plot conflicts, the credits roll to the strains of Jay and the Americans performing "Two of a Kind." You'd never call it soul, but the music for *Wild Wild Winter* was originally recorded for Motown Records, where musical supervisor Frank Wilson worked as a producer and recording artist. (SJM)

SONGS   *Our Love's Gonna Snowball* (Jackie and Gayle); *Just Wait and See* (Beau Brummels); *A Change of Heart* (Astronauts); *Heartbeats* (Dick and Dee Dee); *Two of a Kind* (Jay and the Americans)

WINTER A GO-GO   **(1965)**

CAST: James Stacy, William Wellman Jr., Beverly Adams, Anthony Hayes, Jill Donohue, Tom Nardini; DIR: Richard Benedict; PROD: Reno Carell; SCREENPLAY: Bob Kanter; STUDIO: Columbia; 88 min., color (no video release)

Snow-bun butts wiggle the cheese.
This is Columbia Pictures' follow-up to the surfin' hotshot *Ride the Wild Surf.*

Released on the heels of A.I.P.'s *Ski Party*, *Winter a Go-Go* is perhaps the most incidental of all the *Beach Party*-inspired films. But its appearance on TV a few years back still got a lot of people excited (because it had been buried for so long), which just goes to show that the rockin' fun of any beach exploitation films (even this one) can still cause a buzz. The story here centers on Jeff Forster (William Wellman, Jr.), who inherits an old ski lodge. But that's about all the plot there is. The house band is the Nooney Rickett Four (holdovers from A.I.P.'s *Pajama Party*). The Reflections make a rare appearance. Plenty of cool-lookin' go-go dancers in red ski bikinis jiggle to Hal Blaine's drum beat. (This carries the film.) Of special note is the involvement of future Monkees songwriters Tommy Boyce and Bobby Hart, who chip in two original tunes: "Do the Ski" and the singalong number "The Hip Square Dance." (DP)

SCENES The film opens with a parade of sharply dressed female calves and ankles. Then a red-and-white-polka-dotted ski bunny appears, and suddenly the Hondells start singing "Winter a Go-Go." (This is later Hondells material, never released on disc.)

SONGS *Winter a Go-Go* (Hondells); *Do the Ski* (Nooney Rickett Four, Joni Lyman); *King of the Mountain* (Joni Lyman); *Ski City* (Nooney Rickett Four); *Sweet On You* (Reflections); *Hip Square Dance* (James Stacy)

THE WIZARD OF WAUKESHA (1979)

DIR: Catherine Orentreich; PROD: Catherine Orentreich; STUDIO: Stray Cat; 59 min., color (Direct)

MUSIC ★★★★★
ATTITUDE ★★★★★
FUN ★★★★★

Les Paul invented oxygen.
Not really, but the things that he did develop (like multitrack recording, the solid-body electric guitar, tape echo, overdubbing, and more) are as essential to the recording industry today as oxygen is to life. There was a time in the early 1950s when Les Paul's reputation as an inventor was secondary to his fame as a guitarist, producer, and recording artist. But this documentary pays tribute to all four aspects of Paul's legendary career, especially the enduring popularity of the Gibson Les Paul guitar. First introduced in 1952 (in response to the success of the Fender Telecaster), the Les Paul remains one of the great guitars on the market today. (Since the late '60s, Gibson Les Pauls have been used almost exclusively by hard rock, blues, and metal guitarists, whose sound is about as far removed from Les's own as you can get. That doesn't seem to bother Les.) It's safe to say that anyone interested in popular music will get off on this crazy quilt stitched together from Les's tales. He is a great storyteller (even if he does tend to fib now and again), and his life is the stuff of essential Americana.

If you'd like to hear some of Les's music, try "How High the Moon" by Les and Mary Ford, one of the greatest records every made. And that's just the tip of the iceberg. Check out *Les Paul: The Legend and the Legacy* (Capitol), the mother of all boxed sets. You might also want to look up *Les Paul: An American Original* (Morrow) by Mary Alice Shaughnessy, a biography that explores—among other things—the darker aspects of Les's life that were left out of this film. (MC)

SCENES An interview with late '60s guitar hero Mike Bloomfield, who almost single-handedly revived interest in the Gibson Les Paul when he switched from a Telecaster around '66 or '67

CAMEOS Rick Derringer, Mike Bloomfield, Ivan Kral

WOODSTOCK (1970)

MUSIC ★★★★★
ATTITUDE ★★★★★
FUN ★★★★

DIR: Michael Wadleigh; PROD: Bob Maurice; STUDIO: Warner; 184 min., color (Warner)

What's so funny 'bout peace and love and understanding?
Remembered mostly for the on-site birth of various babies and Hendrix's closing number—a visceral feedback version of "The Star-Spangled Banner"—Woodstock was more than just a Monterey Pop-style music festival: It was a celebration of a generation, for a generation, by a generation (and it shall not perish from this earth). Woodstock became a media focus for all that was right with the dippy hippie world (flower power, flares, freedom, and fornication) *and* all that was wrong with it (flower power, flares, freedom, and fornication).

Since its original release, critics have described the *Woodstock* movie as an endurance test. Its three and a half hours of freakage are guaranteed to exhaust even the fittest viewer. However, with its dramatic wide-pan audience shots and its use of split screens, *Woodstock* is still a fair example of filmmaking on the epic scale. Many rock films don't know where to begin, but *Woodstock* doesn't know when to end. Even so, there are some notable omissions in this film, such as the time Pete Townsend threw Abbie Hoffman off the stage during the Who's *Tommy* medley.

The performances are a mixed bag, from the unbelievable to the unbearable, but the movie does a creditable job capturing the true atmosphere of this half-a-million-people extravaganza with its interviews of townsfolk, policemen, doctors, and refugees from the Love Generation. A Portosan serviceman cheerfully reports that one of his sons is attending the festival, but another couldn't make it because he's fighting in Vietnam. Even more poignant is the scene in which the filmmakers interview a Sullivan County storekeeper. Just over her shoulder, a newspaper headline screams, "SHARON'S PALS BALK AT PROBE." Sharon Tate had just been murdered, while an as-yet-unknown Charles Manson still walked the streets. Watching this film, one can't help but be reminded that Woodstock's utopian innocence never made it to the second reel. (DR)

SONGS   *Freedom* (Richie Havens); *Joe Hill, Swing Low Sweet Chariot* (Joan Baez); *See Me Feel Me, Summertime Blues* (Who); *At the Hop* (Sha Na Na); *A Little Help from My Friends* (Joe Cocker); *Rockin' Soul Music* (Country Joe and the Fish); *Comin' into Los Angeles* (Arlo Guthrie); *Suite: Judy Blue Eyes* (Crosby, Stills and Nash); *I'm Going Home* (Ten Years After); *Younger Generation* (John Sebastian); *Fixin' to Die Rag* (Country Joe McDonald); *Soul Sacrifice* (Santana); *I Want to Take You Higher, Hey Music Lover* (Sly and the Family Stone); *The Star-Spangled Banner, Purple Haze* (Jimi Hendrix)

THE WORLD'S GREATEST SINNER (1963)

MUSIC ★★★★★
ATTITUDE ★★★★★
FUN ★★★★★

CAST: Timothy Agoglia Carey, Gil Baretto, Titus Moody, Betty Rowland, James Farley, Gail Griffin, Gene Koziol, Paul Frees; DIR: Timothy Agoglia Carey; PROD: Timothy Agoglia Carey; SCREENPLAY: Timothy Agoglia Carey; 102 min., b/w (Absolute)

Music like the worst nightmare the Cramps ever had.
Timothy Carey—the charismatically malevolent "heavy" of *The Killing, The Wild One, Paths of Glory*, and *East of Eden*—single-handedly made this film between 1960 and 1963 in and around the town of El Monte, outside Los Angeles. Its plot centers on forty-year-old Clarence, who quits his job at an insurance company so that he can don the mantle of a rock star and run for public office as God. Carey's portrayal of a rock star in a gold suit backed by a ragtag Mexican band is so fantastically bizarre that it puts Salvador Dali (Carey's idol) to shame. During his main performance, which is sour and atonal, Carey falls to his knees and

screams, "Please! Please! Please!" (Without ever having seen or heard of James Brown!)

The World's Greatest Sinner isn't a music movie per se, but its soundtrack stands out. For the background music, Carey hired a young, unproven local odd-ball, Frank Zappa, to compose a full orchestral score. Their association was short-lived, however. Appearing on the Steve Allen show playing a bicycle, Zappa made disparaging remarks about the film that earned Carey's lifelong enmity. (Still, they both made cameo appearances in the Monkees' *Head.*) Although this crude but uniquely imaginative undertaking was ignored by major distributors when it first came out, history has heaped kudos on *The World's Greatest Sinner*—and on Carey for his bravery, wit, and vision. Fans, take note: Still alive, Carey makes occasional film and TV appearances. He also pops up at showings of his films at revival hous-es around L.A. In early 1991, he was completing a stage play, *The Insect Trainer*, about a postal worker killed by a fart. (AF)

Yellow Submarine

YELLOW SUBMARINE *(1968)*

CAST: The Beatles; DIR: George Dunning; PROD: Al Brodax; SCREENPLAY: Lee Minoff, Jack Mendelsohn, Al Brodax, Erich Segal; ANIMATION: Peter Max; STUDIO: Apple; 86 min., color (MGM/UA)

MUSIC ★★★★★
ATTITUDE ★★★★★
FUN ★★★★

In which the Blue Meanies are vanquished and love reigns supreme.

Yellow Submarine stands as the crowning cinematic achievement of '60s psyche-delia, and decades later it's as watchable and enjoyable as ever. In this fantastic, Peter Max-animated film, the Beatles are spirited away in the eponymous yellow submarine to save Pepperland from the dreaded Blue Meanies. Along the way, the singing saviors encounter a surreal feast for both the eyes and ears: phantasmagorical creatures, outrageous landscapes, and colors that throb and vibrate to each and every Beatles song on the soundtrack. It's a drug-free, hallucinogenic journey for the armchair tripper, the peak of which is undoubtedly (and not surprisingly) the "Lucy in the Sky with Diamonds" sequence. An incredible film on all levels, *Yellow Submarine* manages to capture exquisitely and in visual form the beauty and madness of the incomparable Beatles. It's second only to Walt Disney's *Fantasia* for animated musical insight. (EC)

LINES   Jeremy, the Nowhere Man: "Ad hoc, ad loc, and quid pro quo, so little time, so much to know." His Blueness: "Max, it's no longer a blue world. Where can we go?" Max: "Argentina?"

SONGS   *Yellow Submarine, Eleanor Rigby, All Together Now, When I'm Sixty-Four, Only a Northern Song, Nowhere Man, Lucy in the Sky with Diamonds, Sgt. Pepper's Lonely Hearts Club Band, All You Need Is Love, Baby You're a Rich Man* (Beatles)

YOU ARE WHAT YOU EAT   (1968)

MUSIC ★★★
ATTITUDE ★★★
FUN ★★

CAST: Tiny Tim, Peter Yarrow; **DIR:** Barry Feinstein; **PROD:** Peter Yarrow, Barry Feinstein; **STUDIO:** Commonwealth-United; 75 min., color (no video release)

The first film made to sell a soundtrack album.

When I was a youngster, while browsing the record bin of the local department store, I happened upon the soundtrack of *You Are What You Eat* and tried to make sense of it. *You Are What You Eat* didn't look like any movie I had seen, nor had it ever played in my neighborhood. Was this strange film a put-on? Twenty five years later, I finally got to see it, but I still can't make much sense out of this rambling, crazy-quilt look at the late-'60s counterculture.

You Are What You Eat was created at a time when underground cinema was a hot commodity, and the entertainment business was scrambling to grab a piece of the rapidly changing youth market. Director Barry Feinstein, a top album-cover photographer of the '60s, was apparently given license to aim his movie camera at whatever he deemed interesting, then score the results with rock music and call it a movie. Viewed today, *You Are What You Eat* plays like a "1960s lifestyles" sample reel from a stock footage library with scenes of be-ins, body painting, surfing, bikinis, rock concerts, Beatlemania, and even Tiny Tim. One highlight is footage of a "Teen Fair," those now-forgotten sales shows that used rock groups and go-go dancers to sell everything from Detroit's latest wheels to Nazi helmets. The rapid-fire cast of characters listed at the end of this, uh, documentary reads like a Who's Who of Southern California groovy people (i.e., most of the names from the liner notes of *Freak Out* and *Buffalo Springfield Again*). The soundtrack offers some occasionally interesting music from the likes of Harper's Bizarre, record producer John Simon, Paul Butterfield, David Crosby, Peter Yarrow (who co-produced this movie), and others. (JS)

SCENES   Tiny Tim's campy duet of "I Got You Babe" with some girl who sounds like Nico, intercut with footage of madly screaming fans at a Beatles concert

CAMEOS   Barry McGuire, the Family Dog, David Crosby, the Mothers of Invention, Ringo Starr (and countless others, no doubt)

SONGS   *Be My Baby, Memphis Tennessee, I Got You Babe* (Tiny Tim)

THE YOUNG ONES (1962)

ALTERNATE TITLE: *Wonderful to Be Young*
CAST: Cliff Richard and the Shadows, Carole Gray, Robert Morley, Teddy Greene; DIR: Sidney J. Furie; PROD: Kenneth Harper; SCREENPLAY: Ronald Cass, Peter Myers; STUDIO: Associated British; 92 min., color (no video release)

MUSIC	★★★
ATTITUDE	★
FUN	★★

Cliff Richard makes nonsense of adolescence.
This is where Cliff Richard's screen career took off—and went wrong. After playing a key supporting role in his first picture, a major part in his second—both serious, gritty dramas—Richard hit it big on screen in this bright, innocuous drama. He plays the son of a wealthy developer who saves a youth center from his father's wrecking ball. He not only wins his father's respect, and gets the girl (Carole Gray) in the finale, but manages to sing a hit song (the title tune). The presence of color and CinemaScope made this an important movie for the British picture industry, although overall the film is flaccid and silly. It made a fortune at the box office in England, anyway, and was issued in the U.S. as *Wonderful to Be Young*. It heralded the beginning of Cliff Richard's main body of movies, which rapidly declined in quality. Incidentally, the choreography of this movie (and that of his follow-up, *Summer Holiday*) was devised by feature film director Herbert Ross. (BE)

The Young Ones, What Do You Know We've Got a Show, Nothing's Impossible, All for One, Peace Pipe, The Savage, Got a Funny Feeling, We Say Yeah (Cliff Richard and the Shadows)   **SONGS**

ZACHARIAH (1971)

CAST: John Rubinstein, Pat Quinn, Don Johnson, Elvin Jones; DIR: George Englund; PROD: George Englund; SCREENPLAY: The Firesign Theater; STUDIO: ABC; 93 min., color (Playhouse)

MUSIC	★★★★
ATTITUDE	★★★★
FUN	★★★★

Drugs, guns, and rock 'n' roll in the Old West.
They called this hodgepodge of Old West gunslingers and '70s rock opera "the first electric western." Fortunately, the creators of *Zachariah* had the wit, irreverence, and irony necessary to pull it off. The two gunslingers here are friends, torn by the realization that someday one will have to kill the other to prove he's top dog. The plot is, of course, full of other cliches as well, but the fact that country-rock bands seem to pop up everywhere provides a sufficient distraction. The original songs by the James Gang and the New York Rock 'n' Roll Ensemble hold up well today and give the film a slapstick edge. (ALa)

Country Joe and the Fish, the James Gang, the New York Rock 'n' Roll Ensemble, Dick Van Patten, Doug Kershaw   **CAMEOS**

We're the Crackers, All I Need, Poor But Honest Crackers (Country Joe and the Fish); *Country Fever, Laguna Salada* (James Gang); *Drum Solo* (Elvin Jones); *The Ballad of Job Cain* (Doug Kershaw); *Grave Digger* (New York Rock 'n' Roll Ensemble); *Down in the Willow Garden* (White Lightnin'); *Camino Waltz* (John Rubinstein)   **SONGS**

APPENDIX

YES, IT'S TRUE. WE *WEREN'T* able TO review every rock-related film in the preceding section. The laws of time and space simply wouldn't allow it. Instead, we've compiled the following appendices to fill in the gaps. They make *Hollywood Rock* the most complete guide possible to rock'n'roll on film. For our purposes, "on film" means that you can actually see the rock'n'roll on the big screen. Most movies nowadays use some rock songs in their soundtracks, but that doesn't necessarily make them *rock* movies. With a few significant exceptions, these soundtrack-only films have been left out.

We also chose to exclude films released directly to videocassette, mostly sticking to celluloid films that were shown at some point in movie theaters. Although it suited our purpose, we realize that this is quickly becoming an obsolete definition. Sadly, many of the college film societies, repertory theaters, and midnight movie palaces that were once the prime venues for rock films are disappearing rapidly, losing their audiences to home video. The video format has already become the primary means of exhibition for rock concert films. Made-

for-video tapes like *R.E.M. Tourfilm* already boast higher production values than most of the concert films in this book. In narrative films as well, the line between video and film continues to blur. However, for the moment, we will remain purists—if only to keep this book to a manageable size. Our one compromise has been to include a few made-for-TV movies that were simply too rock-oriented to ignore. (Most of these were later shown theatrically in foreign markets.)

So what's left? A lot! The *Concerts & Rockumentaries* appendix includes nonfiction rock films, both features and shorts, that were not included in the main review section. There were just too many of these to give a full review to each. We trust the comprehensive listing that follows will make it up to you. However, no attempt was made to include rock videos or promotional clips of individual songs, because that would require another book.

The *More Rock Films* appendix includes films that aren't *primarily* rock films but that contain relevant footage. If you've ever seen a dramatic film whose only rock content was a band playing a couple of songs in a nightclub scene, you'll probably find it listed here. Ditto films that include rock musicians making cameo acting appearances or starring in dramatic roles. You'll find that these odds and ends include some of the most surprising and enjoyable viewing in this book. Crude local garage bands that probably never released a record can sometimes be found playing in obscure '60s adult movies. And who knew there were so many *Mexican* films with rock'n'roll bands in them?

While reading these appendices, you might find some listings that seem to deserve a fuller review. In many cases, we would agree with you, but we've been unable to locate copies. If anyone has a tape of *Disk-O-Tek Holiday* or *Los Chicas con las Chicas*, please write to us!

In addition to those rock stars who have taken the odd walk-on role in a Jonathan Demme film, some rock musicians have actually built second careers as actors. Because most of this work has been in non-rock films, we've condensed their performances into the *Rock Actors Filmography*. Here you'll find a complete list of the *acting* jobs, both large and small, taken by folks who made their names in rock'n'roll. Rockers who acted in just one or two films can be found in the *More Rock Films* listings.

Working on any reference book can be a maddening experience. Inevitably, the goal of utter completeness is compromised at some point by real-world deadlines. I'm sure there are some accidental omissions in these lists, not to mention the new rock films always coming out (several have been released in the last month alone!). Still, the main review section of this book, combined with the appendices that follow, detail well over a *thousand* rock films. They should keep everybody busy until the next edition of *Hollywood Rock* comes out.

Jay Schwartz

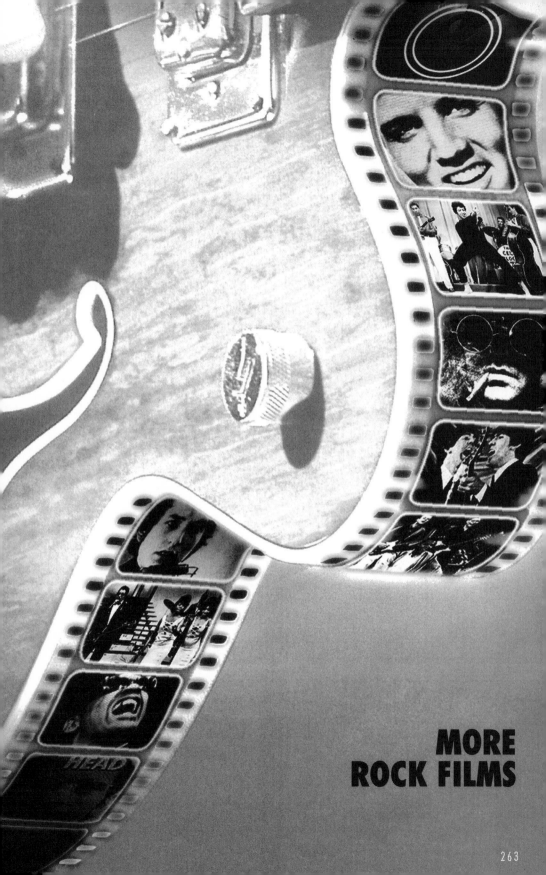

**MORE
ROCK FILMS**

A Ritmo de Twist (1962)   Mexican juvenile-delinquent film with appearances by Los Rebeldes de Rock, Los Beatniks, and Los Teen Tops.

ABC: Mantrap   "The Look of Love" crooner Martin Fry gets to fulfill his matinee idol fantasies in this narrative mystery.

Adventures of the Son of Exploding Sausage (1969)   Film starring British comedy-rock troupe the Bonzo Dog Doo-Dah Band.

Al Compas del Rock'n'Roll   Mexican film with Martha Roth, Joaquin Cardero, and Rosiata Arenez.

Alice in the Cities (1974)   Wim Wenders film with Chuck Berry singing "Memphis, Tennessee" in a concert scene.

All This and World War II (1976)   Made during a revival of Beatles fandom, this consists of nothing but newsreel footage set to '70s all-star covers of Beatles songs, ostensibly to sell the deluxe soundtrack package.

The Allnighter (1987)   Terrible teen sex comedy starring Susanna Hoffs and directed by her mother. Includes appearance by Louis and Clark (with Louis Guitierrez, ex-Three O'Clock and ex-Susanna boyfriend).

American Pop (1981)   Ralph Bakshi's animated history of American music, from vaudeville to Bob Seger.

Americathon (1979)   Elvis Costello is glimpsed performing "(I Don't Want To Go To) Chelsea" and "Crawlin' to the U.S.A.," and Eddie Money sings "Get a Move On" and "Open Up Your Heart" in this Neil Israel (*Tunnelvision*) satire.

Angels from Hell (1968)   The Peanut Butter Conspiracy perform "Mr. Madison Avenue," "Shake Off The Chains" and two more in this biker film.

Apotheosis (1971)   One of countless arty shorts by John Lennon and Yoko Ono.

The Baby Maker (1970)   With the Single Wing Turquoise Bird Light Show.

Babylon (1980)   Reggae drama about a West Indian (Aswad guitarist Brinsley Forde) competing in a London DJ contest and struggling with family problems, police brutality, and racism in his Brixton neighborhood. Score by Dennis Bovell.

Back to the Future, Part III (1990)   Time travel sequence has appearance by ZZ Top, playing music at an Old West campfire. Also includes Flea cameo as the less-than-sane dude in the pickup truck scene.

Backtrack (1988)   Cameos by Bob Dylan and Neil Young.

Battle of the Mods (1966)   Italian film of mods and rockers stars German Ricky Shayne, singing "Crazy Baby, I Got You" and "No No No No" (originally by British group the Sorrows).

Beat Street (1984)   Break-dancing musical includes rap talents Grandmaster Melle Mel and Afrika Bambaata.

The Beatniks (1959)   Leader of juvenile delinquents Peter Breck is heard singing to a jukebox and offered a chance at rock stardom. Directed by cartoon voice actor Paul Frees.

Bedazzled (1967)   Dudley Moore's character gets his pop-stardom wish answered and appears on a "Ready, Steady, Go"-type TV show, singing the Tom Jones-y "Love Me," in this Cook/Moore farce.

Better a Widow (1969)   Italian comedy with British group the Mike Stuart Span.

Between the Lines (1977)   Jeff Goldblum plays a rock critic in this ensemble piece about an underground paper. Appearance by Southside Johnny and the Asbury Jukes ("We're Havin' a Party").

Bikinis y Rock (1970)   Hippie-era remake of another Mexican youth film, *El Mundo Loco de los Jovenes*. With lots of "Laugh-In"-type humor, a guru, a go-go dancing cleaning lady, and El Loco del Ritmo, who play "Roll Over Beethoven."

Birth of the Beatles (1979)   Made-for-TV docudrama of the teething pains of the Four Lads Who Shook the World. Not bad, but some scenes are bound to raise a giggle ("Bri, any luhv is good luhv"). Beatles songs played by Rain.

Black Box (1978)   Beth & Scott B short with Lydia Lunch threatening some guy with a torture device.

Blame It on the Night (1985)   Nick Mancuso stars as rock singer getting in touch with a conservative son he never met. Story co-written by Mick Jagger; songs by Ted Neeley.

The Blank Generation (1980)   Not the CBGB concert epic, but a narrative film by German director Ulli Lommell (*Cocaine Cowboys*), professionally shot in 35mm color. Richard Hell is the leading man in this Godard-style romance (with Carol Bouquet), yet he still finds time to do some songs with the Voidoids, onstage and in the studio. Andy Warhol appears briefly. This movie had a *very* limited theatrical run, then disappeared.

The Bliss of Mrs. Blossom (1968)   With an appearance by British revivalists the New Vaudeville Band.

Blood Orgy of the Leather Girls (1988)   Low-budget horror film produced in San Francisco by Michael Lucas of the Phantom Surfers, who provide the instrumental score. Also appearing are David Nudleman and the Wild Breed.

Blues for Lovers (1966)   British film starring Ray Charles as himself. He befriends a blind boy in London and sings "I Got a Woman," "Let the Good Times Roll," "Talkin' about You," "Unchain My Heart, "What'd I Say," and five more, with the help of the Raeletts.

The Bodyguard (1992)   Whitney Houston stars as a singer/actress who hires Kevin Costner as a bodyguard when she's stalked by a disturbed fan.

Bongo Wolf's Revenge (1970)   Documentary about a Sunset Strip eccentric, whose exploits here include visiting a Mike Bloomfield recording session (of "George Swing" and "People Are Strange") and recounting his U.K. tour with P.J. Proby.

Born in Flames (1983)   Lizzie Borden's radical-feminist future fantasy about a revolution led by women guerrillas. The film co-stars Adele Bertei, with music from her band the Bloods and the Red Crayola.

Born Reckless (1959)   Johnny Olenn and his Group sing "You, Lovable You" in this Mamie Van Doren rodeo drama.

Born Wild (1968)   A.I.P. movie about racial problems on campus, with the American Revolution (doing "Love Has Got Me Down" at the teen club) and the Orphan Egg (playing "In Big Letters" at a pool party). Alternate title: *The Young Animals.*

Bound for Glory (1976)   David Carradine offers a sensitive, if not always accurate, portrayal of Woody Guthrie. Carradine does his own vocals, and Haskell Wexler's photography won an Oscar.

Bravos II (1968)   Los Bravos' second feature film, including the Easybeats cover "Bring a Little Lovin'."

Bread (1971)   Story of British hippies who are inspired by the Isle of Wight Festival to hold their own concert at a country home while the owner is away. Appearances by Juicy Lucy, Web, and Crazy Mabel.

Buddy's Song (1992)   Roger Daltrey stars in this drama of a rock star whose son wants to follow in his footsteps.

Bunny Lake Is Missing (1965)   Ponderous Otto Preminger mystery that includes a teasingly brief scene in which the Zombies are glimpsed on a telly in the corner of an English pub, performing soundtrack-only tracks "Remember You," "Nothing's Changed," and "Just Out of Reach." An alternate version of the latter song called "Come On Time" is sung in the film's trailer, which features the band hyping up the movie ("Laurence Olivier is… immense!").

The Burglar (1987)   Soviet film about a Russian punk rocker (Konstantin Kinchev) in an MTV T-shirt longing for exposure to the world outside.

The Butterfly Ball (1976)   An Albert Hall presentation of Roger Glover's multimedia extravaganza, based on fantasy illustrator Alan Aldridge's Carroll-Tenniel inspired book. With costumed dancers, animation, Vincent Price narration, and rock music performed by members of Deep Purple, Roxy Music, and Fancy.

C.C. and Company (1970)   Joe Namath biker film with Wayne Cochran and the C.C. Riders performing "I Can't Turn You Loose."

C'mon, Let's Live a Little (1967)   Bobby Vee stars as a country boy gone to college. He romances Jackie DeShannon and plays songs, a talent soon exploited by a campus rabblerouser. With performances by DeShannon, Eddie Hodges, and the Pair Extraordinaire. Numbers include "Instant Girl," "Baker Man," "What Fool This Mortal Be," and "Let's Go Go."

Calypso Heat Wave (1957)   Sam Katzman goes island in this tale of calypso singer Johnny Desmond leaving a record label infiltrated by jukebox mobsters. With Joel Grey (!), the Hi-Los, the Tarriers (with Alan Arkin), the Treniers (doing "Rock Joe" and "Day Old Bread and Canned Beans"), and Maya Angelou.

Calypso Joe (1957)   Pre-ska music from Herb Jeffries's Calypsomaniacs, Lord Flea and his Calypsonians, Terry Gilkyson and the Easy Riders, Duke of Iron, and Lady T.

Candy Goes to Hollywood   Hardcore porno film starring a pre-Plasmatics Wendy O. Williams, doing rude things with ping-pong balls.

Captain Milkshake (1970) Hippie movie with lots of music, including an appearance by Trans Love Airways.

Carny (1980) Producer Robbie Robertson stars in this story of carnival life. He also contributed soundtrack songs.

Catch My Soul (1974) Nutty Patrick McGoohan directed this rock opera *Othello*, set in a hippie commune and starring Richie Havens and Tony Joe White. The cast also includes Delaney and Bonnie, and everyone gets to sing songs like "Chug a Lug," "I Found Jesus," "Open Our Eyes," "Working on a Building," and "Backwoods Preacher." McGoohan acted in a jazz *Othello* in 1961, *All Night Long*, which featured Dave Brubeck and Charles Mingus.

CB4 (1993) "The *Spinal Tap* of rap." The title group, featuring Stabmaster Arson and Dead Mike, perform an N.W.A. parody, "Straight Out of Locash."

Cha Cha (1979) Herman Brood and his Wild Romance star in this Dutch film about a bank robber turned rocker. With lots of songs by Brood and other Amsterdam talent such as The Meteors, Inside Nipples, the Dulfergang, and Floor Van Zutphen, plus Nina Hagen.

Cha-Cha-Cha Boom (1956) Sam Katzman mambo package about an A&R man going to Cuba in search of new talent. Playing themselves are Perez Prado, the Mary Kaye Trio, Helen Grayco, Luis Arcarez, and Manny Lopez. Songs include "Cuban Rock and Roll," "Voodoo Suite," "Crazy Crazy," and "Mambo No. 8."

Changes (1968) Counterculture drama co-starring soul singer Kim Weston—with music by Neil Young, Tim Buckley, and Judy Collins.

Chappaqua (1966) Autobiographical tale of director/star Conrad Rooks's heroin addiction. Including such guests as the Fugs, Ravi Shankar, Ornette Coleman, William Burroughs and Allen Ginsberg. Photographed by *Cocksucker Blues* director Robert Frank.

Chastity (1969) Hard-to-see tour-de-force by Sonny Bono, who produced, wrote, and scored this A.I.P.-released vehicle for Cher. She plays a runaway who runs into some seamy characters in this film that shares a name with their child. Cher performs "Band of Thieves."

The Chelsea Girls (1966) Nico acts in one of the more successful of Andy Warhol's underground movies, originally shown with two projectors side by side. Mostly shot at the Chelsea Hotel, but with some scenes shot at the Velvet Underground's West Third Street home. The band plays music off-camera in some scenes, alternately pretty and ambient.

The Christian Licorice Store (1972) Tennis film with Tim Buckley singing "Pleasant Street."

Christiane F. (1981) German drama of teenage junkies throws in a brief David Bowie concert scene, with Bowie performing "Station to Station" and "Heroes."

Cinema Pas Mort Monsieur Godard (1978) Documentary with footage of Patti Smith and the Doors.

Cisco Pike (1972) Kris Kristofferson, in his first film, plays a rocker coerced into dealing drugs. Includes a recording session scene with the Sir Douglas Quintet, in which Sir Doug cops some dope.

Climb Up the Wall (1960) Hokey story of U.K. DJ Jack Jackson screening films of old musical greats as his son Malcolm persuades him that teen music also has value. With performances by Craig Douglas, Mike Preston, Cherry Wainer, and Neville Taylor.

Coffee and Cigarettes (1992)   Jim Jarmusch short film of a conversation between Iggy Pop and Tom Waits.

The Color of Money (1986)   Iggy Pop cameo as a pool player.

The Committee (1968)   Former Manfred Mann singer Paul Jones plays a wayward hitchhiker in this surreal psychological drama. The Crazy World of Arthur Brown perform "Nightmare." Unreleased soundtrack music by Pink Floyd.

Concrete Angels (1987)   A group of boys in 1964 Toronto form a band hoping to win an opening slot for the Beatles.

Connecting Rooms (1969)   Michael Redgrave and Bette Davis live in a rooming house with a pop songwriter. Appearances by the Lady-Birds and Eyes of Blue.

Cool As Ice (1991)   Feature stars white rap flash-in-the-pan Vanilla Ice as a traveling musician who falls for a high school honors student.

The Cool Mikado (1963)   British film with an appearance by the John Barry Seven.

Copenhagen Call Girls (1966)   Danish-made, squalid soft-core sex film with Danish instrumental combo the Sharks, who entertain a group of hookers and their johns while backing a girl singer, and provide Ventures-like incidental music throughout.

Corrupt (1983)   John Lydon co-starred in this violent psychological drama as a prisoner held by bad cop Harvey Keitel.

Cosmic Ray (1962)   Bruce Connor short set to Ray Charles's "What'd I Say?"

Cracking Up (1977)   Comedy about an earthquake with Fee Waybill and the Tubes performing "White Punks on Dope" and "Proud to Be an American."

Crazy Ridiculous American People (1976)   Mondo documentary of sex shops, mud wrestling, and male go-go dancers, with the Dictators singing "America the Beautiful." Alternate titles: *Jabberwalk* and *This Is America.*

Creature of Destruction (1968)   Grade-Z horror from the crazed director of *Beyond the Doors*, with garage solo guy Scotty McKay playing "Watch Out for the Batman" and Little Willie John's "All Around the World" at an outdoor club, then later a folk song on the beach before he is felled by the creature.

Cuckoo Patrol (1965)   Freddie and the Dreamers vehicle with the group dressing as Boy Scouts (!).

Cucumber Castle (1967)   Possibly unfinished Bee Gees project described in a 1967 BBC interview with drummer Vince Melouney as a 40-minute film starting with the band in the studio, then turning into a Camelot-era comedy. With songs from *Bee Gees First* album and guests Adam Faith and Lulu (later Mrs. Maurice Gibb). The 1970 *Cucumber Castle* album cover shows band in King Arthur costumes.

Cult of the Damned (1969)   Jordan Christopher of the Wild Ones (see *The Fat Spy*) as "Bogart" fronts a rock band that includes Roddy McDowall and Lou Rawls. Christopher worms his way into a wealthy family, seducing the teenage daughter (Holly Near) and her middle-aged mother (Jennifer Jones), and people start to die in gruesome ways. The plot resembles the Manson slayings, which were concurrent with the film's release. The songs are by Barry Mann/Cynthia Weil; the producer is Jerome Katzman, Sam's son. Not to be confused with *Guyana: Cult of the Damned*. Alternate title: *Angel Angel Down We Go*.

D'Ou Viens-Tu Johnny (1963)   Film vehicle for French rockabilly king Johnny Halliday.

Dateline Diamonds (1965)   British film about a diamond robber who blackmails a successful pop manager into smuggling his loot via a pirate radio ship. Musical talent includes the Chantelles, Kiki Dee, Mark Richardson, and the Small Faces, who perform in a Dutch nightclub. With British DJ Kenny Everett.

Days of Heaven (1978)   Doug Kershaw appears playing "Swamp Dance."

Daytona Beach Weekend (1965)   16mm production, shot on location during spring break. Del Shannon performs "Searching," "Runaway," and "Stranger in Town," and local acts the OffBeets ("Hey Little Girl"), Rayna Leggett ("Hopelessly"), and Houston & Dorsey (a Homer & Jethro-type country comedy duo) appear.

The Deadly Bees (1967)   British horror film with a great clip of mod band the Birds (Ronnie Wood on guitar) performing the unreleased "It's Not What I Need You For" in a a TV studio, followed by star Suzanna Leigh lip-synching to an Elkie Brooks track.

Deadman's Curve (1978)   TV biopic of Jan and Dean's rise and tragic fall, starring Richard Hatch and Bruce Davison. With Dick Clark, Wolfman Jack.

Dealing (1971)   John Lithgow plays a dope-smuggling Harvard student. Buzzy Linhart plays "Buzzy."

Death May Be Your Santa Claus (1969)   Short political fantasy directed by British Black Power leader Frankie Dymon, Jr., with an appearance by Second Hand.

Death Valley 69   R. Kern short made with Sonic Youth.

The Decline of Western Civilization (1981)   Penelope Spheeris's documentary captures the energy of L.A.'s unique punk-rock scene at its most furious, combining interviews of promoters and fanzine publishers (including Slash Records founder Bob Biggs) with in-the-pit concert footage worthy of any combat photographer. The lineup includes X, Black Flag (pre-Henry Rollins), Circle Jerks, Fear, the Germs, the Alice Bag Band, and Claude Bessy's group Catholic Discipline.

The Decline of Western Civilization Part II: The Metal Years (1988)   Penelope Spheeris's often-hilarious film showcases the inhabitants of L.A.'s then-burgeoning metal culture. Chris Holmes (of Wasp) gives a frightening poolside monologue, while Ozzy Osbourne, seen at home frying eggs, is charming. Also seen are Alice Cooper, Poison, and members of Aerosmith, KISS, and Motörhead. With live footage of Megadeth, Faster Pussycat, Lizzie Bordon, London, Odin, and Seduce.

The Delinquents (1957)   This JD movie with Tom Laughlin was the first film directed by Robert Altman. It includes Kansas City R&B singer Julia Lee belting out "Dirty Rock Boogie."

Devil Rider! (1970)   Florida-made biker film includes an appearance by Miami band Heroes of Cranberry Farm.

Diaries, Notes, and Sketches (1970) Jonas Mekas film that includes footage from *Psychiatrist's Convention EPI Show.*

Diary of a Mad Housewife (1970) Brilliant film of unhappy yuppie couple, with the Alice Cooper Band performing at a party and destroying their gear.

Digital Dreams (1983) Feature film by Bill and Astrid Wyman about Bill's life, with James Coburn and animated sequences.

The Dirty Dozen (1967) Rock god Trini Lopez acts and plays "The Bramble Bush."

Disco 9000 (1977) Obscure movie about a disco/record-label owner fighting the mob with music created by former Stax soul man Johnny Taylor (then riding high on the mega-success of "Disco Lady"). Taylor also appears as a producer.

Disk-O-Tek Holiday (1966) The U.S. re-edit of the British film *Just for You.* Mixed in with the British acts are the Chiffons ("Nobody Knows What's Goin' On"), the Vagrants, the Rockin' Ramrods ("Play It"), Freddie Cannon ("Tallahassee Lassie") backed by the Rockin' Ramrods, and Casey Paxton and Catherine Quine ("East Is East"), also backed by the Rockin' Ramrods!

Disco Fever (1979) German disco/sex comedy with performances by Boney M ("Rivers of Babylon"), Eruption, the Teens, and La Bionda.

Disorderlies (1987) "Three Stooges of rap" the Fat Boys star in this comedy farce and perform just one song: The Beatles' "Baby You're a Rich Man."

Doctor Detroit (1983) James Brown sings at a pimp's ball. Main title song by Devo.

Doctor, You've Got to Be Kidding (1967) Comedy with the Wild Affair performing a number at a club, then backing up star Sandra Dee.

Dogs in Space (1986) Michael Hutchence of INXS stars in this song-filled Australian film about the hedonistic lifestyle of the early punk scene in Melbourne.

Dracula AD 1972 (1972) Christopher Lee/Hammer horror flick with an appearance by Stoneground playing "Alligator Man" and "You Better Come Through." Score by Mike Vickers (ex-Manfred Mann).

Dragon (1993) Bruce Lee biopic has some people playing the Mamas and the Papas.

The Dream Makers (1975) Surprisingly downbeat TV movie starring James Franciscus as a college professor turned record executive. Actually pretty good. With Kenny Rogers and the First Edition.

Dreams of Glass (1969) Obscure film with the Smokestack Lightning, probably the same blues rock group that had an album on Bell Records.

Dudes (1987) Penelope Spheeris drama starring Red Hot Chili Pepper Flea as a doomed punker and Lee Ving as a mean villain. Hardcore band the Vandals appear in concert.

The Duke Wore Jeans (1958) Tommy Steele has hijinks with his double and a beautiful princess. Songs include "It's All Happening," "Happy Guitar," and "Hair Down Hoedown."

An Early Clue to a New Direction (1966) Underground short with an appearance by girl garage band the Unidentified Flying Objects playing "I'm a Woman."

Earth Girls Are Easy (1989)   Musical satire of '50s sci-fi films, with Miss Julie Brown singing some campy numbers.

East Is East (1966)   One-time title to *Disk-O-Tek Holiday*, or so we surmise from the record label info on Casey Paxton's 45 of the same name.

Easy Come, Easy Go   Aborted comedy film starring Mel Brooks, Terry-Thomas, and Jan and Dean.

Eat the Rich (1987)   British black comedy about a small band of revolutionaries serving human flesh in a posh restaurant. Co-starring Lemmy, whose band Motörhead is seen playing songs like "Dr. Rock" and "Orgasmatron." Cameos include Paul McCartney, Bill Wyman, Angie Bowie, Hugh Cornwall, Sandie Shaw, Jools Holland, and Miles Copeland.

Electra Glide in Blue (1973)   Record producer James William Guercio directed this police drama, co-wrote the score, and gave acting roles to Chicago members Peter Cetera and Terry Kath.

Elvis and Me (1987)   Dale Midkiff stars as the King in this TV movie/miniseries based on Priscilla Presley's book about their turbulent marriage. She exec-produced this one-sided account. Songs sung by Ronnie McDowell.

Elvis and the Beauty Queen (1981)   Don Johnson is Elvis in this TV movie about E.P.'s post-Priscilla affair with Linda Thompson. Singing dubbed by Ronnie McDowell.

The Emperor's New Clothes (1967)   Comedy film shot by *Porky's* auteur Bob Clark, starring John Caradine as the

Emperor and Spanky & Our Gang as "roving musical troubadours." The soundtrack was lost, and the film never got finished.

Erection (1972)   John and Yoko short of building construction.

Europa de Noche   Spanish documentary from the '50s about nightlife in European cities. In addition to looks at the Moulin Rouge and the Lido, there are scenes with the Platters and Colin Hicks y sus Reyes del Rock. English title: *Europe at Night*.

The Exotic Ones (1968)   Horror movie from Grade-Z auteur Ron Ormond about a pot-smoking monster terrorizing strippers. With rockabilly legend Sleepy LaBeef in a nonmusical role.

Falling from Grace (1992)   Directorial debut by John Cougar Mellencamp, who stars as a country singer visiting his Indiana hometown.

The Family Jewels (1965)   This Jerry Lewis tour-de-force includes a short scene with his son Gary Lewis and the Playboys doing "This Diamond Ring."

The Family Way (1966)   British story of newlyweds featuring a score by Paul McCartney.

Fans, Fans, Fans   Unreleased second film starring German group the Rattles (see *Hurra Die Rattles Kommen*).

Farewell Performance (1963)   British film about an unpopular singer who is murdered and then replaced by platinum-haired vocalist Heinz Burt. With the Tornadoes. Music written and produced by Joe Meek.

The Fastest Guitar Alive (1967)   Roy Orbison stars as a Confederate soldier who slings a rifle-guitar, robs a mint, and sings several original songs—including "Pisotolero," "Good Time Party," "Medicine Man, " and the title tune. With Sam the Sham as "First Expressman." Produced by Sam Katzman.

Feelin' Good (1966)   Independent, regionally released obscurity produced and directed in Boston by Jim Pike, a successful maker of industrial films and TV commercials. It stars his son Travis, interracial group the Montclairs, the Brattle St. East, and "folksinger Brenda Nichols" in a lighthearted story of romance and rock'n'roll. The Montclairs, who released a few rare singles, scored their part by winning the Massachusetts Jaycees' Battle of the Bands. Travis (who recorded a rare garage single with Travis Pike's Tea Party) wrote eight songs for the film, including "Watch Out, Woman," "Ute Ute," and the title song. Also heard are the Gershwin standard "Summertime" and Nichols's "Ride the Rainbow." The widescreen, color film was the only theatrical feature Pike Films ever made, and a 45 of the theme song was sold in theaters. A documentary short from the same company, "Demo Derby," was previously booked in theaters and also featured a theme song 45 (recorded by the Rondels).

Finders Keepers (1966)   Cliff Richard and the Shadows vehicle about a missing atom bomb. Songs include "My Way," "Time Drags By," "Washerwoman," "La La La Song," and the title tune.

Fingered   Graphic R. Kern short starring Lydia Lunch as a phone sex girl who meets wild-man client Marty Nation.

Fire in the Water (1977)   A filmmaker edits his film in a remote cottage while his girlfriend explores the surrounding country. The footage he views is from *Charlie Is My Darling*, *Tonite Let's All Make Love In London*, and other rock films made by this film's director, Peter Whitehead.

The Fish That Saved Pittsburgh (1979) Basketball comedy starring real players, with appearances by the Spinners and the Sylvers.

Five Minutes to Live (1961)   Rock gods Johnny Cash and Vic Tayback kidnap a banker's wife. Cash gets to sing "I've Come to Kill" and the title song, and country guitar giant Merle Travis plays a bowling alley proprietor. Re-released with added footage as *Door-To-Door Maniac*.

The Fly (1971)   Another Yoko/John artpiece, this one following a fly crawling across a girl's naked body. They also filmed the casting sessions.

Follow Me (1969)   Surfing movie about a worldwide search for the ultimate wave, with Dino, Desi & Billy. Briefly released on video as *Surf Party*.

Follow the Boys (1962)   Connie Francis film in which she sings the title song, "Sleepyland," "Waiting for Billy," and three more.

For Singles Only (1968)   Katzman youthfluff about the swinging goings-on in a singles apartment complex. Onscreen music provided by Cal Tjader, the Nitty Gritty Dirt Band, the Sunshine Company, and Colgems recording artists the Lewis and Clarke Expedition performing "Destination Unknown."

Forbidden Zone (1980)   Bizarre live-action film shot in the style of Max Fleischer animation, with Herve Villechaize as ruler of an underground kingdom. Songs by Danny Elfman and Oingo Boingo. Danny's brother Richard Elfman directs.

The Foreigner (1978) Underground film by Amos Poe about terrorist agent. Performances by the Cramps, Debbie Harry (who sings Brecht's "Bilbao Song"), and the Erasers. Music by Ivan Kral (Patti Smith Group).

Forever Young (1983) British drama of two former teenage rockers who meet up years later and reminisce.

Four Flies on Grey Velvet (1971) Italian horror film from Dario Argento starring Michael Brandon as a rock drummer caught up in blackmail and murder.

Four Stars (****) (1967) Andy Warhol feature with Nico in several roles.

Foxes (1979) Former Runaway Cherie Currie stars, Adam Faith plays Jodie Foster's concert-promoter father, and white-costumed metal band Angel appear performing "Virginia."

Free, White, and 21 (1962) Drama about the interracial rape of a Swedish girl in the South. Joe Johnson and his Orchestra play "The Hobo Twist" in an all-black nightclub.

The Freshman (1990) A mafia comedy with Was Not Was appearing as a wedding band, backing Bert Parks on "Maggie's Farm."

Gamera This famous Japanese monster flick has a short but enjoyable scene of a Jap Ventures-type group in a teen club refusing to flee monster and then getting stomped.

Gang of Souls (1988) Documentary on the impact of the '50s beat generation with Richard Hell, Lydia Lunch, Marianne Faithfull, and Jim Carroll, as well as the expected William S. Burroughs and Allen Ginsberg.

Gas-s-s-s (1970) Roger Corman's hippie sci-fi satire with Country Joe McDonald as "F.M. Radio," emceeing a concert and singing "World That We All Dreamed Of." Also seen performing are star Robert Corff, the Gourmet's Delight, and Johnny and the Tornadoes.

Geek Maggot Bingo (1983) Gory underground horror film by cult director Nick Zedd starring Richard Hell and DJ/horror host Zacherley.

Ghosts of the Civil Dead (1988) Nick Cave stars in this weird Australian film about a three-tiered desert prison that's a cesspool of hate.

Gidget (1959) James Darren sings "The Next Best Thing to Love," and the Four Preps sing "Cinderella" in the first entry in this venerable beach-fun series.

Girl in Gold Boots (1968) T.V. Mikels flick about a voluptuous waitress who becomes a go-go dancer in the same "dragon's mouth" nightclub seen in *It's a Bikini World* (and featured on the jacket of Pat and Lolly Vegas's *At The Haunted House*). Chris Howard and the Third World are seen performing several songs, including "Cowboy Santa" and "Minnie Shimmy."

The Girl, the Body, and the Pill (1967) Another H.G. Lewis classic about bad kids vs. good kids. Chicago garage-band the Fly-By-Nites appear at a barbecue playing live.

Godspell (1973) Filmed version of one entry in the religious rock opera sweepstakes, with the hit "Day by Day" and many more.

Goin' Coconuts (1978) Rock deities Donny and Marie Osmond travel to Hawaii, get mixed up with diamond smugglers, and sing several songs. Sadly, none are from the ass-kicking *Crazy Horses* album.

The Gold Guitar (1966)   New York gangsters go to Nashville to discover the secret of the Sound (but the film's really shot in Atlanta). With Del Reeves, Skeeter Davis, Hugh X. Lewis, Roy Drusky, and more.

Good to Go (1986)   Art Garfunkel stars as a reporter covering crime within Washington, D.C.'s "go-go" funk music scene. This movie was produced by Island Records' film division in an attempt to popularize a musical subcult (see *The Harder They Come*), but go-go remained a local phenomenon. With Trouble Funk, Redds and the Boys, and Chuck Brown and the Soul Searchers.

Grease 2 (1982)   More campy '50s music in this bomb sequel, minus the stars of the original.

The Groove Tube (1974)   Satirical skits of fictitious TV programming with Buzzy Linhart singing "Fingers." Also with an early appearance by former Chameleon Church drummer Chevy Chase.

The Gun Is Loaded (1989)   Underground film starring Lydia Lunch, who addresses the state of America and attacks everyone.

The Guru (1969)   Early film from the Merchant/Ivory team (*Howard's End*) about British pop star Michael York who temporarily escapes his frenzied life to study sitar in India. An Indian garage band plays "Somebody To Love" and an original song at a party, and another Indian rock combo plays an instrumental at a beauty contest. A psychological study that's not as lightweight as it sounds.

The Gutter Girls (1964)   British film with an appearance by Merseybeat group the

Embers. Alternate titles: *The Thrill Seekers* and *The Yellow Teddybears*.

Hanging Out (1985)   German teen flick starring Nena ("99 Luftballons").

Hard to Hold (1984)   Aussie-born Rick Springfield, whose recording career dates back to the late '60s, was a soap-opera heartthrob when he got his first starring film role in this musical melodrama.

Harry and Ringo's Night Out (1974)   Short with Harry Nilsson and Ringo Starr.

The Heartbreakers (1983)   Nostalgic comedy from West Germany about four German youths buying guitars and forming a band, Die Heartbreakers, in the wake of Beatlemania.

Heathers (1989)   Great black comedy featuring the song "Teenage Suicide—Don't Do It" (by Big Fun), which becomes a huge hit after the apparent suicides of several high school co-eds. The track was recorded by Don Dixon, Mitch Easter, Angie Carlson, and Marti Jones.

Heaven Tonight (1993)   Australian drama of a father-and-son rock band. Music by Warren Zevon.

Heavy Petting (1989)   Documentary look at instructional dating films from the '50s and '60s, with commentary from celebrities, including Hall and Oates, David Byrne, Laurie Anderson, and Ann Magnuson.

Hell's Angels '69   A.I.P. biker film with loungey rock band the Stream of Consciousness.

Hell's Angels Forever (1983)   Documentary on the cycle gang, produced by the Angels themselves in a bid for good PR. Bo Diddley performs at a biker gathering.

The Hellions (1962)   Marty Wilde co-stars and sings the title song.

Heroes and Villains (1992)   TV movie based on the Beach Boys biography of the same title.

Hey Boy! Hey Girl! (1959)   Louis Prima, Keely Smith, and Sam Butera and the Witnesses star in this tale of a band helping out at a church bazaar. Songs include "A Banana Split for My Baby" and "Oh Marie."

Hi-Way (1969)   35mm featurette about a hitchhiker, co-directed by Jim Morrison.

Hollywood Boulevard (1976)   Corman-produced self-satire of drive-in movies with an appearance by Commander Cody and the Lost Planet Airmen.

Homer (1970)   Canadian production about a misunderstood rock group leader (Don Scardino) relating to his parents and his best friends. Soundtrack music by Led Zeppelin, the Byrds, Cream, and others.

The Hooked Generation (1968)   Dope smuggling melodrama with Steve Alaimo as an informant and an appearance by the Bangles (no, not those Bangles).

Hootnanny Hoot (1963)   A TV exec plans a country/folk music program in this Katzman package featuring Johnny Cash, the Brothers Four, Judy Henske, Sheb Wooley, the Gateway Trio, George Hamilton IV, Joe and Eddie, Cathie Taylor, and Chris Crosby.

Hot Rods to Hell   Inadvertently hilarious JD movie with an appearance by Mickey Rooney, Jr., and his Combo, sort of a poor man's Bobby Fuller Four. They play a couple of songs in the background at a teen club.

Hound-Dog Man (1959)   Fabian stars in this country-set romance and sings "I'm Growing Up," "Hayfoot, Strawfoot," "Single," and many more.

How Does It Feel? (1976)   Documentary about the human senses with footage of an Elkie Brooks recording session and soundtrack music by Pink Floyd and Jack Nitzsche.

How I Won the War (1967)   Confusing, very-British World War II satire from Beatles director Richard Lester, co-starring John Lennon as Private Gripweed. Lennon wound up keeping the wire-frame glasses from his costume.

How to Commit Marriage (1969)   Bob Hope comedy with an appearance by the Comfortable Chair, whose Ode Records album was produced by John Densmore and Robby Krieger.

Hurra Die Rattles Kommen (1965)   *A Hard Day's Night*-type feature following German beat group the Rattles on a tour of Denmark.

I a Man (1967)   Andy Warhol film with Nico.

I Am a Groupie (1970)   British film about a girl taking off in a pop band's van and leaving her dull life behind. With the Opal Butterfly (a band that once included Lemmy from Motörhead) singing "You're a Groupie Girl" and "Gigging Song." Also appearing are the Sweaty Betty. Directed by Derek Ford.

I Was a Teenage Mummy   Low-budget film with the A-Bones performing "Mum's the Word."

I'll Take Sweden (1965)   Bob Hope comedy with Frankie Avalon and an appearance by Swedish group the Vulcanes.

I'm a Groupie (1970)   European softcore sex film partially directed by Jack Hill (not to be confused with *I Am a Groupie*). The credits list Fred Williams as director and say "presented by Roger Corman," which later led to a financial settlement with Corman.

I've Gotta Horse (1965)   Billy Fury picture about a racehorse he actually owned. This songfest includes "I've Gotta Horse," "I Like Animals" (obviously!), and backup group the Gamblers doing "I Cried All Night."

Idle on Parade (1959)   Anthony Newley stars as Jeep Idle, an Elvis-like rock star who gets drafted. Songs include "Idle Rock-a-Boogie" *and* "Saturday Night Rock-a-Boogie."

If It's Tuesday, This Must Be Belgium (1969) Donovan sings "Lord of the Reedy River" in a youth hostel. Beware TV cuts!

The Image   Arty short film circa 1969 that stars David Bowie as the ghost of an artist's model. The part mostly consisted of standing outside a window under a simulated rainfall, and Bowie caught a cold in the process.

Imitation of Christ (1970)   Andy Warhol film with Nico.

The "In" Crowd (1988)   A look at an "American Bandstand"-type dance show, starring Donovan Leitch (Junior).

The Incredibly Strange Creatures Who Stopped Living and Became Crazy Mixed-Up Zombies (1964)   Among the songs heard in Ray Dennis Steckler's infamous "monster musical" are "The Mixed-Up Zombie Stomp."

Injun Fender   Obscure indie feature about a Native American rock musician/murderer. Music by the Magic Tramp Midnight Opera Company. Produced by Duke University's Department of Foreign Language.

Inner Scar (1971)   Big budget experimental film shot in Cinemascope, with Nico walking across exotic locales and singing music from her *Desert Shore* album.

Intimacy (1966)   Jackie De Shannon plays a hooker in this tawdry blackmail drama.

Into the Night (1985)   Cameo-filled John Landis adventure with David Bowie as a convincing villain and Carl Perkins as a bodyguard who gets into a vicious fight with him.

Invocation of My Demon Brother (1969) Satan-worshipping Kenneth Anger short includes original footage of the Rolling Stones at their Hyde Park concert and a synth score by Mick Jagger.

It Couldn't Happen Here   Murder mystery starring the Pet Shop Boys.

It's All Happening (1962)   Tommy Steele, Shane Fenton and the Fentones, John Barry, the Clyde Valley Stompers, Marion Ryan, and more U.K. acts entertain in this story of a record label putting on a fundraising concert.

It's All Over Town (1963)   British film about a stage worker daydreaming of acts he'd like to see. With Acker Bilk, the Springfields (including Dusty), the Bachelors, the Hollies ("Now's the Time"), and Wayne Gibson and the Dynamite Sounds.

J.D.'s Revenge (1976)   Funny blaxploitation film with an early appearance by none other than Prince, who sings "I Will Never Let You Go."

The Jacksons: An American Dream (1992) Jacksons-approved TV miniseries about the musical family following its long career from Gary, Indiana, through Motown to Michael's superstardom. There's no mention of any *serious* family problems.

The Jazz Singer (1980) This modern version of the Jolson relic finds Neil Diamond as the nice Jewish boy who abandons cantorial singing to wear blackface and rock out. Sir Laurence Olivier gives an outrageous, scenery-chomping performance as Diamond's *Yiddishe* papa. Songs include "My Name is Yussel" and "Kol Nidre" (which was once given a psychedelic treatment by the Electric Prunes), in addition to the smash hits.

Jenny, Wife, Child (1968) Rural sex comedy filmed in 1965 as *Tender Grass*. A new theme song was added, performed onscreen by Davie Allan and the Arrows, who also contribute instrumental music.

John & Yoko: A Love Story (1989) This TV movie, with a script approved by Yoko, has a somewhat biased view of life with the Lennons. It covers their relationship from their first meeting to its tragic conclusion. In one scene, John observes that the B-52s and "all these new bands" sound like Yoko's old records. Decent performances by the leads. The original actor set to play John was nixed when Yoko learned his name was Chapman.

Jovenes de la Zona Roja (1966) Mexican production with juvenile delinquents, bikers, go-go girls, and appearances by Los Johnny Jets and Los Max. English title: *Teenagers from the Red Zone*.

Jovenes y Rebeldes Mexican juvenile delinquent movie with a guest appearance by Bill Haley and the Comets, who perform a few songs.

Junior High School (1977) Musical featurette about teen romance, shot on location at Van Nuys Junior High School with actual students, among them 14-year-old Paula Abdul.

Just for the Hell of It (1968) Herschell Gordon Lewis movie about nihilist teenagers who enjoy destroying property. A garage band that includes Lewis's son Robert on guitar plays a frantic, fuzzed-out instrumental in a South Side Miami bar called the Ale House. Robert also wrote the music to the haunting folk-rock theme song "Destruction Inc." (Dad wrote the words as "Sheldon Seymour"), sung by Tary Rebenar and heard repeatedly. The cast includes two garage musicians from *Blast-Off Girls*, Steve White (of Benedict Arnold and the Traitors, Charlie, and Capitol recording artists Food) and Faded Blue drummer Ralph Mullin.

Just for You (1964) British potpourri of songs framed by DJ Sam Costa, who is shown watching the performances on TV. Acts on hand include Peter and Gordon ("Leave Me Alone," "Soft as the Dawn"), Freddie and the Dreamers ("Just for You," "You Were Made for Me"), Millie Small ("Sugar Dandy"), the Merseybeats ("Milkman"), The Warriors (with Jon Anderson of Yes doing "Don't Make Me Blue"), Band of Angels, the Orchids, Doug Sheldon, Roy Sone, Johnny B. Great, the Applejacks, and more. Some of this footage appeared in the U.S. film *Disk-O-Tek Holiday*.

Kill Me Tomorrow (1957) British thriller with an appearance by Tommy Steele as himself playing "Rebel Rock."

Killers Three (1968) Dick Clark plays an explosives expert who plans a robbery and becomes a murderer. Merle Haggard acts and performs with the Strangers.

The King of Comedy (1983)   In one very brief scene, all four members of the Clash supposedly play "street trash" who bother Sandra Bernhard (but I can't really identify them, even with digital freeze-frame!).

Knights of the City (1985)   Action film about Miami street gang the Royals, who are also a pop group. With the Fat Boys and Smokey Robinson.

Kona Coast (1967)   Hawaiian melodrama with Duane Eddy as "Tiger Cat."

Krush Groove (1985)   This all-star rap story parallels the rise of Def Jam Records. With Run-DMC, the Fat Boys, Sheila E., Kurtis Blow, and 16-year-old L.L. Cool J. as an auditioning rapper, plus record execs Russell Simmons and Rick Rubin as themselves, more or less.

L.A., My Home Town (1977)   Music historian, DJ, and one-hit-wonder Ian Whitcomb presents a travelogue of Los Angeles's British community. He sings "You Turn Me On" and visits Peter Asher.

La Dolce Vita (1959)   Fellini classic including a 15-year-old Nico, who sneaked onto the set while vacationing in Rome, and an unnamed Italian rock band, who put their stamp on "Ready Teddy."

Las Automatas de la Muerte (1963)   Mexican wrestler/sci-fi epic, with mat-king Neutron fighting death robots. Nightclub scenes with Los Rebeldes de Rock, Trio Los Diamantes, and Los Tres Ases. English title: *Robots of Death.*

Las Sicodelicas (1968)   Wild Peruvian movie about a group of girls who start a protection racket to raise money for their dorm mother and kill anybody who won't pay up. Complete with surfing, bowling, and wrestlers. Surf-rock band Los Shains play "Felicidada," "Adoro," and "Cuando Estoy Contigo." English title: *The Psychedelic Ones.*

Leadbelly (1976)   Roger E. Mosely portrays Huddie Ledbetter, the troubled pioneer of country blues and popularizer of the 12-string guitar. Songs (sung by Hi-Tide Harris) include "Rock Island Line" and "The Midnight Special." Directed by Gordon Parks.

The Lemon Grove Kids Meet the Monster (1966)   Ray Dennis Steckler's Bowery Boys spoof co-stars rocker Ron Haydock, but his musical scenes were cut.

Leningrad Cowboys Go America (1990)   Finnish comedy about a rock group that travels to the U.S. in search of fame and fortune, instead finding wedding gigs and the seamy side of American life.

Let's Make Love (1960)   Marilyn Monroe musical with a scene of auditions for Elvis imitators. One hopeful is Dick Dale.

Lethal Pursuit (1989)   Mitzi Kapture stars as a rocker who gets stalked on vacation.

Lisztomania (1975)   Ken Russell's crazed, rock version of the life of Franz Liszt, starring Roger Daltrey as the flamboyant composer. With Ringo Starr as the Pope and Rick Wakeman, who also arranged the music.

Little Malcolm (1974)   John Hurt stars in drama about a confused student revolutionary—the first film executive-produced by George Harrison. Dark Horse recording artists Splinter appear singing "Lonely Man." Alternate title: *Little Malcolm and His Struggle against the Eunuchs.*

The Lively Set (1964)   James Darren plays a Bonneville race car driver in this follow-up to *For Those Who Think Young.* Joanie Sommers appears singing "If You Love Him" and "Casey Wake Up," and the soundtrack includes the Surfaris' "Boss Barracuda." Songs written by Bobby Darin, Terry Melcher, and Randy Newman.

Living Legend (1980)   Earl Owensby stars as an Elvis-like rocker, lip-synching songs recorded for the film by Roy Orbison.

The Lone Ranger (1968)   A prizewinning student film with otherwise unavailable instrumental numbers contributed by Pete Townshend.

Look In Any Window (1960)   Paul Anka stars as a teenage peeping tom who's the product of an alcoholic dad and a promiscuous mom. Anka also sings his self-penned title song.

Looking for Love (1964)   Connie Francis musical about a singing switchboard operator. She performs "Let's Have a Party" and many more.

Los Chicos con las Chicas (1967)   Spanish feature vehicle for that country's top group, Los Bravos.

Lost Angels (1989)   Adam Horovitz of the Beastie Boys stars as a troubled teenager.

Made (1972)   British unwed mother drama with Roy Harper as a horny folksinger. Harper performs some original songs.

Made in Heaven (1987)   Alan Rudolph film with cameos by Neil Young, Tom Petty, and Ric Ocasek.

Made in U.S.A. (1966)   Jean-Luc Godard film with Marianne Faithful singing an a capella "As Tears Go By" in a cafe.

Mad Max: Beyond Thunderdome (1985)   Mel Gibson post-apocalyptic adventure co-starring Tina Turner as Auntie Entity, ruler of Bartertown.

The Man Behind the Beatles (1966)   It's not Brian Epstein or George Martin, but Richard Lester, in this promotional short for *How I Won the War.*

Married to the Mob (1988)   With cameos by Chris Isaak, David Johansen, and Sister Carol.

Masculin-Feminin (1966)   Jean-Luc Godard film with a scene of the recording session for a French pop hit.

A Matter of Degrees (1991)   Dramatic comedy about a soul-searching college DJ at graduation time, with cameos by John Doe and the B-52s.

Medium Cool (1969)   With an appearance by garage band the Litter, who are seen playing but not heard (Mothers of Invention music was dubbed over them).

Menudo...La Pelicula   Comedy musical starring the interchangeable Latin teen group.

The Minx (1969)   Dull sex/crime caper film with an entire soundtrack by the Cyrkle, including a few vocal songs (the soundtrack LP amounted to the third and final Cyrkle LP). The band appears doing the wonderful "Murray the Why" dressed in Sgt. Pepper gear. The film's release was delayed for two years.

The Model Shop (1969)   L.A.-set film from French director Jacques Demy has Jay Ferguson as "Jay" and rehearsing with his band Spirit.

Mods and Rockers (1966)   Short film with the Cheynes performing three Beatles songs, plus staged fights between the title characters. *Mods and Rockers* is one of the films included in the compilation *Go-Go Big Beat.*

Mondo New York (1988)   Documentary that intercuts various arty New Wave performers with faked scenes of shocking street life in the Big Apple. With Joey Arias, John Sex, Dean and the Weenies, Phoebe Legere, Lydia Lunch, and Ann Magnuson.

Money-Go-Round (1967)   Educational short sponsored by the London Stock Exchange. The Koobas perform "Ballad of the Stock Exchange," "Champagne and Caviar," "The Stocktaking Stockbroker," and the title song.

Mongoloid   Experimental short film by avant-garde director Bruce Connor, set to the Devo song, before the band had any records out. Not the promo clip.

The Monkey's Uncle (1965)   Disney comedy with a great main title sequence featuring Annette Funicello and the Beach Boys performing the title song.

Monster a Go Go (1965)   Herschell Gordon Lewis bought the sci-fi film *Terror in Halfday* and then added a few scenes, including people dancing to the band the Other Three, who are barely seen behind the gyrating throng. The Other Three also recorded the trash-rock title song.

The Monster Club (1981)   Vincent Price stars in this multi-episode horror film set in a monster disco. Appearances by the Pretty Things (doing the title tune), B.A. Robertson, and Night.

The Moonshine War (1970)   With Joe Williams and Lee Hazelwood in acting roles.

More (1969)   Barbet Schroeder film with a score by Pink Floyd.

More American Graffiti (1979)   Country Joe and the Fish play "I-Feel-Like-I'm Fixin'-to-Die Rag," Doug Sahm performs "I'm a Man" and "The Race is On," and Wolfman Jack appears in this sequel to *American Graffiti.*

Motorama (1993)   Small parts for Meat Loaf, Flea.

Mr. Mike's Mondo Video (1979)   Michael O'Donoghue's theatrically released comedy special with Debbie Harry, the "My Way" footage from *The Great Rock'n'Roll Swindle,* and New Wave opera singer Klaus Nomi.

Murderers' Row (1967)   Dean Martin's second Matt Helm spy spoof includes his son's band Dino, Desi & Billy performing "If You're Thinking What I'm Thinking."

Musical Mutiny (1970)   A pirate returns from the dead to find a pirate-themed amusement park where his old hideout used to be. Posing as a park official, he turns the day's concert by Iron Butterfly into a free event, causing the band to walk off until they get paid. A rich hippie saves the day, and the band plays "In-a-Gadda-Da-Vida," "Soul Experience," and "In the Time of Our Lives." Also includes appearances by South Florida bands Fantasy, the New Society Band, and the Grit. The trailer for this obscure drive-in film made no mention of the silly plot.

The Name of the Game Is Kill! (1968) Strange drama starring Jack Lord and the transvestite from *Head.* The Electric Prunes appear doing "Shadows," a great psych song that was only released on a one-sided promo single.

Nashville Rebel (1966)   Waylon Jennings stars as a singing veteran battling the bottle. With Tex Ritter, Sonny James, Faron Young, Loretta Lynn, Porter Wagoner, the Wilburn Brothers, and Henny Youngman.

The Nashville Sound (1970)   A singer arrives in Music City hoping to be discovered. Performances by Johnny Cash, Doug Kershaw, Bob Luman, Bobby Goldsboro, and Tracy Nelson and Mother Earth.

Ned Kelly (1970)   Mick Jagger stars as an Australian outlaw, and sings "The Wild Colonial Boy."

Neutron Contra El Dr. Caronte (1962)   Mexican film in the Neutron wrestler series with appearances by Trio Los Diamantes and Los Tres Ases. English title: *Neutron Versus Dr. Caronte.*

Neutron el Enmascardo Negro (1962)   Film debut of Mexico's black-masked wrestler superhero with appearances by Trio Los Diamantes and Los Tres Ases. English title: *Nuetron the Black Mask.*

Never Too Young to Rock (1975)   TV talent scouts investigate a plethora of English glitter-pop bands, among them Mud, the Glitter Band, the Rubettes, and Slik (with future Ultravox vocalist Midge Ure). With Peter Noone.

New York Stories (1989)   Peter Gabriel has a cameo in the Scorsese segment, and toy-instrument band Pianosaurus play at a rich kids' party in the Coppola segment.

Nightmare in Wax (1969)   Awful horror film with an appearance by the T-Bones.

No Surrender (1986)   Elvis Costello has a cameo as a bad magician in this charming British film.

Nothing But the Best (1964)   Alan Bates comedy with an appearance by British instrumental band the Eagles.

The Offenders (1980)   Super-8mm retelling of the Patty Hearst saga from underground filmmakers Scott and Beth B, originally presented as a weekly serial at Max's Kansas City. Starring Adele Bertei, John Lurie, Lydia Lunch, Kristian Hoffman, and other musicians from New York's No Wave elite, including members of the Contortions, DNA, and the Bush Tetras.

Oh Alfie (1975)   Quasi-sequel to *Alfie* starring Alan Price, who also contributed the score.

Old Boyfriends (1978)   John Belushi plays an aging rock singer whose drummer is Jim Keltner.

Once Upon a Coffeehouse (1965)   Miami-shot romance about a singing coffeehouse waitress. With Karen Thorsell, the Goldebriars, the Freewheelers, and Jim, Jake, and Joan.

One P.M. (1969)   Jean-Luc Godard began a political film called *One A.M.* with D.A. Pennebaker and then abandoned it. Pennebaker added footage to the film of Godard at work and called it this. With footage of the Jefferson Airplane.

Otley (1969)   British spy spoof with a ridiculously short appearance by the Herd (with Peter Frampton).

Out of Bounds (1986)   Anthony Michael Hall thriller has two brief bands-in-club scenes with Siouxsie and the Banshees ("Cities In Dust") and Tommy Keene ("Run Now").

Paint Your Wagon (1969)   Musical with the Nitty Gritty Dirt Band performing

"Hand Me That Can o' Beans" with honorary rock star Lee Marvin.

Parachute to Paradise   With an appearance by Boston group the Bagatelle (featuring scene legend Willie Alexander, post-the Lost).

The Patsy (1964)   Jerry Lewis sings the rock parody "I Lost My Heart in a Drive-In Movie." With DJ/rock TV host Lloyd Thaxton.

Patti and Valli (1973)   Short film of Patti Smith getting her kneecap tattooed.

Peggy Sue Got Married (1986)   Francis Ford Coppola's comedy about Kathleen Turner returning to her high school days, where future husband Nicholas Cage has a Fabian fixation and badly wants to be a rock singer. It all starts at her high school reunion, where the cameo musicians are Marshall Crenshaw and his band. They play "You Belong to Me," "The Stroll," "I Ran All the Way Home," and other hits of 1959.

Pelvis (1975)   Comedic send up of Elvis Presley.

The People Next Door (1970)   Suburban-daughter-on-acid drama with appearances by the Bead Game ("Sweet Medusa," "My Life in Review") and the Glass Bottle ("Mama, Don't You Wait Up for Me").

Percy (1971)   Score by the Kinks includes rock-jam instrumentals as well as several specially written songs.

A Perfect Couple (1979)   Robert Altman comedy about a mismatched computer date between straight-laced guy and rock singer Marta Heflin, whose rock-fusion band Keepin' 'Em Off the Streets performs throughout.

Permanent Record (1988)   Drama of teenagers, some of whom are in a rock band. Lou Reed makes a cameo appearance in a recording studio.

Permissive (1970)   British drama of groupies with appearances by Forever More.

Petulia (1968)   Classic Richard Lester film set in San Francisco, with brief appearances by the nascent Big Brother and the Holding Company and the Grateful Dead.

The Phynx (1970)   The Super Secret Agency puts together a rock group to rescue kidnapped show-biz stars from Albanian communists. The unbelievable cast of cameo stars includes James Brown, Trini Lopez, Dick Clark, Rudy Vallee, Leo Gorcey, and Colonel Sanders.

Pickup on 101 (1972)   Hitchhiking girl and hobo take off with rock star played by Martin Sheen.

The Pied Piper (1972)   Jacques Demy's scary version of the classic fable, starring Donovan as the musical rat-catcher. Donovan also wrote the music.

Pipe Dreams (1976)   A romance starring Gladys Knight, with music by the Pips.

The Plastic Dome of Norma Jean (1966) Obscure independent film shot in the Ozarks, about a 15-year-old girl and a rock star who start a tent show featuring the girl's clairvoyant powers. With Sam Waterston and Marco St. John.

Platinum High School (1960)   Mickey Rooney drama with Conway Twitty and Jimmy Boyd.

Play Misty for Me (1971)   Jazz DJ Clint Eastwood witnesses appearances by the

Johnny Otis Show and Cannonball Adderley.

The Playgirl Killer (1965)   Canadian movie about a deranged painter who kills models who won't stand still. J.B. and the Playboys perform "Leave My Woman Alone," then back up Neil Sedaka on "If You Don't Wanna, You Don't Hafta" and "Do The Waterbug." Alternate title: *Decoy for Terror.*

Please Stand By (1972)   Lennon hanger-on David Peel stars as a New York activist using stolen radio equipment for pirate broadcasts. With "Dylanologist" A.J. Weberman.

Pop Down (1968)   Psychedelic sci-fi about visiting aliens starring Zoot Money as Sagittarius and Andy Ellison (of John's Children) as Mr. Love. With music by Brian Auger, the Idle Race, Dantalion's Chariot, and Blossom Toes.

Portrait of a Woman Drinker   German film with Nina Hagen.

The President's Analyst (1967)   Brilliant satire with scenes of Barry McGuire as the Old Wrangler singing "Inner Manipulations" and the Clear Light playing "She's Ready to Be Free" in the Cafe Wha?. The home video version replaces both songs with modern approximations of sixties music.

The Prime Time (1958)   Early Herschell Gordon Lewis film about restless teenagers and a beatnik artist. With Karen Black and an unnamed rockabilly band playing "She's a Teenage Tiger" in a club.

Primitive London (1965)   Mondo tour of swinging London with strippers, key-swap parties, and mods and rockers, plus Billy J. Kramer.

The Private Lives of Adam and Eve (1960) Paul Anka sings in this notorious Albert Zugsmith-made "all-star" sex farce.

Psycho a Go-Go! (1965)   Al Adamson horror movie with an appearance by the Vendells.

Pufnstuf (1970)   Feature version of the Krofft TV kiddie show with Mama Cass as Witch Hazel.

Punk Rock (1979)   Hardcore porno film with non-sexual scenes of black punk rockers Pure Hell and Neon Leon, plus the Fast performing at Max's Kansas City.

Purple People Eater (1988)   Children meet a monster and form a band in this film loosely based on the 1958 Sheb Wooley song. Little Richard plays the mayor and Chubby Checker is a singer.

Radio On (1977)   German film about a London DJ investigating his brother's death. Sting appears as an Eddie Cochran-obsessed mechanic and sings Cochran's "Teenage Heaven."

Rappin' (1985)   Gang drama/rap musical starring Mario Van Peebles. With Ice-T.

Rat Fink (1965)   The story of a rock singer's ruthless rise with appearances by the Futuras (possibly an Ohio garage group) and Don Snyder.

Repo Man (1984)   Ska band the Untouchables appear as the Scooter Boys and get their car repossessed by Emilio Estevez. The Circle Jerks do a lounge band rendition of their old song "When the Shit Hits the Fans." Incidental music by the Plugz, plus a cameo by Rodney Bingenheimer.

Return to Waterloo (1985)   Ray Davies's directorial debut is a 61-minute musical fantasy thriller about a businessman day-dreaming on his daily train. Ray also stars and wrote eight songs.

Rhythm'n'Greens (1964)   Robert Morley narrates the history of England, told through skits and songs by the Shadows (minus Cliff Richard). Tunes include "The Lute Number," "Ranka Chank," and the title number.

Riding High (1981)   Zoot Money acts in this film starring British stunt motorcyclist Eddie Kidd.

Roadside Prophets (1993)   Road movie starring John Doe (from X) and Adam Horovitz (from the Beastie Boys) as two motorcycling truth-seekers. Includes a cameo by Arlo Guthrie.

Robert Having His Nipple Pierced (1973)   Robert is Mapplethorpe, in this accurately titled documentary with a voiceover by Patti Smith, reminiscing about her past.

Rock'n'Roll Mom (1988)   Dyan Cannon stars in this TV movie about a mother who becomes a rock star to the embarassment of her kids. With Waddy Wachtel.

Rock and Rule (1986)   Animated fable of post-apocalyptic society with voiceovers by Iggy Pop, Debbie Harry, and Cheap Trick. Music by Lou Reed and others.

Rock and Torah (1983)   French film about a 30-year-old man who leaves his parents' store to enter showbiz—by forming the eponymous combo, who monopolize the Jewish wedding band market with reggae versions of Jewish folk songs. I didn't make this one up!

Rock-a-Bye Baby (1958)   Jerry Lewis sings "Rock My Baby Rock" with a Comets-lookalike band in plaid coats. He also does "In the Land of La La La" with his 12-year-old son, Gary, the future Playboy.

Rockabye (1972)   National Film Board of Canada short about the business of rock. Seen are the Rolling Stones at the Montreal Forum, the Stampeders in the studio, Michel Pagliaro on a TV show, Ronnie Hawkins, hard rock group Crowbar, and a burned-out Zal Yanovsky giving an expletive-filled account of why he was thrown out of the Lovin' Spoonful.

Rockers (1978)   Jamaican session drummer Leroy "Horsemouth" Wallace takes on some crooks after getting his bike stolen (shades of *The Harder They Come*). With Big Youth, the Mighty Diamonds, Gregory Isaacs, Robbie Shakespeare, Dillinger, Prince Hammer, Jacob Miller, Errol Brown, and Jack Ruby.

Rockin' Road Trip (1985)   Comedy about a Boston band traveling through the South, with an appearance by Guadalcanal Diary. Music by Love Tractor and Pylon.

Rocktober Blood (1984)   An executed rock star returns from the grave, seeking vengeance against his old bandmates.

Rockula (1990)   Musical comedy about a love-starved vampire. With Bo Diddley, Thomas Dolby, and Toni Basil.

Roller Boogie (1979)   Linda Blair stars in a roller-disco update of the old-folks-closing-down-the-kids'-hang-out plot.

Rollercoaster (1977)   Sensurround disaster movie with an amusement park concert by Sparks during the climactic chase scene, but few close-ups of the band.

Rome '78 (1978)   Latter-day underground film starring No Wave personalities Lydia Lunch and James Chance in a parody of spectacle films.

Rumble on the Docks (1956)   James Darren melodrama with an appearance by Freddie Bell and the Bellboys playing "Get the First Train Out of Town."

Run Home Slow (1965)   Latter-day B western with a score by Frank Zappa.

Run with the Wind (1966)   Shawn Phillips plays a singer-songwriter in a love triangle; with appearances by the Nashville Teens and Hedgehoppers Anonymous.

The Running Man (1987)   Arnold Schwarzenegger film with Mick Fleetwood as an aged resistance leader.

Salsa (1988)   Ex-Menudo member Robby Rosa stars in this Latino version of *Dirty Dancing*.

Salvation! (1987)   Former underground filmmaker Beth B directed this drama of a phony TV evangelist. Exene Cervenka (of X) plays one of the believers.

Salmonberries (1992)   Canadian drama starring K..D. Lang as a young woman flirting with lesbianism.

Satan's Bed (1965)   Weird exploitation film about a sunglassed teen gang that rapes women and kills them for kicks. A young Yoko Ono appears as a kidnapping victim.

Saturday Night Out (1963)   British story about sailors on leave with an appearance by the Searchers.

Scandal (1989)   Small acting part for Roland Gift of the Fine Young Cannibals.

Scenes from the Goldmine (1987)   A female songwriter falls for a rock singer and joins

his band but finds she is being used. With Fee Waybill.

Scott Joplin (1977)   Motown Films production with Taj Mahal, the Commodores, and Denise Gordy as a hooker.

Scream for Help (1986)   Thriller featuring a soundtrack by Led Zeppelin bassist and keyboardist John Paul Jones.

Senior Prom   A teenager makes a hit record and appears on Ed Sullivan. With Louis Prima, Keely Smith, Sam Butera and the Witnesses, Mitch Miller, Toni Arden, and Tom "Billy Jack" Laughlin.

Sergeant Deadhead (1965)   Frankie Avalon and the rest of the beach party gang appear in this wacky tale of chimpanzees in space. Donna Loren sings "Two Timin' Angel" in a nightclub and "How Can You Tell" in a WACS barracks with a bunch of comely recruits.

Sex Kittens Go to College (1960)   Conway Twitty sings a couple songs in this infamous Mamie Van Doren comedy.

Shock Treatment (1981)   Flop sequel to the midnight surprise hit *Rocky Horror*. Few saw this rock musical, which starred Cliff De Young, formerly of the psych band Clear Light (see *The President's Analyst*), in the "Brad Majors" role.

Short Cuts (1993)   Robert Altman multi-storied epic with Lyle Lovett and Huey Lewis (seen relieving himself in full-frontal glory!).

Short Eyes (1977)   Harrowing prison story with dramatic parts for Curtis Mayfield and Freddy Fender, who also sings "Break It Down."

The Shot (1969)   Swedish movie with an appearance by British band Mandrake

Paddlesteamer. Alternate title: *The Skottet*.

Shout (1991)   John Travolta plays a music teacher in '50s Texas, using rock'n'roll to help kids express themselves.

Shout! The Story of Johnny O'Keefe (1985)   Miniseries from Down Under starring Terry Serio as '50s rocker O'Keefe, sort of the Australian Cliff Richard.

Side by Side (1975)   British comedy about two competing nightclubs with appearances by Mud, the Rubettes, Desmond Dekker, Fox, and Kenny.

Side by Side: The True Story of the Osmond Family (1982)   TV movie about the Mormon entertainment conglomerate that started as a barbershop quartet. An Osmond-produced project starring Marie Osmond as Mom.

Silver Dream Racer (1980)   David Essex stars as a motorcycle racer and sings "Looking for Someone," plus the title song.

Simon of the Desert (1965)   Mexican featurette from surrealist master Luis Buñuel with the Mexican band Los Sinners, although the upbeat music heard probably isn't theirs.

Sing (1989)   Musical about a song-and-dance competition in the Brooklyn high schools. With Patti LaBelle.

Sir Henry at Rawlinson End (1980)   Comedy written by Viv Stanshall of the Bonzo Dog Band, based on his old song. Trevor Howard stars as a wealthy man haunted by ghosts. With music by Stanshall.

Skateboard (1977)   Jefferson Starship's Craig Chaquico does a skateboarding cameo.

Skaterdater (1966)   Short film with music by Davie Allan and the Arrows.

Skatetown U.S.A. (1979)   Roller disco film with a wacky cast. Dave Mason appears performing "Feelin' Alright," "I Fell in Love," and the title song.

Skidoo (1968)   Otto Preminger farce with Frankie Avalon, Groucho Marx, and an LSD-tripping Jackie Gleason. Harry Nilsson plays a guard and supplies the music.

The Skydivers (1963)   Independent feature with an appearance by Jimmy Bryant and the Night Jumpers, who play "Ha-So," "Tobacco Worm," and "Stratosphere Boogie."

Slacker (1991)   Improvised scenes by Austin layabouts include ex-Butthole Surfers drummer Teresa Taylor in the keynote "Madonna pap smear" scene, three members of Glass Eye, and the Ed Hall band playing at the Continental Club.

The Slender Thread (1965)   *Pebbles* heroes the Sons of Adams appear in a discotheque playing an instrumental.

Slipstream (1974)   Canadian picture about an FM rock DJ broadcasting from a shack in the wilderness.

A Smell of Honey, A Swallow of Brine (1966)   Campy softcore porno with a fascinating, primitive folk/Velvets soundtrack by "et cetera," who appear in a coffee house for a few numbers.

Some People (1962)   David Hemmings stars in this U.K. film about bikers who form a band. With an appearance by instrumental group the Eagles.

The Sorcerers (1967)   Psychedelic, psychological horror film with Boris Karloff, a mod zombie, and a London nightclub scene featuring Columbia recording artists the Moquettes.

Speed Crazy (1959)   Auto racing melodrama with rock singer Slick Slavin as Smiley performing "Ghost Town Rock" and the title tune.

Spring Break (1983)   Girl band Hot Date performs "Friends."

A Star Is Born (1976)   Tiresome "rock" remake of the oft-filmed story of a destructive star in decline (Kris Kristofferson) and his affair with a rising talent (Barbra Streisand). Kris's band includes Booker T. and other heavy players.

Staying Alive (1983)   John Travolta is back in this Sylvester Stallone-directed sequel to *Saturday Night Fever* that failed to ignite a disco revival. Music by Frank Stallone.

Stony Island (1978)   Chicago ghetto kids form a band and get advice from bluesman Gene Barge (Gary "U.S." Bonds's old sax man). With a young Susanna Hoffs. Produced by her mom.

Stunt Rock (1978)   Dramatic feature focusing on Swedish hard rock band Sorcery and an Australian stunt man.

The Subterraneans (1960)   MGM film of Kerouac's beatnik opus with poetry, cool jazz, and Arte Johnson. Songs include "Coffee Time" and "Look Ma, No Clothes." Musicians include Art Farmer, Shelley Manne, Red Mitchell, and Art Pepper.

Summer Love (1958)   Sequel to *Rock Pretty Baby* with John Saxon as a band leader, Rod McKuen as Ox Bentley, Fay Wray (!), Molly Bee, Shelley Fabares, Troy Donahue, Jill St. John, and Jimmy Daley's Dingalings.

Superstar   Stop-motion animation biopic of Karen Carpenter, using a cast of Barbie dolls. For this effort, director Todd Haynes was sued by Richard Carpenter and by Mattel. He has since made the critically acclaimed *Poison*.

The Swan (1956)   Child actor Van Dyke Parks made his only feature film appearance in this Grace Kelly starrer. Parks was twelve at the time.

The Sweet Ride (1968)   Major flop "youth" movie with Moby Grape doing their unreleased (until 1993) title song, plus a cameo by the great Lee Hazelwood.

The Swinger (1966)   Ann-Margaret sings "The Swinger," "Oh So Bad," and more.

Swinger's Paradise (1964)   Cliff Richard and the Shadows make their own musical version of a stodgy director's movie project. Songs include "All Kinds of People" and "We Love a Movie." Alternate title: *Wonderful Life*.

A Swingin' Affair (1963)   College movie with an appearance by surf guitar maestro Dick Dale and his band, the Del-Tones.

Swingin' Along (1962)   Tommy Noonan/Peter Marshall comedy about a songwriting contest, originally released in 1961 as *Double Trouble*. Scenes were added of Ray Charles (doing "What'd I Say") and Bobby Vee.

Swinging U.K. (1964)   Short British film with Millie Small, the Merseybeats, the Wackers, and the Four Pennies. Later used in the compilation picture *Go-Go Big Beat*.

Tailhouse Rock   Porno film starring Sonic Youth T-shirt icon Traci Lords as one member of a girl punk trio. With "Sticks" (the drummer from *Happy Days*), and real drumsticks put to novel uses.

Take a Giant Step (1959)   Johnny Nash stars as a black teenager struggling in a white world. He also sings the title song.

Take Me High (1973)   Cliff Richard stars as a banker who opens a hamburger restaurant. Richard also provides soundtrack songs.

Taking Off (1971)   Milos Forman's first American film, this generation gap comedy features appearances by the Ike and Tina Turner Revue (doing "Goodbye, So Long") and Carly Simon (as an auditioning singer performing "Long Term Physical Effects").

Teenage Gang Debs (1966)   Juvenile delinquent epic shot on location in Brooklyn with real gang members. There's an almost-appearance by Tom Jones-esque singer Lee Dowell, performing "Don't Make Me Mad" and "The Black Belt," but Lee is hard to find amongst the dancers and musicians. A promotional 45 was made available for theater lobby play.

Ten Girls Ago (1962)   Supposedly an unreleased Canadian film starring Dion, with Buster Keaton and Bert Lahr.

Teruchi's Movie   We don't know the real title of this movie starring Teruchi, the king of Japanese surf guitar, who played in such Ventures-inspired bands as Terry and the Bunnies and Terry and the Bluejeans. This time he's with Terry and the Launchers, in a story about a talent contest whose entrants also include a Beatlish group who hold their guitars like rifles and play martial rock.

Thank God It's Friday (1978)   Hit disco exploiter with appearances by the Commodores and Donna Summer (doing "Last Dance").

That Tennessee Beat (1966)   Great country film with Merle Travis and Minnie Pearl.

Third Reich and Roll (1978)   Strange stop-motion film by the Residents.

Thrashin' (1986)   Skateboard gangs take time out to watch the Red Hot Chili Peppers in concert.

Three for All (1974)   British comedy about the group Billy Beethoven touring Spain as their girlfriends try to catch up with them.

Thunder Alley (1967)   Stock car movie starring Fabian and Annette Funicello. With an appearance by the Band Without a Name, a garage group with a few records on the Tower label, who later became the American Revolution (see *Born Wild*).

Thunder Alley (1985)   When a farm boy's bandmate falls to drugs, his newfound rage helps his act. With Leif Garret.

Thunderbirds Are Go   Space-travel movie in Super-Marionation—i.e., animated puppets and miniature props. A pilot dreams of visiting an intergalactic nightclub where puppets of the Shadows play a haunting instrumental before they are joined by a puppet Cliff Richard for "Shooting Star,." The puppets look like the actual musicians, and even the miniature guitars are accurate. Maybe the coolest rock clip ever.

Tokyo Pop (1988)   Charming cross-cultural comedy about a girl leaving her punk band in New York for Japan, where she meets a longhaired rocker who wants a Western girl for his band. After a spat, he tells a co-worker, "I'm better off without her. Like Bob Marley said, 'No woman... no cry.'"

Tommy the Torreador (1959)   Tommy Steele becomes a bullfighter for a day and sings many songs, including "Little White Bull."

Toomorrow (1970)   Olivia Newton-John stars as a member of the title rock band, who are kidnapped by aliens picking up vibes from their amplifier.

The Touchables (1967)   Brilliant, screwball film set in pop art England about four swinging girls in an inflatable dome who kidnap a pretty-boy pop singer for fun. No music performances, but a great theme song, "All Of Us" by Nirvana (no, not...), plus music by Wynder K. Frog, Roy Redman, and the Ferris Wheel. The only feature directed by Beatles photographer Robert Freeman.

Train Ride to Hollywood (1975)   Fantasy stars Bloodstone as a group heading for an audition in a train filled with Humphrey Bogart, W.C. Fields, and other film legends (played by British impressionists). Songs include "Train Ride," "Rock'n'Roll Choo Choo," and "Toot-Toot-Tootsie Goodbye."

The Trip (1967)   Famous drug film with the International Submarine Band, who are seen but not heard.

True Stories (1986)   David Byrne's directing debut, inspired by tabloid newspaper stories, pokes fun at eccentric Texans—or does it just celebrate our diversity? Either way, a pointless bore.

Tuff Turf (1984)   Jack Mack and the Heart Attack perform, and star James Spader sings a laughably nauseating ballad.

Twist All Night (1961)   Another vehicle for Louis Prima, the man who mixed swing and R&B with the Neapolitan slang of his youth. This time he's running a twist club, and he gets mixed up with an art-theft ring. Songs include "Fool Around," "When the Saints Go Twistin' In," "Twistin' the Blues," and "Tag That Twistin' Dollie." With June "the Bosom" Wilkinson and Sam Butera and the

Witnesses, natch. Originally coupled with the short *Twist Craze.*

Twist Locura de Juventua (1962)   Mexican twist film with appearances by Los Locos de Ritmo and some squeaky-clean Mexican kid who sings "A Hundred Pounds of Clay."

Two a Penny (1967)   Cliff Richard stars as a pop singer dealing drugs, in this religiously themed drama. Cliff performs "Questions," "Twist and Shout," and more.

Two Little Bears (1961)   Eddie Albert finds his daughters turn into bears at night. Brenda Lee sings "Speak to Me Pretty" and "Honest Bear."

Two Moon Junction (1988)   Pretentious sex film with a cameo by Screamin' Jay Hawkins.

2000 Years Later (1969)   Comedy about a time-traveling Roman soldier with Monte Rock III as Tomorrow's Leader, plus Casey Kasem.

Two Tickets to Paris (1962)   Joey Dee and the Starlighters appear in this French-set romance. Their songs include "Twistin' on a Liner" and "Willy Willy."

Two-Lane Blacktop (1971)   Dennis Wilson and James Taylor star in this arty road movie about a crosscountry race.

U.K. Swings Again (1964)   Follow-up short to *Swinging U.K.*—with the Animals, the Hollies, Lulu and the Luvvers, Brian Poole and the Tremoloes, the Swingin' Blue Jeans, the Tornadoes, and the Applejacks doing one song each. Used in the compilation *Go-Go Big Beat.*

Uncle Scam (1981)   Philadelphia-produced comedy about the Abscam political scandal co-starring James E. Myers, co-writer of "Rock around the Clock."

Underground U.S.A. One of many underground films by Eric Mitchell, with help from and starring many early *New York Rocker*-scene minicelebrities including James White and the Blacks, Walter Steding, and the Lounge Lizards.

The Unholy Rollers (1972) Roller derby movie with Louis and the Rockets.

Untamed Youth (1957) Totally rockin' Mamie Van Doren film about a juvenile prison farm that co-stars Eddie Cochran (singing "Cottonpicker"). Mamie sings "Salamander," "Go, Go Calypso," and "Oobala Baby."

Up in Smoke (1978) This first film by doper comics Cheech and Chong climaxes with them crashing the stage at an L.A. punk concert. Appearing are the Dils, the Whores, the Berlin Brats, and Rodney Bingenheimer.

Up the Junction (1967) Drama of working-class in London with an appearance by the Delecardos and a score by Manfred Mann.

The Valley (1972) The second Barbet Schroeder film to use Pink Floyd score.

Vanishing Point (1971) This car-chase drama includes a scene with Delaney, Bonnie, and Friends portraying gospel group J. Hovah's Singers and performing "You Got to Believe."

Venus in Furs (1965) Underground film by Piero Heliczer starring Lou Reed, John Cale, and Angus MacLise, with soundtrack music by same. Not to be confused with the 1970 A.I.P. drama.

Venus in Furs (1970) Weird horror/mystery with James Darren and Barbara McNair. This "masterpiece of supernatural sex" includes a party scene with Manfred Mann.

The Virgin Soldiers (1969) Dry comedy about British army recruits with David Bowie in a blink-and-you'll-miss-him bar fight scene and a march theme by Ray Davies.

Vision Quest (1985) Drama of high school wrestler Matthew Modine with a brief shot of Madonna performing "Crazy for You."

Voices (1968) Documentary about director Jean-Luc Godard that shows him at work on *One Plus One*, including footage of the Rolling Stones not used in that film.

Vortex (1981) Campy 16mm (a step up!) film noir by Scott and Beth B, with a New York underground cast that includes singer/poet Lydia Lunch, performance artist/Bongwater member Ann Magnuson, and onetime Danceteria doorman Haoui Montaug. Music by Richard Edson (now a busy character actor), Lunch, and others.

Voyage of the Rock Aliens (1984) Musical comedy starring Pia Zadora, who sings a duet with Jermaine Jackson. Also appearing are Jimmy and the Mustangs.

Walker (1988) This fanciful bio of 19th-century soldier-of-fortune William Walker has usual cameos from director Alex Cox's musician pals: Edward Tudorpole (Tenpole Tudor), Zander Schloss (Circle Jerks), and Joe Strummer, who composed the score.

Welcome to L.A. (1976) Absorbing multi-character film from Robert Altman protege Alan Rudolph in his art-film mode (i.e., not *Roadie*). A *Nashville*-like look at the strange '70s world of singer-songwriter worship, *Welcome to L.A.* relies on the hypnotic, soporific music of Richard Baskin.

What a Whopper (1961)   U.K. film starring Adam Faith.

What's Good for the Goose (1969)   British Norman Wisdom comedy includes an appearance by the Pretty Things. What's unusual is that the songs come from the "needle drop" library of DeWolf Music, a supplier of canned music for films. In their late-'60s pop-psych period, the Pretty Things recorded three 10" albums for DeWolf under the name the Electric Banana. One of these albums included the five songs the band does here: "Alexander," "It'll Never Be Me," "Eagle's Son," "Blow Your Mind" and the title track. Unfortunately, the Pretty Things appear mostly in the background of a nightclub scene.

What's Up, Tiger Lily? (1966)   Woody Allen's comic redubbing of a Japanese spy movie. The Lovin' Spoonful, who supplied the soundtrack, are shown in a new scene playing in a club.

Where Angels Go, Trouble Follows (1968) Includes a scene with teenage band the In Group, lip-syching at a dance to the Boyce and Hart title track.

White Rock (1976)   Sports film about the Winter Olympics, with an appearance by soundtrack creator Rick Wakeman. The filmmakers had planned to use Yes, whom Rick had just left.

Who Is Harry Kellerman and Why Is He Saying Those Terrible Things about Me? (1971)   Dustin Hoffman plays a rock singer/songwriter.

Who's the Man (1993)   The "first Hip-Hop whodunnit" starring *Yo! MTV Raps* hosts Dr. Dre and Ed Lover—plus Ice-T,

Kriss Kross, Run DMC, Queen Latifah, Heavy D, and Salt'n'Pepa.

The Wild Rebels (1967)   Biker film with Florida acts Steve Alaimo, who stars as a car racer helping cops catch some bikers (and sings "You Don't Know Like I Know"), and the Birdwatchers (singing "Can I Do It?").

Wild West (1992)   Winning British comedy about the struggles of a Pakistani country-rock band living in London's "Little India."

The Wild Westerners (1962)   Duane Eddy stars in this oater and contributes the title tune.

The Wild Wild World of Lydia Lunch   Underground film by Nick Zedd with the No Wave princess running around and chasing sheep.

The Wild Wild World of Jayne Mansfield (1968)   Bizarre (and posthumously released) *Mondo*-type documentary showcasing sex hot spots around the world. Jayne dances on the beach at the Cannes Film Festival while expatriate, Italy-based soul combo Rocky Roberts and the Airedales blast out "The Bird." Later we visit a Las Vegas dive where the topless all-girl band the Ladybirds play a great song called "I Just Can't Stand It."

The Wild World of Batwoman (1966) Insane camp comedy about a gang of female superagents, with lots of go-go dancing and a brief scene of the Young Giants playing an uptempo instrumental on the beach. Alternate title: *She Was a Hippy Vampire.*

Wings of Desire (1988)   Wim Wenders art-house hit with performances by Nick Cave and the Bad Seeds and Crime and the City Solution (both spin-offs of Australia's the Birthday Party).

With Six You Get Eggroll (1968) This Doris Day/Brian Keith family comedy includes a nightclub scene in which the Grass Roots perform their cool song "Feelings."

The Wiz (1978) Filmed version of the all-black stage play updating of *The Wizard of Oz*. Diana Ross stars as Dorothy and a pre-op Michael Jackson is the scarecrow. The film includes music by Quincy Jones and Ashford and Simpson.

Wombling Free (1978) Feature film spinoff of TV's *The Wombles*, sort of the British *Banana Splits*. Furry costumed creatures clean up trash and perform '70s bubblegum music composed by Mike Batt, ex-keyboardist of Hapshash and the Coloured Coat.

Wonderwall (1968) George Harrison contributed the Indian and rockabilly score, which has more Clapton guitar work than the soundtrack LP (which was the first album on the Apple label).

Xanadu (1980) Infamous, big-budget flop remake of the 1947 musical *Down to Earth*, starring Olivia Newton-John as a goddess of dance who comes to life off a mural to help Gene Kelly open a roller disco. With music by ELO and Cliff Richard and an appearance by the Tubes at a battle of the bands.

Yesterday's Hero (1979) This Jackie Collins story casts Adam Faith as a soccer team manager and Paul Nicholas (ex-Screaming Lord Sutch and the Savages) as the team's Elton John-esque rock-star owner. Nicholas sings "We've Got Us" with Suzanne Somers.

You Killed Me First R. Kern film short of arguing family starring Lydia Lunch and Karen Finley.

The Young Graduates (1971) A female high school teacher drops out and becomes a hippie. With an appearance by Pat Russell and the Spare Change.

The Young Runaways (1968) Sam Katzman film about restless youth with an appearance by the Gordian Knot, a Harper's Bizarre-sounding group with an album on MGM. (Jim Weatherly, who wrote "Neither One of Us," was a member.)

The Young Swingers (1963) Rod Lauren, Gene McDaniels (of "A Hundred Pounds of Clay" fame), and Molly Bee (a would-be Lesley Gore) star in this tale of nice kids who run a dance club and mean adults who want to develop the property. Songs include "Come to the Party," "Watusi Surfer," "Mad Mad Mad," and "Greenback Dollar."

Zakary Thaks (1966) Self-produced film of the titular Texas garage band, shown plowing through seven live songs in some room, in front of their geeky fans. The songs include "Mustang Sally," "My Little Red Book," and "My Back Pages."

CONCERT FILMS & ROCKUMENTARIES

Sign O' the Times

AC/DC: Let There Be Rock (1980) Feature-length concert film shot during 1978 Belgium and Paris shows, intercut with fictional scenes starring these kings of metal bubblegum.

American Music—From Folk to Jazz to Pop (1967) Documentary with scenes of a Supremes recording session and the Dave Clark Five.

Amougies Music Power (1969) Concert film from the Amougies Festival in France, featuring performances by Captain Beefheart, the Pretty Things, Soft Machine, Frank Zappa, East of Eden, the Nice, and the Art Ensemble of Chicago.

Andy Warhol's Exploding Plastic Inevitable (1966) Ron Nameth's 30-minute film of Warhol's multimedia happening reportedly has rather murky photography of the Velvet Underground performing. Lou Reed was in the hospital, so the lineup had Angus MacLise on percussion, Maureen Tucker on bass, and John Cale and Sterling Morrison on vocals. They perform "Heroin" and "Venus in Furs" but are only seen for a few seconds.

Aretha Franklin: Soul Singer (1969) Lady Soul is seen at home working out steps with her backup singers, in the studio with her manager, and onstage in this short film.

Banjoman (1975) Earl Scruggs is honored in this filmed concert, intercut with interviews. Songs performed include "Amazing Grace" and "You Ain't Goin' Nowhere" (Joan Baez), "Roll Over Beethoven" and "Mr. Tambourine Man" (Byrds), "Diggy Liggy Lo" (Nitty Gritty Dirt Band), and more by David Bromberg, Ramblin' Jack Elliot, Tracy Nelson, Doc and Merle Watson, and the Earl Scruggs Revue.

Be Glad for the Song Has No Ending (1969) Brit folk-rock ensemble the Incredible String Band star in this documentary, performing "All Writ Down," "Mercy, I Cry City," and "The Iron Stone." The band also appears in a mime performance of *The Pirate and the Crystal Ball.*

Beatlemania (1981) You may not have been able to see the Beatles live, but you can see the Film of the Stage Show of the Incredible Simulation. Mimicking the Fab Four through different eras and various hair lengths are Mitch Weissman, Tom Teely, David Leon, and Ralph Castelli—one of several casts that toured in the national company of the Broadway show. They perform songs from "I Want to Hold Your Hand" to "The Long and Winding Road."

The Beatles Come To Town (1963) Cinemascope, color Pathé newsreel of a Beatles concert in Manchester with backstage footage.

Bird on a Wire (1972) This documentary follows Leonard Cohen on tour through Europe as he visits the Eiffel Tower and Dutch canals. Onstage, the old croaker delivers "Suzanne," "Famous Blue

Raincoat," "Chelsea Hotel," and ten more.

Black and Blue (1980)   Concert film with sets by Black Sabbath (doing "Iron Man" and "Paranoid") and Blue Öyster Cult (singing "Cities on Flame with Rock and Roll" and "Born to Be Wild").

Black Wax (1982)   Robert Mugge documentary of political jazz poet Gil Scott Heron and the Midnight Band. Scott-Heron gives an alternative tour of D.C. and performs in concert.

Blank Generation (1976)   Black-and-white, non-sync concert footage from the glory days of CBGB, showcasing the fresh new sounds of Patti Smith ("Gloria," "We're Gonna Have a Real Good Time Together"), Television ("Little Johnny Jewel," "Mi Amore"), the Talking Heads ("Psycho Killer," "Last Weekend"), plus the Ramones, Blondie, Tuff Darts (still with vocalist Robert Gordon), the Heartbreakers (still with Richard Hell), the Shirts, the Dolls, Wayne County, and Harry Toledo. Directed by underground filmmaker Amos Poe and Patti Smith Group guitarist Ivan Kral.

Blitzkrieg Bop (1979)   Concert film of Blondie, the Ramones, and the Dead Boys at CBGB.

Blue Suede Shoes (1979)   Documentary about the British rockabilly revival. Matchbox and Crazy Cavan and the Flying Saucers perform, and there is archival footage of Bill Haley, Cliff Richard, Gene Vincent, Eddie Cochran, and Tommy Steele.

The Blues According to Lightnin' Hopkins (1979)   Les Blank documentary on the legendary bluesman, seen in conversation and song. A 10-minute addition called

Sun's Gonna Shine, with the song "Trouble in Mind," was released in 1980.

The Blues Band (1981)   Short road documentary following the title supergroup (Paul Jones, Dave Kelly, Tom McGuinness, Hughie Flint, Gary Fletcher), who perform "Suss Blues," "Come On In" and the Thatcher-inspired rewrite of "Down on Maggie's Farm" (a pun that predated U2's similar idea).

Bob Marley and the Wailers Live! (1978) Island Records produced this grainy concert film that includes "Trenchtown Rock," "I Shot the Sheriff," "Lively Up Yourself," "Them Bellyful," "Crazy Baldhead" and eight more. The band includes Junior Murvin, Rita Marley, and Judy Mowatt.

Born Too Late (1978)   Another documentary short about London's rockabilly revival, with fan interviews and performance by Matchbox.

Bowie '73' (1973)   D.A. Pennebaker-filmed record of David Bowie's final "Spiders from Mars" concert on July 3 at the Hammersmith Odeon in London. At one point Bowie tells the saddened glitter kids that this will be his last live show ever, which garnered headlines in music press around the world. He later mumbled that he was only speaking in character. The film, as seen on ABC-TV in January 1974, included Jeff Beck's guest spot on "The Jean Genie/Love Me Do." This was cut from the 1982 re-release *Ziggy Stardust and the Spiders from Mars*, which added other footage. Songs include "Suffragette City" and "Changes." Alternate title: *A London Show.*

Braverman's Condensed Cream of Beatles (1973)   Clever short film shows the history of the Beatles in flash-frame technique.

Bring on the Night (1985)   Lavish, self-important documentary of the formation of Sting's new solo band, shown rehearsing in a grandiose mansion in Paris as they prepare for the bleached-blond millionaire's *Dream of the Blue Turtles* tour. The direction by Michael Apted and the musicianship (of Branford Marsalis, Darryl Jones, Kenny Kirland, and Omar Hakim) are first class. This exercise in rampant egotism climaxes with the actual on-screen birth of one of Sting's offspring.

Buddy Knox at the 100 Club (1969) Fifteen-minute documentary with interview and performances of "Party Doll" and "Hula Love." Made at the London club by DJ/*Sound of the Cities* historian Charlie Gillett.

Carry It On (1970)   Documentary on the life of folksinger Joan Baez, shown in concert and with husband David Harris. Songs include "Cinnamon Girl," "Last Thing on My Mind," and "Hickory Wind."

Celebration at Big Sur (1971)   Concert film of the 1969 Big Sur Folk Festival, featuring Joni Mitchell; Crosby, Stills, Nash, and Young; the Flying Burrito Brothers; Joan Baez; Mimi Farina; John Sebastian; Dorothy Morrison; the Combs Sisters; Chris Ethridge; the Struggle Mountain Resistance Band; and the Edwin Hawkins Singers. Highlights of this "celebration" include Stephen Stills blowing his cool onstage when accused by a heckler of selling out, then returning to express his gratitude for the friends who "loved him out of" his bad attitude. Also scenes of David Crosby splashing around in some hot springs with some hippie chicks.

Christmas on Earth Continued (1967) Unreleased film of all-night British concert featuring the Jimi Hendrix Experience, the Soft Machine, Pink Floyd, the Who, the Move, Tomorrow, Sam Gopal's Dream (with Lemmy of Hawkwind and Motörhead fame), and many more. This footage turned up in the home video *Jimi Hendrix: Live In Monterey 1970*.

Chulas Fronteras (1981)   This Tex-Mex music/social documentary by Les Blank features Los Allegres de Teran, Flaco Jiminez, and Lydia Mendoza.

Cliff—Flip Side (1980)   Short documentary made for the TEARfund charity, with born-again rocker Cliff Richard talking about the Third World and singing at a 1979 Albert Hall concert.

Colosseum and Juicy Lucy (1970)   Short video-to-film coverage of a progressive and jazz-rock concert at Questor's Theatre in Ealing. JL perform "I'm a Pimp."

Concerts for the People of Kampuchea UNICEF benefit featuring old and New Wave talents—including the Who, the Pretenders, Elvis Costello and the Attractions, Rockpile, the Clash, Queen, Paul McCartney and Wings, and Paul's Rockestra (an improvised group with members of the above, Led Zeppelin, Ronnie Lane, and others).

Crash'n'Burn (1979)   Short film made at the Toronto punk club, featuring CBGB stars the Dead Boys and the Boyfriends, plus homegrown talent the Diodes and Teenage Head.

Cream's Farewell Concert (1968)   Straightforward filming of the psychedelic supergroup's last show at the Royal Albert Hall in July 1968. In addition to songs like "I'm So Glad," "Sunshine of Your Love," "Crossroads," and "White Room," there are snippets of interviews with the band. The film has been released in 40-, 52-, and 90-minute versions, on film and video (often in grainy, unauthorized dupes). This footage is also used extensively in the *Strange Brew* home video.

The Cure in Orange (1987)   Live concert film shot in the French Cote d'Azur. Robert Smith is seen pontificating while applying makeup before a show that's relatively intimate compared to the arena spectacles the Cure now sell out. The gloomy gusses deliver such beloved underground hits as "Killing an Arab," "Shake Dog Shake," "Strange Day," "Faith," "Boys Don't Cry," and more.

Cure Show (1993)   Robert Smith said that his band's music had changed so much since *The Cure in Orange* that another full-length concert film was needed "for history's sake." Songs here include "Open," "High," "Friday I'm in Love," "Inbetween Days," "Never Enough," and "Just Like Heaven."

Dance Craze (1980)   Concert feature that collects an assortment of performances by top-rank bands of the then-hot Two-Tone British ska revival. All the bands were caught live in various large halls. On hand are scene creators the Specials—plus the Selecter, Madness, the [English] Beat (seen in Cherry Hill, N.J.'s mammoth Emerald City rock disco), Bad Manners, and the Bodysnatchers (who became the Belle Starrs when ska fizzled out).

The Day the Music Died (1977)   Odds-and-ends concert footage with Jimi Hendrix, Mountain, the Beatles, the Doors, and many more. Hosted by Murray the K.

Depeche Mode 101 (1988)   Fascinating look at the hugely successful techno-fash-ion outfit, co-directed by D.A. Penne-baker. The film follows the band on a huge U.S. tour, and a bus load of suburban fans follow the band, having won a contest from a "Rock of the Eighties" radio station. *Depeche Mode 101* is like an update of the punk tour shown in *Another State of Mind*, only this time the band has a huge expense account. Essential viewing for marketing students. Songs include "Master and Servant," "Black Celebration," and "Just Can't Get Enough."

Dread, Beat, An' Blood (1978)   Documentary on reggae poet Linton Kwesi Johnson. Songs include "Come Wi Goh Dung Deh," "It Dread inna England," and the title number.

Dream Deceivers   A video-created (but shown theatrically on film) examination of the lawsuit filed by the family of James Vance against Judas Priest. Vance's parents claimed that their teenage boy blew his brains out under influence of JP's nihilistic lyrics. (The song in question was a cover of Spooky Tooth's "Better By You, Better Than Me.")

Dynamite Chicken (1971)   Richard Pryor and the Ace Trucking Company provide comedy, intercut with a grab bag of old music footage including John and Yoko at a bed-in, Leonard Cohen reading "What Am I Doing Here?", Joan Baez, and more. This was campus screening fodder made for a film circuit that is now extinct.

ELO: Discovery   Concert film capturing the Electric Light Orchestra at their late-'70s peak.

Elvis on Tour (1972)   Presley's final concert film follows the King on a U.S. tour using the same split-screen style as *Mad Dogs and Englishmen* (filmed by the same crew). The thirty-eight-year-old Presley sings 29 songs spanning his lengthy career, joins in a gospel sing, and is shown backstage and at a recording session. There's also old footage, including an Ed Sullivan appearance. Vocal backing is provided by the Sweet Inspirations, Kathy Westmoreland, and the Stamps Quartet.

Emerson, Lake, and Palmer in Concert (1981)   Video-to-film concert feature shot at Montreal's Olympic Stadium, complete with a 65-piece orchestra.

Eno (1973)   Short documentary on the influential art rocker. Songs include "Needles in the Camel's Eye" and "The Paw Paw Negro Blowtorch." Also seen are Roxy Music and Chris Spedding.

Eric Clapton and His Rolling Hotel (1980) Slowhand and company hire Hermann Goering's luxury railroad car for a tour of Germany. Their set includes "Layla," "Cocaine," and a finale of "Further On Up the Road," for which Clapton is joined by George Harrison and Elton John. Opening act Muddy Waters performs "Mannish Boy" and "I've Got My Mojo Working."

European Music Revolution (1970)   Concert film with Pink Floyd and the Nice.

Experience   Concert film of the Jimi Hendrix Experience live at London's Royal Albert Hall. This film was to be released around 1971, when *two* soundtrack albums came out on the Bulldog label (*Experience* and *More Experience*). Alas, it didn't, and the footage went unseen until the recent release of the home video *Live at the Royal Albert Hall.*

Fairport Convention and Matthew's Southern Comfort (1970)   Short concert film from

a benefit show in Maidstone, Kent. The Fairport lineup consisted of Richard Thompson, Dave Pegg, Dave Swarbrick, Simon Nicol, and Dave Mattacks.

Fillmore (1972)   Documentary of the last days of San Francisco's Fillmore Auditorium, with Bill Graham reminiscing behind the scenes. Seen live in concert are Santana, the Grateful Dead, Jefferson Airplane, Hot Tuna, Cold Blood, It's a Beautiful Day, Boz Scaggs, Quicksilver Messenger Service, the Elvin Bishop Group, and Lamb. The New Riders of the Purple Sage and the Rowan Brothers are seen rehearsing. Creedence Clearwater Revival were filmed but not included in the movie.

Free (1973)   Concert film of the 1970 Randall's Island Music Festival with Jimi Hendrix, Steppenwolf, Van Morrison, Mountain, and Dr. John. This footage was also used in *The Day the Music Died.*

Fugs (1966)   Twelve minutes of the lovably-offensive Village combo doing their thing for businessmen at the Waldorf-Astoria. Songs include "Slum Goddess," "Group Grope," and "Kill for Peace."

Genesis—A Band in Concert (1976)   This concert featurette of the freshly Gabriel-less band also includes newsreel footage. The songs includes "I Know What I Like," "Fly on a Windshield," "Supper's Ready," and four others.

Gettin' Back (1974)   Documentary of the Ozark Mountain Folk Fair—with the Ozark Mountain Daredevils, Clifton Chenier, John Lee Hooker, Leo Kottke, Michael Murphy, and Big Mama Thornton.

Glastonbury Fayre (1973)   Delayed concert film from the eponymous 1971 gathering at Worthy Farm in the English countryside. Performers include Daevid Allen and Gong, Arthur Brown and Kingdom Come, Fairport Convention, Family, Linda Lewis, Magic Michael, Melanie, Quintessence, Terry Reid, and Traffic. There's also a lecture by Guru Maharaj J. Filmed but not included were Marc Bolan, David Bowie, and Pete Townshend.

The Grateful Dead (1967)   Short film of the band performing at a gig, including its arrival and departure, all shown in fast-motion.

Grave New World (1972)   Short film featuring the Strawbs in conceptual performances of "Benedictus," "The Flower and the Young Man," and several more.

Greenbelt Live! (1980)   Coverage of a religious rock festival with Cliff Richard, Bryn Haworth, Giantkiller, Lamb, After the Fire, and many more.

Halber Mensch (1985)   Japanese production focusing on the German industrial/noise outfit Einstürzende Neubauten [English translation: Collapsing New Buildings]. The film cuts between footage of the band in concert, microscope shots of molecules, and scenes of pile drivers and sledgehammers.

Half Japanese: The Band That Would Be King (1993)   Feature documentary on primitive art-rockers Jad and David Fair (HJ), examining their 17-year history and small yet fanatical following. With Maureen Tucker, Penn Jillette, and "indie rock philosophers" Gerard Cosloy and Byron Coley.

Harlem Jazz Festival (1955)   An all-black revue that includes dancers, comedians, and music from the Larks, the Clovers, Amos Milburn, Dinah Washington, Martha Davis, and more.

Heartland Reggae (1980)   Concert film of the 1978 event celebrating the anniversary of Haile Selassie's visit to Jamaica. With Bob Marley and the Wailers, Peter Tosh, Althea and Donna, Dennis Brown, U-Roy, Jacob Miller and the Inner Circle, Little Junior Tucker, and the I-Threes.

Home of the Brave (1986)   Multimedia concert film of performance artist/musician Laurie Anderson.

Hot Pepper (1972)   Les Blank documentary about zydeco accordionist Clifton Chenier and the Louisiana music scene.

I Promise to Remember   Documentary about the tragic life of Frankie Lymon.

If It Ain't Stiff, It Ain't Worth a... (1977) Filmed record of the first Stiff Records package tour, with Elvis Costello and the Attractions, Ian Dury and the Blockheads, Nick Lowe's Last Chicken in the Shop (soon to be called Rockpile), Larry Wallis (ex-Pink Fairies and Motörhead), and Wreckless Eric.

Isaac Hayes: Black Moses of Soul (1973) Feature-length concert film shot in Atlanta. The sweaty, chain-wearing soul man's songs include "Light My Fire" and "I Don't Know What to Do With Myself."

It's Your Thing (1970)   Video-to-film Yankee Stadium concert film, produced by the Isley Brothers—starring themselves, Ike and Tina Turner, Patti Austin, the Five Stairsteps, the Edwin Hawkins Singers, the Clara Ward Singers, Judy White, the Winstons, the Young Gents, Moms Mabley singing "Abraham, Martin and John," and the Brooklyn Bridge (what's wrong with this picture?).

James Brown: The Man   A short look at James's public service work, business activities, and personal philosophy—plus live footage. Released by Sterling Educational Films.

Jimi Plays Berkeley (1971)   Featurette filmed on Memorial Day, 1970. Songs include "Voodoo Chile," "Machine Gun," and "Johnny B. Goode"—plus footage of demonstrations and street life.

Jimmy Cliff—Bongo Man (1985)   Portrait of the reggae star as a champion of the people as well as a musician.

Jiveasp (1975)   Feature documentary on Larry Raspberry and the Highsteppers. With Jerry Lee Lewis, Leon Russell, and Professor Longhair.

Johnny Cash! The Man, His World, His Music (1969)   The Man in Black seen in his hometown, in the studio with Dylan (recording "One Too Many Mornings"), and onstage. Sun Records compadre Carl Perkins appears performing "Blue Suede Shoes."

The Kids Are United (1980)   A look at the punk-dominated 1978 Reading Rock Festival, named after a Sham 69 song. Other talent includes the Jam, Ultravox, Penetration, and wizened veterans the Pirates.

Ladies and Gentlemen, Mr. Leonard Cohen (1966)   A National Film Board of Canada documentary on that nation's master of depression. Cohen delivers a humorous monologue and reflects on the writing process. "The subject of this film study is articulate and witty and represents the kind of creative artist who is reaching young people today" (from a film rental catalog).

Ladies and Gentlemen—the Rolling Stones (1974)   Nonstop concert film, recorded in then-essential quadrophonic sound (the Stones must love these fad processes —witness their IMAX film and 3-D TV concert). The film premiered not just as another midnight movie, but as a substitute for a real concert, at prices to match. It was filmed during the band's 1972 U.S. tour, while *Cocksucker Blues* was being made backstage. The 14 songs include "Brown Sugar," "Tumblin' Dice," and "Jumpin' Jack Flash."

Land of Look Behind (1982)   A "magical meditation" on Jamaican life, this reggae concert/fantasy film evolved from a planned documentary on Bob Marley's funeral. With performances by Gregory Isaacs and reggae poet Mutabaruka.

The Legend of Bo Diddley (1966)   Documentary short shows Bo visiting his old Chicago neighborhoods, recording, and playing in Toronto. Songs include "I'm Gonna Get Married," "I'm a Man," and "Bring It to Jerome." Produced by Checker Records.

Let's Join Together (1973)   Religious-themed concert film featuring Cliff Richard with a guest appearance by Johnny Cash.

Let's Spend the Night Together (1982)   Hal Ashby directed this film of the Rolling Stones 1981 tour, one of the biggest ever. The complicated stage set-up was shot at Sun Devil Stadium in Arizona and Brendan Byrne Arena in New Jersey. Songs include "All Down the Line," "Little T and A," "She's So Cold," "Brown Sugar," and "Twenty Flight Rock."

Lol Coxhill (1973)   Documentary short on the British improvisational musician who has collaborated with the likes of Kevin Ayers, Henry Cow, and Hugh Hopper.

The London Rock and Roll Show (1973) British documentary of the Wembley

R&R Revival Show, featuring Chuck Berry, Little Richard, Bill Haley and the Comets, Jerry Lee Lewis, Bo Diddley, Screaming Lord Sutch, and Heinz and the Houseshakers. Also included is an interview with Mick Jagger.

Lonely Boy (1962)   Influential cinema verité short showcasing Paul Anka on- and offstage (even in his underwear) at Atlantic City's Steel Pier, the Copacabana nightclub, and Freedomland Amusement Park. His manager offers comments like "God gave Paul something I don't think has been given to anyone in the last 500 years." With lots of weeping, hysterical fans. You can sense how primed these girls were for the Beatles. Songs include "Diana" and "Put Your Head on My Shoulder."

Love You Till Tuesday (1969)   Fascinating half-hour collection of promo-type clips, made by David Bowie's then-manager who thought the BBC would show it. No such luck. Seen with Bowie are the other members of Feathers, a multimedia performance trio that included girlfriend Hermione Farthingale (of "Letter to Hermione" fame). With unreleased compositions "Ching-a-Ling" and "When I'm Five" (which was recorded by the Beatstalkers), an alternate "Space Oddity," and a mime piece. Bowie wore a mod wig as his hair was freshly shorn from his bit in *The Virgin Soldiers.*

Mad Dogs and Englishmen (1971) Sprawling look at Joe Cocker's massive 1970 U.S. tour, comprising 42 musicians plus their families. The band includes many of organizer Leon Russell's heavy-weight session-man pals, who back up the spastic, gravel-throated song-stylist on "Delta Lady," "Feelin' Alright," "A Little Help from My Friends" and 11 more. There are also songs from Russell and Claudia Linnear.

Magical Mystery Tour (1967)   TV film never officially released in the U.S. until home video, though long a midnight movie staple via washed-out bootlegged prints. The Beatles' first post-Epstein project, largely Paul's baby, was also the group's first critical misfire. Following a bus load of eccentric characters on a magic journey through the English countryside, it works better as a series of acid-drenched promo clips than as a unified narrative. Two days after it was screened by the BBC (on Boxing Day), Paul admitted to a reporter, "We goofed." The Bonzo Dog Doo-Dah Band are seen in a strip club playing "Death Cab for Cutie."

Medicine Ball Caravan (1971)   Warner Brothers, hoping for another *Woodstock*, financed this film and the massive concert tour it documents. Traveling through middle America are headliners Stoneground (featuring ex-Beau Brummel Sal Valentino)—plus B.B. King, Alice Cooper (doing "Black Juju"), Doug Kershaw, Delaney and Bonnie, and the Youngbloods. A promotional trailer played up the traveling circus aspect and named none of the performers. Martin Scorsese was associate producer (actually he was brought in at the editing stage).

The Mekons Movie   Documentary about the long-lasting British punk outfit, shot in 1991. (Soon to be released?)

Millie Jackson—Live (1979)   Short concert film featuring the risque soul singer.

Mississippi Blues (1987)   French director Bertrand Tavernier and American writer Robert Parrish team up for this documentary look at the shanty towns of the deep South and the blues music bred there.

Money Madness (1977)   Documentary showcase for Eddie Money, shown behind the scenes and performing.

No Nukes (1980)   Coverage of the 1979 benefit concerts for Musicians United for Safe Energy. The politically correct lineup includes Bruce Springsteen ("The River," "Thunder Road," "Quarter to Three," "Devil with the Blue Dress On"); James Taylor; Jackson Browne; the Doobie Brothers; Crosby, Stills and Nash; Nicolette Larson; Bonnie Raitt; Gil Scott-Heron; Carly Simon; Jesse Colin Young; and various combinations of the above. Besides the Madison Square Garden shows, a Battery Park rally is seen.

Out of the Blacks into the Blues (1972) French documentary on Mississippi Delta blues—with Sonny Terry, Brownie McGhee, B.B. King, Arthur "Big Boy" Crudup, John Lee Hooker, Albert Collins, Lightnin' Hopkins, and Aretha Franklin.

Pete Seeger—A Song and a Stone (1971) Eighteen months in the life of the out-spoken folksinger. With Johnny Cash and Don McLean. Songs include "Turn Turn Turn" and "Where Have All the Flowers Gone?"

Pictures at an Exhibition (1972)   Video-to-film concert of bombastic prog-rock trio Emerson, Lake, and Palmer. Songs include "Knife Edge," "Take a Pebble," and Kim Fowley's "Nut Rocker."

Pink Floyd (1971)   The group plays seven extended songs in a deserted Roman amphitheater, witnessed only by the camera crew. There are ponderous cutaways to the surrounding ruins and interviews with the band. Songs include "Echoes," "Careful with That Axe Eugene," "Set the Controls for the Heart of the Sun," and "Dark Side of the Moon." Alternate title: *Pink Floyd at Pompeii.*

Playing the Thing (1972)   Short film about harmonica playing—with Sonny

Terry, Duster Bennett, John Sebastian, James Cotton, and Larry Adler.

Popcorn—An Audio-Visual Thing (1969) Hodgepodge of documentary footage of Twiggy, hippies, and cremations. Includes an interview with Mick Jagger and promo films from the likes of the Stones and the Small Faces. Also seen are Jimi Hendrix, the Bee Gees, and Vanilla Fudge.

Portsmouth Sinfonia (1975)   Concert of a classical orchestra made up of musicians playing instruments they can't play, including Brian Eno on clarinet.

Psychiatrist's Convention EPI Show (1966) Jonas Mekas's underground film record of a special booking of the Warhol/Velvet Underground collaboration. No synchronized sound, but Gerard Malanga's whip dance, Edie Sedgwick, and more.

Punk Can Take It (1979)   Julien Temple directed this elaborate U.K. Subs film short that takes the form of a Humphrey Jennings WWII propaganda film.

Punk in London (1977)   German produced documentary with interviews and performances by the Jam ("Carnaby Street"), X-Ray Spex, the Jolt, the Killjoys, Subway Sect, the Adverts, Chelsea, Mark Perry, Jean-Jacques Burnel, Miles Copeland, and more. The Clash were filmed but refused their consent to have the performance included.

Punking Out (1977)   A 25-minute look at the CBGB scene—with performances by the Dead Boys, Richard Hell and the Voidoids, and the Ramones. With a cameo by Lydia Lunch, who claims that the Dead Boys' song "I Need Lunch" was written about her.

Radio Wonderful (1973)   Documentary short on the BBC's Radio One—including interviews with Keith Moon, Jonathan King, Steeleye Span, Doris Troy, and John Peel.

Raga (1971) Documentary feature on the life and music of Ravi Shankar. With George Harrison and Micky Dolenz.

Reality 86ed Super 8 documentary of Black Flag's final tour, made by David Markey (the drummer for opening band Painted Willie and director of *1991: The Year Punk Broke*). Currently unreleased.

Reggae (1970) Coverage of the Caribbean Music Festival at Wembley, England. Seen are: Desmond Dekker; the Maytals; the Pyramids; the Pioneers; Black Faith; John Holt; Count Prince Miller, Millie, Bob and Marcia; Darcus Owusu; Junior Lincoln; Dave Hatfield; Graham Goodall; Lee Gopthall; and Graham Walker.

Reggae Sunsplash (1980) German production filmed at the second Sunsplash Festival in Montego Bay. With Bob Marley and the Wailers, Peter Tosh, Burning Spear, and Third World.

Remember Me This Way (1974) Gary Glitter documentary. Songs include "Leader of the Gang," "I Love You Love Me Love," and the title song.

Right On! Feature documentary starring original rappers the Last Poets. The militant poets perform "James Brown," "Jazz," and "Little Willie Armstrong Jones" from New York rooftops.

Roberta Flack (1971) Half-hour look at the singer performing and discussing the problems of her mixed marriage.

The Rock and Roll Movie (1981) Imaginatively named collection of promo clips and concert footage packaged for mid-night showings. With Jimi Hendrix (taken from *Free*), Meatloaf's "Paradise..." promo touted as the "best rock clip ever made," and various Stones, Beatles, Zeppelin, and Faces clips, all spliced together without rhyme or reason.

Rock City (1973) Like director Peter Clifton's *Popcorn*, this is a rock clip stew with concert footage and promos from Hendrix, the Stones, Otis Redding, the Crazy World of Arthur Brown, Blind Faith, Cat Stevens, and more. Plus an interview with Pete Townshend. Alternate title: *Sound of the City*.

Rock: The Beat Goes On Encyclopedia Brittanica short covering the history of rock, including kinescopes of '50s greats and Beatles footage with a muzak soundtrack. In the film's mid-'70s present, we see Otis Blackwell, Frankie Valli, a Utopia sound check, Seals and Crofts, Linda Ronstadt, James Taylor, and corporate pop band the Dirty Angels (seen at CBGB and described as "punk"). The humorless narration has a bias towards light rock singer/songwriters. Co-edited by Amy Heckerling.

Rockshow (1979) Straightforward concert film starring Paul McCartney and Wings, filmed at their 1976 Seattle show. They plow through "Band on the Run," "Jet," and "Maybe I'm Amazed," as well as "I've Just Seen a Face" and "Yesterday." Band member Denny Laine steps forward for "Go Now" (but no "Japanese Tears").

Rod Stewart and Faces and Keith Richards (1974) Concert film of Kilburn Theatre show in London with Keef sitting in. Songs include "Twistin' the Night Away" and "Maggie May."

The Rolling Stones at the Max (1992) Concert film of the Rolling Stones' "Steel Wheels" tour, the first in a decade for these 50-year-old men. It was filmed in IMAX, a process using a huge curved screen to dominate peripheral vision. Aerial and band point-of-view shots make good use of IMAX, as do whole-stage shots allowing the viewer to focus where he pleases, but the close-ups look silly. The special format of this film limited its release to the few museums equipped with IMAX theaters, resulting in a minor controversy over whether scientific institutions should be used for rock'n'roll films.

The Rolling Stones Gather Moss (1964) Pathé wide-screen newsreel of the band on a British tour.

The Rolling Stones Rock and Roll Circus Show (1968) Legendary film shot for TV and never released. John and Yoko, Eric Clapton, Jethro Tull, and the Who join the Stones in a circus-tent setting, along with a full orchestra and a host of animal and juggling acts. All were fitted with lavish costumes, with Mick as the ringmaster. The Stones played seven songs, but Jagger was dissatisfied with his band's performance, so the project was shelved. A clip of Lennon leading an all-star jam of "Yer Blues" has circulated, the Who's scene showed up in *The Kids Are Alright*, and other footage appeared in the *25 X 5* home video, but the complete show exists only as a bootleg.

Roots Rock Reggae (1978) This documentary of the Kingston music scene drops in on radio stations, record labels, and concerts. Appearing are Bob Marley, Junior Murvin, Jimmy Cliff, and the Mighty Diamonds. Songs include "Trenchtown Rock" and "Lively Up Yourself."

Rope Ladder to the Moon (1969) Robert Stigwood-produced documentary on Jack Bruce, with music from *Goodbye Cream* and Bruce's *Songs for a Tailor* solo album. With John Mayall and Tony Williams.

Rory Gallagher—Irish Tour (1974) Concert footage of the blues guitarist and former Taste-leader playing in Belfast, Cork, and Dublin.

Rough Cut and Ready Dubbed (1982) British Film Institute-funded look at the 1980 state of punk's decline. With concert and interview footage of Patrik Fitzgerald, Stiff Little Fingers, the U.K. Subs, Cockney Rejects, John Peel, and Colin Peacock.

Salsa (1976) Concerts in Yankee Stadium and San Juan include performances by Mongo Santamaria, Manu Dibangia, and Billy Cobham.

Save the Children (1973) Concert for the People United to Save Humanity, intercut with footage of atrocities against children. With Marvin Gaye ("Save the Children," "What's Going On"), the Temptations ("Papa Was a Rolling Stone"), Curtis Mayfield ("Give Me Your Love"), the Jackson Five, the Chi-Lites, the O'Jays, Main Ingredient, Isaac Hayes, Bill Withers, Jerry Butler and Brenda Lee Eager, Cannonball Adderley, Sammy Davis Jr., Nancy Wilson, Gladys Knight and the Pips, and more.

The Secret Policeman's Ball (1979) Amnesty International comedy gala with music from Pete Townshend (acoustic versions of "Pinball Wizard" and "Won't Get Fooled Again") and Tom Robinson.

The Secret Policeman's Other Ball (1981) This follow-up to the first *Ball* film has footage from both concerts. With Sting, Phil Collins, Eric Clapton, Jeff Beck, and Pete Townshend, plus comedy from Monty Python.

Shell Shock Rock (1979) Documentary on punk rock in politically-charged

Belfast. With the Undertones, Stiff Little Fingers, and the Idiots.

Sign O' the Times (1987)   Prince concert film shot in Holland, which mixes in surreal vignettes. Musicians include Sheila E., Cat Glover, and guest Sheena Easton. Songs include "U Got the Look" and "Little Red Corvette."

Sing Sing Thanksgiving (1974)   Film of a Joan Baez-organized prison concert with Joe Williams, B.B. King, Mimi Fariña, and Jimmy Walker and the Voices of East Harlem.

Slits Pictures (1979)   Don Lett co-directed this short film about the female punk/dub outfit, with the girls performing several songs and cavorting in a supermarket.

Somewhere Between Heaven and Woolworth's   Short documentary about the Easybeats in England, directed by Peter Clifton. Last known sighting was at a 1970 concert in Australia. Alternate title: *Easy Come Easy Go*.

Son of Stiff Tour Movie (1981)   Documentary of the second Stiff Records package tour. The eccentric musicians include Any Trouble, Tenpole Tudor, ska band the Equators, and American signings Dirty Looks and Joe "King" Carrasco and the Crowns.

Sound of a City (1964)   Short look at the Merseybeat scene in Liverpool. With the Swingin' Blue Jeans, the Zephyrs, and the Aces.

Steppin' Out (1979)   Short film of London nightlife includes mod revivalists Secret Affair and the Merton Parkas, plus a visit to a roller disco.

Sun's Gonna Shine (1980)   See *The Blues According to Lightnin' Hopkins*.

Supershow (1970)   Jazz and rock concert with Eric Clapton, Jack Bruce, Colliseum, Buddy Miles, and Roland Kirk, who jam in various combinations. Led Zeppelin does a scorching "Dazed and Confused." Also appearing are the Misunderstood, Stephen Stills, Dallas Taylor, Glen Campbell, Duster Bennett, Chris Mercer, and the Modern Jazz Quartet.

Superstars in Film Concert (1971)   Another grab bag of footage from rock filmmaker Peter Clifton (see *Popcorn—An Audio Visual Thing* and *Rock City*).

Take It or Leave It (1981)   Feature-length cinema verité look at the British ska band Madness. The "nutty" boys search for musicians and perform "Bed and Breakfast Man," "One Step Beyond," and seven more. Directed by Stiff Records founder Dave Robinson.

TG Psychic Rally in Heaven (1981)   Concert film with industrial music pioneers Throbbing Gristle.

The Road to God Knows Where (1990)   Road film of Nick Cave and the Bad Seeds (Mick Harvey, Blixa Bargeld, and Kid Congo Powers) on tour.

Third World—Prisoner in the Street (1980)   French-made feature-length documentary of the reggae group. With interviews and songs including "African Woman," "Street Fighting," and "Third World Man."

This Rockin' Globe (1978)   Starring the Jack Bruce Band.

To Russia with Elton (1979)   Dudley Moore narrates this travelogue look at Elton's pre-*glasnost* tour behind the Iron Curtain. Songs include "Crocodile Rock," "Pinball Wizard," and "Back in the U.S.S.R."

Twist Craze (1961) Eight-minute short of a twist demonstration for the stodgy patrons of a posh Chicago supper club. Tobin Matthews and the All-Stars, a band with a cross-eyed drummer, play the same instrumental number several times in the swank setting (which even has a swimming pool).

Urgh! A Music War (1981) Marathon concert collection showcasing 33 early-'80s New Wave acts, most of whom were affiliated in some way with Miles Copeland's management firm, his I.R.S. record label, or his brother's F.B.I. booking agency. Probably no one else would have thought to put John Cooper-Clarke, Jools Holland, Chelsea, Wall of Voodoo, John Otway, and Skafish on the big screen. The roll call also includes Toyah Wilcox, Orchestral Manoeuvres in the Dark, Oingo Boingo, Echo and the Bunnymen, XTC, Klaus Nomi, Athletico Spizz 80, the Go Go's, the Dead Kennedys, Steel Pulse, Gary Numan, Joan Jett, Magazine, Surf Punks, the Au Pairs, the Cramps, Invisible Sex, Pere Ubu, Devo, the Alley Cats, Gang of Four, 999, the Fleshtones, X, Splodgeness Abounds, and UB40—plus Miles's brother's band, the Police, who are the only act who get to do more than one song (they play "Driven to Tears" and "Roxanne").

Van Morrison in Ireland (1980) Concerts from Belfast and Dublin include "Moondance," "Tupelo Honey," "Wavelength," and "Gloria."

The Velvet Underground and Nico: A Symphony of Sound (1966) Andy Warhol's film of the band rehearsing at the Factory and eventually being halted by the police. With Mary Woronov and Gerard Malanga.

Welcome to My Nightmare (1975) Grainy concert film from Alice Cooper's British tour, showing a *Hollywood Squares*-safe Alice well past his prime, both musically and theatrically. Couldn't someone have filmed the *Killer* shows?

What's Happening! The Beatles in the U.S.A. (1964) Long-neglected Maysles Brothers chronicle of the Beatles' first U.S. tour, which finally turned up as most of the *First U.S. Visit* home video. The cinema verité scenes of the lads traveling, greeting the press, etc., were surely seen by the makers of *A Hard Day's Night*, which this film strongly resembles.

Why Should the Devil Have All the Good Music? (1972) Religious concert starring a born-again Cliff Richard.

The Wild World of Hasil Adkins Documentary about the West Virginia primitive rockabilly singer, who has been releasing his own records for over thirty years and has just recently gained some notoriety.

Yessongs (1973) Lackluster concert film with the Rick Wakeman/Alan White lineup of the prog-rockers, shot from just a few camera angles. The animation by onetime best-selling poster artist Roger Dean provides occasional diversion. Songs include "All Good People," "Close to the Edge," and "The Clap."

Ziggy Stardust and the Spiders from Mars (1982) Re-edited, re-released version of *Bowie '73.'*

Zydeco Les Blank's Creole documentary features Bebee Carriere, Amedee Ardoin, and Alphonse "Bois Sec" Ardoin.

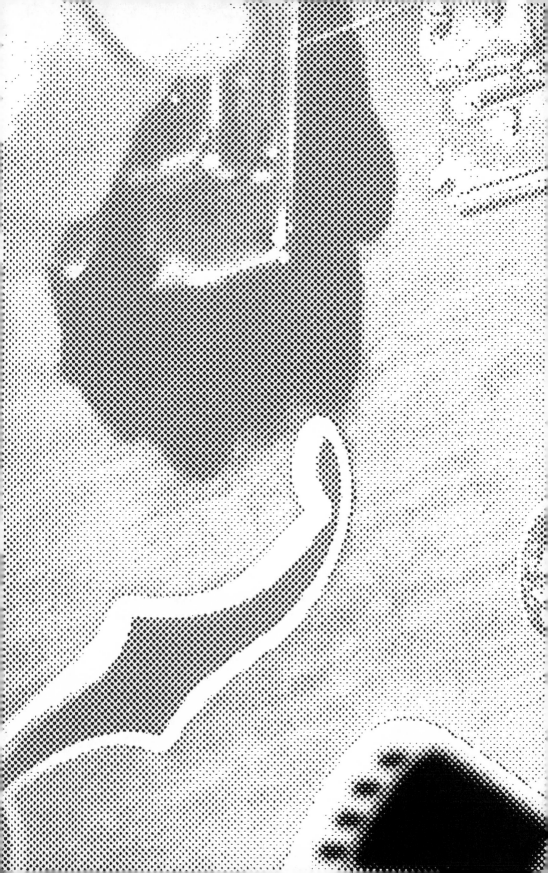

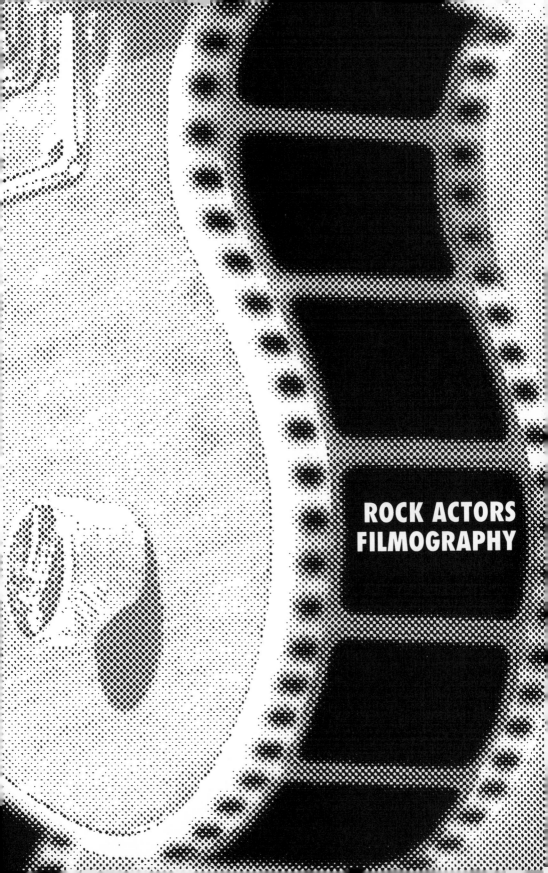

ROCK ACTORS
FILMOGRAPHY

ADAM ANT

Jubilee (1978)
Nomads (1986)
Slamdance (1987)
Cold Steel (1988)
World Gone Wild (1988)
Trust Me (1989)
Spellcaster (1991)
Sunset Heat (1992)

FRANKIE AVALON

Jamboree (1957)
The Alamo (1960)
Guns of the Timberland (1960)
Alakazam the Great! (1961)
Sail a Crooked Ship (1961)
Voyage to the Bottom of the Sea (1961)
Panic in Year Zero (1962)
Beach Party (1963)
The Castilian (1963)
Drums of Africa (1963)
Operation Bikini (1963)
Bikini Beach (1964)
Muscle Beach Party (1964)
Pajama Party (1964)
Beach Blanket Bingo (1965)
Dr. Goldfoot and the Bikini Machine (1965)
How to Stuff a Wild Bikini (1965)
I'll Take Sweden (1965)
Sergeant Deadhead (1965)
Ski Party (1965)
Fireball 500 (1966)
The Million Eyes of Su-Muru (1967)
Skidoo (1968)
Horror House (1970)
The Take (1974)
Grease (1978)
Blood Song (1982)
Back to the Beach (1987)

SONNY BONO

Good Times (1967)
Murder on Flight 502 (TV) (1975)
Escape from Athena (1979)
Vals (1985)
Balboa (1986)
Troll (1986)
Airplane II: The Sequel (1987)
Dirty Laundry (1987)
Under the Boardwalk (1988)
Hairspray (1988)

PAT BOONE

April Love (1957)
Bernadine (1957)
Mardi Gras (1958)
Journey to the Center of the Earth
  (1959)
All Hands on Deck (1961)
The Main Attraction (1962)
State Fair (1962)
The Yellow Canary (1963)
Goodbye Charlie (1964)
The Horror of It All (1964)
Never Put It in Writing (1964)
The Greatest Story Ever Told (1965)
The Perils of Pauline (1967)
The Cross and the Switchblade (1972)

DAVID BOWIE

The Virgin Soldiers (1969)
The Image (1969)
The Man Who Fell to Earth (1976)
Just a Gigolo (1979)
The Hunger (1983)
Merry Christmas, Mr. Lawrence (1983)
Yellowbeard (1983)
Into the Night (1985)
Labyrinth (1986)

Absolute Beginners (1986)
The Last Temptation of Christ (1988)
UHF (1989)
The Linguini Incident (1992)
Twin Peaks: Fire Walk with Me (1992)

CHER
Wild on the Beach (1965)
Good Times (1967)
Chastity (1969)
Come Back to the 5&Dime, Jimmy Dean,
    Jimmy Dean (1982)
Silkwood (1983)
Mask (1985)
Moonstruck (1987)
Suspect (1987)
The Witches of Eastwick (1987)
Mermaids (1990)

PHIL COLLINS
Buster (1988)
Yellowbeard (1983)
Hook (1991)
Frauds (1993)
And the Band Played On (1993)

ROGER DALTREY
Tommy (1975)
Lisztomania (1975)
The Legacy (1979)
McVicar (1980)
Murder: Ultimate Grounds for Divorce
    (1985)
Cold Justice (1989)
Mack the Knife (1989)
Forgotten Prisoners (1990)
If Looks Could Kill (1991)
Buddy's Song (1991)

FABIAN [FABIAN FORTE]
Hound-Dog Man (1959)
High Time (1960)
North to Alaska (1960)
Love in a Goldfish Bowl (1961)
Five Weeks in a Baloon (1962)
The Longest Day (1962)
Mr. Hobbs Takes a Vacation (1962)

Ride the Wild Surf (1964)
Dear Brigitte (1965)
Ten Little Indians (1965)
Dr. Goldfoot and the Girl Bombs (1966)
Fireball 500 (1966)
Thunder Alley (1967)
Maryjane (1968)
The Wild Racers (1968)
The Devil's 8 (1969)
A Bullet for Pretty Boy (1970)
Little Laura and Big John (1973)
Soul Hustler (1975)
Baby Love (1983)
Get Crazy (1983)

ADAM FAITH
Never Let Go (1960)
What a Whopper (1961)
What a Carve Up! (1962)
Mix Me a Person (1962)
Stardust (1974)
Yesterday's Hero (1979)
McVicar (1982)

MARIANNE FAITHFULL
Made in U.S.A. (1966)
I'll Never Forget What's 'Is Name (1967)
Girl on a Motorcycle (1968)
Hamlet (1969)
Ghost Story (1974)
Assault on Agathon (1976)

FLEA
Dudes (1987)
Back to the Future, Part III (1990)
My Own Private Idaho (1991)
Motorama (1993)

ART GARFUNKEL
Catch-22 (1970)
Carnal Knowledge (1971)
Bad Timing: A Sensual Obsession (1980)
Good to Go (1986)

ARCH HALL, JR.
The Choppers (1961)
Wild Guitar (1962)

The Sadist (1963)
The Nasty Rabbit (1964)
Deadwood '76 (1965)

DEBORAH HARRY
The Foreigner (1978)
Mr. Mike's Mondo Video (1979)
Union City (1980)
Videodrome (1983)
Forever, Lulu (1987)
Hairspray (1988)
Satisfaction (1988)
Tales from the Darkside: The Movie (1990)
Intimate Stranger (1991)

ISAAC HAYES
Three Tough Guys (1974)
Truck Turner (1974)
It Seemed Like a Good Idea at the Time
   (1975)
Escape from New York (1981)
Jailbait: Betrayed By Innocence (1986)
Counterforce (1987)
Dead Aim (1987)
I'm Gonna Git You Sucka! (1989)
Guilty As Charged (1991)
Prime Target (1991)
Posse (1993)

LEVON HELM
Coal Miner's Daughter (1980)
The Right Stuff (1983)
Best Revenge (1984)
The Dollmaker (1984)
Smooth Talk (1986)
End of the Line (1988)
Man Outside (1988)
Staying Together (1989)

ICE-T
New Jack City (1991)
Ricochet (1991)
Trespass (1992)
Who's the Man (1993)

CHRIS ISAAK
Married to the Mob (1988)

The Silence of the Lambs (1991)
Twin Peaks: Fire Walk with Me (1992)
Little Buddah (1993)

DAVID JOHANSEN
Candy Mountain (1987)
Scrooged (1988)
Let It Ride (1989)
Desire and Hell at the Sunset Motel (1990)
Tales from the Darkside, The Movie (1990)
Car 54, Where Are You? (1992)
Freejack (1992)

GARY KEMP
The Krays (1990)
The Bodyguard (1992)
Paper Marriage (1992)

CYNDI LAUPER
Vibes (1988)
Life with Mikey (1993)
Off and Running (unreleased)

MADONNA
A Certain Sacrifice (1978-1981)
Desperately Seeking Susan (1985)
Vision Quest (1985)
Shanghai Surprise (1986)
Who's That Girl (1987)
Bloodhounds of Broadway (1989)
Dick Tracy (1990)
Shadows and Fog (1992)
A League of Their Own (1992)
Body of Evidence (1993)

MEATLOAF
The Rocky Horror Picture Show (1975)
Americathon (1979)
Roadie (1980)
The Squeeze (1987)
Leap of Faith (1992)
Motorama (1993)

RICKY NELSON
Here Come the Nelsons (1952)
The Story of Three Loves (1953)
Rio Bravo (1959)

The Wackiest Ship in the Army
(1961)
Love and Kisses (1965)

DIANA ROSS
Lady Sings the Blues (1972)
Mahogany (1975)
The Wiz (1978)

TOMMY SANDS
Mardi Gras (1958)
Sing, Boy, Sing (1958)
Babes in Toyland (1961)
The Longest Day (1962)
Love in a Goldfish Bowl (1962)
Ensign Pulver (1964)
None But the Brave (1965)
The Violent Ones (1967)

RINGO STARR
A Hard Day's Night (1964)
Help! (1965)
Candy (1968)
The Magic Christian (1970)
200 Motels (1971)
Blindman (1972)
That'll Be the Day (1974)
Son of Dracula (1974)
Lisztomania (1975)
Sextette (1978)
Caveman (1981)
Princess Daisy (1983)
Give My Regards to Broad Street
(1984)

STING
Quadrophenia (1979)
Radio On (1979)
Brimstone and Treacle (1982)
Dune (1984)
The Bride (1985)
Plenty (1985)
Julia & Julia (1987)
The Adventures of Baron Munchausen
(1988)
Stormy Monday (1988)
Resident Alien (1990)

FRANKIE VALLI
Grease (1978)
Sgt. Pepper's Lonely Hearts Club Band
(1978)
Dirty Laundry (1987)

LEE VING
Flashdance (1983)
Get Crazy (1983)
Streets of Fire (1984)
Wild Life (1984)
Black Moon Rising (1986)
Oceans of Fire (1986)
Dudes (1987)
Scenes from the Goldmine (1987)
Grave Secrets (1989)
The Taking of Beverly Hills (1991)

TOM WAITS
Paradise Alley (1978)
One from the Heart (1982)
Poetry in Motion (1982)
The Outsiders (1983)
Rumblefish (1983)
The Cotton Club (1984)
Down By Law (1986)
Ironweed (1987)
Candy Mountain (1987)
Bearskin: An Urban Fairytale (1989)
Cold Feet (1989)
At Play in the Fields of the Lord (1991)
The Fisher King (1991)
Queen's Logic (1991)
Bram Stoker's Dracula (1992)
Short Cuts (1993)

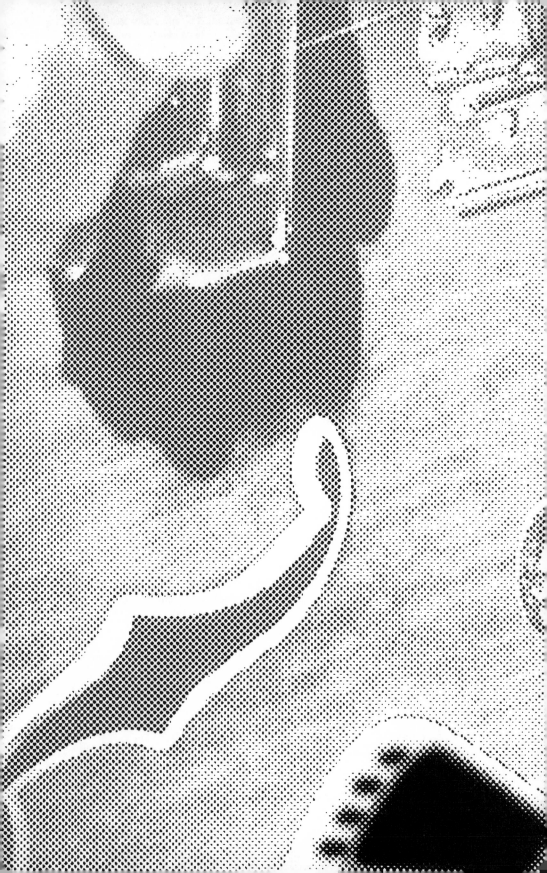

**CAMEO
GLOSSARY**

Franklin Ajaye '70s stand-up comic who was never quite as funny as Freddie Prinze.

Alice in Chains Seattle grunge band.

Steve Allen hosted the "Tonight" show before Jack Paar, Johnny Carson, and Jay Leno.

Keith Allison Paul McCartney-lookalike who played with Paul Revere and the Raiders.

Allan Arkush directed *Rock'n'Roll High School.*

R.G. Armstrong played Tanner's father in "Tanner '88."

Asleep at the Wheel Texas band that revived popular interest in western swing.

Ed Asner played Lou Grant on "The Mary Tyler Moore Show."

Fred Astaire danced his way to stardom with Ginger Rogers.

Frankie Avalon Annette Funicello's sidekick in the *Beach Party* movies.

Barbara Bain starred alongside husband Martin Landau in "Mission: Impossible" and "Space: 1999."

Paul Bartel directed and acted in *Eating Raoul* and *Scenes from the Class Struggle in Beverly Hills.*

Warren Beatty Shirley MacLaine's brother.

Ed Begley, Jr. pale-haired, pink-faced actor who starred on TV's "St. Elsewhere."

Paul Benedict played the British fellow on "The Jeffersons" and the film professor in *The Freshman.*

Sandra Bernhard ex-Madonna gal-pal who starred in her own one-woman show, *Without You I'm Nothing.*

Chuck Berry had a film career, too. (See the February 1993 issue of *SPY* magazine.)

Jello Biafra led a punk band called the Dead Kennedys.

Rodney Bingenheimer one-time stand-in for Davy Jones on "The Monkees" and now a fixture on the L.A. music scene.

The Blasters fundamental L.A. rock band that hit with "Marie, Marie" and "Border Radio."

Mike Bloomfield late-'60s guitar hero who worked with Bob Dylan on "Like a Rolling Stone."

The Blues Brothers two characters invented by John Belushi and Dan Aykroyd for a "Saturday Night Live" sketch that became a record and then a movie.

Gypsy Boots early hippie health-food advocate who danced wildly at Sunset Strip clubs who now hangs out at Dodger Stadium.

Joe Bob Briggs writes syndicated movie reviews for the Bubba crowd.

Alice Brock the Alice of "Alice's Restaurant."

James Brown the Godfather of Soul.

Julie Brown starred in her own *Truth or Dare* spoof, *Medusa: Dare to Be Truthful.*

Jimmy Buffett wears Hawaiian shirts and sings "Margaritaville."

Dez Cadena former member of Black Flag.

Cab Calloway Cotton Club star who wrote "Minnie the Moocher."

Timothy Carey career Hollywood villain who starred in *The Killing* and *One-Eyed Jacks*.

Nell Carter sitcom actress who got her start in the musical "Ain't Misbehavin'" on Broadway.

Dana Carvey played Garth in *Wayne's World*.

Dick Cavett famous talk-show host.

Ray Charles well-known Pepsi spokesman (or is it Coke?).

Tom Cherwin proofread this book.

Tommy Chong doper half of the Cheech and Chong comedy team.

Eric Clapton played with the Yardbirds and helped to found the psychedelic band Cream before going solo.

Dick Clark hosted "American Bandstand" and "The $20,000 Pyramid."

George Clinton funk guru who formed the Parliament/Funkadelic.

Iron Eyes Cody inspired guilt as the crying Native American in a famous early-'70s anti-pollution commercial.

Elisha Cook, Jr. played opposite Humphrey Bogart as Sydney Greenstreet's gunsel in *The Maltese Falcon*.

Rita Coolidge subject of Leon Russell's "The Delta Lady" who hit with "Higher and Higher."

Caroline Coon pioneering British punk journalist.

Chris Cornell lead singer of Soundgarden.

Elvis Costello worked as a computer operator before making his debut album *My Aim Is True* in 1977.

Kevin Costner the auteur of *Dances with Wolves*.

Country Joe and the Fish sang "I Feel-Like-I'm Fixing-to-Die Rag" at Woodstock.

Marshall Crenshaw has a bulldog named Lassie.

Frankie Crocker longtime New York soul DJ who hosted NBC's "Friday Night Videos."

Steve Cropper lead guitarist for Booker T. and the MGs who co-wrote "(Sittin' on) The Dock of the Bay."

David Crosby played with the Byrds before hooking up with Stephen Stills Graham Nash, and Neil Young.

Alvin Crow Austin fiddle player.

Cameron Crowe wrote an article for *Rolling Stone* about high school life that became *Fast Times at Ridgemont High*.

Billy Crystal starred in *When Harry Met Sally* and *City Slickers*.

Warren Cucurullo Frank Zappa's guitarist before joining Zappa alumni Terry Bozzio in Missing Persons.

Willem Dafoe acted at New York's experimental Performing Garage with the Wooster Group before starring in *Platoon* and *Mississippi Burning*.

John Densmore drummer for the Doors.

Rick Derringer played lead guitar in the McCoys ("Hang On Sloopy"), then with Johnny Winter, and later produced some of Weird Al Yankovic's pop parodies.

Pamela Des Barres the groupie with a brain who wrote *I'm with the Band* and *Take a Little Piece of My Heart*.

Devo animated the New Wave scene with their hit "Whip It."

Jim Dickinson eccentric southerner who produced Big Star, the Replacements, and the Spin Doctors.

Pat DiNizio fronted the Smithereens, one of Jersey's finest bands.

Carol Doda San Francisco Condor Club stripper who became famous during the '60s for the size of her breasts.

Fran Drescher played Bobbi Flekman in *This Is Spinal Tap*.

Richard Dreyfuss played the marine biologist in *Jaws*.

Dr. John New Orleans piano player who sings "Aiko-Aiko."

Olympia Dukakis is the sister of presidential runner-up Michael Dukakis. She played Cher's mom in *Moonstruck*.

Ian Dury British rocker who sang "Sex and Drugs and Rock and Roll" with the Blockheads.

Ronnie Dyson member of *Hair*'s original cast who sang "I Just Don't Want to Be Lonely."

John Entwistle played bass for the Who.

Bob Eubanks hosted "The Newlywed Game."

Shelley Fabares played Mary Stone on "The Donna Reed Show" and sang "Johnny Angel."

The Fabulous Thunderbirds Austin band that hit in 1986 with "Tuff Enuff."

The Family Dog commune-like group that produced the first concerts in the Haight-Ashbury.

Mike Farrell played B.J. Cunningham on "M*A*S*H."

Joe Flynn played Captain Binghamton on "McHale's Navy."

Ellen Foley female voice on Meatloaf's "Paradise by the Dashboard Light."

Frankie Ford New Orleans rocker who sang "Sea Cruise."

Harrison Ford played Indiana Jones in *Raiders of the Lost Ark*.

Fabian Forte early-'60s teen idol manufactured by Bob Marcucci of Philadelphia's Chancellor Records.

Douglas Fowley father of Kim Fowley and a regular on "The Adventures of Wyatt Earp."

Peter Frampton came alive during the mid-'70s with "I'm in You" and "Show Me the Way."

Aretha Franklin first lady of R&B who sang "Respect" and "A Natural Woman."

Annette Funicello former Mouseketeer who starred with Frankie Avalon in the *Beach Party* movies.

Leata Galloway member of the original cast of *Hair*.

Jerry Garcia plays lead guitar with the Grateful Dead.

Teri Garr played Gene Wilder's assistant in *Young Frankenstein* and Dustin Hoffman's worried friend in *Tootsie*.

Crispin Glover played Michael J. Fox's father in *Back to the Future*.

Jean-Luc Godard French New Wave director of *Breathless* and *Alphaville*.

Jack Good British TV executive who produced "Oh Boy" in the U.K. and "Shindig" in America.

Bill Graham the late San Francisco concert promoter.

George Harrison played himself in *Help!*.

Debbie Harry fronted the New York art band Blondie.

Screamin' Jay Hawkins sprang from a coffin to wail "I Put a Spell on You."

Flora Hayes was once Hawaii's territorial representative to the U.S. Congress.

Buck Henry created "Get Smart" with Mel Brooks.

Howard Hesseman played Dr. Johnny Fever on "WKRP in Cincinnati."

John Lee Hooker famous Chicago bluesman.

Dennis Hopper played Billy in *Easy Rider*, the photographer in *Apocalypse Now*, and Frank in *Blue Velvet*.

Peter Horton played Gary Shepherd on "Thirtysomething."

Sean Hughes British alternative comic.

Anjelica Huston played John Cusack's mom in *The Grifters*.

Henry Jaglom directed *Eating* and *Someone to Love*.

The James Gang Ohio-based power trio that featured Joe Walsh.

Janet the Planet famous Zappa audience participant.

Jim Jarmusch wrote and directed *Stranger Than Paradise*, *Down By Law*, *Mystery Train*, and *Night on Earth*.

Michael Jeter plays the assistant coach in "Evening Shade."

Elton John stage name of Reginald Kenneth Dwight who formed his first band, Bluesology, in 1966. (He took his stage name from the first names of Bluesology members Elton Dean and John Baldry.)

Anissa Jones played Buffy on "Family Affair" and later died of a Quaalude overdose.

Grace Jones Amazonian creature of the night who played a strikingly costumed villain in the 1985 James Bond film *A View to a Kill*.

Will Jordan famous Ed Sullivan impersonator.

The Jordanaires Nashville-based vocal group who backed Elvis, Patsy Cline, and others.

Boris Karloff horror legend who played Frankenstein in *Frankenstein* and the Mummy in *The Mummy*.

Howard Kaylan sang with partner Mark Volman in the Turtles, with Frank Zappa and the Mothers of Invention and later Flo and Eddie.

Dave Kendall bewigged former host of MTV's "120 Minutes."

Patricia Keneally ex-girlfriend of Jim Morrison.

Doug Kershaw Cajun musician who sang "Louisiana Man" with his brother Rusty.

Bobby Keyes played saxophone with the Rolling Stones.

Bruno Kirby played Billy Crystal's best friend in *When Harry Met Sally* and *City Slickers*.

Danny Kortchmar session guitar player who produced Don Henley.

Ivan Kral played guitar with the Patti Smith Group.

Stuart Lancaster member of the Russ Meyer acting company.

John Lennon Yoko Ono's husband.

Phil Lesh plays bass with the Grateful Dead.

Jerry Lee Lewis married his 13-year-old cousin Myra.

Arto Lindsay New York avant-rock musician who played with the Lounge Lizards and formed the Ambitious Lovers.

Sonny Liston former heavyweight boxing champion.

Los Lobos Mexican-American band that topped the charts with their cover of the title track from *La Bamba*.

Courtney Love wife of Nirvana frontman Kurt Cobain and leader of Hole.

Darlene Love lead singer of the Ronettes who married and then divorced Phil Spector.

Tony Machine plays drums for Buster Poindexter.

Johnny Maestro Italian-American vocalist who sang with the Crests ("Sixteen Candles") and then the Brooklyn Bridge ("The Worst That Could Happen").

Joe Mantegna played the Jewish cop in *Homicide*.

Ray Manzarek played organ with the Doors.

Rocky Marciano former heavyweight boxing champion.

Herbert Marshall appeared in *The Fly*, *Midnight Lace*, and *Blonde Venus*.

Steve Martin played the jerk in *The Jerk*.

Victor Mature played Samson in Cecil B. De Mille's *Samson and Delilah*.

Maureen McCormick played Marcia on "The Brady Bunch."

Van McCoy produced and arranged disco prototype "The Hustle."

Xavier McDaniel plays small forward in the NBA.

Barry McGuire folk-rock singer with the New Christy Minstrels who hit solo with "Eve of Destruction."

Howard McNear played Floyd the barber on "The Andy Griffith Show."

Meatloaf sang the teen-hormone hit "Paradise by the Dashboard Light."

Jonas Mekas underground filmmaker and critic for the *Village Voice* during the early '60s.

Keith Moon played drums for the Who.

Paul Mooney former Richard Pryor writer with a stand-up act of his own.

Melba Moore member of the original company of *Hair*.

Keith Morris singer of the Circle Jerks

The Mothers of Invention band founded by Frank Zappa in 1964 and disbanded in 1971.

Bob Mould fronted Husker Dü.

Mudhoney Seattle band who first recorded for Sub Pop.

Cookie Mueller member of the John Waters's acting company who appeared in *Female Trouble* and *Multiple Maniacs*.

Murray the K influential New York DJ who called himself the "Fifth Beatle."

The New York Rock'n'Roll Ensemble classical rock fusion band from the late '60s.

Jack Nicholson made countercultural films in the '60s and millions in the '80s.

Mojo Nixon human embodiment of Foghorn Leghorn.

Peter Noone Herman of Herman's Hermits.

Chris Noth plays the handsome young detective in TV's "Law and Order."

Don Novello Father Guido Sarducci on "Saturday Night Live" and the author of *The Laszlo Letters*.

William Obanhein Officer Obie from "Alice's Restaurant" who took the 8x10 color glossy photographs with the circles and arrows on the back.

Roy Orbison the guy with the dark glasses who sang "Pretty Woman."

Bruce Pabitt co-owner and founder of Sub Pop records

Jack Palance played the leather-skinned Marlboro Man in *City Slickers*.

Tony Paris wrote the reviews of *D.O.A.* in this book.

Alan Parker directed *Midnight Express, Fame, Pink Floyd: The Wall, Birdy, Angel Heart,* among other films.

Pearl Jam Seattle grunge band fronted by Eddie Vedder.

Vicki Peterson played lead guitar with the Bangles.

Tom Petty Dylan soundalike and founding member of the Traveling Wilburys.

Slim Pickens rode a nuclear bomb in *Dr. Strangelove* and played Harvey Korman's hired gun in *Blazing Saddles*.

The Pogues radical British folk-rockers.

Vincent Price played Egghead on TV's "Batman."

Jimmy Pursey punk rocker who sang with Sham 69.

Joe Pyne right-wing talk-show host who served as a model for Morton Downey, Jr.

Charlotte Rae played Mrs. Garrett on "The Facts of Life."

Dee Dee Ramone founded and played bass for the Ramones.

Nicholas Ray directed *Rebel without a Cause*.

Maureen Reagan daughter of the star of *Cattle Queen of Montana*.

Leon Redbone gravel-voiced Canadian folksinger who appeared on "Saturday Night Live" during the mid-'70s.

Rockets Redglare New York performance artist.

Lou Reed former member of the Velvet Underground who hit solo with "Walk on the Wild Side."

Carl Reiner straight man for Mel Brooks and father of Rob who created and produced "The Dick Van Dyke Show."

Rob Reiner Meathead on "All in the Family" and director of *Stand by Me* and *This Is Spinal Tap*.

REO Speedwagon first topped the charts with "Keep On Loving You."

Trent Reznor founder of Nine Inch Nails.

Don Rickles comedian who makes a living insulting people and specializes in impressions.

Sam Riddle L.A.-based DJ and teen music-show host of the '60s.

Geraldo Rivera opened Al Capone's vault and hosted other memorable events on live television.

Jason Robards played Ben Bradlee in *All the President's Men*.

Mimi Rogers ex-wife of Tom Cruise who starred in *Someone to Watch Over Me*.

Linda Ronstadt topped the charts in 1975 with "You're No Good."

Tony Rosato veteran of "SCTV" and "Saturday Night Live."

Brenda Russell veteran session vocalist who had a solo hit with "Piano in the Dark."

David Sanborn saxophone player who hosted TV's "Night Music."

Colonel Harlan Sanders goateed fried-chicken impresario.

John Sayles directed *The Return of the Secaucus Seven* and *Matewan*.

John Sebastian sang with the Loving Spoonful.

Pete Seeger helped popularize folk music during the '50s with the Weavers.

Brian Setzer fronted the Stray Cats and played in the Honeydrippers.

Paul Shaffer David Letterman's sidekick and bandleader.

Harry Shearer played Derek Smalls in *This Is Spinal Tap.*

Bobby Sherman late-'60s teenybopper idol who appeared regularly on "Shindig."

Michael Shrieve played drums for Santana.

Charles Martin Smith played Toad in *American Graffiti* and the accountant in *The Untouchables.*

Tommy Smothers the taller Smothers brother.

Suzanne Somers played the blonde Chrissy on "Three's Company."

Soundgarden Seattle grunge band.

Terry Southern wrote the cult novels *Candy* and *The Magic Christian.*

Phil Spector "Wall of Sound" record producer whose hits include the Crystals' "He's a Rebel," the Righteous Brothers' "Unchained Melody," and John Lennon's "Instant Karma."

Harry Dean Stanton played Emilio Estevez's mentor in *Repo Man.*

Ringo Starr drummed for the Beatles but later found his calling as a caveman.

Daniel Stern played Ellen Barkin's husband in *Diner* and the tall burglar in *Home Alone.*

Joe Strummer led the Clash.

Grady Sutton character actor who appeared in numerous W.C. Fields films.

Tad modern rocker in the Meatloaf mode who recorded on Sub Pop.

Rufus Thomas Memphis-based R&B singer who hit with "Walking the Dog" and "Do the Funky Chicken."

Tiny Tim falsetto-voiced ukulele player who sang "Tip-Toe Thru' the Tulips with Me" and married Miss Vicki on the "Tonight" show.

Su Tissue lead singer with the SoCal New Wave band Suburban Lawns.

Rudy Toombs R&B songwriter who penned "One Scotch, One Bourbon, One Beer. "

Robert Townsend wrote, starred in, and directed the *Hollywood Shuffle* and *The Five Heartbeats.*

Pete Townshend destroyed many guitars while playing with the Who.

Ellen Travolta John's sister.

Doris Troy R&B singer-songwriter who hit with "Just One Look" and sang back-up vocals on Pink Floyd's *Dark Side of the Moon* album.

Edward Tudorpole sang with the British band Tenpole Tudor.

Tina Turner inducted into the Rock'n'Roll Hall of Fame (with her former husband Ike) in 1991.

John Turturro played the title role in *Barton Fink.*

Ultraviolet appeared in Factory-era Andy Warhol films.

Jimmie Vaughan Texas-based blues guitarist (the older brother of Stevie Ray Vaughan) who played with the Fabulous Thunderbirds.

Dick Van Patten played the dad on "Eight Is Enough."

Lee Ving lead singer of Fear.

Tom Waits gravely voiced Renaissance man.

M. Emmet Walsh played the bad guy in *Blood Simple.*

Andy Warhol initiated the Pop Art movement with his paintings of Campbell's Soup cans.

John Waters iconoclast director of *Pink Flamingos, Hairspray,* and *Cry Baby.*

Chuck E. Weiss title character in Rickie Lee Jones's "Chuck E.'s in Love."

Raquel Welch '60s sex symbol is best remembered for her roles in *One Million Years B.C.* and *Fantastic Voyage.*

Frank Welker voice talent for TV cartoons.

Red West member of Elvis's Memphis Mafia.

Fred Willard played Martin Mull's co-host Jerry Hubbard on "Fernwood 2-Night."

Hank Williams, Jr. son of honky-tonk icon Hank Williams who sang the "Monday Night Football" theme song.

Paul Williams short, blond songwriter who penned "Old-Fashioned Love Song."

Walter Winchell newspaper columnist who was narrator of the original "Untouchables" TV show.

Mare Winningham Brat Pack actress who appeared in *St. Elmo's Fire.*

George "Foghorn" Winslow was once a well-known, frog-voiced child actor.

Wolfman Jack legendary deep-voiced DJ.

Ron Wood onetime Faces guitarist who replaced Mick Taylor in the Rolling Stones.

Mary Woronov member of director Paul Bartel's acting company.

Steven Wright moribund stand-up comedian and man of few words.

Rudy Wurlizer -wrote the screenplay for *Pat Garrett and Billy the Kid* and co-wrote *Candy Mountain* and *Two Lane Blacktop.*

Bill Wyman played bass with the Rolling Stones.

Skip Young played Wally Plumstead on "The Adventures of Ozzie and Harriet."

Frank Zappa formed the Mothers of Invention in 1964.

Moon Unit Zappa Frank's daughter who hit with the 1982 novelty record "Valley Girl."

Annette Zilinskas original bass player with the Bangles.

**WHERE
TO FIND IT**

SALES AND RENTALS

Eddie Brandt's Saturday Matinee
P.O. Box 3232
North Hollywood, CA 91609
818-506-4242
Mail-order rental and sales. Over 28,000 titles. Excellent selection of black-and-white films.

Evergreen Video
228 West Houston Street
New York, NY 10014
212-691-7362
Mail-order rental and sales. Large collection of out-of-print tapes for rental only.

Facets Video
1517 West Fullerton Avenue
Chicago, IL 60614
800-331-6197
Mail-order rental and sales. Catalog lists over 17,000 films.

Movies Unlimited
6736 Castor Avenue
Philadelphia, PA 19149
215-722-8298
Mail-order sales only. Catalog lists 35,000 popular and hard-to-find films on video.

Something Weird Video
P.O. Box 33664
Seattle, Washington 98133
206-361-3759
Mail-order sales only. A one of a kind source, specializing in exploitation/sexploitation films from 1948-1972. For a catalog, send $3 with a statement of age (must be 18 or older).

The Video Beat
107 University Place, Suite 6H
New York, NY 10003
212-505-0459
Mail-order sales only. Specializing in hard-to-find rock'n'roll films from the '50s and '60s.

Video Finders
4401 Sunset BoulevardLos Angeles, CA 90027
900-860-9301
Primarily mail-order sales but some rentals. Nearly 100,000 titles available. Each call costs 2$ for first minute, so have your titles ready!

Video Library
7157 Germantown Avenue
Philadelphia, PA 19119
800-669-7157
Mail-order sales and rental. About 9,000 titles ranging from little-known cult flicks to Hollywood favorites.

Video Oyster
62 Pearl Street
New York, NY 10004
212-480-2440
Mail-order sales of out-of-print tapes. Over 10,000 titles in stock. Send $3 for Half Shell magazine, which contains updated listings.

Video Search of Miami
P.O. Box 1917
Miami, FL 33116
305-279-9773
Mail-order sales only. Specializing in European and Asian films.

MAGAZINES/FANZINES

Ads in these publications offer obscure videos for sale and trade.

Filmfax
P.O. Box 1900
Evanston, IL 60204
Bimonthly guide to cult and unusual films and television shows (including a catalog of B movies). $4.95/issue

Film Threat Video Guide
P.O. Box 3170
Los Angeles, CA 90078-3170
Underground film guide and catalog with a different theme each month (gore, angry women, banned films, etc.). $4.95/issue

The Joe Bob Report
P.O. Box 2002
Dallas, Texas 75221
A biweekly newsletter published by that mysterious guru of American dross, Joe Bob Briggs. Send your name and address for a complimentary issue.

Kicks Magazine/Norton Records
P.O. Box 646
New York, NY 10003
Great source for information on obscure rock'n'roll films.

Psychotronic Video
3309 Rt. 97
Narrowsburg, NY 12764-6126
Quarterly guide to psychotronic (underground, rebellious, cult, schlock, teen, etc.) film. Classified ads geared to rare-video seekers. $4/issue

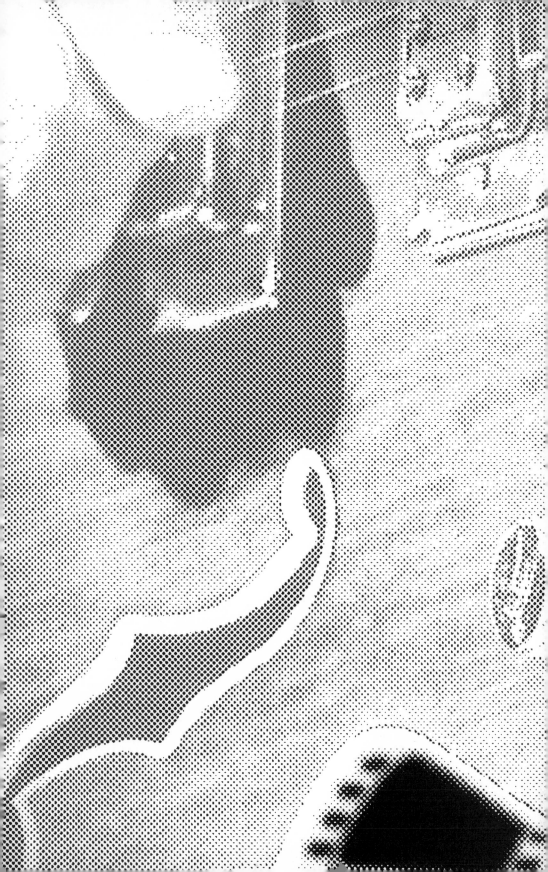

PERFORMER INDEX

Marshall Crenshaw is a recording artist with six albums to his credit, a songwriter whose tunes have been recorded by numerous artists, an actor who has had cameo performances in several films, a student of rock'n'roll history, and the author of many articles on the subject.